AXIS OF
CONVENIENCE

AXIS OF CONVENIENCE

MOSCOW, BEIJING, AND THE NEW GEOPOLITICS

Bobo Lo

CHATHAM HOUSE
London

BROOKINGS INSTITUTION PRESS
Washington, D.C.

Chatham House, 10 St. James's Square, London SW1Y 4LE
(www.chathamhouse.org.uk); charity registration no 208223.

Axis of Convenience: Moscow, Beijing, and the New Geopolitics
may be ordered from:
BROOKINGS INSTITUTION PRESS
c/o HFS, P.O. Box 50370, Baltimore, MD 21211-4370
Tel.: 800/537-5487; 410/516-6956; Fax: 410/516-6998
Internet: www.brookings.edu

Library of Congress Cataloging-in-Publication data
Lo, Bobo, 1959–
    Axis of convenience : Moscow, Beijing, and the new geopolitics / Bobo Lo.
      p.   cm.
    Includes bibliographical references.
    ISBN 978-0-8157-5340-7 (cloth : alk. paper)
    1. Russia (Federation)—Foreign relations—China.   2. China—Foreign relations—Russia
(Federation)   3. Geopolitics—Russia (Federation)   4. Geopolitics—China.   I. Title.
    JZ1616.A57C45 2008
    327.47051—dc22   2008028108

9 8 7 6 5 4 3 2 1

The paper used in this publication meets minimum requirements of the
American National Standard for Information Sciences—Permanence of Paper
for Printed Library Materials: ANSI Z39.48-1992.

Typeset in Minion and Univers Condensed

Composition by R. Lynn Rivenbark
Macon, Georgia

Cartography by Meridian Mapping
Minneapolis, Minnesota

Printed by R. R. Donnelley
Harrisonburg, Virginia

To my gorgeous Siriol

CONTENTS

Maps

Tables

Figure

ACKNOWLEDGMENTS

When I first contemplated a career of creative endeavor, I little imagined how arduous the road would be. There was, I recognized, more to the matter than just thinking "great thoughts" while quaffing a glass (or several) of a fine Sancerre. But I must confess to underestimating the grueling nature of the process. This book has been more than usually demanding. That I have managed to survive the experience is almost entirely due to many wonderful people who have suffered with me, pushed me, and helped me every step of the way.

My wife, Siriol, has shown extraordinary patience, putting up with all manner of unreasonable behavior, as well as offering numerous critical suggestions on various versions of the book. James Nixey is the heart and soul of Chatham House's Russia and Eurasia Programme. He has borne my mood swings with great stoicism, while finding the time to balance a huge administrative workload, pursue his own research interests, and read the text with painstaking thoroughness. Margaret May, head of publications at Chatham House, performs miracles in sustaining the institute's intellectual reputation—a feat not adequately recognized. Her sharp editorial eye, vast knowledge, and superb judgment are every author's dream. I owe her an especially large debt.

A number of outstanding (if slightly terrifying) experts have offered invaluable advice and insights, and made many improvements to the text. They have striven mightily on my behalf. Thank you to Kerry Brown, Mary Dejevsky, Peter Duncan, Aage Espedal, Feng Shaolei, Peter Ferdinand, Phil

Hanson, Shoichi Itoh, Akihiro Iwashita, Natasha Kührt, John Lough, Andrew Monaghan, John Mitchell, Magnus Norman, Keun-Wook Paik, Anthony Phillips, Alex Pravda, Andy Rothman, Alexandra Siddall, Volker Stanzel, Angela Stent, Jonathan Stern, Kyle Wilson, and Andrew Wood.

This book is the product of numerous research trips, during which I have had the good fortune to meet and get to know some leading authorities on Russia, China, and Central Asia. In addition to people already mentioned, I should like to single out Viktor Larin, Jörg Wuttke, Zhao Huasheng, Yu Bin, Paul French, and Birgit Brauer.

I have benefited enormously from the enthusiastic research assistance of some excellent interns at the Russia and Eurasia Programme, most notably the remarkable Alex Nice, Botagoz Shantemirova, Ilze Gelnere, and Irina Ghaplanyan. Thank you also to Abdujalil Abdurasulov, Szymon Ananicz, Khurshid Faizullaev, Artem Kossenko, Eteri Mamrikishvili, and Yulia Oleinik. The work of the interns has been greatly assisted by senior librarian Mary Bone, another of the unsung heroes of Chatham House.

I am very grateful to the team at Brookings Institution Press: Bob Faherty for inviting me to write for such a prestigious publishing house; Janet Walker for her many wise suggestions to improve the text; Chris Kelaher, Robin Becht, and Susan Soldavin for the great publicity; Susan Woollen for producing such a cool cover design; and Larry Converse for expert management of the typesetting and printing.

Over the years, I have been blessed to enjoy the love and wholehearted support of great friends. Thank you to Bruce and Lyn Minerds, Linda Kouvaras and Richard Ward, Steve Shay and Nicola Cade, Lizzy Fisher and Rohit Jaggi, Liz Scott and Dusan Mihajlovic, Ole and Berit Lindeman, Emily Gale, Alex Pravda and Riitta Heino, Kostya and Natasha Eggert, Herbie Flowers and Claire Lacey, Glenn and Agnes Waller, Justine Braithwaite and Dave Peebles, Guy Chazan, Andrei Ryabov, Deborah Bronnert and Alf Torrents, and Dmitri and Vera Trenin.

I should like to thank my family, new and old. In addition to my wife, Siriol, I am proud to count as my "own" Hugh and Helen; Gweno, Rhian, and Gary; Luke, Alex, and Nicholas; my mother; Helen, Hsiao, Didi, and Ping; Hung Koon and Kathy; Hwa Ching and Fred; Han Ching and Mei-yu.

Finally, in the course of writing this book, I have drawn inspiration from some wonderful music, particularly the premiere recordings of Shostakovich's first violin and cello concertos, played by David Oistrakh and Mstislav Rostropovich.

Вово Lo

AXIS OF
CONVENIENCE

Russia and China

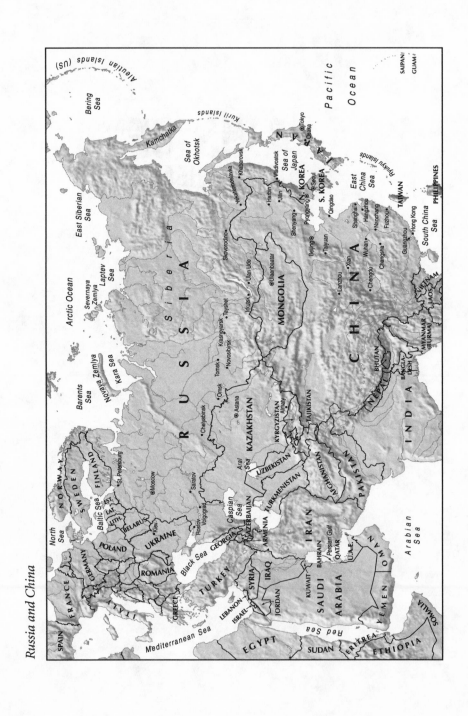

CHAPTER ONE

COOPERATION, AMBIGUITY, AND TENSION

"The pure and simple truth is rarely pure and never simple."
—OSCAR WILDE, *The Importance of Being Earnest*, Act I

Few relationships have provoked such polarized views as the Sino-Russian "strategic partnership." Moscow and Beijing portray it as the very model of international cooperation—pragmatic, enterprising, and innovative. In a world still marked by Cold War–era tensions, it embodies the promise of a new "global multipolar order," not dominated by American "hegemonism" but centered in the "democratization of international relations."[1] Such bullishness testifies to an extraordinary transformation. Less than forty years ago the two countries were seemingly implacable enemies on the verge of nuclear confrontation. Today they can rightly claim that ties are better than at any time in their history. Ancient antagonisms and suspicions appear to have given way to an unparalleled convergence across multiple policy agendas.

On the other hand, the rude health of the relationship has generated mounting concern in the West about its longer-term aims. Although Russian and Chinese leaders deny that their partnership is directed against third parties, many observers in Washington view it as an anti-American alliance in all but name. For such critics the convergence of Russian and Chinese positions on a range of international issues is not merely unhelpful, but represents a concerted challenge to the United States' global leadership.

It is perhaps inevitable that such black-and-white views should flourish in an unstable international context, one characterized by growing geopolitical tensions and security uncertainties. The temptation to extol or demonize the

1

Sino-Russian relationship is all the more powerful given that so little is understood about the motivations and forces shaping it. Despite its prominence it remains a subject on which there is far more heat than light.

Inconveniently for advocates and critics alike, the real picture is ambiguous, full of contradictions both implicit and explicit. Moscow and Beijing speak the language, and undertake many of the actions, of a multifaceted partnership. Yet practical cooperation is hamstrung by historical suspicions, cultural prejudices, geopolitical rivalry, and competing priorities. Despite satisfaction with the growth of "partnership relations," there is lingering doubt about their sustainability.

Such uncertainty is rooted in history, but is fueled also by the emergence of an increasingly confident and assertive China. Beijing has worked hard to allay the fears of the international community by emphasizing concepts such as "peaceful rise," "peaceful development," and a "harmonious world." It has adopted a restrained posture on Taiwan, engaged with the United States, and stepped up participation in multilateral organizations. But the sheer speed and scale of China's transformation from regional backwater into influential global actor have made it an object of concern for many countries, not least Russia.

This anxiety has been accentuated by the turnaround in the strategic fortunes of the two countries since the collapse of the Soviet Union. At the beginning of the 1990s the outlook for Yeltsin's democratic Russia appeared much more promising than that of a Chinese Communist regime shaken and isolated following the international outcry at the brutal suppression of the 1989 Tiananmen Square protests. Russia seemed destined to remain the "older brother" and China the "younger brother," as in the "unbreakable" Sino-Soviet friendship under Joseph Stalin and Mao Zedong. But over the course of the 1990s the momentum within the relationship shifted inexorably in favor of Beijing, first to an "equal partnership," and then to one in which China became seen as ascendant by many on both sides.

The changing dynamic reinforced a long-time mutual ambivalence. For Moscow, China has symbolized a "good" and "bad" East—on the one hand, one of the world's great civilizations; on the other, a barbarous presence that lapsed into decrepitude and medievalism for much of the nineteenth and twentieth centuries. For Beijing, Russia/the Soviet Union was at different times avaricious imperial power, patronizing mentor, and indispensable backer. At no stage in the two countries' common history has there been a period of unalloyed good relations. As Russian leader Vladimir Putin has pointed out, even during the period of "unbreakable friendship" there was considerable ill-feeling beneath the veneer of Sino-Soviet solidarity.[2] While many Russians envy China its political stability and economic success, the notion of a "China threat" persists. Perceptions of China and the Chinese may be more nuanced and positive than in the past, but Sinophobia continues to exert a significant pull. On specific issues, such as the right of Chinese to live, work, and acquire property in Russia, public responses are strongly negative. And most Russians believe that China benefits far more from the relationship.[3]

By contrast, the Chinese have a relatively benign if faintly dismissive view of their largest neighbor. They value it as a supplier of advanced weaponry to the People's Liberation Army (PLA), as an important source of crude oil, and as a useful ally in balancing American power in Central Asia. Unlike many in the West, they do not regard a resurgent Russia as a serious threat to their national interests. They are somewhat bemused at Moscow's obsession with "great power-ness" (*derzhavnost*) and frustrated by its double-dealing on issues such as the East Siberian oil pipeline (see chapter 8), but they recognize the need for accommodation in order to concentrate on more important priorities elsewhere. Generally speaking the Chinese attitude toward Russia combines Middle Kingdom *hauteur*, pragmatism, and cynicism. Russophobia, although it exists, is less of an issue than indifference, as China's governing elite and society increasingly turn their attention to the West.

Axis of convenience

This asymmetry and ambivalence call into question the conventional wisdom that Russia and China enjoy a bona fide strategic partnership. Although the two countries have come a long way in recent years, they share neither a long-term vision of the world nor a common understanding of their respective places in it, a disjunction reflected in differing perceptions of the bilateral relationship.

This book argues that the dynamic between Russia and China is one of strategic convenience—an *axis of convenience*. It suits Moscow and Beijing to talk up the quality of ties, both for intrinsic reasons and as a significant factor in regional and global politics. But such interaction falls well short of strategic cooperation, which implies not only a common sense of purpose across the board, but also the political will and coordination to translate broad intent into meaningful action. The rationale of the Sino-Russian axis of convenience is often tactical and instrumental, and expediency and opportunism are more relevant considerations than an often illusory likemindedness. Tellingly, the

Kremlin assigns greater resources to the countries of the former Soviet Union (FSU) and to relations with key EU member-states (such as Germany), while the Chinese leadership is much more focused on engagement with the United States, Japan, the ASEANs (Association of Southeast Asian Nations), Africa, and the European Union.

The secondary importance of the bilateral relationship reflects critical differences in the two countries' center of gravity and strategic orientation. Russian foreign policy arises out of an indigenous imperial tradition, a European cultural-historical heritage, and an Americacentric geopolitical culture. The West continues to supply the principal external reference points, even if many of these are perceived negatively. At the same time the longevity of Russia's imperial tradition and recent memory of the Soviet superpower era have ensured that Moscow retains a globalist mindset, despite a much diminished capacity to project power and influence. Within this world-view China has traditionally occupied a peripheral place. Even at the height of Sino-Soviet friendship and later during the U.S.-Soviet-Chinese triangularism of the 1970s, its importance to the Kremlin was more auxiliary than independent, a source of leverage in a bipolar world rather than valued in itself.

China is still in the early stages of evolution from a regional to a global power and from a developing into a developed nation. It is no surprise, then, that its principal foreign policy priorities are essentially inward-looking: to create the most favorable external conditions for domestic modernization; and reunification with Taiwan. The same introspection characterizes its imperial mentality, which reflects the dynastic nature of Communist Party rule rather than empire-building ambitions or irredentist designs.[4] The global extension of its foreign policy in recent years is motivated not by a desire to assert a great power presence on the world stage, but by concrete and fairly narrow goals, such as maximizing access to overseas markets, energy sources, and other raw materials necessary to sustain growth. Although China has shown signs of assuming greater international obligations and becoming a "responsible stakeholder," its approach to global affairs remains utilitarian.[5]

Contrasting foreign policy agendas have not prevented Moscow and Beijing from coordinating positions in certain circumstances. Crucially, however, what binds them is a largely defensive agenda: stability and confidence-building along the common border; resisting the influence of "alien" Western values;[6] emasculating UN action over Iran's nuclear program; and excluding or weakening an outside strategic presence in Central Asia. The axis of convenience is in many respects an "anti-relationship," directed more at containing undesirable developments than creating new structures and mechanisms for cooperation.

Much of the impetus behind its development has come from a desire to restrain the "hegemonic" power of the United States. In the immediate post–Cold War era, the arrival of the "unipolar moment" encouraged the reassertion of American internationalism, missionary in its zeal and seemingly unchallengeable.[7] This America was seen to threaten regional as well as ex-global powers and provided a natural locus for Sino-Russian convergence. After a brief period of introspection in the first year of George W. Bush's presidency, 9/11 reawakened Washington's foreign policy activism. The U.S.-led military operations in Afghanistan and Iraq have drawn Moscow and Beijing together in a common purpose—not in combating international terrorism, as Washington had hoped, but in countering the geopolitical presence of the hegemon in their "spheres of vital interests."[8] Even here, however, the two countries' approaches are scarcely identical. At a time when Russia is taking every opportunity to contest America's global leadership, China has adopted a more restrained approach. The contrast between the escalation of Russia-U.S. tensions and the generally positive interdependency between the U.S. and Chinese economies is stark.

The new geopolitics

In challenging the assumption of a Sino-Russian "strategic partnership," we should not underestimate its wider implications. Perceptions of the national interest can be short-term, but they have regional and global consequences nonetheless. Moscow and Beijing may be "dreaming different dreams,"[9] but this has not stopped them from working together, often to considerable effect, in many areas: Iran, Central Asia, countering missile defense, North Korea.

Such cooperation, more opportunistic than strategic, is facilitated by an international environment where no single world order—unipolar, bipolar or multipolar—predominates, but in which a Hobbesian "anarchy" reigns.[10] George W. Bush's presidency has seen a spectacular decline in the authority of the United States, with Washington's global leadership coming under attack from all sides. Yet it will be decades before rising powers such as China and India have the capacity—or will—to compete with it for preeminence. The much-vaunted "multipolar world order" remains more aspiration than reality, while an equitable, more "democratic" international system based on the primacy of the UN and other multilateral institutions is similarly elusive. There is an "international society" of sorts, in that certain rules of behavior continue to govern interstate relations,[11] but the Helsinki "big idea" of universal rights and norms[12] has become so eroded in recent years as to be meaningless as a frame of reference. In addition to the growing fractiousness of states and proliferation of value-systems, new non-state actors have emerged to undermine established institutions and norms.

A new geopolitics is challenging the Western-driven, positive-sum interdependency that has become discredited in many parts of the world. It is a hybrid phenomenon, reflecting the transitory nature of the contemporary international system. Traditional constructs of space and influence remain influential, but a revolution of means is taking place. This geopolitics is flexible in approach, employing both hard and soft power and making use of multilateral, bilateral, and unilateral mechanisms. And it is flourishing in circumstances where classical conceptions of the balance of power are interacting with new security and economic challenges—international terrorism, the proliferation of weapons of mass destruction (WMD), the globalization of trade, energy security, climate change. The new geopolitics is not based on fixed and long-lasting "strategic partnerships," let alone alliances, but on much more supple arrangements that are frequently opportunistic, non-committal, and volatile.[13] Such arrangements are highly susceptible to changing international circumstances and evolving perceptions of the national interest.

That Sino-Russian relations are driven by interests and not ideology (as under Stalin and Mao) is both a strength and a weakness. On the one hand, it enables Moscow and Beijing to escape some of the baggage of the past, focusing instead on what unites rather than divides them. The disparateness and lack of clarity of the current geopolitical environment also enables their partnership to punch above its weight, in conditions where the illusion of power is often mistaken for genuine clout.

On the other hand the fluidity of the international context makes the relationship a hostage to fortune. While it can strengthen the axis of convenience in dealings with other actors, it feeds tensions and uncertainties within the relationship itself. With so little to be taken for granted, there is no inclination in Moscow and Beijing toward mutual reliance. The notion of a "normative convergence" between them has become popular recently,[14] yet this supposed convergence is fragile and superficial and in no way approximates the shared values that exist within bodies such as the EU.

For all the public packaging, the Sino-Russian relationship is defined by tangible interests and the realities of power. And herein lies its greatest source of vulnerability. China's rise as the next global superpower threatens Russia, not with the military or demographic invasion many fear, but with progressive displacement to the periphery of international decisionmaking. Although it is fashionable to bracket Russia and China together as emerging powers, along with India and Brazil,[15] the trajectory of their development foreshadows different fates.[16] The aggregate bilateral balance of power—economic, political, technological, strategic—has already shifted in Beijing's favor, and the disparity will only become more marked with time. More than any other single factor, it is this growing inequality in an uncertain world that will inhibit the development of a genuinely close partnership.

The policy context

Some clarification on the nature of the policy process in this highly ambivalent relationship may be useful. Policymaking is opaque, even in the most transparent and accountable of Western democracies. It is much more so in states where a culture of confidentiality is pervasive, input is limited to the select few, and dissimulation is more often than not a virtue.[17] We can rarely be sure who initiated or influenced particular decisions; a measure of clarity emerges only with time and, in a few lucky instances, with the publication of indiscreet memoirs.[18]

In this connection, it is vital to distinguish between those who drive policy and those who merely articulate it. The recent transfer of the Russian presidency from Vladimir Putin to Dmitry Medvedev illustrates the dangers of a literal approach to the study of policymaking. On the face of things, President Medvedev has become the new power in the land, with direct responsibility for running foreign policy. Yet it is Putin, albeit as prime minister and party leader, who remains the supreme arbiter of Russia's affairs at home and abroad. His personal domination of the body politic and control of elite networks outweigh the institutional assets of a nominally strong presidency.

This book makes liberal reference to "Russia" and "Moscow," "China" and "Beijing," more or less interchangeably. The reader should not interpret this as implying the existence of uniform views, but as shorthand for *the dominant policy line at a given moment*. The abstract concept of "the national interest" has little meaning, except at the most general level—"territorial integrity," "national security," "economic prosperity." In practice, the national interest is a matter of interpretation and perspective. Different groups within the policy elite—big business, economic ministries, the security and intelligence community, the

military—may (and do) view it in different ways. The issue is further complicated by the blurring of public and private interests, especially in Russia. Policy outcomes reflect the interplay of competing interests and agendas; in Russia and China, even more than in the West, they are the product of multiple
compromises.

With this in mind, several scholars have adopted an interest-group approach, associating certain attitudes and policies with particular constituen-
cies.[19] But this, too, is not without its problems. Interests and allegiances cut
across institutional lines.[20] The Russian military, for example, is sharply
divided in its views of China. Some senior officers regard it as the greatest
long-term threat to national security, others as an actor of limited military
capabilities, while a third group adheres to the Kremlin line that China is a
key strategic partner and customer for the Russian arms industry. Divining
the inner workings of Chinese policy is more challenging still, since the
extreme secrecy surrounding decisionmaking there makes it very difficult to
identify distinct policy strands with any confidence. Mark Leonard has cate-
gorized Chinese thinking about international affairs in terms of "liberal inter-
nationalists," "neo-comms," and "pragmatists."[21] However, it is unclear how
far these intellectual currents influence specific government policies. The
most plausible, if somewhat unsatisfactory, answer is that they probably all
feed into the policy process, but in ways that are extremely hard to gauge.

Part of the problem is that perceptions and attitudes fluctuate. The
numerous contradictions in the bilateral relationship have translated into
inconsistent policymaking over the years, particularly in the Kremlin. Just as
there is no such thing as *the* national interest, so the hackneyed phrase "permanent national interests" is inadequate in explaining the complex motivations behind Sino-Russian interaction. Interests alter in response to changing
domestic and international circumstances. Events intervene to change the
"normal" course of things. 9/11, for example, disrupted the positive momentum of Sino-Russian relations. Putin seized on the opportunity to re-engage
with the United States, leaving the Chinese in little doubt as to their second-
class status in the Kremlin's world-view. Subsequently, the Iraq war and the
Orange revolution in Ukraine helped swing the pendulum back toward Beijing. No relationship evolves in a vacuum, especially one between two countries struggling to redefine their place in the international system. Evolution
of the "strategic partnership" is inseparable from larger trends in a rapidly
globalizing world.

In the end, much of foreign policymaking is ad hoc and reactive, notwithstanding the best intentions of leaders to assert a long-term vision. Although

the talk is of "pragmatism," this is rarely more than a bland certificate of endorsement (the obverse of pragmatic are the pejorative terms "ideological" and "romantic"). States may be "rational actors" for the most part, yet many of their actions are influenced by irrational considerations; myopia and prej-udice often outweigh clear-sighted views of national (or even group) inter-ests. We should not underestimate, too, the role of miscalculation and mis-perception—especially pertinent in relationships where there is little tradition of trust, as between Moscow and Beijing.

The many faces of Sino-Russian relations

The Sino-Russian axis of convenience operates on several levels—bilateral, regional, and global—that constantly intersect. The following chapters exam-ine key dimensions of this multi-layered relationship: its historical and ideational setting; critical bilateral issues, such as the situation in the Russian Far East and the military balance; the relationship in its regional context (Central Asia, East Asia); and the nexus between the development of Sino-Russian ties and larger global realities, in particular the world's growing resource hunger and the continuing primacy of the United States. Some of the themes are geographical in focus, others functional, and they frequently overlap. Together they reflect the increasingly complex interaction between two of the world's leading powers.

Chapter 2 looks at the impact of history and of historical memory. Over the past two decades, Russian and Chinese leaders have sought to transcend a contentious past. These efforts have met with considerable success and are responsible in large part for the generally healthy state of bilateral ties today. However, the burden of history continues to weigh heavily. Many of the underlying tensions and uncertainties in Sino-Russian relations have their roots in a series of historical "episodes": the thirteenth-century Mongol inva-sion of Russia and three centuries of Mongol rule; the Tsarist imperial expan-sion into China in the nineteenth century; the "unequal treaties," under which the Qing dynasty was forced to cede 1.5 million square kilometers of Chinese territory; the enormous disappointments of the Sino-Soviet "unbreakable friendship" in the 1950s; the border clashes of 1969; and the sharply contrasting experiences of modernization in post-Soviet Russia and post-Mao China.

These episodes are signposts in a relationship that has rarely been com-fortable and has frequently been bitter. They have left a mixed legacy: on the one hand, anxiety, alienation, and mistrust; on the other, accommodation, calculation, and pragmatism. Historical animosities and suspicions have softened, but not disappeared. The outcome of this ambivalent condition is a selective and wary engagement. Enduring Russian fears of Chinese irredentism in the Far East highlight the extent to which history still impinges on the relationship, notwithstanding the best efforts of governments to set the past aside. The longer-term outlook for partnership hinges on the capacity of Moscow and Beijing to embrace present and future opportunities with an open mind.

Chapter 3 lays out the ideational context by addressing the central question of what Moscow and Beijing understand by "strategic partnership." For Russia, in particular, this has become a near-universal rubric applied to all manner of relationships. Sino-Russian ties have improved beyond recognition in the last fifteen years, and the degree of political, normative, and foreign policy convergence is unprecedented. Yet there are serious questions to be asked about both sides' expectations of partnership and the extent of their likemindedness.

Although they appear to espouse virtually identical views on many issues, major differences of perspective and emphasis continue to divide them. For Russia, a good relationship with China serves immediate security interests and global geopolitical ambitions. It reinforces the security of its far eastern regions by establishing a common interest in cooperation. It also gives Moscow the confidence to pursue an assertive ("independent") foreign policy and to challenge Washington's global leadership. In this sense, China is less a strategic partner to Russia than a strategic counterweight to the United States. Beijing sees its relationship with Moscow differently. Its chief priorities are more practical and less ambitious: to secure its "strategic rear" in the northeast in order to concentrate on domestic modernization and Taiwan; to ensure the continued flow of energy and other commodity imports; and to work with Moscow (and others) toward stability in Central Asia. Although the Communist leadership values Sino-Russian solidarity on international issues, it treats Russia less as a global strategic partner than as a secondary and "limited" partner in niche areas.

The Sino-Russian dynamic is consequently not equal but asymmetrical, a fact that has generated some tensions between them. For the most part the image of "strategic partnership" enables Moscow and Beijing to gloss over its limitations. However, the disjunction between sweeping rhetoric and modest achievement is becoming more difficult to sustain, especially in areas such as energy where real cooperation has fallen well short of expectations. In coming years the relationship faces several major challenges: managing demographic tensions in the Russian Far East (RFE); translating a largely rhetorical convergence into tangible outcomes; and balancing between cooperation and competition in Central Asia. Such challenges are all the more formidable given the fluid international environment.

Few issues touch the Russian psyche as deeply as the idea of the land (*zemlya*). Territorial integrity is central to notions of Russian national identity and of "Russian-ness."[22] The specter of a Chinese take-over of the Russian Far East, the subject of chapter 4, goes to the heart of these issues. In its most primitive form, the "China threat" is reflected in the xenophobic image of the "yellow peril"—the Chinese invading in their millions to fill the vast expanse of Siberia and Russia's Far East. But the issue is more than just about vulgar racism. Even Vladimir Putin, the driving force behind the expansion of relations with China, has suggested that if Russia does not manage to settle the RFE then it may one day lose it.[23] The fate of Russia's eastern lands is thus of pivotal importance in the evolution of the bilateral relationship. Tensions over "illegal migration" are exacerbated by the widening demographic imbalance between the RFE and China's northeastern provinces, by Russia's larger population crisis, and by the growing Chinese economic influence in eastern Russia. Beijing denies any irredentist ambitions, yet many Russians believe that it has not abandoned hope of recovering these territories through surreptitious means—namely, the gradual build-up of a large and influential Chinese presence on Russian soil.

In fact, the real problem in the RFE is the bankruptcy of Soviet and post-Soviet policy toward the region. Decades of neglect and half-baked schemes have truly made this Russia's forgotten land. Despite Putin's public commitment to development of the RFE, there has been minimal progress in resolving fundamental problems of corruption, misgovernment, and economic backwardness. In these circumstances the Chinese serve a dual purpose: as chief supplier of essential goods and services to the local population and convenient scapegoat. The combination of socioeconomic dependency and political expediency leaves Sino-Russian relations in the RFE (and beyond) especially vulnerable to changing conditions at home and abroad.

China's spectacular transformation in the post-Mao era elicits mixed feelings among Russians. For some it proves the wisdom of the Chinese model of socioeconomic development—the "Beijing consensus"[24]—compared with the attempts of Gorbachev and Yeltsin to follow "inappropriate" Western political and economic prescriptions. There is a strong sense of *schadenfreude*, too, at American discomfiture in the face of a rapidly emerging global power that would challenge the Western-dominated international order. Set against this, however, is the worry that China's rise, "peaceful" though it may be, will eventually threaten Russian interests across the board. The bilateral balance of power in its various dimensions therefore looms large in Moscow. Chapter 5 focuses on two critical aspects of this question. It assesses, first, the two countries' respective military capabilities and potential. Of particular interest here are their contrasting experiences of reform, where the PLA's comprehensive modernization compares strikingly with the failure of successive Russian governments to develop effective modern fighting forces. Although it is inconceivable that China would attack Russia in the foreseeable future, the former's ongoing "revolution in military affairs" is the subject of close scrutiny in Moscow (as well as Washington).

Still more important are the consequences of China's rise as a civilian power, particularly if it becomes the world's leading economy by 2040, as some predict.[25] Moscow frets that Russia is becoming a raw materials appendage of an ever more hi-tech China. Yet the key issue here is the fungibility of Chinese economic might, which is translating into a much enhanced ability to project power across the globe, including in regions where Russia has been accustomed to exercising a dominant influence. The transformation is nowhere more apparent than in the economic sphere. In a world dominated by economic power, the growing asymmetry of the bilateral relationship threatens to accentuate Russia's marginalization from international decisionmaking.

One of the most sensitive areas of the relationship is former Soviet Central Asia, the subject of chapter 6. For well over a century Russia has been the imperial power and (largely) unchallenged hegemon.[26] This continued to be the case even after the break-up of the Soviet Union and the independence of the five Central Asian republics. During the 1990s, American involvement in the region was low-key, while Beijing was content to defer to Moscow, partly because their interests coincided and partly because it lacked the capacity to play a more independent role. 9/11 nullified these strategic understandings. Virtually overnight America became the leading power in Central Asia, reinforced by a long-term troop presence; the limits of Russian influence were severely exposed; and the Chinese leadership realized it could no longer rely on Moscow to take care of business. The emergence of an environment that was "anarchic" (in the Hobbesian sense) established a natural setting for renewed geopolitical competition.

Although some commentators speak of a new Great Game and a de facto Sino-Russian alliance against the United States, the real picture is much more confused, involving many players with their own individual agendas. Beijing, supported by Moscow, has promoted the Shanghai Cooperation Organization (SCO) as an "international organization of a new type," a purported alternative to geopolitics. But so far the SCO has raised more questions than answers. Is its "Shanghai spirit" of positive-sum cooperation in response to universal threats, such as international terrorism, merely a cover to legitimize a shared determination to force America out of Central Asia? Should the SCO be viewed as an institution of growing stature, or as yet another in the long line of ineffectual multilateral organizations in the former Soviet space? If the SCO is becoming a serious player, then where does it fit in the overall scheme of Sino-Russian relations—as an additional layer that consolidates progress at the bilateral level, or a competitive arena in which Moscow and Beijing vie for the loyalties and resources of the Central Asian states?

Chapter 7 focuses on the dynamics of the Sino-Russian relationship in East Asia. This region represents a unique strategic environment. It is fractured and possesses no collective identity. It encompasses four of the world's leading powers—the United States, China, Japan, and Russia—three of which are nuclear weapons states that have often been at loggerheads. Rival bilateral alliances rather than multilateral mechanisms have traditionally predominated. And culturally and normatively it is exceptionally diverse, a place where Huntington's thesis of a "clash of civilizations" is more applicable than anywhere else on the planet.[27] In this unstable context, the key question is not the supposed threat of a Moscow-Beijing axis directed at U.S. interests, as in Central Asia. The real tension is between China's emergence as a real force in the Asia-Pacific, and the desire of other powers, including Russia, to preserve the strategic status quo. Beneath the surface of apparently convergent interests, there is a fundamental conflict between Moscow's vision—a Concert of Great Powers, in which Russia is a full and valued member—and Beijing's determination to carve out a leadership role.

It is no coincidence, then, that Putin has emphasized the importance of "strategic diversity." He has attempted to improve relations with Japan; raised Russia's level of participation in Asian multilateral organizations such as APEC (the Asia-Pacific Economic Cooperation grouping) and the ASEAN Regional Forum (ARF); brought Russia into the Korean Six-Party talks; and engaged actively in the ASEAN-plus dialogue and the East Asia Summit (EAS).[28] His interest in a strategic architecture of checks and balances has led him to flirt with ideas of Russia as a "swing power" between China and Japan, and between China and the West. But this approach carries risks. It undermines Chinese trust in Moscow's good faith and could, in certain circumstances, be interpreted as part of a larger project of "neo-containment" and "keeping China down." In the latter eventuality, the outcome would not be a Concert of Asia, but heightened bilateral tensions, destabilization of the Korean peninsula, and aggravation of existing fault-lines in the region.

The geopolitics of energy is the subject of chapter 8. Energy has become a central plank of the bilateral relationship and of the two countries' foreign policies more generally. Moscow regards control of oil and gas resources as its most effective means of power projection in the post-bipolar age. For Beijing the quest for energy has become an all-encompassing priority, the engine of China's modernization. Sino-Russian energy cooperation is emblematic of the potential, but also of the shortcomings of their partnership. It offers a vision of the future as the most plausible avenue for taking relations to the next level, with political and strategic, as well as economic, benefits. However, progress has been slow. Prolonged delays over the East Siberian oil pipeline and the Kovykta gas pipeline have highlighted numerous problems: confusion over routing, pricing disagreements, uncertain levels of investment, and denial of Chinese access to Russian energy equity. Such difficulties reflect Moscow's reluctance to become too China-dependent in terms of markets, as well as concern that Russia is turning into a resource-cow for Chinese modernization. For its part Beijing has reacted to the Kremlin's erratic behavior by widening the search for new suppliers of energy. Resource hunger has become the main driver of the Chinese push into Central Asia, one that has led it into growing competition with Russian interests.

Thus energy offers both opportunity and risk for the development of relations. And the same is true of the use of energy as a foreign policy tool. The political elite in Moscow has made much of Russia as an "energy superpower" and attempted to exploit control of energy (especially gas) resources as leverage on the West. In fact, the threat to "go East" by diverting exports away from primary European markets is a bluff. Russia has neither the inclination nor the capability to make good on such threats. In the meantime, however, its reliability as a long-term supplier has been called into question, including in Beijing. The Chinese find they have more in common with energy consumers like the United States than with exporting countries such as Russia.

The Kremlin's use of energy as a foreign policy tool is consistent with a view of the world as a competitive, often hostile place, where geopolitics is becoming more rather than less important. For all the talk about interdependency and positive-sum cooperation in counterterrorism, WMD nonproliferation and conflict resolution, concepts such as the balance of power and spheres of influence have lost none of their salience. Chapter 9 revisits the idea of the "Grand Chessboard," put forward by Zbigniew Brzezinski in

1997.[29] Now, as then, the Eurasian continent is the main sphere of geopolitical contestation, while the principal actors—the United States, Russia, and China—remain the same. However, much also has changed in the intervening decade: the advent of a long-term Western presence in Central Asia; the Iraq war; the erosion of American political and normative influence; skyrocketing energy prices that have enabled Russia's resurgence; and the spectacular rise of China.

Against this background the Sino-Russian relationship has taken on a global character. For the Kremlin, geopolitical triangularism retains a special place, even if good relations with China have come to be valued for intrinsic as well as instrumental reasons. The nature of this triangularism—and the global chessboard—remains unclear. Russia and China share a profound distaste for American "hegemonic" behavior and seek to constrain it. But beyond that general objective the two sides differ substantially. Moscow plays up the "strategic partnership" with Beijing in order to maximize its foreign policy options and compensate for the deterioration of relations with the United States. Making common cause with China is critical to Russia's larger vision of reasserting itself as a global player.

China's perception of the grand chessboard, while also colored by geopolitical thinking, is more flexible. It does not deem it necessary to contest Western interests and influence wherever it finds them. Beijing's commitment to closer relations with Russia has not been prompted by worsening ties with the United States and the EU—indeed, these have improved significantly in recent years—but by the need to achieve specific political, economic, and security goals. It operates on the assumption that China can and must engage with the United States and Europe while maintaining a "strategic partnership" with Moscow. As its cautious approach toward Iraq demonstrates, it is unwilling to jeopardize China's far more substantial ties with the West for the sake of a partner whose actions at times seem motivated by visceral anti-Americanism. The case for flexibility is reinforced by a sober understanding of the limits of Sino-Russian friendship. The Communist leadership has few illusions that Moscow would offer more than moral-political support in the event of a major crisis in China's relations with the United States, such as over Taiwan. More important still, it understands that it is not Russia, but America, that is truly China's indispensable partner.

In spite of many unresolved issues, the short- to medium-term prognosis for the Sino-Russian relationship is good. There is no problem so serious as to lead to an early change for the worse, let alone a crisis. The axis of convenience will hold for some years, as both sides continue to find compelling reasons to cooperate: maintaining a solid front against Western "interference" in domestic affairs, developing energy ties, and countering American "hegemonism." Beyond the next decade, however, the future is much less clear. Chapter 10 considers five scenarios for the longer-term evolution of relations: strategic convergence and the continuation of current positive trends; a political-military alliance; the "end of history" based on democratization in both countries; military confrontation; and a state of strategic tension. The last of these scenarios seems the most probable, although by no means inevitable. It envisages a gradual widening of policy differences, but within controlled parameters. The relationship would lose much of its luster, talk of "strategic partnership" would become perfunctory, and the opportunistic nature of ties would be widely evident. Nevertheless, dealings between Moscow and Beijing would remain more or less businesslike, and even effective in certain areas.

This final chapter concludes with some thoughts on the implications for the West of present and future trends in the relationship. As noted at the outset, there is a tendency to portray Sino-Russian convergence in melodramatic terms, as the most serious long-term strategic threat to the West. This alarmist picture is based on a misreading of developments, be they summit communiqués, occasional military exercises, or formulaic declarations on the multipolar world order. Contrary to conventional wisdom, good relations between Moscow and Beijing can contribute to a more stable world and should be welcomed rather than feared. Indeed, historical experience has shown that a souring of Sino-Russian ties is a major destabilizing factor in Eurasian and global security. Western policymakers should therefore examine the axis of convenience on its merits, not through the lens of geopolitical stereotypes or the self-serving rhetoric of "strategic partnership."

CHAPTER TWO

THE BURDEN OF HISTORY

O Rus! Forget your former glory:
The two-headed eagle is ravaged,
And your tattered banners passed
Like toys among yellow children
He who neglects love's legacy
Will be overcome by trembling fear . . .
And the third Rome will fall to dust.
Nor will there ever be a fourth.
　　　　　　—From "Pan Mongolism," VLADIMIR SOLOVIEV, October 1894[1]

At a time when their partnership is flourishing as never before, Moscow and Beijing are understandably eager to claim that they have consigned past antagonisms to the metaphorical dustbin of history. Relations, it is said, are developing on the basis of mutual trust, pragmatism, and the national interest.[2] If neither side would agree with Henry Ford's dictum that "history is more or less bunk," then they have nevertheless exerted strenuous efforts to minimize its impact. For both, the key to the rapprochement of recent years lies in their ability to transcend a dark and often tragic shared history.

These efforts have reaped considerable dividends. By concentrating on present-day realities and future opportunities, Russia and China have raised cooperation to unprecedented levels. The notable improvement in Russian public perceptions of the Chinese, in particular, demonstrates how the underplaying of past animosities, together with the growing identification of common interests, can erode the most stubborn of prejudices.[3]

For all that, however, historical memory continues to play a crucial role. Its impact is understated but unmistakable. History matters, and nowhere more so than in two countries that share many psychological traits: a strong if not always well-articulated national consciousness; a sense of destiny; painstaking (and painful) remembrance of the past; a culture of grievance and "national humiliation"; and a quasi-permanent feeling of strategic vulnerability.

This chapter does not intend to offer a comprehensive historical account of the relationship. Its purpose, rather, is to demonstrate how certain episodes, from the Mongol invasion of Russia to the collapse of the Soviet Union, have influenced Russian and Chinese attitudes toward each other. History, or rather the use of history as icon, *cause célèbre*, and intellectual rationale, has served as both stimulus and hindrance to the development of relations. Its presence is all-pervasive, touching on every aspect—political, economic, strategic, and civilizational.

Russia's "Mongol complex"

The first, and in many respects most defining, of these historical "moments" is the Mongol invasion of the Russian city-states in the thirteenth century and the subsequent three centuries of the "Mongol yoke" (*mongolskaya iga*). The Mongols wreaked enormous devastation on the local population, establishing in the process the notion of the East as an abiding source of threat in the Russian mind. Soloviev's apocalyptic vision encapsulates Russia's Mongol complex, a subliminal but existential fear that resonates strongly to this day. The notion of a "yellow peril," which he and a number of other writers articulated at the turn of the nineteenth and twentieth centuries,[4] conjures up the nightmare of a barbarian horde sweeping through Russia, impervious to all reason and humanity.

The Mongol effect amounted to more than the scarring impact of its sheer destructiveness. Unlike most conquering empires, the Mongols left little by way of culture, civilization or even governance in Russia. The tributary system of indirect rule, the absence of arts and letters, and the overwhelming focus on military might ensured, from the outset, a fundamental separateness between the Russian population and their conquerors. Growing intermarriage did little to challenge a predominantly negative view of the Mongols as not only dangerous, but also ignorant and uncivilized. A relationship defined principally by the obligation to pay tribute was scarcely conducive to a fuller, more positive engagement.[5]

Russia found itself largely isolated from mainstream European civilization. Later writers were to view this period as the Dark Ages, in which a "Chinese wall" separated Russia from the rest of Europe.[6] The Mongol occupation became both allegory and rationalization for political tyranny and economic backwardness, while a clear divide arose between the West as the incarnation of progress and a savage East.[7] Even those who opposed the influence of Western ideas sought inspiration not from Asia, but in indigenous Russian values. The Slavophile movement of the mid-nineteenth century thus emphasized the triad of autocracy (*samoderzhavie*), Orthodoxy (*pravoslavie*), and nationhood (*narodnost*).[8] Such introspection reflected a hostile attitude toward all alien influences, not just those from Europe.

The distinction between the West as the embodiment of advanced civilization and a backward but threatening East has proved remarkably durable,[9] if somewhat paradoxical. Modern (that is, post-medieval) Russia has suffered far more from invaders coming from the west, most famously Napoleon in the early nineteenth century and Hitler in 1941–45. Such traumas, however, have been counterbalanced by constructive contributions. France and Germany, for example, are associated with the supreme achievements of European civilization and have been instrumental in Russia's political, economic, and intellectual development. The greatest Russian rulers, such as Peter the Great and Catherine the Great, looked to Europe for inspiration and knowledge, even while they fought against the European powers. (For Catherine, who began life as a German princess, the connection was even more intimate.) For better or worse, over the past four centuries it is the West that has established the external standards of reference against which Russians—elite and public—have measured themselves. No such argument has been mounted in relation to the East.

In recent times, China's rise post-Mao has challenged the traditional stereotype of a barbarian Asia. There is greater public awareness of Chinese civilization as well as of its recent achievements, and the Kremlin's determination to talk up the "strategic partnership" has softened perceptions of the "China threat" (*kitaiskaya ugroza*). But it will be many decades, if ever, before Russia loses its "Mongol complex." The recentness of China's emergence, not to mention the unevenness of its development, ensures that many Russians will continue to view their largest neighbor as alien, lacking in important respects, and more than a little menacing.[10]

Mutual isolation

One may ask how Russia tarred one of the world's great civilizations with the Mongol brush, particularly as imperial China was even more a victim of barbarian depredations.[11] The chief explanation lies in the extremely limited engagement between Russia and Asia. Although the Russian city-states experienced the full force of the Mongol invasion, they had virtually no contact with mainstream Asian cultures. From the thirteenth to the sixteenth centuries, there was minimal opportunity for more nuanced images of the East to emerge in the Russian mind. Perceptions of different Asian peoples—Mongols, Central Asian nomads, Han Chinese—were more or less conflated, a homogenization reinforced after the Mongol conquerors of China transformed themselves into the Yuan dynasty (1271–1368).[12]

On the Chinese side there was little disposition to export the civilization and values of the Celestial Empire, even after the expulsion of the Mongols by the Ming (1368–1644) in the late fourteenth century. Although the early Ming rulers extended China's northern and western frontiers, like their predecessors they were content with the tributary system and limited direct contact with foreigners. By the fifteenth century even this was waning, as the dynasty increasingly turned in on itself and reduced links with the outside world to a minimum. The age of destruction had given way to a prolonged period of mutual isolation and indifference in Sino-Russian relations.

This remained the case until the second half of the nineteenth century. There was intermittent contact between the Romanov Empire (1613–1917) and Qing dynasty (1644–1911) from the mid-seventeenth century onward, as Russia's push into Siberia and the Manchu expansion northward led to several armed skirmishes, the development of trading links, and eventually the Treaty of Nerchinsk in 1689.[13] However, over the next 200 years interaction took the form of a tentative engagement between peripheries rather than a clash of empires. The vast region east of the Siberian city of Chita—which now constitutes the Russian Far East—was neglected by both capitals. For the Qing, these were vassal lands, populated by "barbarians."[14] There was no interest in engagement, and official contact was sporadic and motivated almost entirely by defensive considerations. Russia lay within the purview of the Lifan Yuan (Office of Border Affairs), which managed relations with other difficult northern neighbors, such as the Mongols and the nomadic Zunghars.[15] Similarly, with the partial exception of Peter the Great, successive Tsars were unpersuaded by the wisdom of penetrating into unknown territory several thousand kilometers away.[16] Russia's gaze was directed almost entirely toward Europe, and it was left to a few enterprising individuals to sustain even a modicum of interest in East Asia.

The age of imperialism

The real collision between Russia and China did not occur until the mid-nineteenth century. The corruption and decay of the Qing dynasty, the new-found assertiveness of modern imperial powers such as Great Britain, and Russia's rapid settlement of Siberia generated tremendous pressures for change. Although the imperial government in St. Petersburg was sometimes embarrassed by the enterprise of explorer-adventurers such as Count Muraviev-Amursky,[17] it was anxious not to miss out on the carve-up of China and the allocation of lucrative foreign trade concessions. The terminal decline of Manchu rule added urgency to Russia's eastward expansion, which was motivated as much by a desire to protect its interests against other foreign powers as by opportunism.

The period of mutual isolation gave way to renewed engagement, albeit one that was extremely unequal. Russia was able to dictate terms to a China it held in profound contempt.[18] The Tsar's imperial project in the Far East was consummated by the three "unequal treaties" of Aigun (1858), Peking (1860), and Tarbagatai (1864), under which the Qing emperor surrendered some 1.5 million square kilometers of territory.[19] The 1880s saw the further loss of Chinese lands in the west, while the Imperial Russian Army took advantage of the crushing of the Boxer Rebellion by the foreign powers in 1900 to reinforce its presence in Manchuria, gaining the ports of Dalian and Port Arthur (Lüshun).

Sino-Russian relations were never more unbalanced than during this period: on one side, a self-confident and prosperous empire; on the other, a dynasty destroyed by corruption, internal rebellion, and foreign intervention. At the time this asymmetry strongly favored Russian interests. In the longer term, however, it reinforced extant prejudices and suspicions and ensured that the bilateral relationship would remain dysfunctional for the next century.

The "unequal treaties," in particular, had three major consequences. They fostered, first, a lasting Russian assumption of superiority that has only softened—partially—in recent years. The Russian political elite has frequently underestimated China's capabilities, unsurprising given that its first substantial contact with Chinese civilization was when the latter was on the point of collapse. Second, the loss of enormous territories became a potent symbol of China's "century of humiliation" between the end of the First Opium War in 1842 and the final Communist victory in 1949. Russia came to be seen as no less exploitative than the other imperial powers, taking unconscionable advantage of Chinese weakness.[20] Third, and most important, the treaties

Changes in the Sino-Russian Border, Nineteenth Century

(A) Area lost in the treaty of Aigun, 1858 (>600,000 sq km.)
(B) Area lost in the treaty of Peking, 1860 (400,000 sq km.)
(C) Area lost in the treaty of Tarbagatai, 1864 (440,000 sq km.)
(D) Area lost in the 1880s (70,000 sq km.)

China's northern boundary, 1850
Modern boundaries

0 — 1,000 Kilometers

established a territorial question which for many in both countries remains unfinished business. Moscow and Beijing may have agreed on formal demarcation of the common border, but the Russian Far East (RFE), along with Taiwan, represents the last "unreturned" territory taken from China in the nineteenth century. This has led some Russians to believe that Beijing will turn its attention to recovering the RFE after it has completed Taiwan's reunification with the mainland.[21]

"Fraternal" relations and the Sino-Soviet split

Few periods so encapsulate the ambivalence of relations as the decade of "unbreakable friendship" between 1950 and 1960.[22] During this period the Soviet Union metamorphosed from China's greatest friend into its most bitter enemy. Yet the roots of this duality date back much earlier, to the May Fourth movement of 1919, the founding of the Chinese Communist Party in 1921, and the beginnings of Sino-Soviet cooperation in the 1920s.

The May Fourth movement began with student demonstrations against the decision of the Western powers at the Versailles Peace Conference to transfer the German colonial possessions of Jiaozhou and Qingdao and part of the Shandong peninsula to Japan instead of returning them to China. The disturbances, which began spontaneously, spawned a much larger political and cultural movement committed to national revival and the eradication of foreign imperialism and domestic warlordism.[23] During the 1920s the movement was a broad church, with one strand supporting Western democratic models, a second the semi-authoritarianism of Chiang Kai-shek, and a third taking inspiration from the Bolshevik revolution and its subsequent victory in the civil war against the Whites and foreign powers.[24]

This last strand gained tremendous impetus from the acute sense of betrayal in the wake of Versailles. Japan's diplomatic triumph highlighted Chinese weakness and isolation, but also the perfidy of the West; Wilsonian principles of self-determination had counted for nothing in the face of international *realpolitik*. In a highly charged, increasingly nationalistic atmosphere, many educated Chinese turned to alternative sources of inspiration. The recent experience of the Bolsheviks, in seizing and then holding on to power, appeared to offer a ready model for emulation.[25]

Moscow responded quickly to such aspirations, paving the way for the early establishment of the Chinese Communist Party (CCP) and its inclusion in the Communist International (Comintern). It sent advisers, such as Mikhail Borodin, to assist in the CCP's development; invited Party delegates to Moscow for training and ideological guidance; and provided considerable financial, logistical, and material support throughout the 1920s.

From the outset, however, the relationship between these fellow communists was difficult. On the plus side, a nascent CCP saw the Russian Revolution as an example of what could be achieved by a committed political-intellectual elite supported by the masses. The Party relied heavily on Kremlin funding and derived legitimacy from Comintern membership. But there was a constant tension between the need for Soviet assistance (money, arms, technical advice) and the desire to preserve independent decisionmaking in the face of Kremlin attempts to direct CCP affairs. This tension was never satisfactorily resolved during the four decades of Soviet involvement in China (1921–60).

Another major source of difficulty was the Soviet refusal to return territories gained by the Russian Empire in the nineteenth century. Although Moscow initially promised to relinquish its political and economic rights in Manchuria, it soon reneged on this commitment. Despite earlier condemnation of the great powers' imperialist policies and secret treaties, it clung on to the Russian Far East and even established a client-state in the form of a nominally independent Mongolia.[26] There appeared to be little difference between the imperialist ambitions of the new and old regimes.

The relationship between the Bolsheviks and the Chinese Communists was further complicated by Moscow's reluctance to offer unequivocal support and by the dubious quality of much of its advice. During the 1920s and 1930s, Stalin provided assistance to Chiang Kai-shek's Nationalists (Guomindang) as well as to the CCP, and insisted that the latter rein in its activities.[27] The consequences were occasionally disastrous, as when Chiang Kai-shek massacred the Communists in Shanghai in April 1927 and again in Canton (Guangzhou) in December that year. Subsequently, at Soviet insistence the CCP launched ill-fated frontal assaults on the southern cities of Nanchang, Changsha, and Wuhan in 1930—the outcome of which was a near-fatal weakening of the Party.[28] Most crucially, Stalin was instrumental in ensuring that Chiang Kai-shek would continue to lead China, even after he was kidnapped by the northern warlord Zhang Xueliang in December 1936.[29] Soviet policy was motivated by the strategic imperative of containing the rise of Japan rather than by ideological likemindedness with the Chinese Communists. The upshot of the Kremlin's double-dealing was that in the years before the final Communist victory in 1949, relations between the "fraternal" parties were notably lacking in trust.

Following the founding of the People's Republic of China (PRC) in October 1949, the Soviet Union became the country's number one, indeed sole partner. Mao's inclination to "lean to one side"—toward Moscow—was confirmed by his decision to intervene in the Korean War (1950–53). The bitterness of the conflict, in which nearly a million Chinese soldiers were killed, destroyed any hope of a functional relationship with the United States and its allies, and cemented the PRC's dependence on the USSR. The 1950 Treaty of Friendship, Alliance and Mutual Assistance initiated the period of "unbreakable friendship" and led to a flood of Soviet technical assistance, including the transfer of atomic weapons technology.[30]

However, relations were never easy between the "older brother" in Moscow and the "younger brother" in Beijing. Mao chafed under slights, real and perceived, and resented Stalin's attempts to control China by exploiting its dependence on Soviet aid. He was especially disappointed by the Kremlin's consolidation of the Mongolian People's Republic as a client-state. Nevertheless, in the early years of the PRC Mao had little option but to accept Stalin's direction as the price of Soviet assistance.

The situation changed after Nikita Khrushchev came to power, although initially relations improved as Moscow stepped up its assistance programs.[31] Mao regarded Khrushchev as a buffoon and a traitor to the Stalinist tradition. The dislike was cordially reciprocated. Personal tensions were exacerbated by widening ideological differences, especially after Khrushchev denounced Stalin's "excesses" in his "Secret Speech" at the 20th Soviet Communist Party Congress in 1956. An insecure Mao worried that Khrushchev's attack had set a dangerous precedent that would loosen his own hold on power.[32] Further disputes—over Soviet overtures to the Eisenhower administration and the fiasco of Mao's Great Leap Forward (1958–61)—fueled animosities to the point where, in June 1960, Khrushchev withdrew all 1,390 Soviet advisers working in China, leaving a number of major industrial and infrastructural projects in limbo.[33]

It is tempting to over-personalize the Sino-Soviet split and view it largely as the product of erratic behavior by two egocentric leaders. But while the personal dimension was important, the differences between the Soviet Union and China had deeper causes. The most important was Moscow's belief in its mission as the leader of the socialist camp, and insistence that China should acknowledge its own subordinate status. This was unacceptable to Mao, still smarting from the disasters of the "century of humiliation" and keen to restore China's self-esteem, not to mention reinforce his political authority at home.

The second major reason for the deterioration in relations was a deep-seated mutual mistrust. Part of this was historical, a legacy of developments

described earlier. But there were also concrete disagreements over the demarcation of the common border,[34] the pulling back of Russian assistance to
China's nuclear weapons program,[35] and Moscow's attempts to pursue some
measure of cooperation with the United States and Western Europe—all of
which aggravated Chinese fears of strategic encirclement.[36] For its part the
Kremlin became increasingly disturbed by Mao's foreign policy adventurism—exemplified by China's 1962 border war with India—and his pretensions to leadership of the communist bloc and the Non-Aligned Movement
(NAM). On an ideological level there was a disjunction between the Chairman's continuing attachment to hardline Marxist-Leninist doctrine and the
Soviet leadership's less doctrinaire approach to international affairs. This
found an outlet in very public quarrels over Soviet "revisionism."[37]

From tension to confrontation and back

Khrushchev's removal from power in 1964 alleviated tensions briefly, but
did not lead to substantive changes for the better. Indeed, relations soon
worsened. Both countries built up troop levels, so that by 1969 there were
twenty-one Soviet divisions and twenty-eight Chinese divisions along the
common border.[38] The combination of huge troop deployments, an
intractable territorial dispute, and acute domestic instability in China arising out of the Cultural Revolution proved combustible, and in 1969 Soviet
and Chinese troops were involved in a series of bloody border clashes.[39]
Although the full details of the crisis have yet to be revealed, it is estimated
that nearly a thousand soldiers died, mainly on the Chinese side. Most seriously, Moscow contemplated using nuclear weapons in the event of a Chinese "mass attack" across the border.[40]

Apart from the danger of nuclear confrontation, the 1969 crisis confirmed
long-held prejudices on both sides. For the Russians it reinforced the terror-
image of the "yellow peril"—millions of Chinese flooding across the border,
threatening to overwhelm Soviet defenses through sheer force of numbers.[41]
In Beijing it reaffirmed the idea of Russia as an imperialist power that was
determined to keep China down, and whose allegiance to communist ideals
was a sham.

Tensions eased somewhat after 1969, but less as a result of bilateral initiatives than because of changes in the wider international environment. American president Richard Nixon's overtures, first to Beijing and then to Moscow,
established strategic triangularism as an integral element of Sino-Soviet relations. Fears of being the odd one out in the process of détente with Washing-

ton encouraged a slight softening of attitudes.[42] Nevertheless, relations remained cold for the next two decades.[43] There was no perceptible movement on the territorial issue and economic links were very modest (trade turnover was a fraction of Soviet-Japanese trade over the same period[44]). Subsequently, fresh tensions arose in connection with Moscow's support for the Vietnamese military intervention in Cambodia in 1978, the ensuing war between China and Vietnam, and the Soviet invasion of Afghanistan in December 1979.

Gorbachev's initiatives

Mikhail Gorbachev's visit to China in May 1989, the first by a Soviet leader for three decades,[45] is frequently cited as the event that ended the Sino-Soviet split and launched a new era in relations.[46] In fact, this judgment confuses cause and effect. The real shift occurred three years earlier in July 1986, during his speech in the far eastern port city of Vladivostok, home of the Soviet Pacific fleet. Gorbachev emphasized the importance of good-neighborly relations between the "two largest socialist states," on whom "a great deal in international development depends." He expressed the hope that the Sino-Soviet frontier would "become a zone of peace and friendship" and called for enhanced economic cooperation. To this purpose he offered the first territorial concession by a Russian/Soviet leader since the "unequal treaties" were concluded more than a century earlier, proposing that the border run through the middle of the main channel of the Amur river rather than along the Chinese shore.[47] Gorbachev was conciliatory on the Sino-Vietnamese conflict, advocated a reduction of troop levels on either side of the Sino-Soviet border—a key Chinese demand—and proposed a range of security confidence-building measures, including opening up Vladivostok, then a closed military city.[48] Two years later he followed up the Asia-Pacific theme in an address in the central Siberian city of Krasnoyarsk. Claiming that bilateral ties were increasingly characterized by "good-neighborliness and trust," he declared that the USSR supported the "full normalization" of relations and foreshadowed a Sino-Soviet summit meeting.[49]

Gorbachev's address at Vladivostok revealed his "new thinking" on relations with the outside world.[50] The emphasis on cooperation instead of competition, on shared interests rather than past antagonisms and existing policy differences, provided the philosophical foundation for a radically different China policy. Although many difficulties lay ahead in realizing good intentions, not least Beijing's tough stance,[51] Vladivostok marked the point when the Soviet Union moved from its previous policy of containment to one of engagement.

Unfortunately, tangible progress was slowed by developments in both countries. In China, the Tiananmen Square massacre in June 1989 led to a period of introspection as the CCP set out to restore its authority. The bloody suppression of the demonstrations led to Western sanctions, which in turn caused the Chinese leadership to adopt a resolutely defensive international posture. Later that year Beijing was disconcerted by the "velvet" revolutions in Eastern Europe and the populist example these appeared to give to its own restive urban population. It had previously noted that Gorbachev's visit to China had provided encouragement to protesting students and workers.[52] In these fraught circumstances the improvement of Sino-Soviet relations became a marginal priority.

The rapid decline of Gorbachev's authority and the disintegration of the Soviet Union meant also that the Kremlin could not devote the time and resources to build on rapprochement. There was a modest expansion of bilateral trade, and in May 1991 the two countries agreed on demarcation of the eastern section of the boundary. However, the agreement left in abeyance several disputed areas,[53] and relations remained cool.

During this turbulent period (1989–91), China and the Soviet Union appeared to be traveling in opposite directions. The former reversed much of the political and social liberalization—"bourgeois liberalization"—that had followed in the wake of economic reforms in the 1980s.[54] Meanwhile the USSR was undergoing an extraordinary transformation as a result of the changes Gorbachev had initiated but was no longer able to control. For the Chinese leadership, the failure of Gorbachev's reforms provided—and still provides—a model lesson in how *not* to implement change, with its "mistaken" and subversive emphasis on political democratization over economic reform.[55] To the Russian liberal elite, on the other hand, the CCP's crushing of the Tiananmen Square demonstrations reinforced the traditional image of a despotic East. Beijing's premature endorsement of the August 1991 putsch in Moscow only seemed to confirm China's identification with repressive forces everywhere. In short, while Gorbachev played a crucial role in the improvement of Sino-Soviet relations in the second half of the 1980s, his policies and their consequences highlighted a growing values gap between the two countries. The relationship may have become more pragmatic in its focus on practical cooperation and security confidence-building. But this did not signify any warmth, rather the reverse. Few regretted the passing of the Soviet Union more than the Chinese government. Despite finding it an overbearing and often hostile neighbor, Beijing found comfort in its relative predictability. By contrast, it knew little about the new Yeltsin administration, other than that it had promised to introduce far-reaching political and economic reforms and had set the country on an avowedly pro-Western course. China once again appeared to be threatened by strategic encirclement.

The Yeltsin-Jiang years

Chinese fears proved to be misplaced. Yeltsin's reforms began radically, but soon ran into trouble. The Russian population suffered tremendous hardships in the transition from a planned system to a market-based economy, and the Kremlin's authority came under growing challenge from the federal legislature (Duma) and Russia's regions. The accumulation of problems— new and inherited—encouraged factionalism within the elite, crippled policymaking, and undermined regime confidence. It also contributed to an ever more erratic foreign policy. Unrealistic expectations of Western assistance and investment, and "equal partnership" with the United States, gave way to bitter disappointment and a profound sense of betrayal. The perceived failure of Western economic prescriptions—the "Washington consensus"[56]—was accentuated by conspiracy theories alleging that these were intended to weaken, not reform, Russia. Under mounting domestic pressure and resentful of what he saw as the West's ingratitude for his part in ending the Soviet Union, Yeltsin moved Russian foreign policy toward a more "multi-vectored," less obviously Westerncentric approach.[57] This entailed, in the first place, returning to rapprochement with Beijing.

Yeltsin described his first state visit to China in December 1992 as ushering in "a new era in Russia-China relations."[58] For once, the hyperbole was appropriate. During the 1990s the momentum of bilateral ties was uniformly positive. By 1994 the two sides were already speaking of a "constructive partnership," upgraded two years later to a "strategic partnership of equality, mutual confidence and mutual coordination for the 21st century."[59] Such descriptions reflected the transformation of a formerly adversarial relationship into one of increasing warmth.

Significant progress was achieved on border issues. After delimitation of its eastern section in 1991, there followed demarcation of the western section in September 1994 and, in April 1996, an agreement on confidence-building measures along the whole length of the former Sino-Soviet frontier. The Agreement on Strengthening Mutual Military Confidence in the Border Region, signed in Shanghai by Russia, China, Kazakhstan, Kyrgyzstan, and

Tajikistan, provided for the withdrawal of all armored troops and heavy weaponry from a 100-km-wide frontier zone. The five signatories became known as the "Shanghai Five" and in 2001 evolved into the Shanghai Cooperation Organization, a development that reflected the tightening links between them.

There was also substantial progress in developing economic ties. Joint communiqués lamented that bilateral trade was not commensurate with the extent and warmth of political relations.[60] Yet China once again became a major Russian trading partner, displacing Japan from first position among Asian countries. After an initial surge in which two-way trade reached nearly U.S.$8 billion in 1993, it hovered around the $5–6 billion mark for the rest of the decade.[61] Although Yeltsin's boast that trade would reach $20 billion by 2000 was not fulfilled, this still compared impressively with levels reached during the previous three decades.

The 1990s were notable for the extent of convergence between Russian and Chinese positions on a number of domestic and international issues. After a brief early flirtation with Taiwan,[62] Moscow reiterated its commitment to the "one China" policy. In return Beijing was supportive during Yeltsin's first war in Chechnya (1994–96), at a time when the Kremlin was being roundly condemned in the West. The two sides adopted similar positions on the guiding principles of international relations—promoting "multipolarity," criticizing American "hegemonism," condemning the West's "double standards" and "interference in [their] domestic affairs"—as well as on more specific issues: the Balkans, Iraq, the Middle East peace process, relations with Iran.[63]

On a personal level, Sino-Russian rapprochement was facilitated by the chemistry between Yeltsin and Chinese president Jiang Zemin. The latter had trained as an electrical engineer in Moscow in 1955 and spoke fluent Russian. His gregarious personality also jelled with Yeltsin's extrovert manner, and the two enjoyed a trouble-free relationship.[64] More broadly, bilateral ties benefited from the presence of a strong "Russia lobby" within the Chinese leadership. Like Jiang, Premier Li Peng and Vice Premier and Foreign Minister Qian Qichen[65] had studied in the Soviet Union during the 1950s.

Great expectations, partial achievements

By the end of the Yeltsin presidency, Sino-Russian relations were developing well. Both sides lost little opportunity to proclaim the merits of their "strategic partnership," and even experts in the West spoke of "strategic convergence" between Moscow and Beijing.[66] Progress appeared to be seamless, with movement on key bilateral questions and consensus on international issues. But beneath the surface, problems persisted. Some were related to unresolved matters from the past, such as border demarcation, Chinese "illegal migration," and Russian perceptions of the "China threat." Others arose out of differences in political and business culture. Most important, Moscow and Beijing still devoted far greater attention to building up relations with the West than with each other.

The most serious outstanding issue was the common border. Officially the two governments had largely settled this by 1996, with the exception of some disputed islands near Khabarovsk.[67] But closure was sabotaged by the behavior of provincial administrations in the RFE. The weakness of Moscow's remit meant that it was unable or unwilling to bring them into line with the intergovernmental agreements it had concluded with Beijing. Primorye governor Yevgeny Nazdratenko and his counterpart in Khabarovsk, Viktor Ishaev, managed to slow down the work of the joint boundary commission, and the former even succeeded in regaining part of the Tumen river basin for Russia.

Similar tensions arose over Chinese "illegal migration." The Primorye and Khabarovsk administrations, supported by influential elements in Moscow, played up fears of a mass demographic invasion of the RFE. Allegedly authoritative sources spoke of "millions" of "illegals" settling in the region, bringing with them crime and disease and threatening Russia's territorial integrity. There was growing animosity toward Chinese shuttle-traders (*chelnoki*) who brought essential goods across the border. The local population, neglected by Moscow and faced with the collapse of the Soviet system of subsidized goods and services, became almost entirely dependent on Chinese imports. Regional politicians stoked up local resentment to divert attention from endemic corruption and misgovernment. The Chinese became a scapegoat for plummeting living standards, a natural target for envy and xenophobia.

Chauvinism in the RFE was only part of a more general anti-Chinese sentiment among large sections of the Russian elite and population. Fears about frontier security and "illegal migration" were supplemented by concerns about the changing military balance. Throughout the 1990s arms exports to China remained controversial. The military-industrial complex, crippled by the demise of the USSR, needed the China market to ensure the survival of factories and whole one-industry towns.[68] But Westernizing liberals and senior military figures worried that the sale of hi-tech weaponry to China could come to haunt Russia, as such arms might one day be used against it.[69] The Kremlin firmly rebutted the notion of a "China threat," but even as late as 1996 Defense Minister Igor Rodionov identified China in precisely those terms.[70]

Politicians and intellectuals highlighted the cultural threat of Sinification—the erosion of Russia's way of life by Chinese economic and demographic influence. The concentration of Chinese migrant workers in self-contained enclaves fueled suspicions of a fifth column undermining Russia from within.[71] On a marginally more sophisticated level, liberals feared that the Kremlin's commitment to expanding the "strategic partnership" with Beijing would distract Russia from integration with the West. The more the Yeltsin administration engaged with an authoritarian China, so the argument ran, the less it would stay true to its original commitment to political democracy, liberal market reforms, and a civil society.[72] The China relationship became a barometer of Russia's post-Soviet evolution and its place in the international community. The alleged normative threat posed by China was reinforced by the stark contrast between a stable and prospering state, on the one hand, and a fragile and destitute Russia, on the other. As in the nineteenth century, even those who believed that the country was selling out to the West were little interested in too close an embrace with China. Like Slavophilism, the fashionable concept of Eurasianism was a Russian, not Asian, choice. It emphasized Russia's unique values and individuality (*spetsifika*), its transcontinental dimensions, and its globalist perspective in international affairs.[73]

Geopolitics and instrumentalism

Throughout the 1990s Beijing adopted a pragmatic approach to doing business with Moscow. Although irritated by the dysfunctionality of Russian decisionmaking, it took a long view of the relationship. It reconciled itself to the Kremlin's Westerncentrism and accepted that the Russian establishment would, for all sorts of historical and practical reasons, look primarily to the United States and Western Europe. What mattered more to Beijing was that the "strategic partnership" should serve concrete priorities: backing for its position on Taiwan, Tibet and Xinjiang; security-building on China's northern and western frontiers; ensuring a steady stream of advanced weaponry; and political support for China's efforts to play a more active role in the world. To achieve these aims, the Communist leadership could (and did) put up with a lot.

Nevertheless, Yeltsin's increasingly erratic management of foreign policy inhibited the development of the bilateral relationship. His fixation with the United States, whether as "equal partner" or strategic rival, proved especially damaging. He yearned for "integration" with the West,[74] yet clung to Soviet-era ideas of bipolarity, the balance of power, and privileged spheres of influence. Sino-Russian relations became hostage to extraneous geopolitical considerations. The "China card," not partnership with China, became the Kremlin's priority, as strategic direction gave way to a series of ad hoc responses and a lowest common denominator approach to international relations.[75]

The failure of competitive multipolarity

The return of geopolitics reflected the Kremlin's conviction that international politics was competitive by its very nature. If Russia was to find its niche in the post–Cold War environment, then it could not do so as a "junior partner" of the United States, but must instead maneuver between different major actors—the United States, Europe, China, Japan, India. This assumption underpinned the emergence of competitive multipolarity in the early 1990s.[76] The world might no longer be formally bipolar following the collapse of the Soviet Union, but Moscow nonetheless retained a bipolar mentality: on one side, the United States and its NATO allies; on the other, the major non-Western power centers—Russia, China, India, and the Islamic world. This competitive multipolarity amounted to a "revised" form of bipolarity and rested on the principle that hegemonic power should always be counterbalanced.[77]

In these circumstances China became Yeltsin's "balancer" of choice. He envisaged, at a minimum, that the "strategic partnership" would force the West to take greater account of Russian interests. Better still, Russia might aspire to become the "swing power" between the United States and China, moving to and from each according to requirements. In performing the role of counterbalancer, it would thus be able to fulfill its strategic and civilizational destiny as "bridge" between East and West.

Unfortunately for the Kremlin, others refused to play Moscow's game. Periodic threats to "go East" lacked credibility in Western capitals, nowhere more so than in Washington where the Clinton administration was increasingly committed to comprehensive engagement with China. Far from maximizing Russia's standing, Yeltsin's clumsy use of the China card betrayed Russia as an awkward but weak "partner," whose appetites greatly exceeded its modest capacities. The limits of Sino-Russian "likemindedness" were evident everywhere. Whereas Moscow envisaged their partnership as leverage against

Washington and a check on American "hegemonism," Beijing viewed it in more practical terms—as a means of realizing concrete objectives in the bilateral relationship.

Contrasting foreign policy approaches

This divergence highlighted the two countries' very different approaches to foreign policy in general. While Beijing underplayed China's rise, Moscow demanded that the West respect Russia's birthright as a great power. This sense of strategic entitlement drew it into a debilitating series of quarrels with the United States and Europe—over Western "encroachment" in the newly independent states (NIS); NATO enlargement into Central and Eastern Europe; the Balkan crises in Bosnia and Kosovo; economic sanctions and military intervention against Iraq; Russian nuclear cooperation with Iran; and strategic disarmament. Force of habit led Moscow to adopt vocal positions even where its interests and influence were peripheral.

The contrast with Chinese foreign policy over the same period is striking. There were relatively few crises in Beijing's interaction with the West. Significantly, when problems did occur, they concerned core Chinese interests: the 1996 crisis over PLA military exercises in the Taiwan straits and the subsequent dispatch of the U.S. Seventh Fleet; the diplomatic quarrel and violent demonstrations following the American bombing of the Chinese Embassy in Belgrade in May 1999; accusation and counter-accusation over human rights in China; theatre missile defense in East Asia. Even then such crises were short-lived. On larger international questions—the situation in the Balkans, Iraq, the Middle East peace process—Beijing maintained a very low profile. Although it agreed with Moscow on much of the policy substance, it was not prepared to invest political capital in pursuing secondary priorities.

Russia and China might have been singing from the same song-sheet when they declared that the main purpose of their respective foreign policies was to promote an international environment that would facilitate domestic growth.[78] However, their implementation of this objective could hardly have been in greater contrast. While both spoke of a "global multipolar order," they viewed its realization and composition very differently. Moscow believed, for the most part, that "an international order for the twenty-first century" already existed or would soon come to fruition. It also assumed that Russia would be one of the major poles, at the very least on a par with China. Beijing, on the other hand, saw the world as essentially unipolar, a condition in which it would remain for some decades.[79] Moreover, by the time a multipolar order came into being, it was unlikely that China and Russia would still be equals.[80]

Duality and ambivalence

A number of themes emerge out of the historical experience of the Sino-Russian relationship. The first is *fear and anxiety*. In conflict and in cooperation, the importance of defense and security considerations has been paramount.[81] Thus the Mongol invasion implanted the idea of *the East as threat* in the Russian mind, while the Russian annexation of China's northern lands (the Manchu province of East Tartary) through the "unequal treaties" established it as an exploitative imperial presence in Chinese perceptions. Later the Sino-Soviet alliance and subsequent split were driven first by the fear of a dominant America (supported by a resurgent Japan), and then by growing suspicions regarding each other's strategic intentions and irredentist agendas. The rapprochement of the Yeltsin-Jiang years was motivated, at least in Russia, by the perceived need to "counterbalance" America's growing power in the post–Cold War world. Overall the motivation behind both enmity and partnership/alliance within the relationship has been *defensive*, a response to real and imagined security concerns. Only rarely has a positive vision supplied the motive force for progress; the brief Gorbachev period is the (partial) exception that proves the rule.

The second recurrent theme is *mistrust*. At no stage in the long stretch from the Mongol invasion to the end of the Yeltsin presidency was there a time when the two sides enjoyed a genuinely trusting relationship. On occasions Moscow and Beijing worked together with some success. But there was no honeymoon period; during the "unbreakable friendship" in the 1950s, for example, rhetorical flourishes obscured vast reservoirs of mutual contempt and resentment.

This sense of alienation has resulted in a utilitarian approach to relations, the keynotes of which are *pragmatism and expediency*. The two sides have generally sought accommodation, swallowing antipathy for reasons of state. Thus the Qing dynasty agreed to the loss of its northern territories, more or less without a struggle, in the hope of avoiding an even worse fate—its complete collapse.[82] In the Sino-Soviet period, Moscow and Beijing managed close cooperation despite an obvious lack of trust. During the Yeltsin years the Kremlin did not let its Western leanings stop it from improving relations with China, while Beijing ignored the naked instrumentalism of Russian foreign policy. There may have been no tradition of friendship, but both countries grew accustomed to setting aside personal feelings for the sake of concrete national interests.

At the same time such pragmatism has always had its limits. Throughout history the Sino-Russian relationship has almost invariably been of *secondary importance* to both sides. Even at the height of the "unbreakable friendship," the Soviet Union paid greater heed to the United States and Western Europe than it did to China, while Mao focused overwhelmingly on domestic development at the expense of foreign policy. Soviet assistance was primarily important in facilitating reconstruction after the ravages of a twenty-year civil war (1927–49) and the Japanese occupation (1937–45). When China engaged with the outside world, it often did so in competition with the Soviet Union; witness Beijing's efforts to lead the third world, beginning with the 1955 Asia-Africa summit in Bandung (that led to the creation of the NAM) and continuing with the ideological and political struggle to head the international communist movement.

For all the differences in their respective paths to modernization, China post-Mao and Russia under Gorbachev and Yeltsin each looked to the West for assistance, trade, and investment. Political elites in both countries recognized that neither was able (or committed enough) to assist the other in the primary tasks of national development. "Strategic partnership" was a mere adjunct to functional ties with the West, which was seen as the fount of real power and influence in the world.

Unsurprisingly Moscow and Beijing have found it useful to promote *positive but misleading images* of their relationship, supported by the appropriate terminology. "Fraternal relations" reached their apogee in 1950 with the grand-sounding Treaty of Friendship, Alliance and Mutual Assistance. Nearly half a century later, in April 1996, public language achieved new heights of optimism with the "strategic partnership of equality, mutual confidence and mutual coordination for the 21st century." Opposition to American "hegemonism and power politics" was expressed in terms of promoting the "multipolarization of the world and the establishment of a new international order." On a more sentimental note, the phrase "forever friends, never enemies"[83] described a "dynamically developing" relationship. Both sides continued to assert, in the face of compelling evidence to the contrary, that the relationship occupied a central place in their foreign policy thinking. Russia, in particular, rejected any suggestion of a Westerncentric bias by asserting that it was committed to a "multi-vectored" and "geographically balanced" foreign policy.

The disjunction between high-sounding phrases and prosaic realities exemplified the *duality* of the relationship. During the Soviet and early post-Soviet periods, it suited Moscow and Beijing to suspend disbelief—their own and that of others. Particularly under Yeltsin and Jiang, both were aware of the limitations and often contradictory character of their interaction,[84] and sought to compensate for this through florid rhetoric and the proliferation of framework agreements. They saw advantage in making their partnership appear more significant and influential than it really was.

But ultimately such dissimulation could not hide the reality of an *ambivalent, half-hearted cooperation*. For every positive, there was a negative. The specter of the "China threat" disturbed the dream of "strategic partnership." Diplomatic rapprochement was limited by the obvious priority of relations with the West. Signal achievements, such as demarcation of the border, were diluted by continuing suspicions and fears for the future. And agreement on many domestic and international issues contrasted with diverging perceptions of their respective roles in the post–Cold War order. These contradictions had their roots in a difficult shared history or, more accurately, in different memories and readings of that history. The challenge for Vladimir Putin, upon succeeding Boris Yeltsin in January 2000, was to transcend this accumulated burden and realize the grand vision of Sino-Russian strategic partnership.

CHAPTER THREE

STRATEGIC PARTNERSHIP—
IMAGE AND REALITY

"Both sides agree that in recent years Chinese-Russian partnership relations of strategic cooperation...have reached a level unprecedented in their history."
—Hu Jintao, Moscow, July 1, 2005[1]

"Relations today are the best they have ever been in our interaction with China....They are of a pragmatic and good-neighborly character. And I think they can continue for a long time to come."
—Vladimir Putin, Novo-Ogarevo, September 9, 2006[2]

Over the last few years, Sino-Russian relations have shown remarkable improvement. Moscow and Beijing have built on the progress of the late 1980s and 1990s to such an extent that ties today are closer and more substantial than at any time in the two countries' history.[3] Every area of the relationship has expanded, and it now has a fully multidimensional character. The agreement formally delimiting the 4,300-kilometer border was ratified in June 2005, and there are no obvious bilateral disputes. The two sides give each other strong moral and political support on priority issues: Moscow backs Beijing on Taiwan, Tibet, and Xinjiang, while the Chinese reciprocate on Chechnya and the North Caucasus. They coordinate efficiently in repelling Western criticisms of domestic political and human rights practices. Trade turnover has increased eightfold since 1999, from U.S.$5.7 billion to U.S.$48 billion,[4] with China now Russia's second largest trading partner after the EU.[5] Russian oil exports to China have risen at double-digit levels,[6] and the arms relationship remains significant. Even in areas where engagement has previously been weak or nonexistent, such as military-to-military cooperation, the partners have made important progress—as demonstrated by the "Peace Mission" joint exercises in 2005 and 2007.

Internationally the two sides give a convincing impression of consensus. They voice concerns about American "hegemonic" tendencies and claim to support the "democratization of international relations," while in practice acting on the great power principle that the big players should deal with the big issues.[7] They attach primary importance to geopolitics, but understand the value of economic instruments in projecting influence. They talk up the primacy of the UN and use multilateral mechanisms to raise their profile as good international citizens. Yet both are highly protective of national sovereignty and mutually supportive in resisting "interference" by supranational institutions and normative regimes. More concretely, Russia and China assign priority to combating the "three evils" of terrorism, separatism, and extremism; would like to see an end to the stationing of American troops in Central Asia; are critical of the U.S. coalition's presence in Iraq; advocate peaceful engagement with Iran and North Korea; and see few moral impediments to close ties with unsavory regimes around the world, from Belarus to Zimbabwe.

This convergence is facilitated by the multiplying of institutional links. In contrast to the Russia-U.S. relationship, which has been under-institutionalized and overdependent on the personal chemistry between Putin and George W. Bush, Moscow and Beijing interact on many levels: presidential and prime ministerial, in joint ministerial and sub-ministerial commissions, and through academic, media, and student exchanges. An estimated 2 million Russians visited China in 2006, with 900,000 Chinese traveling in the opposite direction.[8] The relationship between Putin and Hu Jintao (sometimes called "Pu and Hu" in an echo of the "Bill and Boris" and "Boris and Helmut" friendships of the 1990s[9]) has been of particular importance. It has thrown up interesting similarities in policy approach. Hu's emphasis on a "harmonious society" and Putin's platform of greater social responsibility and justice represent a reaction to the capitalist "excesses" of the previous decade in China and Russia. Likewise, there is considerable common ground in their agendas for recentralizing power following the partial devolution of authority to the regions and provinces in the 1990s.[10]

The radical improvement in the bilateral relationship is due mainly to changes on the Russian side. Moscow is now much more consistent in its engagement with Beijing. Although Putin has remained faithful to the Western-centric tradition of Russian foreign policy, this has not inhibited the growth of bilateral ties as much as it did under Yeltsin. Putin has pursued a genuinely multi-vectored foreign policy, consistent with his vision of Russia's status and potential as a global power. Although there have been various switches of emphasis, one constant has remained: a personal commitment to expanded relations with China.[11] Russia may be a "European civilization," as Putin has asserted on many occasions,[12] but this has not deterred him from striving to take the "strategic partnership" to the next level.

The surge in relations owes much, also, to a greater focus on substance. Although wordy statements continue to issue from the Kremlin, there is much more emphasis on the concrete. Thus the March 2006 summit in Beijing witnessed the signing of 29 separate agreements, many on trade and economic matters.[13] It is symptomatic of Moscow's seriousness that Russian summit delegations invariably include top business leaders negotiating individual contracts.

Defining strategic partnership

These impressive achievements have inevitably spawned claims about the emergence of a fully-fledged strategic partnership—at once a flourishing bilateral relationship and an increasingly influential factor in world politics. To a growing number of observers in the West, not to mention in Moscow and Beijing, the existence of such a partnership has become a self-evident truth. Yet the real picture is altogether more confused. There are clearly strategic dimensions to Sino-Russian relations, and in recent times the two countries have demonstrated a surprising degree of policy coordination. However, in many respects they act in ways that contradict the very essence and spirit of a strategic partnership. To understand this contradiction it is necessary to establish first what we mean by *strategic partnership*.

One of the barriers to understanding is the ubiquity of the phrase itself. During the 1990s, the Russian leadership applied it to every relationship of significance and to many that were not.[14] It was a form of legitimation, often serving to mask a lack of content with the illusion of significance. "Strategic partnerships" were seen as a way of maximizing Russia's "room for maneuver on a global scale."[15] With Russia's weight in world affairs at its lowest since the 1920s,[16] such quasi-formal arrangements were important in bolstering national self-esteem as well as in eliciting greater international consideration. These considerations remain pertinent today. Although Russia is playing a more prominent role in regional and global affairs, its capacity to exercise influence depends on the extent to which it is able to co-opt others in the pursuit of common agendas—or at least give the impression of doing so.

For China, "strategic partnership" fulfills similar functions. It is at once a mark of respect to a valued bilateral partner, an indicator of progress in the relationship, and a potential source of wider influence. Most important, it is consistent with Beijing's theme of a "harmonious world." China's network of "strategic partnerships" with the other major powers—the United States, the European Union (and its leading member-states), Russia, India, and even Japan[17]—proclaim its commitment to peaceful and constructive engagement. Such partnerships enable it to play a more active part in international affairs. For notwithstanding its impressive rise, China does not yet possess the confidence or the capacity to assert itself as a fully independent actor.

The proliferation of "strategic partnerships" has, however, greatly devalued the concept. Indeed, since virtually any significant relationship in Russian or Chinese foreign policy now qualifies as strategic, omission of the epithet has become more noteworthy than its inclusion, most recently in highlighting Moscow's deteriorating ties with the United States.[18] How, then, to distinguish the genuinely strategic relationship from its facsimile?

It is important not to set the bar either too high or too low. It is improbable, for example, that partners will agree on every issue, all the time. Even the closest-knit of alliances, such as the "special relationship" between the United States and the United Kingdom, have their tensions and differences. On the other hand it is reasonable to expect a certain shared vision, both of the world in general and of the partners' respective roles within it. Defining a relationship as strategic implies a long-term reciprocal commitment, one resilient enough to withstand occasional setbacks and misunderstandings. Although there is scope for tactical opportunism, this remains an unstable basis for constructive engagement and cannot be overplayed. Similarly, instrumental considerations—the use of partnership to exercise leverage on third parties—should not exercise a disproportionate influence. For in that event the bilateral relationship would become overly susceptible to changes in the external environment. Ultimately, a bona fide strategic partnership is predicated on a broad consistency of purpose. It succeeds or fails to the extent that both sides are able to identify lasting common interests and to translate these into far-reaching, substantive cooperation.

Sino-Russian "strategic partnership"

Official documents shed little light on the nature of Sino-Russian "strategic partnership," largely because its existence is taken for granted—more a question of faith (and ritual) than reason. The July 2001 Treaty of Good-Neighborliness and Friendly Cooperation certainly appears to operate on this assumption. In the preamble, the rationale for the treaty includes the following standard formulations: "to consolidate friendly and good-neighborly ties and mutual cooperation in all fields"; "promoting and establishing a just and fair new world order"; "to endeavor to enhance relations between the two countries to a completely new level." Article 1 commits the two parties to developing a "strategic cooperative partnership of good-neighborliness, friendship and cooperation and equality and trust . . . from a long-term view and in a comprehensive manner," but does not elaborate further. Nor is it much more precise on the principles on which the treaty is based. These are "universally recognized principles and norms of international law" and China's Five Principles of "mutual respect for state sovereignty and territorial integrity, mutual non-aggression, mutual non-interference in each other's internal affairs, equality and mutual benefit, and peaceful co-existence."[19]

The remaining articles of the treaty rehearse standard positions and policies: mutual non-aggression (Articles 2 and 8); "one China" (Article 5); the abandonment of territorial claims against the other party (Article 6); confidence-building measures along the common border (Article 7); preserving "strategic stability" in nuclear weapons (Article 12); support for the "central role" of the UN in handling international affairs (Article 13); cooperation in various fields—the economy, trade, "military know-how," science and technology, "energy resources," etc. (Article 16); and active cooperation in "cracking down on terrorists, splittists and extremists." There are occasional clues, such as the denial in Article 22 that the treaty—and hence the "strategic partnership"—is "directed against any third country."[20] But for the most part it reads like a shopping list, with some items ticked off and others in the "to do" column.

The joint statement from the December 2002 summit in Moscow is scarcely more enlightening. It speaks of implementing the great strategic idea that the two countries will "forever be good neighbors, friends and reliable partners, and never be enemies." And it declares that "the friendly relations of the two countries are a new type of state-to-state relations based on non-alignment and non-confrontation, and which are not directed against third countries." The 2002 statement is simply a more detailed iteration of the 2001 treaty. It was not until the Beijing summit of March 2006 that the two governments set out the principles underpinning partnership, instead of merely restating well-known policy positions. The summit communiqué notes that ten years have passed since the establishment of "relations of equal and trusting partnership and strategic interaction." In that time "reciprocal political trust" has "constantly deepened" and a "multifaceted mechanism of interaction" now functions in all spheres of cooperation. As for the basic principles of the bilateral relationship, these include: "mutual respect, equality, mutual support, the maximum promotion of mutual political trust, complementarity, mutual benefit, taking a long-term perspective, striving for joint development, the exchange of experience, the broadening of human contacts, and strengthening the social base of bilateral relations." In external affairs, both sides promised to "adhere to the line of coordinating and deepening strategic interaction . . . with the aim of creating a favorable international situation."[21]

This unwieldy set of principles is little more than a cobbled-together amalgam of China's Five Principles of Peaceful Co-existence and other platitudes. They do not provide a detailed, let alone accurate, picture of the ideational context of the relationship or of Moscow's and Beijing's objectives. For contrary to the seamless consensus they seek to convey, Russian and Chinese approaches to their partnership differ in significant respects.

The Russian agenda

Russia's rationale for partnership with China is essentially twofold. The first is what might be called "global strategic." In its most primitive form this means using the partnership to counterbalance the dominance of the West, and America's hegemonic power in particular. In that sense it is an "anti-relationship," driven by the urge to neutralize or negate. However, while Moscow's agenda is colored by visceral anti-Americanism in some quarters, it is informed by positive considerations as well. Russia in 2008 is far more stable and prosperous at home, and more influential abroad, than under Gorbachev and Yeltsin. But it remains a relatively minor player on the world stage, notwithstanding Kremlin claims to the contrary. Putin understands that Russia needs to make common cause—tactical or strategic as the case may be—with other powers if it is to exert a serious influence in international affairs.

From Moscow's perspective, China represents both the present and the future. A formidable power already, it seems to have unlimited economic, political, and military potential.[22] If China rises as quickly as many believe, then the leverage from partnership with it will become correspondingly greater, and the sooner America's irksome global leadership will be undermined. Of course, few Russians would like to see one hegemon replaced by another. But the expectation is that this will not happen, and that instead China and the United States will effectively balance and contain one another, with the involvement of other major actors—India, the major European powers, and above all Russia. Putin's pursuit of a "multi-vectored" foreign policy is driven by the desire to maximize Moscow's options. Russia would become the strategic, as well as civilizational, bridge between East and West, and possibly even the "third pole" in the multipolar world of the future, alongside the United States and China.[23]

In the meantime the China relationship gives the Kremlin an "alternative" to the West. It is argued in chapter 9 that this supposed alternative is bogus. Nevertheless, growing ties with Beijing are of considerable comfort at a time when Russia's relations with a number of Western countries (the United States and the United Kingdom) and organizations (the European Union) are going through a very rough period. The "strategic partnership" serves as an important psychological crutch; after energy-driven economic prosperity, it is the most compelling explanation for the confident face Russia presents to the world. Whether strategic or not, a successful relationship with China is key to the "independent" foreign policy Putin has consistently promoted.

Partnership with Beijing, however, is more than just about geopolitical maneuvering. It serves critical security interests as well,[24] ensuring a stable border and, by extension, the security of the Russian Far East (RFE) and Russia's territorial integrity. The Sino-Soviet freeze highlighted the undesirable consequences of poor bilateral relations: strategic confrontation on two fronts and the threat of encirclement; the requirement to station large numbers of troops along an extremely tense frontier; and the huge expense of sustaining armed forces capable of meeting the challenges posed by an unpredictable China, on top of the Cold War with the United States and its allies.

Today Moscow sees the "strategic partnership" as its most reliable guarantee against a resurgent and potentially aggressive China. To some extent its approach is informed by the adage "keep your friends close, keep your enemies closer." Although China is certainly no enemy, the underlying message is clear: positive engagement enables you to keep tabs on emergent threats and to establish a common interest in peaceful coexistence and cooperation. It offers Russia obvious security, political, and economic benefits. For example, both sides have worked well together to defuse the controversial issue of Chinese "illegal migration"—efforts that have enabled Moscow to escape the full consequences of its neglect of the RFE. China has also been the number one customer for Russian arms—a commercial relationship that has saved much of Russia's military-industrial complex from extinction. And Beijing's friendship offers a potential entrée to the Asia-Pacific community. It is no coincidence that when Moscow speaks of developing Asian energy markets it is China that it has in mind above all others.

Finally, Russia views the bilateral relationship as one between "strategic equals." The frequent references to equality in official communiqués reflect a vital aspiration, if not necessarily reality. Russian attitudes here are somewhat contradictory. On the one hand, there are concerns about China's rapid rise and the changing balance of power between them (see chapter 5); on the other hand, Moscow is incapable of seeing itself as the "junior partner" in any relationship, particularly with a country that it has long regarded with a superior and even dismissive eye.[25] For Putin and the political establishment, Russia is always "equal-plus": equal to the greatest powers, including the United States, but meriting a much higher status than other, "ordinary" states in the international system.

The Chinese agenda

The benefits of partnership are somewhat different for China. One crucial distinction is that Beijing does not view Russia as a strategic counterweight to the United States. It believes that Russia has some international influence, especially in the former Soviet Union, and that cooperating with it in the UN Security Council pays dividends. But Beijing has not attempted to use its friendship with Moscow as a bargaining counter in dealings with the West— and with good reason. Russia is too weak to perform such a role and, in any event, would be reluctant to act on behalf of Chinese interests. Moscow's refusal to become involved in the Taiwan question, beyond formal recognition of Beijing's "one China" policy,[26] highlights its limitations as a partner on crunch issues.

A still more important reason for restraint is that China has no need to engage in balancing games, since it enjoys far greater strategic choice than Russia. Since the late 1990s Beijing has reached out successfully across the Asia-Pacific region to all continents. Relations with the United States and the EU have expanded exponentially; close ties with ASEAN member-states and the Republic of Korea bear no resemblance to the chilly atmosphere prior to the 1997 Asian financial crisis;[27] the Chinese presence in Africa has grown to impressive proportions;[28] and Beijing is making major economic inroads into South America. Meanwhile, the world is coming to China. The lure of "one billion customers"[29] is intoxicating, and nearly all the Fortune 500 companies now have a permanent presence in the country.[30] The dichotomy between a welcoming China and a confrontational Russia is striking—exemplified in August 2008 by simultaneous images of the enormously successful Beijing Olympics and the Russian armed intervention in Georgia. China has many more "friends" than Russia, whose closest partners are restricted to the Central Asian republics, unsavory regimes such as Iran and Syria—and China. China as a partner confers a degree of respectability on Russian foreign policy, whereas the reverse is not the case.

All this means that Beijing has little interest in allowing partnership with Russia to ruin its relations with other key players, above all the United States. Too tight an embrace with Moscow limits rather than expands its options. That is why the Chinese government has shown no interest in a formal alliance and why it has pursued a cautious line on issues such as Iraq (and, more recently, Georgia). Although it opposed the American-led intervention, it did so discreetly; it was more than happy for Russia, along with France and Germany, to make the running in the UN Security Council. The comparison between Russian and Chinese policies toward Iran is similarly revealing. Although China has the much larger commercial relationship[31] and likewise opposes sanctions against Tehran, it is Moscow, not Beijing, that has come to be seen in the West as President Ahmadinejad's leading supporter.[32]

In general, Beijing is committed to portraying the "strategic partnership" in a positive light: as a supplement, not an alternative, to its burgeoning ties with the United States and Europe. The last thing it wants is for these players to interpret Sino-Russian convergence as anti-Western and threatening. For this would contradict the main purpose of contemporary Chinese foreign policy, which is to foster a benign external environment—a "harmonious world"—that would facilitate the country's modernization.[33]

Like Russia, China sees a good bilateral relationship as benefiting vital security interests. However, the two sides differ in their emphasis. Moscow's priority is to secure the RFE from a potential Chinese threat—demographic, military, or economic. China also needs a stable frontier, not to protect itself against an improbable Russian attack, but so that it can concentrate on economic transformation and reunification with Taiwan.[34] A hostile Russia would represent little danger to China's political stability, let alone territorial integrity. But it would represent an unwelcome distraction from more important business elsewhere.

The security relationship is less asymmetrical in the Central Asian context. Beijing is worried about Islamic-based extremism and Uighur separatism in Xinjiang. Good relations with Moscow contribute to a more comfortable security environment, both directly and through Russia's continuing influence on the Central Asian states (Kazakhstan, Kyrgyzstan, Tajikistan) bordering China. Yet Sino-Russian partnership is merely one of many factors in the Central Asian security equation. The significance of the "stans," principally

Kazakhstan, means that Beijing's relations with them are equally important in strengthening regional security.

Taking a broader view, one major difference between Russian and Chinese views of the security dimension in their relationship is that Moscow's main focus is on the border between the RFE and Northeast China (Manchuria), while Beijing's concerns center on the future of its western regions adjoining Central Asia. This difference has obvious implications; it is one reason why China is much more committed than Russia to development of the Shanghai Cooperation Organization (see chapter 6).

Energy is another major dividend of partnership with Russia. There is a causal link between rapprochement and Beijing's policy of diversifying sources of imports. In its quest for the energy and natural resources needed to sustain economic growth, it has stepped up efforts to develop a significant energy relationship with Moscow and pushed hard on projects such as the East Siberian–Pacific Ocean oil pipeline (ESPO). Faced with competition for Russian oil from other energy-hungry Asian powers, notably Japan, China has sought to translate political warmth into negotiating advantage.

This is not to say that Russia and China enjoy a strategic energy relationship or even aspire to build one. As chapter 8 shows, their agendas differ markedly. Moscow sees energy as the twenty-first-century equivalent of nuclear weapons—the main instrument of power projection. Within this vision, China serves as leverage against the West. For Beijing, however, Russia is only one of many suppliers of its energy needs, not a substitute for the Persian Gulf. Although Russia's oil exports to China have grown considerably in recent years, in the energy dimension it is no more a "strategic partner" than Saudi Arabia, Angola, or Iran.[35]

Latent tensions

The overall picture of the two partners' respective agendas is one of asymmetry. For Moscow, partnership with Beijing is crucial to its ability to conduct an "independent" foreign policy and to secure Russia's return as a global great power. For China, it is a relationship of secondary importance, lagging well behind its more substantial ties with the United States, the European Union, and the countries of the Asia-Pacific region (Japan, the Republic of Korea, the ASEAN states). Many Russian policymakers are uncomfortable with China's rise and believe that a "China threat" could re-emerge one day. The Chinese, on the other hand, do not feel threatened by Russia, although they are sometimes irritated by Moscow's actions. Russia seeks every opportunity to use the

China card in international relations; China has no interest in the partnership becoming a tool of Kremlin revanchism. Finally, Russia sees the partners as "strategic equals." Beijing, however, sees Russia as having few friends and as a country that it is overtaking, indeed has overtaken, in many areas.

The disjunction between the smooth façade of "strategic partnership" and its underlying tensions is especially apparent at the bilateral level. Notwithstanding the impressive progress of recent years, many achievements are fragile and, in some cases, superficial. Take the issue of Chinese "illegal migration." Moscow and Beijing claim this is no longer a source of tension, yet the evidence suggests that the problem has been only temporarily and partially defused. Although Russian media coverage of this issue has become less emotive,[36] the Russian public retains a negative view of Chinese influence on everyday life. A 2007 survey by the All-Russian Centre for the Study of Public Opinion (VTsIOM), for example, found that 62 percent of respondents believed that the participation of Chinese firms in the RFE economy would be dangerous for Russia; 58 percent had a negative view of Chinese goods appearing in Russian shops; 85 percent were opposed to Chinese entrepreneurs and companies owning property in Russia; and 78 percent were against any increase in the numbers of Chinese laborers working in Russian firms.[37] These figures are hardly consistent with the claim that border and migration questions have been definitively resolved.

And neither are Putin's warnings about the consequences of depopulation in the Russian Far East. Although he has refrained from criticizing Beijing, the notion of a China threat is implicit in his emphasis on an active demographic policy for eastern Russia. The call to populate the RFE is a throwback to the Soviet era, only with an even weaker economic basis. What drives Kremlin policy is not the necessity for additional labor to exploit the region's resources, but the political fear of demographic, economic, and cultural Sinification, and the possible loss of the RFE.[38]

The tension between public face and discomfiting reality is evident in another much publicized area of the relationship: military-to-military cooperation. In August 2005 Moscow and Beijing hailed "Peace Mission 2005" as heralding a new era in the "strategic partnership."[39] This was true insofar as it was the first time the two militaries had participated together in exercises. But this unity was more notional than real. In the months leading up to the exercises, Moscow and Beijing engaged in protracted negotiations over their location and scale. The PLA pressed hard for the exercises to take place in Zhejiang province, a proposal rejected by Moscow as too provocative owing to the province's relative proximity to Taiwan.[40] The two sides compromised by holding the exercises off the Shandong peninsula southeast of Beijing. The Russian Ministry of Defense (MOD) had originally wanted to send only a token number of troops but was persuaded eventually to send a sizeable contingent.[41] Most significant, "Peace Mission 2005" was run as two separate exercises rather than as a single joint exercise, with no interoperability between the 7,000 Chinese troops and 1,800 Russians.[42] While it undoubtedly marked an important step forward in the relationship, it also highlighted the limits of cooperation and trust.

A similar wariness was evident in the build-up to "Peace Mission 2007." Beijing rejected out of hand a Russian MOD proposal to undertake military exercises under the combined auspices of the Shanghai Cooperation Organization and the Collective Security Treaty Organization (CSTO). The ostensible reason was the lack of a legal provision enabling the exercises to take place on that basis. In reality, the Chinese feared that the SCO would be shown up by the CSTO's greater military capabilities and thereby lose ground as the premier multilateral institution in Central Asia. Beijing—and Moscow—viewed the joint exercises through a competitive as well as cooperative lens.[43]

The gulf between image and reality is most apparent in the energy relationship. Chapter 8 reviews in some detail the tortuous course of cooperation in this sphere. It is important to note, however, that the Russians and Chinese have scarcely behaved toward each other in the manner of strategic partners. Moscow finds it irksome that Beijing is always trying to extract oil and gas at concessionary rates and believes that the Chinese abuse their position as the largest energy market in Asia. Accordingly Putin would like Russia to diversify to other Asian customers rather than risk a neo-colonial subservience as raw materials supplier to the Chinese economy.

For their part the Chinese resent Moscow's double-dealing over pipeline routes, which has seen it renege on intergovernmental agreements. They find it difficult to cope with its dysfunctional decisionmaking, which has seen it swing between China and Japan on the routing of the East Siberian oil pipeline. Another sore point is the Kremlin's refusal to allow Chinese firms to buy significant equity in Russian energy companies. Although the resistance to foreign ownership of "strategic resources" now applies across the board in Russia, this was not always the case.[44] Before the Yukos affair in the summer of 2003, the Russian government appeared to operate on the principle of "anyone but the Chinese."[45] Western companies such as BP, Exxon-Mobil, and Shell were welcomed,[46] while CNPC (China National Petroleum Company) and other Chinese companies were excluded.[47]

The shortcomings of cooperation have not only inhibited mutual trust but have also constrained the economic relationship. Despite impressive growth since 2000, trade remains modest in volume and unbalanced in structure. China accounts for about 6 percent of Russia's total trade volume, while Russia's share of Chinese trade is a meagre 2 percent. Oil and natural resources (principally timber) dominate Russian exports, while industrial and consumer goods make up the bulk of Chinese exports. In the economic sphere Russia and China are niche partners, not strategic partners. Moscow supplies 11 percent of Beijing's oil imports and nearly all of its arms purchases (nearly $2.5 billion in 2005[48]). But each looks elsewhere for the economic relationships that really matter: Moscow to Europe and the CIS countries, Beijing to the EU, the United States, and the Asia-Pacific.

The myth of identical views—the case of strategic stability

It has been easier for Moscow and Beijing to preserve the illusion of likemindedness in international relations. They agree on its guiding principles, and their positions on many issues broadly coincide. As noted earlier, however, their attitudes towards multipolarity, relations with the United States, the Iraq war, and Iran reveal important differences in perspective, emphasis, and interests.

The theme of "similar, but different" is well illustrated by their contrasting approaches to the question of strategic stability. Both countries have criticized Washington's unilateral withdrawal from the 1972 Anti-Ballistic Missile (ABM) Treaty; its plans to develop a theatre missile defense (TMD) system in the Asia-Pacific; and, most recently, the decision to deploy a limited missile defense and early warning system in the Czech Republic and Poland. Yet their motives and objectives differ in important respects. Russia's opposition has been directed principally at strategic missile defense, China's at theatre missile defense.[49] In 1999 Moscow opposed American plans to expand a national missile defense system, not because of doubts about its ability to respond to a possible American first strike but because such a system undermined the arms control agreements that were the last bastion of Russia's "parity" with the United States. Concrete security concerns are similarly marginal in the ongoing dispute over missile defense installations in central Europe. Moscow knows that these would have negligible impact on its nuclear strike capabilities, but interprets the Bush administration's plans as evidence of a continuing refusal to give Russia its due—that of a global great power.[50] The Kremlin also sees an opportunity to exploit divisions between the United States and major European powers such as Germany.[51]

China's objections to missile defense are more concrete. Beijing believes that a TMD system in East Asia would reassert America's strategic presence, strengthen Japan's military position, and bring Taiwan closer under the American umbrella, thereby further postponing its reunification with the mainland.[52] Unlike Russia, China does not have a sufficiently large nuclear arsenal to be confident that missile defense systems would not nullify its ability to launch a retaliatory strike.[53] Its fears are existential rather than psychological.

The debate over strategic stability highlights the relevance of historical and geographical perspective. Russia's stance is shaped by the legacy of Cold War bipolarity and its own globalist outlook. In the past it has not been much concerned about TMD; indeed, it has attempted to persuade Washington to move away from building a strategic network toward developing regional systems of tactical defense, and even to include Russia in joint projects.[54] China's focus, on the other hand, is almost exclusively regional. Its interest in American missile defense has no Cold War origin and is not founded in any desire to compete with the United States globally. But it fears that a regional missile defense system would severely limit its capacity to achieve primary national security objectives.

These different perspectives—global versus regional, psychological versus existential—are not necessarily incompatible with a common purpose in countering U.S. plans. For example, in February 2008 Russia and China proposed a new international treaty banning the use of weapons in outer space— a direct response to the intended missile defense deployment in central Europe.[55] But such differences have in the past generated tensions between Moscow and Beijing. In December 2001 the Chinese felt betrayed when the Kremlin barely reacted to Washington's announcement of withdrawal from the ABM Treaty. Putin underplayed the significance of this step,[56] and then resumed negotiations on the Strategic Offensive Reductions Treaty (SORT) as if nothing had happened. Moscow's insouciance contradicted the letter and spirit of the 2001 Sino-Russian summit declaration, which committed both parties to strongly opposing any unilateral American withdrawal.[57] More recently, there has been talk of a possible Russia-U.S. accommodation over missile defense, whereby the Russian military would be given substantial access to the installations in the Czech Republic and Poland and might even participate in developing a joint system with the United States and Europe. The very fact that these ideas are being discussed points to the shallowness of the much-vaunted "identity of views" between Moscow and Beijing.[58]

The disjunction between Russian and Chinese positions on strategic stability issues highlights a larger problem of consultation. Moscow's casual acceptance of the U.S. position on ABM withdrawal is not the only time it has failed to show solidarity with Beijing or keep it fully informed. Putin's decision, two weeks after 9/11, to endorse a U.S. troop presence in former Soviet Central Asia came as an unpleasant surprise to the Chinese leadership,[59] while the conclusion of SORT in May 2002 left Beijing once again out of the loop on frontline issues. The importance of the treaty may have been largely symbolic, but for the Chinese the symbolism was telling. In the early 1990s Andrei Kozyrev, the then Russian foreign minister, used to complain about Washington's failure to consult the Kremlin on important international decisions;[60] ten years later the same criticisms could be leveled at Moscow's sometimes cavalier attitude to partnership with Beijing.

The values gap

It has become fashionable to speak of a normative convergence between Russia and China, centered on preserving national sovereignty and norms against the intrusive influence of Western-dominated supranational regimes.[61] Such theories are supported by the apparent shift in Russia away from core "Western" values—political democracy, a transparent market economy, and open civil society—toward a more "Asiatic" conception of political, economic, and civil rights.[62] Putin and other senior figures routinely reiterate their commitment to democratic and accountable government, but invariably add that this must reflect Russia's "special" circumstances.[63] "Democracy" is an increasingly malleable phenomenon, defined principally by the Kremlin's political exigencies. In this respect Russia scarcely appears to differ from China, where the leadership likewise proclaims its commitment to "democracy" and "human rights" and decides how these are to be interpreted.[64]

Analogies between the two systems, however, are misleading. Notwithstanding the reversal of political liberalization and pluralism under Putin, Russia remains a more democratic, pluralistic, and liberal polity than China. It may bear little resemblance to Western democracies, but it is a far cry from the Soviet system to which it is sometimes compared. Crucially the Russian elite do not see themselves as partaking of the same normative tradition as China—ancient, modern, or post-modern. Their insistence that Russia is an integral part of European civilization highlights the extent to which Russians see themselves as existentially intertwined with the West. Conversely, despite the progress in the Sino-Russian "strategic partnership," it remains a relationship between normatively distinct entities.[65]

For their part, the Chinese take a fairly detached, even cynical view of so-called "Russian values," which tend to vary according to the state of Moscow's relations with the West. They understand their relationship with Russia as an interest-driven partnership. While Moscow and Beijing unite in rejecting UN human rights resolutions against China and other countries,[66] this solidarity is motivated by pragmatic reasons of state rather than a confluence of values. The PRC leadership clings to principles of "anti-interventionism" and "non-interference" as a means of insulating its legitimacy from external, as well as domestic, challenges. For to permit Western involvement in China's domestic affairs would be to encourage open criticism of the Communist Party regime, with unpredictable and possibly unmanageable consequences.

The so-called normative convergence between Russia and China, then, is largely formalistic. "Values" and "norms" rationalize rather than influence policy. Of course, as both countries modernize, they may eventually achieve a genuine convergence—as polities and societies in transition toward a more liberal (or more authoritarian) form of government. But for the time being at least, all this remains highly speculative.

A relationship of tactical convenience?

The reality of the much-vaunted "strategic partnership" between Moscow and Beijing falls well short of the mythology surrounding it. The policy differences that continue to separate them cannot be brushed off as mere spats that occur in any relationship. They point to different views of the world, of their respective roles in the international system, and of the nature and purpose of the bilateral relationship itself. But if Russia and China do not enjoy a genuine strategic partnership, with a shared long-term vision and common objectives, then how should one characterize it?

Some commentators define the relationship as one of tactical convenience,[67] driven by instrumentalism and opportunism. Although this judgment seems harsh, given the progress of recent years, it is not without foundation. Moscow's crude attempts to use China as geopolitical leverage against the United States, and more recently against Europe over energy (see chapter 8), suggest that it values its largest neighbor more as strategic counterweight than strategic partner. From time to time the Kremlin's Westerncentrism has asserted itself to the detriment of relations with China, for example when Putin made his "strategic choice" in the aftermath of 9/11.[68] Almost overnight the pretence of geographic evenhandedness gave way to an overtly pro-Western line. Even after Russia-U.S. relations began to sour during the Iraq crisis of 2002–03, Moscow turned in the first instance not to China but to the major European powers, France and Germany. It was only after the "color revolutions" in Georgia, Ukraine, and Kyrgyzstan and the consequent deterioration of relations with the EU that Moscow began to play up China's importance as a strategic partner of the first rank—and then only selectively. Revealingly, the Kremlin has shown little enthusiasm for proposals to expand the G-8 to include China and other non-Western powers such as India.[69]

Beijing's approach to partnership is less transparently opportunistic. After all, it seeks Russian natural resources, especially oil and timber, on a long-term basis. This requires a more strategic approach, one able to ride the bumps of interaction with a sometimes capricious neighbor. Yet Chinese policy too is informed by instrumentalism: Russia as a source for the energy that sustains economic growth; Russia as a stabilizing security presence in Central Asia and, by extension, western China (Xinjiang); Russia and China as the non-Western caucus in the UN Security Council;[70] Russia as deflector of Western human rights criticisms. Although Beijing would like to expand political and economic ties with Moscow for their own sake, this is not a priority of the first importance. And just as Moscow has been reluctant to see China admitted to the G-8 top table, so Beijing has sought discreetly to marginalize Russia in Asia.

The axis of convenience

Despite this somewhat cold-blooded pragmatism, the relationship is nevertheless driven by more than tactical opportunism. It may be a "relationship of convenience," but we can hardly dismiss it as a temporary aberration that will "correct" itself once either or both partners restore "equilibrium" to their foreign policy.

Ultimately, the Sino-Russian relationship is an axis of convenience because it combines tactical expediency with strategic calculus and long views. It is an axis because it is based, first, on a substantial degree of solidarity. Moscow and Beijing believe that it benefits them to resolve or alleviate their differences and to present a united front internationally. Two is better than one, especially in containing the American presence in Central Asia and projecting power and status through the mechanism of the UN Security Council's Permanent Five (P-5).

On the other hand the relationship is not an axis in the sense of being a budding political-military alliance, for the reasons discussed earlier: contrasting perspectives, conflicting priorities, different expectations, and an enduring if often suppressed feeling of mutual alienation. This is an axis born of necessity, real and perceived, not natural inclination. Unlike the fascist axis between Hitler and Mussolini, there is no common ideational foundation, notwithstanding talk of the Beijing consensus.[71] The axis exists and prospers because it is founded in the pursuit of concrete strategic and tactical goals.

Contrary to the naysayers, the axis of convenience has an underlying resilience that sustains it in the face of internal and external pressures. Many core elements are likely to remain in place for decades: cooperation along with competition; pragmatism offsetting distaste and suspicion. The ability of the relationship to survive, if not always transcend, the tensions within it is due above all to two factors. The first is a shared conviction that each country has much to gain from a good relationship, and much to lose from a bad one. The second is a selective suspension of disbelief and the consequent creation of a mythology of relations. For all the debasing of the term, the honorific "strategic partnership" is a useful device. It glosses over many imperfections and the lack of a shared vision, while emphasizing the benefits of long-term engagement. And it reinforces the message to the international community that Russia and China, together as well as individually, are to be reckoned with.

As long as these two factors remain in place, reports of the coming demise of the Sino-Russian "strategic partnership" are premature. But the fluidity of the international environment means that its future is far from assured. The world finds itself in a transitional phase in which "new" positive-sum notions of regional and global interdependency have yet to displace an "old" geopolitics that has reinvented itself, at least in the means it employs. In this anarchical context the relationship faces a diverse and daunting set of challenges: demographic tensions in the Russian Far East; a shifting bilateral balance; emergent competition in Central Asia; contrasting priorities in East Asia; the regional and global geopolitics of energy; and Russia-China-U.S. triangularism in an era of rampant globalization. The prospects for long-term partnership will depend on whether Moscow and Beijing are able to move from an often declaratory convergence to addressing these problems in a practical and above all strategic fashion.

CHAPTER FOUR

THE "YELLOW PERIL"— ENGAGEMENT IN THE RUSSIAN FAR EAST

"If in the short term we do not undertake real efforts to develop the Russian Far East, then in a few decades the Russian population will be speaking Japanese, Chinese, and Korean. . . . The real issue is about the existence of the region as an inalienable part of Russia."
—Vladimir Putin, speech in Blagoveshchensk, July 21, 2000[1]

The Russian Far East (RFE) encapsulates in the most direct sense the ambiguities of the Sino-Russian relationship. Here, more than anywhere else, strategic anxiety and cultural alienation coexist with political rapprochement and economic engagement. Although ties between Moscow and Beijing have become more diverse in recent times, the RFE has lost little of its original salience. It provides at once a barometer of the current state of "strategic partnership" and the key to its future. Forty years ago the region was the theatre of bitter confrontation. Today resolution of the territorial question reflects the positive dynamic between the two countries. But the future remains profoundly uncertain. The RFE has the potential to become the center of a new quality of bilateral and multilateral engagement in Northeast Asia, or a "dead zone" fertile only in suspicion and recrimination.

For Moscow, the region has immense symbolic and practical importance. Along with Eastern Siberia, it is the RFE that gives Russia its "Asian-ness."[2] And yet this persona is heavily distorted by the vagaries of climate, population, and resources. Russia may be Asian in a physical sense, but the historical and civilizational foundations for such an identity are flimsy. Not for nothing has it been said that "while Russia is in Asia, it is not *of* Asia."[3] The contradiction between Asian location and European mentality is particularly evident in the southern part of the RFE,[4] whose development has been driven by imperial and colonial exigencies. As Victor Larin has remarked, "[Russia's] Pacific Rim was and remains not a gateway to Asia, but a natural geographic border for expansion; a frontier and a barrier that has yet to be overcome in either the psychological or political—or even economic— sense."[5] In many respects the RFE is not so much part of Asia as an extension of Europe into Asia.[6]

The region has for long periods been shut off from the outside world, at no time more so than during the seventy years of Soviet rule. It is unsurprising, therefore, that the local population, predominantly migrants from European Russia who came to work in the military-industrial complex or on large infrastructural projects, are more than usually wary of the Chinese. Successive governments have done nothing to allay these feelings of insecurity. The RFE is home to many of the country's leading arms industries, such as the nuclear submarine plant in Komsomolsk-na-Amure, as well as the bases for the Russian Pacific surface and submarine fleets, in Vladivostok and Petropavlovsk-Kamchatsky respectively. These cities and many others in the RFE were closed to foreigners (and most Russians) until the final days of the Soviet Union.

The fall of the USSR proved disastrous for the region. Although it was now open to the outside world, during the 1990s it suffered terribly from neglect by the central authorities, and from chronic corruption, criminality, and misgovernment at the local level.[7] The crisis that accompanied Russia's transition from a planned economy to a market system affected the RFE particularly badly. Whole towns died with the downsizing of the Soviet military establishment and collapse of much of the military-industrial complex. People began to leave the region in ever greater numbers. Those who stayed found themselves relying increasingly on Chinese shuttle-traders for basic consumer items, a demeaning dependence that led them to resent both Moscow and the Chinese. During this decade, the RFE's main identity became that of a "forgotten land"—so forgotten that there was growing talk of it "dropping off" from the rest of Russia.[8] Although fears of secession were overblown, the RFE became emblematic of the most negative feelings in Russian society. The pioneering spirit that lay behind the original settlement of the region had long since given way to fatalism and demoralization. The local population fell back to nostalgia for the Soviet era, xenophobia toward the Chinese, and a "besieged fortress" mentality.

The task facing Putin

Vladimir Putin thus faced multiple challenges on coming to office. Some shortcomings, such as Moscow's ostentatious disregard for the region, were soon rectified. Putin lost little time in traveling east and tapping into the concerns of the local population. His famous speech at Blagoveshchensk in July 2000, during which he condemned Moscow's past neglect and called for urgent remedial action,[9] resonated with an audience anxious about China's "creeping expansion" (*polzuchaya ekspansiya*). More broadly, Putin's statist project, with its emphasis on centralization and the "vertical of power,"[10] demonstrated a heightened commitment to keeping Russia "whole" through tighter political control and national economic integration.

From the outset, however, there were a number of obstacles. The first was the dismal level of governance in key provinces of the RFE; the administration of Primorye governor Yevgeny Nazdratenko, in particular, had become a byword for venal and arbitrary misrule. Although Putin soon moved Nazdratenko sideways to the Fisheries Ministry,[11] he found it much more difficult to address the underlying problems of maladministration.

A second major impediment was the narrowness and dysfunctionality of the local economies. In Soviet times the RFE had been a frontier outpost, prison camp, and supplier of essential raw materials. It was a resource to be exploited to the maximum, with little care for those who lived and worked there. If the Soviet economy was skewed in favor of heavy industry at the expense of the consumer sector, then the RFE was an especially grotesque example of a flawed model. With Yeltsin having largely ignored the region, the old problems remained. There were opportunities for some niche industries, such as advanced weapons, but in much of the region Putin inherited an economic infrastructure that was very poorly adapted to the new market conditions.[12]

The third and potentially most serious problem was demographic. In Soviet times many RFE inhabitants had found themselves there because they or their parents had been sent to the camps, posted with the military, or been lured by the promise of better pay and conditions working on big projects such as the BAM (Baikal-Amur) railway. With the demise of the Soviet Union the element of coercion disappeared, and with the collapse of much of the local economy many inhabitants returned to western Russia. This led to a precipitous fall in the region's population, from 8 million in 1990 to 6.68 million in 2004.[13]

Demographic decline was less an economic than a political and security issue, since there was little justification for maintaining employment at

Soviet-era levels.[14] The real problem was the demographic imbalance between a sparsely populated RFE and the mass of humanity—107 million and rising—in the three northeastern Chinese provinces of Heilongjiang, Jilin, and Liaoning.[15] Russian nervousness at this disparity was aggravated by the opening up of the RFE and loosening of border controls. Suddenly, large numbers of Chinese shuttle-traders began crossing into Russia. Although few of them stayed for any length of time, their ubiquitous presence exacerbated an extant fortress mentality among the local inhabitants.

The demographic issue presented Putin with a real dilemma. On the one hand, he wanted to invest greater substance into the bilateral relationship, which meant maximizing trade and human contacts across the board, including interregional links with China's northeastern provinces. On the other hand, he could not ignore the economic and social tensions arising from anti-Chinese sentiment among the local population and their political representatives. On a more strategic level there was the problem of how best to manage engagement over the longer term. Could Moscow use the injection of Chinese commerce to revive the RFE and satisfy consumer demand without risking a de facto Chinese take-over?

Chinese "illegal migration"

Few issues have been the subject of as much prejudice and falsification as the so-called threat of Chinese "illegal migration" to the Russian Far East. The Chinese presence next door poses clear challenges for Moscow and for Russia's eastern provinces, but this does not explain, let alone justify, some of the extraordinary allegations that have circulated.

The most egregious myth is that there are "millions" of Chinese in the RFE, not to mention in the rest of Russia as well. In a radio interview in 2005, prominent nationalist politician Dmitry Rogozin spoke of a demographic "invasion," claiming—only half-jokingly—that the Chinese were crossing the border "in small groups of five million people."[16] Rogozin's views are shared by many Russians. One common estimate is that there are up to 2 million Chinese living in the RFE alone, which would mean that they account for nearly one-third of the total population of the region—an obviously nonsensical figure.[17] Some Russian officials have been only too willing to fuel such anxieties. In March 2006 the head of the Federal Migration Service, Oleg Romandovsky, told the Russian state Duma (parliament) that there were "between 400,000 and 700,000 illegal Chinese migrants in Russia's Far East."[18] The huge estimated range suggests that Romandovsky had little idea of the actual numbers of Chinese; whether these "migrants" were long-term settlers, seasonal workers, or shuttle-traders; or whether they were legal or illegal.

Such scaremongering has flourished in a climate where the truth is unclear, Sinophobia is rife, and local and federal politicians see advantage in manipulating public opinion on the issue. All the evidence indicates that the number of Chinese in the RFE *at any one time* is far lower than the figures peddled by the more irresponsible politicians and commentators. According to the latest (2002) Russian national census, there were only 35,000 Chinese living in the whole of Russia.[19] Admittedly this figure referred only to permanent residents and excluded seasonal workers, shuttle-traders, tourists, and "illegals." But in 2004 Putin's foreign policy adviser Sergei Prikhodko estimated the size of the Chinese permanent population in the *whole* of Russia at between 150,000 and 200,000.[20] Other estimates put the range at 250,000–400,000, although these latter figures almost certainly counted short-term workers and students as well as permanent residents.

The most exhaustive and reliable research on the Chinese presence in the RFE comes from Mikhail Alexseev and Vilya Gelbras. In a 2004 study of Chinese migration into Primorskii *krai* (Maritime province), Alexseev observed that, when set in the larger global context, the RFE was "just one of several peripheral destinations," and he described the number of "settled" migrants in the province as "statistically insignificant." He emphasized that most so-called migrants were short-term stayers—"tourists, 'shuttle' traders, entrepreneurs, laborers, poachers, smugglers, and students." Compared with the overseas Chinese communities, "the Chinese remained a marginal ethnic segment in Primorskii and in the Russian Far East generally." Alexseev concluded unequivocally that "forecasts of hundreds of thousands, if not millions, of Chinese workers moving into the Russian Far East to develop its vast natural resources so far remain in the realm of fantasy."[21]

Writing at around the same time, Gelbras was more guarded in his assessment of the size and impact of Chinese migration on the RFE. Yet he agreed with the broad thrust of Alexseev's comments. While noting an increase in the numbers of Chinese visiting, and staying in, the region, he wrote that "the bulk of Chinese migrants enter Russia legally" and that the scale of this legal migration was "not big enough to cause panic, let alone speak of a Chinese demographic expansion." Although "a permanent Chinese community is gradually forming . . . in Russia's Far East, this process is slow and limited in scope."[22]

Alexseev, Gelbras, and several other sources stress that the vast majority of Chinese who travel or work in the RFE are not interested in staying. Most workers want to earn good money before returning home or, in a few cases, moving on to the West.[23] As for the traders, the nature of their business requires them to stay on the move, criss-crossing the frontier. Gelbras notes that Chinese migration to Russia is not "some search for a promised land. There has emerged a specific form of the movement of manpower that serves the flow of goods."[24] Gelbras's data from Khabarovsk and Vladivostok—the two largest urban centers in the RFE—reveal that the number of migrants with families in Russia has halved, sure indication that increasing numbers of Chinese see the region as a "get rich quick" working environment and not as a desirable place in which to live.[25]

More recently evidence has been emerging of a decline in the total number of Chinese in the RFE. The Russian law on market trading, which came into force on April 1, 2007, prohibited Chinese (and other foreign) traders from carrying out cash transactions[26] and led to a significant reduction in the numbers crossing the frontier. Shuttle-trading remains a visible part of bilateral commerce, but these days nearly all the shuttle-traders are Russians.[27] Prospective Chinese tourists have also been deterred by a recent law from Beijing requiring them to have a valid external passport when traveling abroad. Previously, many used to cross the border just for the day to gamble in Russian casinos, most notoriously in Blagoveshchensk, capital of Amurskaya *oblast*.[28] Increasingly, too, Chinese business people are sidestepping the RFE because its market is too limited and basic; there is a growing inclination to conclude more ambitious deals farther afield, in Moscow and western Russia.[29]

None of this is to deny that Chinese migration—legal or otherwise—is a serious issue. However, the threat has been misrepresented as a "flood" that foreshadows the occupation and eventual annexation of the RFE. Gelbras argues, instead, that "the main problem . . . lies not in the number of Chinese migrants, but in the economic damage that Chinese communities inflict on Russia."[30] The threat, as he sees it, is twofold. First, the balance of trade between Russia and China is skewed in the latter's favor. China exports cheap consumer goods, many of which would be rejected elsewhere. In return, it imports raw materials, such as timber, non-ferrous metals, and other vital resources. Second, much of the trade in these imports is illegal and is conducted by criminal organizations on both sides of the border. This dual threat undermines Russia's "economic security," inhibits the emergence of "a civilized market economy" in the region, and results in Russia becoming a "raw-material appendage of China."[31]

This last point dovetails with Moscow's increasingly vocal concerns about the "unbalanced" nature of bilateral trade in general.[32] The specter of Russia as a quarry highlights the true nature of the challenge posed by China in the RFE, which is not demographic "invasion," the encouragement of criminality, or even the undermining of "normal" economic relations. The real issue is strategic, part of a larger shift in the overall balance between Russia and China—the subject of chapter 5. Specifically, the region may become part of the East Asian rather than Russian periphery, and increasingly subservient to Chinese requirements.

Social and civilizational challenges

Russians living in the east are acutely conscious of the growing Chinese influence. This is reflected, for example, in survey data showing that most believe that China benefits more than Russia from bilateral cooperation.[33] There is considerable resentment at China's impact on the local economy, whether in the form of undercutting in the construction industry, forcing down prices for consumer goods and services,[34] or acquiring land and property.

Such attitudes have important social and ethno-cultural dimensions. The first is the "culture of envy" that has been a storied feature of Russian life for centuries and the subject of numerous jokes in the Soviet era. Most Chinese who come to the RFE fall into two broad categories: market traders and short-term/seasonal workers. The former are relatively well-off, possess goods in abundance, and are able to trade profitably (if now indirectly) in a market where the customer has few alternatives. The second group may, as one acerbic Russian critic remarked, include the "rural poor of the Chinese hinterland,"[35] but in the RFE they nevertheless find employment in Chinese- and Russian-owned enterprises in construction and agriculture.[36] While the earnings of migrant workers are modest by Russian standards, their income is much higher than it would be back in their homeland.[37]

Second, the Chinese are seen by Russians as far better workers than the indigenous population—industrious, skilled, and sober. The obverse is that they are also viewed as cunning and rapacious.[38] Such perceptions have social as well as economic ramifications. One recent phenomenon in the RFE is the alleged increase in the number of mixed marriages—Chinese men to Russian women[39]—and a corresponding rise in Sinophobia among the Russian adult male population. As one local journalist put it, "the lazy, wife-beating, alcoholic Siberian man hates to see another beautiful Russian girl running into a Chinese man's arms."[40] The issue is not simply one of "raw envy,"[41] but also the fear that this trend, if extrapolated, would see the consolidation and expansion of a long-term Chinese presence in the region—in effect, Sinification through intermarriage. All this is occurring against a background of rising nationalism, characterized by a renewed emphasis on "Russian values." The emerging reality of a more multicultural Russia,[42] in which migrants from different sources—the Caucasus, Central Asia, East Asia—increasingly dominate the Slavic core, has become the new anathema.[43]

This leads to a third problem, that of Chinese enclaves in the RFE and in Russia more generally. Not only do the locals resent the Chinese looking after their own in commerce and employment, they are also suspicious of their reluctance to assimilate.[44] Many regard Chinese expatriates in the same way that Jews were viewed in late nineteenth-century Russia: as a community apart, with their own closed way of life and "dubious" customs. In the context of Russia's larger demographic decline (see below), the Chinese are viewed as a potential fifth column.

Chinese policy

One accusation sometimes leveled at the Chinese government is that it tacitly encourages the migration of its citizens to the Russian Far East. Its motives are said to be various. One is the constant pressure to find millions of new jobs every year for a rapidly expanding working population. James Kynge puts the demand as high as 24 million,[45] and although other figures are somewhat lower, the message is the same: regime stability depends on being able to resolve problems such as rising unemployment and growing income disparities. Since the domestic economy cannot generate sufficient new workplaces to accommodate demand, the government is encouraging migrant workers—estimated at more than 140 million[46]—to seek jobs in other countries, including Russia. In relation to the RFE, some critics claim that despite having agreed in 1994 to a regime regulating cross-border movement, Beijing is turning a blind eye to large numbers of its citizens crossing the frontier illegally or semi-legally (for example, posing as "tourists").[47]

The second motivation behind Beijing's alleged support of migration into the RFE is to facilitate the import of natural resources. The most publicized example of such collusion relates to the vast quantities of timber harvested and exported illegally from Russia. Gelbras estimates that every year 1.5 million cubic meters of timber are cut down illegally in Primorye alone.[48] This timber is critical to China, which has a deficit in this as in most other natural resources except for coal. Overall, an estimated 60 percent of Russia's timber exports go to China.[49]

But for some Russians the most sinister motive informing a covert Chinese migration policy is that Beijing has not given up hope of regaining the RFE and reversing the results of the "unequal treaties."[50] As the overall bilateral relationship has improved so the tenor and frequency of Russian criticisms have become less fraught.[51] Nevertheless, there is lingering suspicion that Beijing sees advantage in building up a substantial Chinese population in the region in order to preserve options for the future.[52]

These views of Chinese policy contain elements of truth. The leadership in Beijing has attempted to alleviate employment pressures by encouraging worker migration to other countries through the "Go Outward" program.[53] China has also been engaged for some years in a worldwide search for essential raw materials. It is not always particular about how it obtains these resources, as demonstrated by the complicity of Chinese business interests in illegal logging in Southeast Asia and the Amazon.[54]

However, most criticisms of the Chinese government are wide of the mark. There is no evidence linking "illegal migration" to policy in Beijing. In the 1990s the increased numbers of Chinese traveling or living in Russia coincided with a period of economic liberalization and labor mobility in China, as well as the opening-up of the frontier. Today "tolerance" of the activities of Chinese firms, criminal organizations, and individuals does not indicate official collusion so much as Beijing's inability to control many areas of economic and social activity. China is not the hermetically sealed monolith it was under Mao; there are far fewer restrictions on people's movements within the country or even to foreign destinations.

In fact, Chinese official involvement has been more cooperative than laissez-faire.[55] The 1994 agreement on visa regulation and border controls reflected a willingness to meet Russian objections and reservations *to the extent possible*. At the March 2007 summit the Chinese agreed to halve the period for visa-free travel from 30 to 15 days in order to cut down on abuses of visit conditions.[56] Beijing has no interest in allowing migration to harm the larger bilateral relationship, knowing how allergic Russians can be on this issue. While increasing numbers of Chinese are traveling outside the country for work, the RFE, indeed

Russia as a whole, remains a much less attractive destination than Europe, the United States or other Asian countries.

Russian attitudes

All this raises the question of why migration continues to be such a delicate issue in Sino-Russian relations. There are several explanations: unreconstructed attitudes towards the Chinese; political imperatives; Russia's larger demographic decline; and Moscow's dysfunctional approach to development of the RFE.

The first of these takes the form of a deep-seated Sinophobia among the local population.[57] This chauvinism not only perceives a political, economic, and civilizational challenge in the Chinese expatriate presence, but equates this more broadly with hostile intent in Beijing. It does not distinguish between the "threat of Chinese migration" and the "China threat" writ large. Since it believes the first proposition to be true, it assumes the second is as well.

The migration question has been fueled by political expediency. During the 1990s, regional leaders such as Nazdratenko and Khabarovsk governor Victor Ishaev exploited popular sentiment by talking up the threat of "illegal migration" and "creeping expansion," condemning the sharp practices of Chinese shuttle-traders, and accusing the Kremlin of selling out to Beijing over the common border. This approach proved highly effective. By blaming all ills on Moscow and the Chinese, the local authorities evaded responsibility for corruption and misgovernment, economic collapse, and failing living standards.[58] Despite a notable reduction in anti-Chinese rhetoric under Putin, the importance of political expediency has not diminished. The difference now is that the emphasis has shifted from the provincial to the federal. Instead of regional administrations currying favor with the electorate, it is the Kremlin that focuses on the migration issue as a subject of both strategic concern and popular appeal.[59]

Anxieties about Chinese migration are magnified in the context of a general decline in Russia's population, which is falling by an estimated 700,000 people a year.[60] According to some projections, it will plummet from 142 million today to around 100–110 million in 2050.[61] The perception of a larger crisis finds a ready focus in China's huge—1.3 billion and rising—population. What Beijing says or does is of relatively little account; the reality that resonates is of contrasting demographic patterns in the two countries.[62]

A failure of strategy

The significance of local xenophobia, political manipulation, and demographic trends pales, however, in comparison with Moscow's continuing failure to implement a viable development strategy for the RFE. Although the Kremlin signed off in 2002 on a Strategy for the Social and Economic Development of Eastern Siberia and the Russian Far East, very little has been achieved. The region continues to be one of the most backward in Russia; the local economy is increasingly reliant on Chinese goods, services, and labor; and local out-migration shows little sign of reversing.[63] For all the early promise under Putin, Moscow's policy toward the RFE is barely more effective than during the dismal Yeltsin years.

This is mainly because the Kremlin has no clear conception of what to do, merely a wish-list. It hopes to stimulate immigration by encouraging working-age people from European Russia and the Caucasus to go east. Indeed, so desperate is Moscow that it has stepped up efforts to persuade ethnic Russians in the Central Asian republics to work in the RFE.[64] Such plans recall the Soviet-era strategy of inducing workers to emigrate to the region through various economic and social incentives. So far, however, these inducements have been half-hearted and unsuccessful. Russian citizens now enjoy considerable freedom of movement and choice of residency and understandably prefer not to live in one of the most depressed regions of the Federation.[65] As long as there is such a large and well-publicized disparity in quality of life, and coercion remains out of the question, there is minimal prospect of attracting potential migrants from western Russia or the former Soviet republics. As Vladimir Portyakov has observed, the key is for Moscow to show a "genuine concern for the transformation of Siberia and the Far East into a really livable place."[66]

But the problem goes further than the government's inability to provide sufficient incentives to prospective migrants. There is also a dearth of suitable jobs. Viktor Larin has noted that "there is no clear economic basis for the widely advertised idea of resettling millions of Russians from the former Soviet republics . . . to Pacific Russia."[67] The work that tends to be available either requires narrowly specialized skills, such as in the arms industry, or cheap labor. Typically, the Chinese do the jobs—in construction and agriculture—that Russians reject because the work is considered too demeaning or low-paid.[68] There is a third disincentive as well: the absence of effective rule of law or even rule by law. High levels of corruption and criminality discourage the development of small and medium-size business enterprises (SMEs).

Putin understands that Moscow's previous neglect of the RFE is unsustainable. Yet although he feels compelled to address the interrelated problems of depopulation and labor shortage, he is afraid to embrace the most practical solutions: bringing in labor from neighboring countries, above all China, and developing the "free trade zones" along the border.[69] The result is policy confusion, with the emphasis on half-baked schemes such as attracting labor from western Russia and prestige projects like Vladivostok's hosting of the 2012 APEC Summit.[70]

The government's lack of ideas is evident also in the return to the Soviet-era chimera of looking to transnational energy projects to help revive the region and integrate it economically with the rest of the country. This notion has several flaws. First, such projects are not labor-intensive, so the effect on employment in the RFE would be marginal.[71] Second, the benefits of cooperation would accrue overwhelmingly to Moscow or the regions where the oil and gas are exploited, rather than the regions through which the pipelines pass.[72] Third, the fate of many of these projects remains uncertain. Moscow has been talking for over a decade about the Kovykta gas pipeline, the extension of the Trans-Siberian railway into the Korean peninsula, and the East Siberian oil pipeline to the Pacific (see chapter 8). But progress on these projects has been glacial. The considerable uncertainties about their future prospects make them a most unreliable basis for the region's economic revival.

Interregional trade

With Moscow largely devoid of inspiration, some of the provinces in the RFE have taken the initiative to expand interregional ties. Local trade with China's northeast has grown considerably. In 2007 Primorye's trade with China was U.S.$2.36 billion, compared to $311 million in 2001,[73] while Khabarovsk's trade with China reached $1.5 billion, accounting for 55 percent of the province's total imports and 44 percent of exports.[74] The increases on the Chinese side have also been significant, if not as impressive. Heilongjiang's trade turnover with Russia, mainly Primorye, reached $3.83 billion in 2004, a more than fourfold increase since 1999.[75]

Although this growth is welcome in some respects, the picture is not all positive. The most disturbing aspect from a Russian standpoint is that interregional trade is tilted heavily in favor of Chinese interests. Local trends confirm the long-standing national fear of Russia being reduced to a raw materials appendage and easy market for Chinese goods. Exports from Khabarovsk in 2007, for example, were dominated by timber (46.9 percent) and oil products (19.5 percent), while the main import items were machinery (44.1 percent) and textiles (30 percent).[76] It is a similar story with Primorye, which is especially dependent on Chinese consumer goods and services.[77] There is no serious Chinese investment in local RFE enterprises,[78] and Russian companies have not managed to break into the Chinese market. Early hopes that cross-border trade might provide a boost to regional economies on both sides—China's rust belt in the northeast as well as the RFE—remain unfulfilled.

The second area of concern is that much of interregional trade is illegal or semi-legal. The large-scale pillaging of Russian forests has already been noted, but the problem goes beyond illicit practices in one particular sector. Primorye's economic life is characterized by flourishing cross-border criminal links, whether in the timber trade, construction, retail, banking, hospitality services, poaching, or people-smuggling. This is not to mention corruption by government and law enforcement agencies, many of whose members participate directly in such activities or are on the take.[79] While other provinces in the RFE are less criminalized than Primorye, they suffer from similar problems.

All this adds up to a growing and unhealthy dependence on China. As one regional academic has pointed out, "an enormous part of the population is already integrated into an economic relationship with China, from the hotel business and retail to construction."[80] While cross-border trade is a naturally occurring phenomenon, the worrying thing from Moscow's perspective is that it has very little control over this since the southern RFE is already more economically integrated with China than it is with the rest of Russia.[81]

This nexus accentuates the ambiguity in local attitudes toward the Chinese. On the one hand, local RFE administrations profit directly from commercial engagement with them. Chinese business keeps the local economies afloat and, through the provision of essential consumer goods, contributes to political and social stability. On the other hand, the Russians are loath to admit the extent of their dependence, both because they fear it and because it is humiliating. This leads to a situation whereby during periods of (relative) prosperity, such as today, the notion of a "China threat" is underplayed, but in times of difficulty or crisis, as in the 1990s, it is quick to surface.[82] The Chinese thus fulfill a dual purpose in the RFE: they mask the policy inadequacies of regional and central government, while serving as a convenient scapegoat whenever necessary.

The Russian Far East and Sino-Russian "strategic partnership"

In recent years Moscow and Beijing have worked hard to minimize tensions over the Chinese presence in the RFE. The Communist leadership has cooperated whenever the Russian government has sought to tighten visa procedures and regulate shuttle trade. Beijing has reiterated on many occasions that it holds no irredentist ambitions, and it has responded with restraint to intemperate accusations from Russian regional and federal politicians. For its part the Kremlin has consistently rejected the notion of a "China threat," whether in general terms or in the specific context of the RFE. It has given its blessing to the growth of interregional ties and canvassed the possibility of Chinese participation in energy and infrastructural projects in the Far East. It has also managed to bring the regions on-message and contain the worst of their Sinophobia. The presence of Ishaev, a once vociferous critic of China, at the signing of the final border agreement in Beijing in October 2004 highlights the extent to which the Russian side is now singing the same tune—at least in public.[83] Such apparent unanimity is in stark contrast to the open discord that prevailed under Yeltsin.

Goodwill on both sides has led to a clear improvement in the dialogue on RFE issues, which has become much more constructive. Crucially there has been substantive progress to back up the fine sentiments. In addition to demarcation of the border, "illegal migration" is less of an issue than at any time since the opening-up of the RFE; interregional trade is growing; and political contacts between provincial administrations on both sides of the border are more frequent and cordial than ever before. It would seem that things could hardly be better.

Paradoxically, however, this is part of the problem. The largely positive state of relations in the RFE relies disproportionately on the "suspension of disbelief" discussed in the previous chapter. It is as if Moscow and Beijing have agreed not to delve too closely into the underlying contradictions for fear of awakening the monster. This softly-softly approach fosters an atmosphere in which both sides can talk through issues. But it also risks sliding into self-deception and complacency. For Moscow, in particular, benign interaction may obscure the importance of finding lasting solutions to unresolved problems.

Thus far there is little sign of the Kremlin implementing the measures needed to make the RFE a viable political and economic entity within the Russian Federation. Instead, the government has adopted a band-aid approach, marked by declarations of intent as impractical as they are vocal. Whether through lack of interest, a failure of comprehension, or absence of political courage, it has not managed to address the region's problems. State investment in economic and social infrastructure remains inadequate.[84] Putin's centralizing political reforms have not significantly reduced corruption and misgovernment by local administrations.[85] Moscow shows little understanding of the different economic conditions across the RFE.[86] There has been no progress in regularizing the importation of Chinese labor for projects in construction, the timber industry, and agriculture. And the federal government continues to play games over the development of transnational energy and infrastructural projects.

An uncertain future

The continuing expansion of Sino-Russian partnership ensures, for the time being, a relatively favorable environment in which to resolve these problems. But time and opportunity are not unlimited. While talk of a crisis is premature, the present state of affairs in the RFE cannot continue indefinitely.[87] A number of variables could change the situation for the worse.

The first is a rise in the overall number of Chinese migrant workers and a corresponding diminution of work opportunities within China. Although Beijing is taking steps to alleviate this problem, the pace of domestic modernization will ratchet up employment pressures for the next decade and perhaps longer.[88] Most workers will continue to gravitate toward China's cities, while others will find employment in various Asian countries, Europe, and America. However, while Russia will avoid the worst of the overflow, an increase in the number of Chinese in the RFE is possible. This would exacerbate tensions between the newcomers and the local Russian population.

The second variable is macroeconomic. The bilateral relationship has benefited from high growth rates in Russia and China. These have not only driven the expansion of trade, but also instilled a new confidence. This begs the question, however, of what might happen in the event of an economic slowdown or worse in either or both countries, with knock-on effects for political and social stability. One potential outcome, already witnessed in the Russia-Japan relationship, is the emergence of an antagonistic nationalism. This could manifest itself in several ways: trade disputes, resource competition in Central Asia, great-power rivalry across the globe. The most plausible theatre of trouble, however, is the RFE, because it is here where the Russian and Chinese sit in direct proximity and where many issues are outstanding.

Third, the rise of nationalism could, in time, see a revival of Chinese claims on parts of the RFE. It was not so long ago that Mao called for these lands to be returned to China. This coincided with the Sino-Soviet freeze and the build-up to the 1969 clashes, and highlighted the extent to which the prominence of such questions rises and falls according to the overall state of the relationship. A serious downturn, whether in the RFE or elsewhere, might dilute previous commitments. With its attention overwhelmingly focused on internal modernization and Taiwan reunification, Beijing has no interest in resurrecting the territorial issue for the foreseeable future. But there may come a time when the Chinese leadership feels either confident or desperate enough to reassess the situation on its northern frontier. Today's academic discussions about the "lost one-and-a-half million square kilometers" could become tomorrow's policy debates.

Even if successive Chinese leaders remain true to their promise not to raise territorial claims, the Russians may not believe them. A number of Russian commentators are asking what happens after Taiwan's reunification with the mainland. There is genuine concern that the RFE could be back on the table some time in the next fifteen to twenty years and that, when the time comes, Moscow will be unable to withstand Chinese pressure.[89] Suspicion of Beijing's intentions will always remain, no matter how often and how vigorously it reaffirms its present position. To skeptics the only way of guaranteeing Russia's territorial integrity is to "trust in capabilities, not intentions"—an attitude that history shows has the potential to generate serious misunderstandings. Other commentators, including several leading Sinologists, posit a scenario whereby the Communist Party loses control of the modernization process and the ensuing chaos sees "millions" of Chinese fleeing across the border. In that event, the territorial question would resurface by force of circumstances.[90]

The widening demographic imbalance, and Russia's larger population crisis, is the final variable. The danger is not so much the decline in the number of working-age Russians, but rather its impact on Russian self-perceptions and views of the outside world. In particular, it could heighten such traditional instincts as the "besieged fortress" mentality and fear of strategic encirclement. In such an atmosphere, even a modest increase in the Chinese presence in Russia's eastern provinces could undermine the larger bilateral relationship.

Of course, one should be wary of assuming the worst. Apocalyptic scenarios make for good copy, but the ordinary course of events is usually calmer and more predictable. A crisis in Sino-Russian relations over the RFE is neither imminent nor inevitable. There is a window of opportunity, while the "strategic partnership" continues to expand, for Moscow and Beijing to cooperate in defusing tensions and resolving problems. But there is little room for irresoluteness. As long as Russia's rulers refuse to face up seriously to the challenge of the region's long-term economic and social development, then notional risks could one day turn into concrete realities. In that event, the Russian Far East would become a focus for escalating tensions rather than an area of mutually beneficial engagement.

CHAPTER FIVE

"PEACEFUL RISE" AND THE SHIFTING SINO-RUSSIAN BALANCE

"Peace and rise, which look quite contradictory, can actually be integrated. In the past, the rise of a big power involved toppling the international order and threatening peace. China breaks this rule. While seeking a peaceful international environment to ensure our development, we are safeguarding world peace through our own development."

—Zheng Bijian[1]

"The rapid growth of the PRC's economy, coupled with its military expansion, has propelled China's emergence as a regional power with an increasingly global foreign policy."

—US Department of Defense's
*Annual Report to Congress on the Military Power
of the People's Republic of China 2006*[2]

Like much of the world, Russia has viewed the extraordinary rise of China since the death of Mao with a mixture of awe and apprehension. This reaction is partly due to the spectacular nature of the phenomenon itself, but also reflects the striking contrast with its own, far more difficult experience of modernization. Whereas China has enjoyed consistent economic growth of around 9 percent a year for the past three decades, Russia has suffered a series of misfortunes: stagnation in the late Brezhnev period; catastrophic economic decline and state collapse under Gorbachev; and political turbulence, hyperinflation, and disintegrating living standards during the 1990s. Only in the last few years has Russia recovered something of its former position, thanks largely to the boom in world oil prices.

For many in the Russian elite, the rise of China offers signal lessons. It "proves" the folly of mechanically following alien recipes for development—"shock therapy" and the so-called Washington consensus—instead of adapting reforms to a country's "special" circumstances. The Yeltsin administration, which attempted to introduce political democratization, liberal market reforms, and civil society into Russia, became increasingly disoriented in the face of mounting crises. China, on the other hand, has stayed true to its legalist and Confucianist traditions and thrived on a diet of political authoritarianism and economic liberalization.[3] The "Beijing consensus" of authoritarian modernization has emerged as an alternative, homegrown template that is not only effective but also psychologically more palatable to the Russian mind. It has provided much of the inspiration for the unapologetic state capitalism of the Putin administration.

Even those who oppose the application of Chinese or other authoritarian models of development to Russia agree on three things at least. First, China has achieved a remarkable transformation from autarkic, backward nation into one of the world's leading economies. Second, domestic modernization has enabled China to become a major regional and, increasingly, global player. Third, the rise of China poses enormous challenges to the international community and to Russia specifically.

In the previous chapter we examined the notion of a "China threat" in the context of the Russian Far East. But for Moscow the challenge of China extends far beyond the border regions. It calls into question many of the understandings that underpin the "strategic partnership." How long can both countries maintain the illusion that theirs is an equal relationship? How far can Russia trust in Chinese assurances about the benign character of "peaceful rise" or "peaceful development"?[4] To what extent has the bilateral balance of power—political, military, and economic—shifted, and what are its implications? Most crucially, does China's rise threaten Russia and, if so, how?

The military balance

The most obvious litmus test of the Russia-China balance is in the military sphere, where two key questions arise. The first centers on the capabilities of the respective armed forces. Is the People's Liberation Army (PLA), long derided as technologically backward and poorly trained, overtaking its Russian counterpart? Second, do China's enhanced military capabilities threaten Russia's security interests? In particular, will Beijing look one day to cash in on its military superiority—real or perceived—to regain territories lost as a result of the "unequal treaties," and to make inroads into Central Asia?

According to some commentators, China has virtually caught up with Russia as a military power.[5] With the demise of the USSR, the Soviet war machine crumbled. The new Russia's armed forces were largely ineffective, undermined by poor leadership, rampant corruption, and severe under-funding. The military's weaknesses were amply revealed in the botched Chechen war of 1994–96, and even its relative success in the second war of 1999 owed more to the efforts of pro-Moscow Chechen militias than to federal forces.[6] The post-Soviet period has seen a litany of scandals, as well as public humiliations such as the accidental sinking of the *Kursk* nuclear submarine in August 2000.[7] Although the Kremlin has repeatedly proclaimed its commitment to "urgent" military reform, in practice this has become an oxymoron. There have been periodic changes of force structure, some progress toward professionalization, and, in the last two or three years, improvements in funding and equipment. But Russia's armed forces remain incapable of meeting many of the demands of a modern military, let alone achieving more ambitious goals such as the projection of power beyond the country's borders.[8]

Contrast this to China, where there has been a comprehensive "revolution in military affairs" (RMA) since the 1991 Gulf War, when the impressive performance of the U.S. military shocked the PLA leadership into action.[9] China's armed forces are virtually unrecognizable from fifteen years ago. They are leaner and more efficient;[10] they are better educated, trained, led, and equipped; funding has increased at double-digit rates every year since 1989;[11] their technological level has improved dramatically; the nuclear arsenal has grown substantially in quantity and quality;[12] and there has been a quantum leap in investment in the indigenous military-industrial complex and in research and development (R&D). Whereas a decade ago the PLA was seemingly light years away from being able to launch an amphibious operation against Taiwan, even without American intervention on behalf of Taipei, today the prospect can no longer be so easily discounted.[13] More broadly, the Pentagon's 2008 *Annual Report to Congress on the Military Power of the People's Republic of China 2008* notes that the PLA is "pursuing a comprehensive transformation from a mass army designed for protracted wars of attrition on its territory to one capable of fighting short-duration, high-intensity conflicts along its periphery against high-tech adversaries."[14]

Such has been their contrasting experience with military reform that it is tempting, but wrong, to conclude that China's aggregate military power now exceeds Russia's or will do so shortly. Despite the decline of the Russian armed forces, they nevertheless continue to enjoy several critical advantages, above all several thousand nuclear warheads.[15] It has become fashionable in the post–Cold War era to minimize the importance of this core element of national defense on the grounds that such power is scarcely usable. Yet while the significance of nuclear weapons as a geopolitical trump, means of power projection, or symbol of great power status has diminished, their ultimate deterrent effect has not. Nor should one assume from the decline in Russia's conventional forces that their condition is terminal. Although the capacity to fight a "two-front war" remains a distant prospect, their sheer size—still around a million—added to advanced weaponry and other technological advantages, constitutes a massive conventional deterrent to any country or countries contemplating an attack on Russian territory.[16]

It would be equally mistaken to view China's military modernization as the finished product, or as a process nearing completion. The 2008 Pentagon report, for example, recognizes that the PLA remains deficient in many respects. It notes a consensus within the U.S. intelligence community that China "will take until the end of this decade or longer to produce a modern force capable of defeating a moderate-size adversary . . . will not be able to project and sustain small military units far beyond China before 2015, and will not be able to project and sustain large forces in combat operations far from China until well in the following decade."[17] The mediocre performance of Chinese troops in the "Peace Mission 2005" joint exercises (see chapter 3)[18] indicates that the PLA has a long way to go before it develops into an effective modern fighting force, let alone one capable of defeating a *large-size* adversary such as Russia. A notional Chinese assault on Russia would also need to consider two other factors. The first is the vast distance between the common border and Russia's main population and command centers. Whereas Moscow could strike very effectively at key Chinese installations and cities, it would be much more difficult for Beijing to retaliate in kind. As in the Great Patriotic War against Nazi Germany, Russia enjoys the advantage of strategic depth, not to mention a huge advantage in nuclear weapons technology. The other major deterrent is that China could hardly hope to fight a limited war to annex the RFE. Russia would not concede 40 percent of its territory without substantially raising the costs of a hostile intervention. Although the region has been neglected by successive Soviet and Russian governments, its importance is greater than ever. Russia owes its position as a re-emerging great power largely to its abundant natural resources, many of which are located in the RFE. It would "accept" the loss of such strategic assets only after a bitter and extremely bloody struggle.

Of course, wars sometimes occur as a result of misunderstandings and accidents.[19] The Pentagon report identifies in this context "three perceptions that could lead to miscalculation or crisis. First, other countries could underestimate the extent to which PLA forces have improved. Second, China's leaders could overestimate the proficiency of their forces by assuming that new systems are fully operational, adeptly operated, adequately maintained, and well integrated with existing or other new capabilities. Third, China's leaders may underestimate the effects of their decisions on the security perceptions and responses of other regional actors."[20]

These warnings make sense, however, only in relation to localized conflicts with Taiwan and in the South China Sea, not Russia. Regarding the first "miscalculation," there is little danger of Russian military planners underestimating the considerable progress the PLA has made over the past ten to fifteen years. If anything, they have erred in the opposite direction. One analyst makes the interesting but far-fetched analogy between the state of China's military today and Soviet capabilities in 1932–33,[21] while in 2003 Mikhail Margelov, then head of the International Affairs committee of the Federation Council (the upper house of the Russian parliament), forecast that the military gap between China and the *United States* would be bridged some time before 2020.[22]

The second concern, that the PRC leadership may overestimate China's military capabilities, is no more plausible. The underlying premise of the concept of "peaceful rise" (and "peaceful development") is that China cannot hope to achieve its foreign and security policy goals through military means and must look to positive engagement instead.[23] Over the past decade, the leadership's approach toward a whole raft of issues—from Taiwan to relations with the United States—indicates that "peaceful rise/peaceful development" is no mere philosophical abstraction, but a practical guide to policy. It would most likely contemplate military action only to defend national borders or for the sake of reunification with Taiwan—and the latter only in very specific circumstances, such as a unilateral declaration of independence by Taipei.[24]

Third, for the most part Beijing is highly sensitive to the security anxieties of China's neighbors. The emphasis on soft power, economic interdependency, and good international citizenship highlights a larger commitment to changing traditionally negative perceptions of China. Although there have been hiccups, such as the furor over the PLA's anti-satellite test in January 2007, the government is far more aware these days of the potential consequences of its actions. This is especially true in respect of Russia, where Beijing's approach toward sensitive issues in the Russian Far East and Central Asia has been careful and even self-effacing.

Chinese military planning

One of the nightmare scenarios canvassed by Russian commentators is that China will turn its attention to the Russian Far East once it has completed its internal modernization and reunited Taiwan with the mainland.[25] Such speculation ignores a number of realities. The first, highlighted above, is the *actual* stage of development of the two countries' respective militaries. Notwithstanding the PLA's progress, it has little capacity to conduct successful operations against Russia, whether in Central Asia or in the RFE. This is likely to remain the case for many years, perhaps even decades.

Second, China's modernization will be an extraordinarily difficult and protracted process. This is not the place to enter into a detailed discussion of the prospects for economic transformation, but suffice it to say that there are numerous obstacles—huge resource constraints, environmental degradation, economic "overheating" and inflationary pressures, rising corruption, widening income disparities, growing unemployment, an ageing population—that could derail or at least slow it down. The question "what happens *after* China's modernization?" is almost entirely speculative—and premature.

Conjuring up post-Taiwan scenarios is similarly moot. Beijing is pursuing a restrained strategy on reunification, based on increased human interaction and economic integration with a view to eventual absorption.[26] Although it has indicated that it will not wait forever and would react forcefully in the event of a unilateral declaration of independence,[27] there is little indication that it is otherwise preparing for early military action. The current PLA build-up in southeastern China is designed primarily to strengthen Beijing's negotiating position vis-à-vis Taipei and pre-empt possible moves toward Taiwanese independence. China dare not risk the consequences of U.S. military intervention, not only because of the destructive impact this could have on the PLA and through it the legitimacy of Communist Party rule, but also because the Chinese economy depends so much on engagement with America.[28] Aggressive action against Taiwan would also incur other serious consequences: an active strategic response from Japan, including the possible development of a nuclear weapons capability; alienation of the ASEAN member-states which Beijing has wooed so assiduously over the past decade; and loss of critical Taiwanese investment in the booming economy of southeastern China.[29]

All this means that the Chinese leadership has given very little thought to post-Taiwan scenarios that might entail confrontation with Russia.[30] The Taiwan question will remain Beijing's overwhelming external preoccupation as long as it is unresolved. Even in the unlikely event of early reunification, the leadership would almost certainly concentrate on other priorities first: the hunt for resources in Southeast Asia, Africa, Central Asia, and Latin America; assuming a leadership role in the Asia-Pacific; boosting Chinese influence in Central Asia; and playing a more active part in global affairs. Compared to these strategic objectives, the RFE is a provincial side-show, hardly worth risking war with the world's second nuclear weapons state.[31]

Examination of the PLA's evolving force structure, budgetary priorities, arms acquisition, and troop deployments reveals how far Chinese military planning is oriented *away* from Russia and toward reunification with Taiwan and building up "comprehensive national power."[32] The emphasis given to naval and air power over land forces reflects these priorities. Mao's mass peasant army is long gone. Instead, Beijing is devoting intensive efforts to developing a blue-water navy that would guard the sensitive sea-lanes through which more than 80 percent of its oil imports pass, and enable China to project power throughout the Asia-Pacific, including in the oil-rich areas of the South China Sea. The PLA emphasis on "local wars under the conditions of informationization" is completely incompatible with planning for a possible attack on Russia, even in the very long term.[33] As the Pentagon's 2006 report on Chinese military power noted, in the post-Mao era "PLA strategists began to conceive of future wars as being short, intense, and of limited geographic scope."[34] A confrontation with Russia would be intense, but certainly not limited in either geographical or military scope.

Russian arms transfers to China

There is growing evidence that the Russian military itself is coming around to the idea that China poses little threat. This is borne out in comments by General Yury Baluyevsky, chief of the General Staff (2004–08), that it would take China until 2050 to become a "mighty, world-class military power," thereby giving Russia plenty of time and opportunity to maintain its military-technological advantage.[35] Baluyevsky's sanguine assessment is reflected in the expansion of Russian arms sales to the PLA in recent years. Far from being intimidated by the PLA's impressive modernization, the Kremlin and the Russian Ministry of Defense have given enthusiastic support to sales of hi-tech weaponry such as Kilo-class submarines, Sovremenny II-class destroyers, and SU-30 MKK fighter aircraft.[36] The U.S. government estimates that Russia has supplied around 95 percent of the arms sold to China over the past decade.[37]

In the 1990s sales to China were critical to the survival of the Russian military-industrial complex; the Chinese market was one of the few remaining after the collapse of the Soviet Union. Today, however, the Russian arms industry is selling to an ever wider range of clients, and yet China remains a pivotal customer.[38] This is due partly to the potential size of the market, but also to Moscow's confidence that even advanced weaponry and systems can be sold to China without jeopardizing national security. The traditional fear that Russian arms may be used one day against Russia's armed forces has become discredited. It helps, of course, that major items such as the Kilo submarines and Sovremenny destroyers cannot be readily deployed in the event of conflict between Moscow and Beijing.

The Russian government's concerns over arms transfers to China are now principally commercial. Beijing has ratcheted up the pressure on Russian firms to sell it design technology instead of military hardware.[39] Moscow is reluctant to accede to such requests, understandably so given China's poor record in safeguarding intellectual property rights and its emergence as one of the leading arms exporters to the developing world.[40] In this connection, Beijing's practice of re-exporting Russian matériel is a potential irritant.[41]

The prospects for the bilateral arms relationship are consequently unclear, but for economic rather than security reasons. Beijing's drive to possess the most advanced weaponry and military technologies begs the question of how long Moscow will be able (or willing) to satisfy its requirements.[42] In recent years, Russia has enjoyed a dominant market position, but largely because the other "big four" exporters—the United States, Britain, and France—have maintained an embargo on sales to China since Tiananmen.[43] It would be unwise for Moscow to assume that the PLA will always be so restricted in its choice of hi-tech hardware and weapons systems. The EU embargo was almost lifted in 2005[44] and will come under mounting pressure as China's modernization proceeds apace and its economy becomes fully integrated into the global system. In a more open international market, Russian arms could be squeezed out unless Moscow can find ways to stay abreast of increasingly stiff competition: by offering discretionary terms, top-of-the-line equipment, and much improved access to design technology through licensing agreements.[45]

China's "peaceful rise" and the implications for Russia

Much of the Russian commentary on the nature of the "China threat" misses the mark by overestimating China's military capabilities and demographic "expansion." Nevertheless, the latter's rise as one of the world's leading powers does represent a tremendous challenge to Russian economic and geopolitical interests. This threat is diverse and difficult to define, but centers in the reality that China's growing ascendancy is likely to come, at least in part, at Russia's expense. Both countries may be "emerging powers," but they are emerging in very different ways.[46]

Sheer geographical extent, a vast nuclear arsenal, the memory of strategic bipolarity, abundant natural resources—these remain the pillars of Russia's sense of "great power-ness" (*derzhavnost*). Even the modern notion of Russia as an "energy superpower" is founded not in a true understanding of the geopolitics of energy (see chapter 8), but in an inherited messianic vision: Russia's timeless identity as a global great power. In good times, such as today's era of high energy and commodity prices, this feeling of strategic entitlement translates into complacency and triumphalism. In times of difficulty, such as the 1990s, the notes are of envy, recrimination, and insecurity. Either way, Russian policymakers tend to view the world through a Cartesian lens: "we think we are a great power, therefore we are." Self-aggrandizement and mythmaking are as important as substance in promoting the idea of Russia as a globally influential actor.[47]

Chinese attitudes differ from Russia's in significant respects. The Communist leadership has few illusions about the country's weaknesses and limitations. China has come a long way in a few decades, but it remains—as Beijing recognizes—"the world's largest developing nation."[48] Although the Chinese are sometimes accused of assuming an innate superiority, they remember well the "century of humiliation" and the country's long decline from the end of the eighteenth century. With recent history providing little to cherish, they look to the substance rather than trappings or tradition of power. Whereas Russia inflates its importance in the world, China underplays its strengths and talks up its shortcomings. This reflects not so much the urge for rigorous self-analysis as a pragmatic desire to minimize opposition to its interests.[49] Yet for all the emphasis on "equality" in their relationship, it is China, not Russia, that is increasingly the dominant partner and influential global player.

The economic balance

The different trajectories in Russian and Chinese development are most apparent in the economic sphere. Judged by size of GDP, China is already the world's fourth largest economy after the United States, Japan, and Germany.[50] If it maintains the 9 percent annual growth it has averaged over the last thirty years, then it will become the world's second largest economy before the decade is out.[51] According to the Goldman Sachs BRICs report and several other estimates, it will reach the number one position by the middle of the century.[52]

Of course, China's per capita GDP remains comparatively low, falling well short of levels in the world's leading industrialized economies.[53] Zheng Bijian speaks of the "two mathematical propositions" of "multiplication" and "division"—the multiplication of sundry problems by 1.3 billion people, and the division of resources among the same.[54] But even with its many difficulties, above all resource constraints, China is making its presence felt as a global economic power. Whereas for much of the modern era its development was dictated by the impact of the West, today China's influence reaches all corners of the earth.[55]

Meanwhile, the Chinese themselves are changing radically. The education system has been transformed over the past ten to fifteen years. The illiteracy rate has fallen from 21.7 percent in 1990 to under 11 percent today.[56] It is estimated that some 200 million Chinese are currently learning English, the international language of business. The most far-reaching changes have been in tertiary education, where there are now some 2,500 institutions with a total enrollment of over 20 million full-time students.[57] This compares with only 1,075 institutions with just over two million full-time students in 1990.[58] On a more specialized level, there are four times as many engineering graduates coming out of Chinese universities as from U.S. establishments.[59] Many problems remain unsolved, and it would be foolish to see China as an "advanced technology superstate" or likely to become one in the near future.[60] Zheng Bijian notes that even after it achieves modernization in the mid-twenty-first century, it will only have reached "the level of a moderately developed country."[61] But the point is that China is heading in that direction, and more rapidly than anyone had anticipated only a few years ago. Its image as a low-technology economy relying almost entirely on the exploitation of cheap mass labor is being challenged, as are assumptions that the Chinese will be unable to make the breakthrough to hi-tech production and exports.[62]

China's international trade reflects the importance the leadership places on qualitative as well as quantitative growth. The worldwide search for natural resources, predominantly but not solely energy, sustains China's industrial growth. But these days the Party's ambitions extend further. It is no longer satisfied with the growth of manufacturing exports, but seeks to develop a knowledge-based economy as quickly as possible. To this purpose the gov-

Figure 5-1. Comparison between Russian and Chinese Gross Domestic Product, 1992–2007

2000 U.S.$ billions

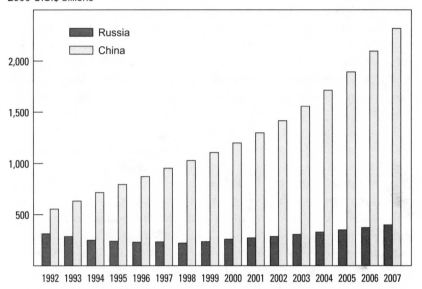

Source: World Bank World Development Indicators, adjusted to 2000 base by the Economic Research Service. See www.ers.udsa.gov/Data/Macroeconomics/.

ernment and Chinese companies are exerting increasing pressure on foreign partners to transfer key technologies, often making this a condition for the completion of deals.[63] The message is clear: China wants to be a world-class, *post-modern* economy.

Russia, by contrast, continues to look to its natural resource assets. Since coming to power in January 2000, Putin has consistently stressed the importance of economic diversification, of not relying on high energy and commodity prices. Russian policymakers point to the impressive expansion of the service sector, as well as to consumption-driven growth. But the Russian economy is as dependent as ever on energy exports. Today these account for over 50 percent of federal budget revenues, more than 60 percent of exports in value terms,[64] and the bulk of exports to Russia's major trading partners— the EU, China, Ukraine, and Belarus.

Although Putin has talked up the importance of Russia becoming a knowledge-based economy,[65] there are few signs of this occurring. On the contrary, the evidence suggests that the importance of the resource sector will only grow. In addition to its vital contribution to budget and export revenues, energy is viewed as the main instrument of Russia's return as a global power (see chapter 8), as well as an indispensable tool of domestic influence. The positioning of senior Kremlin figures such as Igor Sechin and Dmitry Medvedev on the boards of Russia's major oil and gas concerns, Rosneft and Gazprom respectively, reflected not only a blurring of private and public interests but also the extent to which energy is identified with political authority. The anointing of Medvedev as Russian president in May 2008 confirmed the nexus between the Russian energy sector and the highest circles of power.[66]

In the circumstances, the prognosis for a "balanced" or diversified economy is unpromising. As long as world energy and commodity prices remain high, Russia will continue to play to its perceived strengths. Whereas for Beijing modernization is driven by domestic imperatives, for Moscow economic prosperity is at least as important for the international clout that it brings. China's first foreign policy priority is to achieve the most favorable external conditions for domestic development, while Russia sees political stability and economic growth as the springboard for reasserting its influence as a global power as soon as possible. In short, although there is a natural fusion between domestic and foreign policy in both countries, the emphasis and order of priorities are very different.

The trade imbalance

These contrasting perspectives shape the bilateral trade relationship. Russian policymakers view China less as a primary market than as leverage against the West. There is little sense that it represents "one billion customers," a potential El Dorado for the Russian corporate sector.[67] Bilateral trade may have multiplied eightfold during the Putin presidency, but it has done so from a very modest base—a mere U.S.$5.7 billion in 1999. Moreover, much of this increase is due to the combination of high oil prices, escalating Chinese energy and resource requirements, and the explosion of Chinese manufacturing and consumer exports.[68] To put things in proportion, 52 percent of Russia's total turnover is with the European Union, as opposed to 6 percent with China, while China's trade with the EU and the United States—$356 billion and $302 billion respectively—dwarfs that with Russia.[69]

It suits Moscow and Beijing to talk up the expansion of commercial ties, all the more so since this was one of the weakest areas of the relationship during the 1990s. But closer examination reveals how far the two sides diverge in their objectives and capabilities. Official rhetoric speaks of economic complementarity, yet in the Sino-Russian context this means imbalance and inequality. While Moscow hopes that China will become an economic, as well as political and strategic, counterweight to the West, Beijing sees Russia as little more than a resource-cow for Chinese growth and an easy consumer market. With the exception of a few niche areas, such as space and military design, the Chinese have little interest in Russian technology—a huge change from the 1950s when China's industrialization depended almost entirely on Soviet technical assistance. Russia is seen as a second-rate economy, certainly by comparison with those in the developed West. It is indicative that today the vast majority of Chinese graduate students pursue their studies not in Russia but in the United States and Western Europe—a Westerncentric trend reflected also in the ruling elite. The "princelings," the offspring of the current "fourth generation"[70] of Chinese leaders, are educated in the West, as are some of the "fifth generation" leaders expected to come to power at the 18th Party Congress in 2012.[71] Unlike many of their forebears of the "third generation"—notably Jiang Zemin, Li Peng, Qian Qichen—none have spent time in the Soviet Union or Russia.

Such is the unequal nature of the economic relationship that the Kremlin has started to complain openly about the "unbalanced" nature of bilateral trade. At the March 2006 summit in Beijing, Putin remarked on "the raw materials bias of Russian exports to China." He noted specifically that exports of Russian machinery and equipment had nearly halved in 2005, while Chinese exports in the same category had increased proportionately.[72] The figures support his concerns. In the period January–July 2006, for example, Chinese exports of machinery and equipment to Russia were nearly fifteen times higher than imports of the same; by year's end Russia's share comprised no more than 1.2 percent of total exports to China.[73] Even the arms trade, viewed by many as the jewel in the crown, is not as impressive as it seems. Russia has provided the lion's share of Chinese military purchases, but their value as a proportion of total bilateral trade is modest indeed—$2.4 billion out of $29 billion in 2005. Moreover, recent indications are that this once reliable pillar of the relationship may be tottering. In 2006 Russian arms exports to China slumped to $200 million, and there have been no new contracts since then.[74]

Most worrying for Moscow is that the terms of trade are becoming more unbalanced every year.[75] Indeed, the relationship is so asymmetrical that it is beginning to acquire a neo-colonial tinge: a modernizing China exploiting a backward Russia for its energy and timber resources and as a market for low-grade goods unsalable in the more discriminating West. Commercially, Beijing appears to rate Russia more or less on a par with countries such as Saudi Arabia and Angola, its main sources of oil imports, and Sudan, where the China National Petroleum Corporation is developing oil fields in conjunction with the government in Khartoum.

Russia's attempts to broaden the economic relationship have been conspicuously unsuccessful, including in areas where it once enjoyed a strong competitive advantage. In nuclear energy, for example, it is being squeezed out by Western competition, particularly third-generation technology from the United States, France, and Germany; Russia's participation is now restricted to just one area, Lianyugang in Jiangsu province.[76] Exports of electrical energy, an area described by Moscow as extremely promising, have largely stalled. An ambitious agreement to export 60 billion kilowatt hours (kWh) per year remains unfulfilled due to pricing disagreements.[77] Space and arms exports are under mounting pressure as Beijing demands licensing agreements and access to cutting-edge technology. It is symptomatic of the shifting balance that Russia's long-time trade surplus, derived almost entirely from energy and natural resources, has disappeared under the combined effect of China's growing manufacturing exports and diminishing interest in Russian industrial imports. In 2006 Russia still enjoyed a trade surplus—$17.55 billion in exports against $15.83 billion in imports. In 2007, however, the balance shifted decisively toward China. Russian exports grew modestly to only $19.68 billion, largely due to increases in oil prices, while imports from China almost doubled to $28.49 billion.[78]

Asymmetrical partnership

Beijing takes every opportunity to emphasize that China's "peaceful rise"/"peaceful development" poses no threat to other countries. In the words of its architect Zheng Bijian, it is "a new security concept that differs from any traditional concept. . . . Our new paradigm firmly abandons the strategic framework in which big powers in the past vied for spheres of influence, engaged in military confrontation, or exported ideologies. Ours is a comprehensive and strategic concept with peaceful coexistence as its precondition, common interest as its basis, strategic cooperation as its bond, and common development as its objective."[79] The idea of "peaceful rise" fits in with the notion of a "harmonious world," characterized by positive-sum globalization and the absence of conflict.

Beijing's insistence that "China's rise is not a threat but an opportunity"[80] is aimed primarily at allaying American concerns about its implications for

Table 5-1. Sino-Russian Trade, 1992–2007

U.S.$ millions

Year	Total bilateral trade	Russian exports to China	Chinese exports to Russia
1992	5,862	3,526	2,336
1993	7,679	4,987	2,692
1994	5,076	3,495	1,581
1995	5,463	3,799	1,665
1996	6,844	5,152	1,693
1997	6,119	4,086	2,033
1998	5,480	3,640	1,840
1999	5,720	4,223	1,497
2000	8,003	5,770	2,233
2001	10,669	7,959	2,710
2002	11,927	8,407	3,521
2003	15,758	9,728	6,030
2004	21,226	12,127	9,098
2005	29,101	15,890	13,211
2006	33,387	17,554	15,832
2007	48,165	19,677	28,488

Source: *China Statistical Yearbook* (various years).

Washington's global leadership.[81] As such it hardly seems relevant to Moscow. Nowhere in Zheng Bijian's speeches is there any mention of Russia in connection with "peaceful rise," and the steady improvement in bilateral relations would appear to obviate the need for such assurances. Publicly at least, Moscow belongs to the converted when it comes to crediting Beijing with good intentions.

Nevertheless, China's rise, peaceful though it may be, has serious implications for their relationship. The fact that Russia is not explicitly targeted does not insulate it from its effects. In China's transformation, Russia is cast in the role of raw materials supplier. This would matter less if it could position itself as the dominant energy exporter to China—in oil, gas, liquefied natural gas (LNG), nuclear power, or electricity. However, there is no sign of this happening. China's growing economic capabilities not only give it the advantage in bilateral trade but translate into enhanced influence in non-economic spheres as well. In a world increasingly dominated by economic power, China's emergence as a global player is of all-encompassing significance to Moscow.

That Chinese intentions are essentially benign is also of little consolation. Intentionally or not, China's ascent as the next global power threatens to leave Russia at the margins of international decisionmaking. Just when the Putin regime is reasserting Russia's credentials as a global great power, much of its thunder is being stolen by the more remarkable transformation of China and also India. They, not Russia, are the true emerging powers of the twenty-first century. It is a measure of the unequal standing of Russia and China in the world that the former is the focus of attention only in very particular, generally negative circumstances—in relation to tensions in the former Soviet space, proliferation concerns vis-à-vis Iran, conflict in the Balkans, uncertainties over gas supply to Europe. China, on the other hand, is universally recognized as a pivotal player, whose influence will expand dramatically over coming decades. While its performance as a "responsible stakeholder" in the international community remains patchy, no one doubts its central importance in world affairs.

Awareness of these trends explains why Moscow has returned to the open instrumentalism of the Yeltsin years: using the China card to "counterbalance" the West and maximize its own impact on the world stage, and promoting Russia as the interface between East and West. Unlike China, Russia as a self-standing, "independent" actor is viewed by many countries as little better than a spoiler, with neither the capacity nor the inclination to help solve global problems.[82] Moscow thus faces a double conundrum: first, Russia needs China more than China needs Russia;[83] and, second, in order to boost its international influence it must make common cause with a state that is partly responsible, albeit unwittingly, for the common perception of Russia as a second-class power.

Closer to home, China's rise has direct implications for the balance of power within the "strategic partnership." Although Russian economic growth is healthy enough—6–7 percent annually since 1999—China's figures of 9 percent per annum over 30 years are more impressive. Whereas Russia's improved economic fortunes are due largely to the oil windfall, the Chinese performance has benefited from no such lucky circumstance; on the contrary, it has been achieved in the face of increasingly severe resource constraints. Seen through the prism of economic development, this is a partnership between a state ever more reliant on its traditional trumps, and a rising power making significant strides in the transition to a post-modern, knowledge-based economy.

It is a matter of some importance that this contrast is apparent to both parties. It has been said that Russia is "doomed to be a junior partner to everyone,"[84] and this is almost certainly the case in its relationship with China. For the time being Beijing's massaging of Russian sensibilities means that this growing inequality is not yet a major source of tension. But as China engages more with the world, it is questionable how long it will continue to indulge Russia's great power pretensions, a source of considerable if generally private irritation in the past.[85]

Even with the Chinese exercising tact, the Russians are struggling to adapt to the rapid transformation of the bilateral balance. As recently as the early 1990s Russia was still the senior partner in the relationship, in a seemingly natural continuum of the "older brother/younger brother" dynamic between Stalin and Mao. Despite the misfortunes of the Yeltsin era, an embattled Russia could still claim center stage as a major foreign policy priority in Washington and "strategic partner" to Beijing. In the first few years of the new century, however, the illusion of an "equal" relationship with China has become much more difficult to maintain. This shift in power and perception is a bitter pill to swallow. As Yeltsin's erratic relationship with Clinton showed, Moscow has never found it easy to be the "junior partner," not even to the United States.[86] And junior status is all the more unpalatable when Russia's economy is doing well and the "senior partner" is a country it has long regarded as inferior.[87]

China's rise does not threaten Russia's territorial integrity, political stability, economic prosperity, or civilization. Instead, the real "China threat" is dual. First, its rise as a global actor is creating an ever greater asymmetry between Moscow and Beijing. The importance of Russia in China's worldview is diminishing, which means that over time Beijing will take less account of Russian interests. This leads on naturally to the second threat—that of Russia's strategic displacement. Whether in Central Asia, East Asia, or global politics, China's rise calls into question Russia's place in the world. An increasingly confident Beijing is unlikely to respect the old understandings merely because that is the way things have always been. Faced with the twin imperatives of sustaining domestic modernization and strengthening its position in a fluid international environment, it will do whatever it deems necessary and possible. Inevitably, this will entail stepping over many of the "red lines" of the past, such as "spheres of influence," and adopting a single-minded approach to the pursuit of Chinese strategic objectives. Such ruthlessness will not only undermine the prospects for genuine partnership with Moscow, but become the prime source of growing tensions between them.

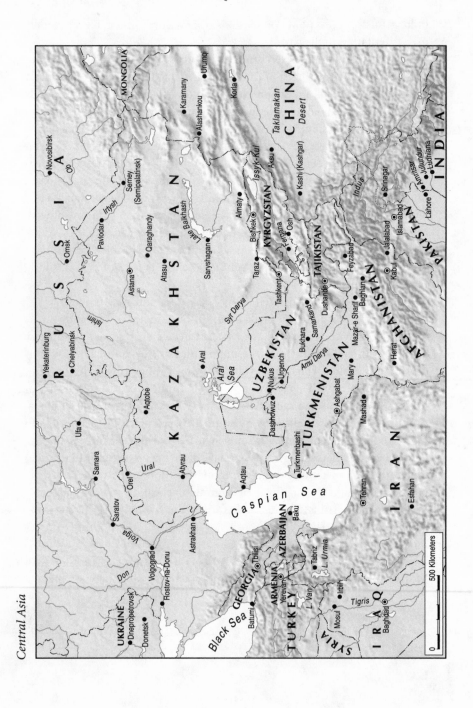

Central Asia

CHAPTER SIX

COOPERATION AND COMPETITION IN CENTRAL ASIA

"The U.S. military presence in Central Asia has deeply affected the strategic structure of the region, and a three-way confrontation may be on [the] horizon."

—ZHAO HUASHENG, February 2005[1]

"The SCO will make a constructive contribution to the establishment of a new global security architecture of mutual trust, mutual benefit, equality and mutual respect."

—Declaration on the Fifth Anniversary of the Shanghai Cooperation Organization, Shanghai, June 15, 2006.[2]

For much of the past two centuries Russia has enjoyed a hegemonic position in Central Asia. Its primacy has been challenged from time to time, most notably by Britain in the "Great Game" of the nineteenth century,[3] but as others have come and gone Moscow has maintained a dominating presence. Whether under the Tsars or Soviet rule or during the post-Soviet period, Moscow has invariably looked upon Central Asia with a patrimonial eye. Indeed, the idea that Russia has always been an empire, and never a modern nation-state in the Westphalian sense, owes much to the physical reality that the region has always either belonged to the Russian/Soviet Empire or been under its hegemonic sway.

Such proprietary feelings have been aided by the acquiescence of great powers and smaller neighbors alike. With the exception of Britain, whose priority was to protect its colonial possession, India, from Russian infiltration, the rest of the world showed little interest in the region. During the Cold War

Central Asia was one of the few areas where the United States did not attempt to compete with Soviet influence; its support for the Afghan resistance after 1979 was a reaction to the Soviet invasion rather than an attempt to assert its own strategic presence. Even after the collapse of the USSR and the ensuing independence of the five Soviet Central Asian republics, the United States paid only modest attention to the region, focusing instead on its relationship with Moscow.

Like the West, China has long recognized Russia's primacy in Central Asia as a historical and geographical fact. Although the Manchus extended their writ deep into the region in the eighteenth century under Emperor Qianlong, the decline of the Qing dynasty in the nineteenth century ensured that there would be no meaningful opposition to Russian expansion. After the fall of the imperial system China was too preoccupied with its own civil war and the Japanese invasion to focus on what was literally a peripheral priority. And during the Stalin-Mao years China's dependence on the Soviet Union meant that it was in no position to challenge the status quo. Stalin's decisive role in the transfer of Xinjiang to the Communists highlighted the extent to which China was beholden to its "older brother," in Central Asia as elsewhere.[4]

Chinese acceptance of Russia's leading position in the region reflected in the first instance a realization that it could do little to challenge it. Despite his strident condemnation of Moscow's "imperialism" and "revisionism" during the Sino-Soviet freeze, Mao understood well the limits of Chinese power. But Chinese attitudes have been conditioned by more than just weakness or lack of interest. There is a strong positive rationale as well. In the 1990s, for instance, Russian primacy in Central Asia represented a comforting constant, a guarantee of stability at a time of otherwise great uncertainty. The Kremlin's aversion to separatist sentiments, whether in Chechnya or the Russian Far East, dovetailed with the Communist leadership's determination to crush Uighur, Tibetan, and other independence movements as well as effect reunification with Taiwan. The confluence of Russian and Chinese regional views was subsequently enshrined in a common commitment to combating the "three evils" of terrorism, separatism, and extremism.[5]

In effect Beijing concluded a tacit bargain with Moscow. It was happy to recognize the status quo in Central Asia and defer to Russia's regional leadership in exchange for the latter continuing to take care of business. With its "strategic rear" covered, China could then focus on domestic modernization and Taiwan.[6] Russia would also help to suppress Uighur separatism, either directly or by pressuring the Central Asian governments to take active measures against groups such as the East Turkestan Islamic Movement.[7]

This accommodation suited Moscow very well. China's compliant attitude contrasted with the West's perceived opportunism in response to Russian weakness. Whereas the United States had exploited the end of bipolarity to strengthen its geopolitical position across the board, particularly in Central and Eastern Europe, China respected Russia's "sphere of vital interests" by not attempting anything similar on the latter's eastern and southern flanks. In Central Asia at least, Russia's hegemonic position seemed secure.

The 9/11 effect—the Russian perspective

Or at least that was until 9/11. In its immediate aftermath, discussion centered on the "global war on terror" and common approaches toward the "new threats and challenges" confronting civilization. In Russia Putin was said to have made a "strategic choice," not just in favor of cooperation with the West, but away from the traditional paradigm of geopolitical competition.[8] His prompt offer of political and intelligence support to the United States and endorsement of an American force presence in former Soviet Central Asia signaled for many observers a new era in Russia-U.S. relations.[9]

Putin's response to 9/11 was predicated on several assumptions. The first was that the Bush administration would come to see Russia as an indispensable partner rather than a secondary priority.[10] Putin was influenced here by the original Yeltsin vision of the United States and Russia standing side by side in cooperation where there had once been confrontation. Second was the realization that Russia was powerless to stop the United States from entering the region, particularly after several Central Asian governments had indicated they would be pleased to host the U.S. military.[11] Putin therefore decided to make a virtue out of a necessity and gain kudos and other benefits for being supportive from the outset. Third, the arrival of American forces in Central Asia meant that Washington would take responsibility for solving problems that Moscow had never been able to manage successfully: the Taliban regime in Afghanistan and its radicalizing impact on the rest of Central Asia. Ideally the United States would do the work, but Russia would remain the hegemon—only strengthened by the removal of the most serious threat to its dominion. This led to the final assumption, which was that the U.S. presence in Central Asia would be temporary, just long enough to defeat the Taliban and reinforce the stability of the Central Asian states.

In backing the American-led intervention, Putin calculated that the pluses of security cooperation with Washington outweighed the geopolitical minuses of "allowing" the United States to become a major player in Central

Asia. This thinking informed Russian decisionmaking over the next eighteen months. Despite the speedy overthrow of the Taliban regime, the Kremlin continued to see Islamic extremism as the chief threat to regional stability and the survival of authoritarian leaders such as Uzbekistan's Islam Karimov. It therefore saw U.S. troops as still fulfilling a necessary function. Importantly, the overall climate of Russia-U.S. relations remained sufficiently positive to soften concerns about the geopolitical consequences of the American troop presence. The Kremlin continued to believe that the region would remain a Russian sphere of interests, albeit not as exclusively as before.

This dynamic began to change, however, when it became evident that Putin's expectations of enhanced cooperation with Washington would not be met and that the United States was in Central Asia for the long haul. Far from scaling down its "temporary" bases in Manas (in Kyrgyzstan) and Karshi-Khanabad (Uzbekistan), it expanded them. At the same time the Bush administration began to promote a Western normative agenda, not so much focused directly on Central Asia but throughout the former Soviet Union. The "color revolutions" in Georgia in October 2003, Ukraine in December 2004, and Kyrgyzstan in June 2005 heightened Kremlin fears that U.S. policy had shifted from fighting Islamic extremism to exporting Western democratic values. The United States changed from being Russia's security partner in Central Asia to becoming an ever more subversive presence—part of the problem rather than the solution. The geopolitical and normative minuses of the American presence now seemed much more significant than an insubstantial and tarnished security cooperation.

Moscow's regional anxieties were exacerbated by the realization that Washington did not appear to value Russia as a full strategic partner in world affairs, but at best as a useful (rather than indispensable) regional supporter in selected areas, such as counterterrorism and the proliferation of weapons of mass destruction (WMD). Russia's secondary importance in the American scheme of things appeared to be confirmed by developments during 2002–04: Washington's casual dismissal of Kremlin objections to military intervention in Iraq; intensified criticisms of Putin's authoritarian tendencies; failure to offer symbolic quid pro quo such as abrogation of the 1974 Jackson-Vanik amendment;[12] and alleged Western complicity in the color revolutions.[13] All this contributed to a review of Russian attitudes toward the United States, and the steady deterioration of bilateral relations.

In the circumstances Moscow had two choices in Central Asia. The first was to attempt to re-establish the status quo ante by going it alone. This was impractical for many reasons, above all because of Russian weakness and the aversion of the Central Asian states to surrendering again to the authority of their former imperial master. While Russia still exerted considerable influence in the region, the great power understandings that had allowed it to enjoy a hegemonic position had broken down irretrievably. Central Asia was no longer a "no-go" or "no interest" zone for others, but a pivotal theatre of the new geopolitics.

The Kremlin therefore turned to the second option: co-opting China and the Central Asian states in the largely negative agenda of constraining "outside" influence. Faced with the post-9/11 reality that the United States would remain a significant player in the region for at least the medium term, Moscow braced itself for the task of geopolitical damage limitation. If Russia could not restore its hegemony, then it could at least aim to ensure that no other power took its place. More ambitiously, it might hope to be the leader of a regional condominium serving Russian security, political, and economic interests. Such a condominium would operate at two levels. The first would be the consolidation of traditional ties with the Central Asian states while supplementing them with new common interests, such as combating Islamic extremism and expanding energy cooperation. The second would be enhanced strategic partnership with China.

The 9/11 effect—the Chinese perspective

Unfortunately for Moscow, 9/11 had a revolutionizing impact on Chinese policy toward Central Asia and, specifically, its approach to regional cooperation with Russia. The causes of this transformation lie as much in Putin's response to 9/11 as in the U.S. presence itself. His speedy endorsement of the American military operation came as a shock to the Chinese leadership.[14] While Beijing did not subscribe to the fiction of "geographical balance" in Russian foreign policy, it could scarcely believe that Moscow would permit, let alone support, the deployment of U.S. troops in Russia's sphere of influence. It was one thing for the United States and other Western powers to override Kremlin objections to NATO enlargement in central and eastern Europe. It was quite another for the West to move, with Putin's blessing, into a region that had been an integral part of the Tsarist and Soviet Empires.

What made things worse was that Moscow gave no advance warning of its decision. There had been some signs of a Russia-U.S. rapprochement after Putin and Bush had held their first summit meeting in the Slovenian town of Brdo in June 2001. But nothing prepared Beijing for the sudden change in Russian policy. Almost overnight the Kremlin switched from a multi-vectored approach to one unambiguously centered on comprehensive cooperation with the United States. Relations with China were unceremoniously pushed into the background. Over the next year, a number of developments confirmed the new "pro-Western" trend. In December 2001 Moscow meekly accepted the unilateral American withdrawal from the ABM Treaty; in April 2002 it concluded the Strategic Offensive Reductions Treaty (SORT) with Washington; and one month later it co-established the Russia-NATO Council.

From the Chinese perspective Putin's response to 9/11 highlighted a number of truths. First, for Russia, relations with the United States (and Europe) would always take precedence. Notwithstanding the rise of China and India, the West remained the principal source of global power in its various dimensions—military might, political influence, economic power, technological superiority, cultural "imperialism," moral authority. As in the Yeltsin years, Russian attitudes toward China were conditioned by a default mechanism. In times of difficulty for Russia-U.S. relations, the Kremlin would play the China card to show that Russia was not without friends and options. But when Moscow enjoyed good relations with the West, as in the first year after 9/11, the "strategic partnership" with Beijing would take a back seat.

To some extent the Chinese leadership had understood this before 9/11. But the Kremlin's ready acquiescence in U.S. troop deployment and the lack of prior consultation with Beijing rammed home the point that Russia would not support Chinese interests in Central Asia, except on a purely coincidental basis. From this it was a short step to concluding that China would have to rely largely on its own efforts to advance its agenda. The tacit bargain in Central Asia was off. A Russia that tilted toward the West could not be counted on, while any Russia-U.S. cooperation in counterterrorism would be on Washington's terms.

The latter became evident after the formal military defeat of the Taliban. Central Asia, once a strategically predictable region with an acknowledged hegemon, had metamorphosed into a much more disparate environment. It was apparent that Russian influence had been severely weakened and that the United States was now a major power in the region. Beijing had to adapt to a very different set of realities. Setting aside any feelings of betrayal, it understood that Moscow was no longer even capable of acting on behalf of Chinese interests.

With the deterioration of Russia-U.S. relations from late 2002, China's position in Central Asia improved considerably. It no longer faced the threat of being the odd one out in the Russia-U.S.-China triangle. The emergence of fresh tensions between Washington and Moscow meant that it could build up its presence in the region on the quiet, without causing undue concern to the other two major powers. Nevertheless, the key lessons of the early post-9/11 period remained. China could not depend on Russia as in the past, since the latter was both untrustworthy *and* weak. It was also important to avoid being sucked into Moscow's growing anti-American agenda. The solution lay in pursuing a more flexible and active policy toward Central Asia, one that involved the accelerated expansion of ties with all states in the region.[15]

A new Great Game?

The re-emergence of a competitive strategic environment in Central Asia has seen geopolitics return with a vengeance. Despite talk of common approaches to universal problems, great-power tensions in the region are at their most acute since the Soviet occupation of Afghanistan. Instead of a shared vision of cooperative security, there is talk of a new Great Game.[16] The positive-sum spirit of the immediate post-9/11 period has given way to elemental "win-lose" instincts and balance-of-power notions, even if these are wrapped up in the language of interdependency.[17]

The geopolitical construct of spheres of influence is at the root of the strategic tension between Russia and the United States in Central Asia. Russia may no longer be the undisputed hegemon, but it continues to believe that it is the leading power in Central Asia "by right" and, increasingly, through its control of energy resources.[18] Washington, on the other hand, explicitly rejects both the principle of a privileged sphere of influence and Russia's right to dominate the former Soviet space.[19] This gulf in perceptions, exacerbated by differences over democratic norms, has intensified geopolitical competition.

That said, it is questionable how far one can take the Great Game analogy. For one thing, there is very little of the "Game" element today; the Boy's Own adventures with their individual freelancing and often amateurish japes belong to a bygone era. Central Asia is now the subject of concerted state policy in Russia and the United States, and both governments invest far more resources into the region than the Russian and British Empires did in the nineteenth century. More importantly, the current "Great Game"—if one can call it that—is a hugely complex affair involving many different state and non-state actors and taking place in an infinitely more anarchic world. The Central Asian states no longer have passive roles, but are important players in their own right.[20] Influence is no longer just a prize to be fought over by two giants confident in their powers, but is shaped by multiple arrangements and agendas.

China's re-entry into Central Asian affairs, after a hiatus of nearly two centuries, has radically altered the strategic picture. This development is likely to be of more lasting importance to the region than the recent American involvement. Whereas the latter may be seen as the product of an extraordinary concatenation of circumstances, China's renewed interest is consistent with more permanent realities: geographical proximity, historical antecedents, and direct security imperatives.[21] The Americans may well leave Central Asia in the not too distant future, and in fact are already scaling down their presence in favor of burden-sharing with NATO troops. But the Chinese are there to stay and, over time, will strengthen their political, economic, and security ties with the region. If one can speak at all of a Great Game, then it is of a game that is being played at several levels and where there are now three strategic "principals"—Russia, the United States, and China.[22]

Competing agendas—the view from Moscow

China's arrival as a major player in the region raises the issue of its impact on the larger "strategic partnership" with Russia. Is Beijing's heightened involvement a source of tension, or does it give both sides the opportunity to strengthen bilateral ties through cooperation on pan-regional issues? Is Central Asia the focus of a lasting convergence of interests or is this Sino-Russian alignment preserved only by a common desire to contain the United States? To what extent are Russian and Chinese objectives reconcilable?

Moscow's approach to Central Asia reveals an essential duality. On the one hand, it is informed by the messianic vision of a return to the pre-9/11 status quo: Russia as the dominant regional player, a compliant China following in its wake, an absent or uninterested West, a subordinate Central Asia, and the defeat of Islamic extremism (Taliban, al-Qaeda). On the other hand, Moscow is aware that this set of outcomes is improbable. So there is also a strong pragmatic dimension to its Central Asian policy that recognizes the limitations of Russian power as well as the strengths of some of the other players—not least China.

This relative pragmatism, however, does not lack ambition. Russia is striving to strengthen ties with the Central Asian states through many avenues. Reciprocal high-level visits are far more frequent than during the Soviet era, let alone under Yeltsin; trade turnover has quadrupled since 2002;[23] Russian energy companies are investing heavily in the region;[24] military and security ties are expanding; and Moscow has injected considerable resources into cultural and public diplomacy.[25] Russia is neither capable of, nor even interested

Table 6-1. Russian Trade with Central Asia, 1994–2007
U.S.$millions

	Kazakhstan	Uzbekistan	Kyrgyzstan	Tajikistan	Turkmenistan	Total
1994	4,194	1,638	202	233	172	6,439
1995	5,230	1,713	206	357	272	7,778
1996	5,591	1,739	306	240	283	8,159
1997	5,215	1,889	316	186	423	8,029
1998	3,777	1,091	264	138	140	5,410
1999	2,623	708	179	179	137	3,826
2000	4,447	937	192	293	177	6,046
2001	4,796	993	145	199	179	6,313
2002	4,349	798	178	134	175	5,633
2003	6,233	998	264	198	252	7,945
2004	8,093	1,380	418	259	285	10,435
2005	9,735	1,763	543	335	301	12,676
2006	12,807	2,379	755	504	309	16,753
2007	16,576	3,180	1,169	771	454	22,149

Sources: *Federal'naia Tamozhennaia Sluzhba and Rossiiskii Statisticheskii Ezhegodnik* (various years).

in, restoring its imperial fiat over the Central Asians, but it does hope to achieve "indirect control" by reinforcing their dependence through various soft power means: political backing for authoritarian regimes, economic investment and assistance, advantageous trade (particularly market access) arrangements, and so on. The endgame is not the restoration of the Soviet Empire, as some Western critics allege, but the maximization of Russian interests across the board.[26]

The emphasis on regional "interdependency" is apparent in Moscow's use of multilateral mechanisms. Russian policymakers have traditionally viewed bilateral relationships as the most effective channels for conducting foreign affairs. But multilateral or rather pseudo-multilateral institutions perform an important supplementary role, providing a veneer of international legitimacy as well as balance. Thus in the 1990s Russia responded to the eastward enlargement of NATO and the EU, and the latter's European Neighbourhood Policy, by promoting the Single Economic Space (*edinoe ekonomicheskoe prostranstvo*) with Belarus, Ukraine, and Kazakhstan.[27] Today Moscow's multilateral balancer of choice is the Collective Security Treaty Organization (CSTO), while it has also bought heavily into the Eurasian Economic Community (EurAsEC) and the Shanghai Cooperation Organization (SCO).

Moscow has been careful to mask its discomfort with China's growing involvement in Central Asian affairs. Publicly it has welcomed its contribution to regional stability and raised no objection to Chinese energy companies building pipelines from Central Asia to western China or buying up equity in Kazakhstan. This complaisance recognizes that a frontal assault on such deals would be counterproductive, not only for the bilateral relationship, but also for Russia's ties with the Central Asians. Instead the Kremlin has sought to counter Beijing's "peaceful offensive"[28] by playing on local apprehension about Chinese economic domination, and piggybacking on Chinese projects. An example of the latter approach is its participation in the Atasu-Alashankou oil pipeline between Kazakhstan and Xinjiang, which came on tap in May 2006. Since the Kazakhstanis are unable to produce enough oil to fill the pipeline, Russia has proposed meeting the shortfall with its own exports to China.[29] This enables it to position itself as a constructive and even indispensable player, while discreetly exposing the inadequacies of Chinese engagement. Although it is already too late to sideline China, Moscow hopes to contain its political and especially economic influence. Tactically this entails a broadly cooperative, soft-power approach, but one with the strategic intent of restoring Russia's pre-eminent, if no longer hegemonic, place in the region.

Such an ambition is premised on counterbalancing the American military presence or, better still, ejecting it from Central Asia altogether. The most promising way of achieving this is to co-opt other regional actors, which means working with, rather than pressuring, the Central Asian republics. Moscow has cleverly exploited the resentment of local regimes against Washington's democracy agenda, in particular their fear of further color revolutions. Following the Andijon killings in Uzbekistan in May 2005, the comparison between Russia's wholehearted support for the Karimov regime and American condemnation of the actions of the Uzbek security forces ensured that Tashkent would switch its favors from the United States to Russia. Karimov's decision to terminate the lease for the American base in Karshi-Khanabad two months later was due to a combination of personal apprehension over the stability of his regime and an acute sense of betrayal.[30]

In Central Asia, as elsewhere, Moscow strives to make the best of its axis of convenience with China. Discomfort with the latter's growing profile in the region pales in comparison with geopolitical concerns over a possible long-term U.S. presence. In effect, it proceeds according to the principle of "my enemy's enemy is my friend." Although the United States is scarcely an enemy, even in today's difficult times, the Kremlin identifies it as Russia's most serious geopolitical competitor in the region. And this means it is keen to develop tactical alliances with the express purpose of undermining the American position. China's strong opposition to Washington's "hegemonic" power makes it a natural candidate for just such an alliance.

Chinese interests, strategy, and tactics

All this presupposes that Beijing is willing to be used as a tool of Moscow's grand strategy and that Russian and Chinese objectives coincide. There are serious doubts on both scores. First, an increasingly self-confident China is no one's instrument, but an independent player. The notion of "older brother/younger brother" outlived its usefulness decades ago, and the changing balance of power within the bilateral relationship makes it improbable that China will subordinate its regional interests to another's agenda. Moreover, the recent memory of Putin's post-9/11 decision to side with the United States gives Beijing little reason to trust in Russian benevolence.

Second, Chinese objectives in Central Asia differ from Russia's in key respects. Beijing, like Washington, is not prepared to concede Russia's regional leadership, at least not in the longer term. With the breakdown of their tacit bargain, it is seeking to expand its own role in Central Asia, one which it has both the capacity *and* the need to fulfill. It is accordingly ready to use all available means—political, strategic, economic, and cultural. One of the notable features of recent Chinese diplomacy has been a readiness to employ, with some skill, soft power in all vectors of foreign policy.[31] Central Asia is no exception.

China has little interest in becoming the regional hegemon,[32] but it aspires to recognition as a strategic principal in Central Asia. Unlike Russia, this goal is driven less by a sense of historical entitlement than by the knowledge that a stronger presence serves its interests. The most important of these is security, particularly in Xinjiang province. There are interesting parallels here with Russian sensitivities over the future of the Russian Far East. Both Xinjiang and the RFE are vast territories with tiny populations; both are frontier regions rather than part of the national heartland; and both are the subject of considerable anxieties over territorial integrity. In much the same way that Moscow views partnership with China as a means of securing the RFE, so Beijing sees the development of close ties with the Central Asian states and Russia as intrinsic to stability in the far west of the country.[33]

For the Chinese a Central Asia made up of authoritarian and semi-authoritarian regimes represents the most favorable context in which to combat Uighur separatism in Xinjiang and preserve security in the longer term. So far governments in the region have supported Beijing's anti-separatist agenda, clamping down on Uighur activists and even extraditing them back to China. But such support cannot be taken for granted, given the considerable sympathy for Uighur self-determination among expatriate communities in

Table 6-2. Chinese Trade with Central Asia, 1992–2007

U.S.$millions

	Kazakhstan	Kyrgyzstan	Uzbekistan	Tajikistan	Turkmenistan	Total
1992	369	35	53	3	5	465
1993	435	103	54	12	5	609
1994	304	105	124	3	11	547
1995	391	231	119	24	18	783
1996	460	105	190	12	11	778
1997	527	107	203	20	15	872
1998	636	198	89	19	13	955
1999	1,139	135	40	8	9	1,331
2000	1,557	178	51	17	16	1,819
2001	1,288	119	58	11	33	1,509
2002	1,955	202	132	12	88	2,389
2003	3,292	314	347	39	83	4,075
2004	4,498	602	576	69	98	5,843
2005	6,806	972	681	158	110	8,727
2006	8,358	2,226	972	324	179	12,059
2007	13,876	3,779	1,129	524	353	19,661

Source: *China Statistical Yearbook* (various years).

Kazakhstan and Kyrgyzstan. The potential growth of democratization and pluralism in Central Asia could undermine previous state-to-state understandings.[34] To forestall this possibility, Beijing has therefore intensified its relationship-building with regional elites.

The second imperative for Beijing is to obtain access to Central Asian energy. The leadership is motivated not only by a general desire to diversify external sources of supply (see chapter 8), but also by the need to expand its options *within* Eurasia. Moscow's unreliability as an energy supplier has led Beijing to look increasingly at Central Asian states such as Kazakhstan, Turkmenistan, and Uzbekistan, as sources in their own right and as insurance to compensate for any shortfall in Russian imports.[35] Diversifying into Central Asia also serves as subtle leverage on Moscow, by hinting that China may be able to satisfy its requirements from other regional sources if necessary. CNPC's purchase of PetroKazakhstan, the opening of the Atasu-Alashankou pipeline, and the concluding of a massive gas deal with Turkmenistan[36] reflect this dual approach of diversification and leverage.

Unsurprisingly Beijing's search for energy in Central Asia has generated some tensions with Moscow. The competition between Russian and Chinese energy interests is becoming more intense. Moscow, for example, attempted unsuccessfully to scupper the sale of PetroKazakhstan to CNPC in 2005.[37] Although this behind-the-scenes struggle has yet to impinge seriously on the larger bilateral relationship, the two sides' agendas are in conflict. Russia wants China to be energy-dependent on it, particularly within Eurasia, while China is anxious to widen its sources of supply. Russian companies are keen to buy up equity in the oil and gas companies of the Central Asian states, which means excluding other outside interests, including China. Moscow also seeks to control the major pipelines traveling east and west out of Central Asia. China resists attempts to exclude it from equity ownership and prefers to deal with the Central Asian energy-producing states directly, free from Russian interference. For the time being these competing agendas are being managed politically, but there are real doubts as to how long this can continue as China's energy hunger grows and Russia's oil and gas giants become ever more predatory.

Beijing's third objective in Central Asia is to ensure a stable geopolitical environment. Although it appears in this respect to be of like mind with Moscow, its understanding of geopolitical stability differs. Whereas Russia envisages itself as the undisputed regional leader, to the Chinese leadership geopolitical stability implies a more equal arrangement. In effect, it hopes for a Concert of Central Asia,[38] characterized by numerous checks and balances that prevent any one power—the United States now, Russia later—from dictating terms. This is not so much a defensive security posture, but derives more from the belief that Chinese interests would be best served by a level playing field. For much the same reasons as Beijing pushes for unrestricted market access globally, so it would like a Central Asia that is "open" to all states in the region (but closed to "outside" powers such as the United States).

At the same time China is aware that the Central Asian states, as well as Russia, fear its potential and suspect its intentions.[39] Beijing has therefore trodden lightly in its dealings with them. In addition to reiterating the self-deprecatory mantra that China is a "developing country," it has abjured great power ambitions and portrayed itself as a team player fully committed to pan-regional cooperation. It has played up the concept of a "prosperous neighborhood" (whereby Beijing provides economic assistance to the Central Asian states)[40] and used other forms of soft power, such as educational scholarships and Confucian Centers. Most critically, in focusing on pan-regionalism Beijing has emphasized cooperation through multilateral institutions, rather than just relying on bilateral relationships. Although this runs against the traditional grain of Chinese foreign policy, in Central Asia it is the most unthreatening avenue for engaging with other states.[41] Within the Shanghai Cooperation Organization, for example, the disparity in power between China and smaller countries is less pronounced. The Central Asian states can take comfort in safety of numbers, as well as in the ample possibilities for maneuvering between Russia and China.

The Shanghai Cooperation Organization

In recent years the Shanghai Cooperation Organization has been at the center of debate about strategic cooperation and competition in Central Asia. To some observers it is a constructive multilateral organization that addresses in a practical way common threats and challenges such as international terrorism. Others, however, see it as a pseudo-multilateral body with a blatantly anti-Western agenda. There is a similar divergence of view regarding its effectiveness. Moscow and Beijing claim that the SCO is making great strides in tackling regional security issues. But its critics argue that the organization is heavy on process and light on substance, and that its importance remains essentially symbolic. As for the implications for Sino-Russian partnership, it can reasonably be argued that the SCO's development at once reflects the strength of bilateral ties and reinforces them. Yet there are signs that as the organization expands and takes on an ever more ambitious agenda, cracks are starting to appear between Moscow and Beijing.

"An international organization of a new type"

According to the rhetoric, the SCO is an "international organization of a new type,"[42] committed to positive-sum cooperation not only in security matters, but also increasingly in the political, economic, and cultural domains. The SCO, its advocates assert, is imbued with the "Shanghai spirit," based on "mutual trust, mutual benefit, equality, consultations, respect for the diversity of cultures and aspiration toward common development." As such it represents "a new and non-confrontational model of international relations, a model that calls for discarding the Cold War mentality and transcending ideological differences."[43] The SCO member-states routinely emphasize that the activities of the organization do "not mean a movement toward the creation of any bloc" and are not directed against "any third parties"—namely, the United States. However, they unambiguously oppose American "hegemonism" and the imposition of Western values, and emphasize the "right of all countries to . . . pursue particular models of development and formulate domestic and foreign policies independently."[44]

Sensitive to accusations that the SCO lacks substance, the member-states have talked up its achievements. Chief among these is the SCO's institutional development, which now includes annual summits and meetings at heads of government and foreign minister level, as well as numerous other interministerial, interagency, and interdepartmental links.[45] The initial establishment of a Permanent Secretariat in Beijing in 2004 has been reinforced by the development of more specialized bodies, such as the Regional Anti-Terrorist Structure (RATS) based in Tashkent and the SCO Business Council. There have been a number of joint anti-terrorism exercises, the most notable being "Peace Mission 2007" (see p. 49). The organization has also been looking to expand its geographical scope. The original six members—Russia, China, Kazakhstan, Uzbekistan, Tajikistan, and Kyrgyzstan—have been supplemented by four observer states: Mongolia in 2004, followed a year later by India, Pakistan and, most controversially, Iran. The SCO has also entered into formal dialogue arrangements with ASEAN and the Organization of the Islamic Conference (OIC).

The overall impression that the SCO member-states seek to convey is of an organization that is growing dynamically, but from a modest base. Originating in the April 1996 "Shanghai Five" agreement on confidence-building measures along the former Sino-Soviet border, the SCO formally came into being only five years later, in June 2001. Official documents note that it has been in existence a relatively short time and is therefore a work in progress with much still to do. Thus the declaration of the July 2005 summit in Astana "underscored the importance of taking necessary measures on the *fulfillment* of agreements." On the RATS, the declaration noted that it was "playing a still more important role, *which must increase further*" and that "measures will be taken to *improve and enhance the effectiveness* of [its] activity" [author's italics].[46]

A year later little appeared to have changed. At the fifth anniversary summit in Shanghai in June 2006, the joint communiqué asserted that the SCO had "completed the building of institutions and the legal framework, which ensures its effective functioning," but was vague on details. It noted that the SCO had "carried out close security cooperation focusing on addressing non-traditional security threats and challenges such as fighting terrorism, separatism, extremism and drug trafficking," and that it had "identified the goals, priority areas and major tasks of economic cooperation among member-states." However, the statement hinted at the absence of tangible progress: "The SCO *will take steps to strengthen* the regional anti-terrorism agency"; "SCO member-states *need to coordinate their efforts* in implementing the Programme of Multilateral Trade and Economic Cooperation"; and "[SCO members] *need to work together* to promote trade and investment facilitation and gradually realize the free flow of commodities, capital, services and technologies" [author's italics].[47]

The Bishkek summit in August 2007 pointed to the recently completed "Peace Mission 2007" exercises as evidence that the organization was finally acting on its ambitious policy agenda. The notion of an "energy club" also elicited some interest in the West.[48] Yet the summit communiqué makes for unimpressive reading. Although it declared that the activity of the RATS was "consistently intensifying," it revealed almost nothing by way of actual achievement. Instead it stressed "the importance of fulfilling the Cooperation Plan of the SCO member states on combating terrorism, separatism, and extremism for 2007–2009" and "the need to step up counteraction against the funding of terrorism and illegal money laundering." The generally lackluster tone of the document is reflected in the surfeit of ritualistic phrases: "the younger generation will take over the cause of promoting friendship among the peoples of the SCO member states"; "the 2008 Summer Olympic Games in Beijing would have an important meaning for strengthening friendship among nations."[49]

Just another CIS?

The language of SCO summit communiqués is reminiscent of the grandiose but empty sentiments expressed by the organization of the Commonwealth of Independent States during the 1990s. In the course of the decade, the CIS signed off on literally hundreds of agreements, almost none of which were ever implemented. The CIS became a standing joke, and not long after Putin came to office he acknowledged that it had become largely ineffectual.[50] There is a natural temptation to view the SCO in the same light and to dismiss it as an inconsequential organization manipulated by Beijing and Moscow.

Such assessments are wide of the mark. True, SCO rhetoric has greatly outstripped achievement. Its statements are full of banalities, many directed at Washington, and they rarely address specific tasks of political, economic, and security cooperation.[51] Parallels with NATO and the EU are obviously absurd.[52] The SCO has yet to develop a genuine collective identity. As Murat Laumulin observes, "there is no SCO policy *per se*"; much of the organization's activity is a "geopolitical bluff," intended to create "the perception (or at least the illusion) of there being a new and serious player on the regional and international stage."[53] It is also undeniable that China and, to a lesser extent, Russia dominate the organization.

For all that, however, the SCO amounts to more than just a mini-CIS plus China. In the first place, it has a degree of cohesiveness on certain issues that sets it apart from the ragtag "collective" of the CIS in the 1990s (and today). There are no openly dissenting members—no Georgia, Ukraine, or Azerbaijan—to mar the image of organizational unity. Although important differences exist between individual member-states, notably between Kazakhstan and Uzbekistan, these have been well managed on the whole. The SCO has demonstrated an impressive solidarity on occasions, as in the call at the 2005 Astana summit for a "final timeline" to be set for the removal of American bases in Kyrgyzstan and Uzbekistan.[54]

The SCO also has real achievements to its name. These are not many and one should not overstate the significance of its institutional and legal development *as an end in itself*. But there has been important progress. In addition to enhanced political coordination, the SCO has contributed to the development of bilateral and multilateral security ties between member-states. The RATS, although in its infancy, retains the potential to serve as a moderately effective coordinating center for counter-terrorism. And there is growing interaction between the militaries of the member-states, involving frequent joint exercises, as well as consultation between security and intelligence agencies.

While China and Russia dominate proceedings, the SCO is not simply a souped-up version of the "Shanghai Five" (whose overriding purpose was to stabilize the old Sino-Soviet frontier). Today the SCO is a genuinely multilateral organization, even if some member-states are more equal than others. The weakest, Kyrgyzstan and Tajikistan, can make themselves heard— another big difference from the CIS in the 1990s when the smaller members were largely ignored. In the SCO, the presence of two great powers rather than a single leader allows the Central Asians to maximize their interests by maneuvering between Moscow and Beijing. Finally there is a level of collegiality that has never existed in the CIS or its constituent bodies. The SCO commitment to a "democratic, fair and rational political and international order"[55] is realized to some degree within the organization itself.

Friend or foe?

As the SCO has grown institutionally and expanded its policy agenda, the West has begun to take it more seriously. There are calls for NATO and the EU to develop formal dialogue arrangements[56] and even for the United States and the EU to seek membership or observer status.[57] The argument for closer ties with the SCO is twofold. It would raise the hitherto mediocre level of international cooperation on common security priorities such as combating terrorism and drug trafficking, while the development of institutional links would contribute to confidence-building in the region. As Richard Weitz puts it, "by enhancing transparency and countering misperceptions, [the region's core multilateral institutions] could help avert an unnecessary great-game security spiral among Russia, China, and the United States."[58]

The fear of a possible Great Game is one shared by critics of the SCO, who see the organization as dedicated to old-fashioned geopolitical competition, albeit using "modern" means. One extreme view describes the SCO as "the most dangerous organization that Americans have never heard of."[59] Although most critics are more measured in their assessment, they nevertheless believe that the organization's chief raison d'être is to undermine the American presence in Central Asia.[60] As such, it is first and last a geopolitical entity, whose zero-sum agenda is wrapped in a thin cloak of positive-sum multilateralism.

Such suspicions are not entirely without foundation. SCO pronouncements sometimes take on the flavor of Soviet-era propaganda. Thus the Astana summit statement of July 2005, in addition to calling for a "final timeline" for American forces to leave, emphasized that "a rational and just world order must be based . . . upon the establishment of true partnership with *no pretence to monopoly and domination in international affairs*" [author's italics]. In an unsubtle reference to Washington's democratization agenda, it asserted that "in the area of human rights it is necessary to respect strictly...the historical traditions and national features of every people and the sovereign equality of all states."[61] The 2006 summit declaration in Shanghai continued in much the same aggressive-defensive vein, calling for the "discarding of the Cold War mentality," condemning "double standards," and warning that "models of social development should not be 'exported'"— a transparent reference to the color revolutions.[62]

It would be wrong, however, to disregard the SCO as simply a blunt geopolitical instrument. Despite the modest progress of its security-building agenda, this nevertheless remains the main priority for most member-states. The Central Asians, in particular, are concerned first by the threat of Islamic-based "terrorism" to political stability and only then by the subversive effect of Western normative influence. It was only after Washington ratcheted up criticism of their internal politics—in Kyrgyzstan during 2004–05 and Uzbekistan after the Andijon killings in May 2005—that they bought into Moscow's overtly anti-U.S. agenda. Similarly, Beijing's first priority is the security of China's far west rather than strategic competition with Washington. And none of the member-states—not even China, which has been the most enthusiastic supporter of the SCO's development—believes that it will evolve anytime soon into an international organization rivaling NATO.

Ultimately the SCO is a modest organization of modest achievements, a reality implicitly recognized by its members, whose main foreign policy activity is either directed elsewhere (in the case of Russia and China)[63] or channeled through bilateral relations (the Central Asian states). For all the bark about "Cold War mentality," "hegemonism," and "double standards," the engine of the SCO's development today is the intrinsic logic of intra-regional cooperation. It is this logic that will ensure its continued growth, regardless of whether the Americans stay in Central Asia. There are enough commonalities in the interests of member-states—regime stability, counterterrorism, trade—for the organization to develop without the reference point of an external enemy, real or artificial.

The predominantly positive impulse motivating the SCO is one reason why there is little to fear from it. Another is that the six member-states are so different from one another that they find it difficult to reach agreement on sensitive issues, especially when this entails firm commitments. For example, after the Astana summit Uzbekistan followed through on the "final timeline" by terminating the lease for the American base in Karshi-Khanabad. Kyrgyzstan, however, extended the lease for the Manas base in return for more money.[64] Even in prestige areas such as military cooperation, policy coordination is very limited. "Peace Mission 2007" was Sino-Russian in all but name, with only token involvement by the other member-states.[65] There is no early prospect of a unified SCO military force or strategic doctrine, and interoperability remains extremely limited.

Diverging interests within the SCO are nowhere more apparent than in the ongoing debate over membership. Russia would like to see Iran and India become full members; India, in particular, would help counterbalance not only the United States in Central Asia, *but also China*. Beijing, on the other hand, has no interest in the accession of a strategic competitor or in the SCO becoming openly anti-American, which would happen if Iran were admitted. The Chinese also fear that expansion and the overt politicization of the SCO would distract the organization from its primary tasks: security-building, political stability, and economic cooperation. This reflects a larger discussion about the SCO's strategic direction: whether to focus primarily on counterterrorism and geopolitical issues, as at present, or reorient itself toward commercial cooperation and economic integration.[66]

The lack of progress on difficult issues—membership, military cooperation, economic integration—highlights the SCO's limitations as a would-be bloc. Not only have member-states rejected the principle of bloc politics, but they have demonstrated no capacity to act as one. Although there is a degree of normative convergence in that all are authoritarian or semi-authoritarian regimes, this does not remotely approximate the consensus on values and interests that exists within NATO, the EU, or even ASEAN. Thus far the relative unity and cohesiveness of the SCO have been preserved through self-moderation, whereby all members, China and Russia included, recognize implicitly that they cannot overtax the capacities of the organization.[67] Far from the SCO posing a strategic threat to Western interests, it is more probable that its expansion—qualitative and quantitative—will generate increasing internal tensions. A radicalized agenda would jeopardize the unity that has been its greatest asset so far, not to mention undermine the SCO's wider legitimacy as an "organization of a new type" supporting international peace and stability.

Russia and China in the SCO

Paradoxically, the more the SCO grows in importance, the greater the potential for Sino-Russian rivalry to emerge. As long as the organization remains a relative sideshow, Moscow and Beijing will be careful to manage their reservations about each other. But if a leadership role within the SCO becomes synonymous with a broader influence in Central Asia, such self-restraint will come under increasing strain. The changing balance in the bilateral relationship (see chapter 5) could spill over and the SCO could become a forum for great power competition.

For the time being, however, the organization serves to reinforce the bilateral partnership. It highlights the commonalities between Moscow and Beijing, such as combating the "three evils" of terrorism, separatism, and extremism, and containing the American presence in Central Asia. Regular contact through the SCO strengthens Sino-Russian institutional links and integrates them with the cooperative ties and channels of communication each country has with the Central Asian states. The fostering of a regional collective identity—even if only a facsimile—ties in nicely with the image of "strategic partnership."

Over the next few years any tensions between Moscow and Beijing over the SCO are likely to be limited, for two reasons. First, the bilateral relationship is too important to risk for the sake of regional influence in Central Asia, a secondary priority for China especially.[68] Second, as long as the United States remains in the region, Russia and China will have a ready focal point. Differences in their general attitudes toward Washington will matter less than the shared conviction that both would benefit strategically from the departure of American (and NATO) forces. Fostering consensus within the SCO supports this objective.

This raises the question of how things may develop as Central Asia increases in importance for both capitals, and if the United States leaves the region or significantly reduces its presence. As China continues its spectacular economic growth and completes its transformation into a global power, it is likely to become more assertive. There are already signs of this in its ambitious proposals for regional economic integration, the end-result of which could be that China supplants Russia as the leading power in Central Asia. Faced with the threat of strategic displacement, Moscow would scarcely remain passive, just as it has strongly resisted Western "encroachment" in the former Soviet space. Accustomed to being the "regional superpower," it is already taking active measures to strengthen its position.[69] It has tightened bonds with the Central Asian elites; it is striving to prevent the SCO from becoming an instrument of Chinese influence; and it is playing on Central Asian fears of Chinese economic domination.

Even with the current healthy state of Sino-Russian relations there is evidence of emergent tensions. Beijing is looking to steer the SCO's activities toward economic cooperation and integration, while Moscow continues to stress security, military, and geopolitical aspects. These divergent visions highlight the relative strengths and weaknesses of Russia and China in Central Asia. Moscow understands that its most effective levers of influence are its personal and political ties with the Central Asian elites.[70] Conversely, it feels most vulnerable in the economic sphere, notwithstanding its control of energy resources and the continuing trade dependence of the Central Asians.[71] Beijing's political, security, and institutional links are modest compared to Moscow's well-developed networks. However, China shows signs of being able to raise its economic influence beyond anything Russia can match, particularly given the vulnerability of the local economies.

The lack of progress over Beijing's proposals for an SCO "free trade zone"[72] indicates that Russia and the Central Asians are conscious of the challenge posed by China. They are unenthusiastic about removing or lowering protectionist barriers, since this would naturally favor the strongest and most dynamic economy in the region. A more transparent commercial environment would accelerate the extension of Chinese influence, undermine Russian interests, and make the local economies "China-dependent" to an uncomfortable degree.[73] It could lead to outcomes similar to those that have already occurred in Sino-Russian trade: China would export increasing volumes of manufacturing products to Central Asia in return for energy and other natural resources.[74] Worse still for Moscow, Beijing might look to import most of its Eurasian-source energy requirements from the Central Asian states (Kazakhstan, Uzbekistan, Turkmenistan), rather than Russia.[75] In that event, the latter would lose even the leverage that comes from being an energy power.

Russian concerns about Chinese influence in the SCO are not limited to a fear of Chinese goods and services swamping Central Asia. There is a more general anxiety as well. Although the SCO began life as the "Shanghai Five," a condominium arrangement established by the big two, it is Beijing, not Moscow, that has been the driving force behind its evolution into "the most important multilateral organization in Central Asia."[76] The growth of the SCO is inextricably linked to China's re-entry as a major player in the region, at once legitimizing and reinforcing its involvement. As a multilateral institution that emphasizes the "democracy of international relations" and "an inclusive environment for cooperation,"[77] the SCO enables Beijing to do what might otherwise be unpalatable and unachievable.

The emergence of the Collective Security Treaty Organization

This explains Moscow's generally lukewarm approach to the SCO—politically supportive, but cautious on practical cooperation. It also explains why the Russians have invested much more effort in the Collective Security Treaty Organization.[78] In most respects, the CSTO is a typical CIS-type organization: it is Moscow's creature; it is anti-Western; and its performance falls well short of its overblown rhetoric. The CSTO covers much the same ground as the SCO, combating "new security threats and challenges" such as terrorism, Islamic extremism, drug trafficking, and transnational crime. Similarly, it condemns Western policies, such as NATO enlargement, missile defense, and recognition of Kosovo, and calls for a "just and democratic world order."[79] It is even branching out into economic cooperation, if just for show.[80]

However, the similarities between the SCO and the CSTO only go so far. The most important difference is in the make-up of the two organizations. Whereas China is the leading player in the SCO, Russia dominates the CSTO. The latter's crowning virtue, viewed from Moscow, is that China is not a member, which means that Russia's pre-eminent position within it can never be challenged. Despite its shortcomings, the SCO has some important achievements to its credit. By contrast, the CSTO has achieved little of significance since its establishment in 2003. The self-serving claims that it is "a key factor of regional stability"[81] do little to mask a lack of substance and a rationale that is almost nakedly geopolitical: to package Russia's return as the leading power in Central Asia.[82]

It matters that the CSTO, as a mutual defense arrangement, has military forces of its own—a Rapid Reaction Force comprising 10 battalions and about 4,000 troops[83]—whereas the SCO, a multilateral security organization, does not. Although the notion of a distinct CSTO military capability is a fiction, it has encouraged Moscow to promote a military agenda within the SCO and in Central Asia more broadly, since this is one sphere where Russia will continue to enjoy a considerable advantage over China. The proposal to conduct "Peace Mission 2007" under combined SCO/CSTO auspices (see chapter 3) was a transparent bid to reassert a leadership role and put the Chinese back in their place.[84]

The SCO and the CSTO thus serve virtually identical purposes for two of the great powers in Central Asia: the SCO is China's multilateral instrument of influence, while the CSTO fulfills the same function for Russia.[85] This similarity of purpose sows the seeds of potential trouble down the line. Despite tentative efforts to coordinate their work, ultimately they are competing organizations that cover much the same ground, but for different sides. Their chief value lies in the extent to which they can be used to support the respective strategic agendas of Moscow and Beijing in Central Asia.

Strategic partnership or emergent competition?

Views of Sino-Russian relations in Central Asia tend to divide into two schools of thought. According to the "optimists," Russia and China are cooperating effectively in countering terrorism and the strategic and normative threat posed by a hegemonic America. Indeed, so the argument runs, the success of this interaction proves the existence of a larger strategic partnership between them. (A more jaundiced variant of this interpretation plays up the partnership's quasi-alliance aspects.)

The contrary argument points to the modest level of *actual* cooperation in security-building and highlights the growing if tacit tensions between two ambitious powers. A key thesis here is that were it not for the presence of a common "foe" in the form of the United States, there would be little to bind them. Stripped to its basics, the "Shanghai spirit" of positive-sum cooperation is an elaborate ruse, whose motivation extends barely further than evicting the Americans from Central Asia. The current accommodation is therefore unstable; Russia and China are not so much strategic partners as strategic competitors, whose rivalry will become increasingly evident.

It is relevant that Central Asia represents something of a new, or at least rediscovered, field in Russian and Chinese foreign policy. Buoyed by a growing self-confidence, Moscow and Beijing are keen to exercise their influence to the fullest extent possible—almost as if to make up for lost time. They are acting not only on the basis of clearly defined national interests, but also with a strong sense of historical mission, particularly in Russia's case.

These circumstances mean that Russia and China will inevitably compete with each other. In a manner of speaking, they are two powers divided by a common purpose—to be the leading power in the region (even if for China this is still a distant prospect). On the other hand, such competition does not stop them from sharing certain interests and coordinating on many issues, most notably in countering the U.S. presence. Both find it useful to emphasize the positives in their relationship for presentational reasons and because it consolidates the idea that Russia and China, not America and its allies, are the primary actors in Central Asia.

In the longer term it is difficult to be sanguine about the prospects of Sino-Russian partnership in the region. Strategic divergence seems more probable than strategic convergence. Moscow and Beijing will become more assertive and even aggressive in promoting their national agendas and in containing or undermining each other's. To this end, they will compete hard for the loyalties of the Central Asian states, which, for their part, will look to exploit this rivalry to maximize their freedom of action. The result will be an increasingly tense regional environment.

But Sino-Russian geopolitical confrontation is not imminent. Both sides have too much to gain from stability and security in Central Asia, and they will continue to cooperate, selectively, with each other and the states of the region in combating Islamic-based terrorism and separatism, expanding existing security arrangements, reinforcing local elites, and repelling Western pressure for greater democratization and human rights. For the time being at least, the *strategic convenience* of continued cooperation remains unimpeachable. In an anarchic world, it represents a logical response to the security and economic challenges of Central Asia and to each country's strategic imperatives.

CHAPTER SEVEN

EAST ASIA—
ARENA OF THE GREAT POWERS

"The economic growth of Asia's largest power increases Chinese influence in the region and the likelihood of China reasserting its traditional hegemony in East Asia, thereby compelling other nations either to 'bandwagon' and to accommodate themselves to this development or to 'balance' and to attempt to contain Chinese influence."

—SAMUEL P. HUNTINGTON, 1996[1]

"China is shepherding its resources for the long-term goal of being a dominant player in East Asia and beyond. As and if Beijing achieves success in this pursuit, it will have enormous, and potentially negative, implications for the current balance of power in the region."

—BATES GILL AND YANZHONG HUANG, 2006[2]

"The development of Russia can only be successful if we participate most actively in the [Asia-Pacific] regional integration process. Constructive involvement in these processes is our strategic choice and a most important task for the foreseeable future."

—VLADIMIR PUTIN, Busan, November 17, 2005[3]

Since coming to power in January 2000, Vladimir Putin has presided over a marked "Asianization" of Russian foreign policy. Unlike Yeltsin, for whom Asia served mainly to counterbalance the United States, Putin has pursued closer relations with China, Japan, the Koreas, and the ASEAN member-states both for their own sake and as building blocks in a larger challenge to American "unipolarity." The slogan of a "multi-vectored" foreign policy has acquired genuine substance, with Moscow's engagement in the Asia-Pacific extending beyond the political to embrace growing economic and security cooperation. The Kremlin has stepped up efforts to integrate Russia into regional structures and processes. Bilateral "strategic partnerships" have been supplemented by membership of, or increasing interaction with, organizations such as APEC, the ASEAN Regional Forum, ASEAN, the East Asia Summit, and the Organization of Islamic Conference, in addition to Central Asian bodies such as the SCO and the CSTO, discussed in the previous chapter.

But despite these efforts geographical balance in Russian foreign policy remains elusive. Judged by any criterion—level of political commitment, economic involvement, security engagement, human and cultural contacts—Moscow's world-view continues to be overwhelmingly Westerncentric. Relations with the major Asian powers have certainly grown in recent years, but from a very low base. If Asia is no longer a neglected theatre of Russian foreign policy, then nor does it rank among the Kremlin's highest priorities.

Much of this is a function of geographical, historical, and demographic *force majeure*. Less than a fifth of Russia's population of 142 million lives east of the Urals, the traditional divide between European and "Asian" Russia. Crucially, fewer than 7 million people reside in the Russian Far East, the only part of the country that could reasonably qualify as lying in the Asia-Pacific region. The core of decisionmaking, Moscow, is many thousands of kilometers west, as are the main centers of economic activity. Since the collapse of the Soviet Union, the vast majority of the nation's armed forces have moved west, so that even a military presence is thin on the ground.[4]

Russia's modest presence in the Asia-Pacific is reflected in the minimal influence it exerts in the region. It is the least important of the participants in the Korean Six-Party talks (the United States, China, the two Koreas, Japan, and Russia) and is a peripheral member of APEC and the ARF. Even in areas where it enjoys a strong competitive advantage, such as energy, its impact is secondary.

"The cauldron of civilizations"

Part of Russia's difficulty in making its voice heard is that the Asia-Pacific, and East Asia in particular, has an unusually high preponderance of great powers. The United States, China, and Japan are not only major players in their own right, but unlike Russia they are also natural members of the Asia-Pacific community—China and Japan by virtue of physical location and history, the United States through its active and multifaceted engagement for more than half a century. This unique context has made it very difficult for Russia to establish a meaningful role for itself after the demise of the USSR and collapse of Soviet military power.

Unlike in Europe, there is no collective regional identity or tradition of cooperation in East Asia.[5] As Huntington puts it, the region is a "cauldron of civilizations."[6] Interaction between states has been characterized by constant competition and often outright hostility. In the last century alone there have been bloody conflicts between Japan and Russia, Japan and the United States, Japan and China, China and the Soviet Union, not to mention the Cold War between the United States and the Soviet Union, dangerous stand-offs between the United States and China, and the three-decades-long Sino-Soviet freeze. It is indicative that the pan-Asian regional structures that do function, such as ASEAN, ARF, and APEC, originated outside East Asia.[7] The Korean Six-Party talks, in particular, have highlighted the considerable problems of multilateral engagement in such an environment.

Given ongoing rivalries and the absence of a larger collective identity, it is hardly surprising that the powers in the region have put their trust in bilateral security arrangements. East Asia is the ultimate geopolitical arena, where zero-sum calculus and the balance of power have greater currency than anywhere else on the planet. Alliances, with their emphasis on concrete commitments, are a natural response to weak transnational political and normative regimes. It is revealing that even with the end of the Cold War, the United States' security agreements with Japan, the Republic of Korea, and ASEAN member-states such as Singapore, Thailand, and the Philippines remain the cornerstone of stability in the Asia-Pacific.

China's emergence

As noted in chapter 1, the instinctive reaction of many observers to Sino-Russian rapprochement has been to view it as a de facto alliance.[8] In fact, this is to misunderstand the nature of the relationship and its implications for the region. The central issue in East Asia is not a putative Moscow–Beijing entente directed at the United States and its allies, but the rise of China as potential regional hegemon and the response of other players to this challenge.

Today China is the sole "revolutionary" or "revisionist" power in East Asia.[9] Of all the powers present, it is the most committed to challenging the existing American-led order, even though it recognizes that it will be a long time before it is able to contest this directly. China's modernization is motivated by domestic imperatives—economic well-being, political stability—yet it also contains the tacit assumption that a developed China can aspire one day to be the leading power in the Asia-Pacific.

Indeed, the very process of China's transformation from middling regional actor to global power is already undermining the established system.[10] It matters only secondarily that China's rise is peaceful and its approach cooperative, since other major players are already responding to "facts on the ground"— the impact of Chinese economic growth, the rapid modernization of the PLA, and Beijing's increasingly active role in international affairs. Faced with these diverse challenges, Washington has reinforced security arrangements with various regional allies, initiated theatre missile defense (TMD), embarked on rapprochement with India, and expanded economic engagement throughout Asia.[11] The other great regional power, Japan, has bought into TMD and maintained high levels of military spending, and is thinking of revising its constitution to allow the deployment of Japanese troops overseas.[12]

China's emergence has had a similarly powerful impact on Russian political consciousness. In much the same way that the United States has been the focus of Russian strategic culture for over half a century, so China dominates Moscow's view of Asia today. And just as Americacentrism does not imply pro-Americanism, so Russia's Sinocentrism in Asia incorporates negative as well as positive elements. Putin sets great store by the "strategic partnership" with Beijing, yet much of his Asia policy is based on the premise that a dominant China would be detrimental to Russian interests.

It might seem that China's emergence as the new power on the block should benefit rather than harm Russia's cause. A well-disposed China might help restrain American "hegemonic tendencies" and assist Russia's integration into the Asia-Pacific, while the strategic uncertainties provoked by China's rise could increase the pressure on Japan to agree a settlement on the disputed South Kurile islands/Northern Territories.[13] In any event, the warmth of their bilateral relationship should mean that Russia has little to fear from a resurgent China.

This logic is plausible, but flawed. First, Russia recognizes the United States as a status quo power in East Asia. Although conceptually it opposes American regional "hegemony," in practice it identifies a number of advantages from its continuing existence. A strong United States provides a check on Chinese ambitions, reins in Japanese nationalism, and represents the most reliable guarantee of stability in the region. The last is especially important, given Moscow's sensitivities about the Russian Far East. Interestingly, some Russian officials acknowledge a security debt to Washington, even while they claim that alliances such as the U.S.-Japan Treaty of Mutual Cooperation and Security and the U.S.-ROK (Republic of Korea) Mutual Defense Treaty "are not the way of the twenty-first century."[14] They distinguish between America's largely conservative approach in East Asia and its revisionist agenda in Europe and the former Soviet Union, where it is unmistakably a "revolutionary" power.[15]

Moscow might conceivably take a different view were it in a position to challenge U.S. leadership in East Asia. But Russia's weakness precludes this for the foreseeable future. In the meantime, it does not want to see one hegemon replacing another, especially since it regards an up-and-coming China as more unpredictable than an America it has long accepted as part of the strategic furniture. It is relevant to note here that for much of the Cold War the Kremlin regarded a fiercely anti-communist United States as a far more congenial partner than an ideologically similar but antagonistic PRC. Even after the normalization of Sino-Russian relations, Chinese actions in East Asia continued to cause concern. During much of the 1990s, periodic crises over Taiwan, ongoing tensions with Japan, and disputes over territorial rights in the South China Sea reinforced China's reputation as a destabilizing actor.

Beijing is striving to overcome this reputation, but its efforts have been undermined, ironically, by the very success of China's modernization. The issue is no longer about Chinese intentions, but about its extraordinary capabilities. As Wang Jisi has noted, "China has yet to convince its regional partners, in particular those with which China has territorial disputes, that a strong Chinese military power will not pose a threat to them."[16] The fear, in Russia as elsewhere, is that if and when China becomes the leading power in East Asia, it may abandon its current restraint.

For Russia specifically the potential danger is twofold. First, policymakers worry that China's rise in East Asia could translate one day into a revanchist intention to recover the RFE. A China unchecked by others is a China that has a free hand to exploit the isolation of Russia's eastern provinces. The question "what happens after Taiwan's reunification?" (chapter 4) can be amplified to "what happens after China becomes the regional hegemon?"

The second concern is more general but also more immediate. China's emergence as the leading power in the Asia-Pacific may undermine Russian attempts to play a more active part in the region's affairs. While Moscow's expectations are relatively modest, it nevertheless sees itself as an increasingly serious player, whether as a primary source of energy, a conduit for Asia-Europe infrastructural projects, or a key party in conflict resolution. A China dependent on, and accountable to, its neighbors would allow scope for the projection of Russian economic and geopolitical influence. An overly powerful China, on the other hand, could constitute an impassable obstacle to Russian interests, either blocking or disregarding them.

Moscow's apprehension has been fueled by the belief that China has done little to facilitate Russian engagement in Asia. While Beijing has made the right noises and been supportive at certain moments, such as over APEC membership,[17] hopes that China might assist Russia's integration into the region have proved fanciful. As the East Siberian oil pipeline project has shown, Beijing does not want to "share" Russia with others. Its interest is in maximizing imports of energy and natural resources, not in assisting the (re-)entry of another great power into a region already groaning under the strain. If Russia has geopolitical utility for China in East Asia, then it is in the limited guise of cheerleader, for example on the Korean question, or in selling the arms that enhance the PLA's power projection capabilities.

Ultimately, Moscow's interest in strategic continuity is founded in the realization that the growing asymmetry in Sino-Russian relations is nowhere more pronounced than in East Asia. As the bilateral balance continues to shift in favor of Beijing, so Moscow will look to others to help preserve an environment that protects Russia's security interests and enables it to exploit any opportunities that may arise. It will hope for a stable and secure China, but one which is not so strong or self-confident as to upset the current strategic balance or exclude Russia from it.

Russian policy toward East Asia

Moscow understands it is not Russia but the other major players—the United States, China, Japan—that will determine the regional strategic context. Nevertheless, Russian policymakers have not remained passive. Since Yeltsin's first substantial engagement with Asia, his visit to China in December 1992, they have pursued three broad approaches with the aim of raising Russia's profile and influence in the Asia-Pacific: (i) strategic diversity; (ii) the "Concert of Asia"; and (iii) multilateral engagement.

Strategic diversity

Strategic diversity is intrinsic to the "multivectorialism" that defines contemporary Russian foreign policy.[18] It derives from the assumption that it is dangerous to rely overmuch on one "vector" or "partner" and that, consequently, national interests would be best served by a "flexible policy of diverse partnerships with individual countries or groups of countries interested in building ties with Russia."[19] In the East Asian context this means refraining from excessive Sinocentrism[20] by building closer relations with Japan, the two Koreas, ASEAN member-states, and regional multilateral structures. The "strategic partnership" with China would remain critical, but would be balanced by substantial ties with other centers of power.

Given ongoing problems in Russia-U.S. relations, and Moscow's aversion to (publicly) supporting the American force presence in East Asia, Japan is the most plausible subject for such a policy. Despite an often difficult relationship, punctuated by several wars over the past century,[21] Russian attitudes toward Japan are surprisingly positive, with little of the negativity that accompanies views of China.[22] Japan is not regarded as an aggressive power with irredentist ambitions—a paradoxical state of affairs given the bilateral territorial dispute and the number of wars its leaders have initiated in the modern era. Japan is held in high esteem as one of the world's most advanced economies and purveyor of high-quality goods and services. Here it compares especially well with China, which Russians see as much more backward. Japan is viewed as geographically Asian, but also as part of the developed West; it is a founding member of the G-8, the group of the world's most industrialized countries. It is symptomatic of the contrast in Russian attitudes toward its two most important Asian neighbors that Moscow should welcome Japanese foreign direct investment, yet be very wary of Chinese attempts to buy equity in Russian enterprises.[23] In many respects Japan stands as the epitome of the "good East," an East at once politically sophisticated, economically prosperous, technologically ambitious, and strategically unthreatening.[24] It represents a model of a nation that has become as developed and influential as the Western powers, but that has managed to preserve its own distinct identity and values—a vision Putin aspires to for Russia.

Ideally China and Japan would neutralize one another. Such a balance would, in the first instance, greatly reduce the potential for Chinese aggression against the Russian Far East. Second, it might offer Russia opportunities to act as the "swing" power in East Asia. Maneuvering between the two Asian giants, it would be able to maximize its political and economic clout and obtain recognition as a major regional player. Third, Sino-Japanese rivalry is likely to translate—indeed, is already translating—into intense competition for Russian natural resources. Both countries are highly dependent on energy imports and are seeking to develop alternative sources of supply. This resource competition, not to mention an underlying mutual antipathy, is to Russia's advantage, always assuming that it does not overplay its hand.

Such calculations have been evident in Russia's handling of its relations with China and Japan since the beginning of the post-Soviet period. During the Yeltsin presidency the Kremlin flirted with Beijing and Tokyo in turn. Although China was the main beneficiary of Russia's attention in the 1990s,

Japan also had its moments, especially at the informal "no ties" summits of Krasnoyarsk and Kawana, in November 1997 and April 1998 respectively. For a brief period Japan rivaled China as Russia's chief foreign policy priority in Asia, as liberal Westernizers enjoyed a temporary ascendancy in the Yeltsin administration.[25]

In recent years Putin has tried to pursue an even-handed approach, reflecting the view that, all other things being equal, this is likely to reap greater dividends than a policy that favors one or the other Asian power. He has offered to settle the territorial dispute with Japan on the basis of the 1956 Khrushchev formula, involving the return of the two smallest islands, Shikotan and the Habomais.[26] He has presided over a considerable expansion in bilateral trade—from U.S.$4.3 billion in 2003 to U.S.$20.1 billion in 2007.[27] And he has kept his options open over the routing of the East Siberian oil pipeline. This last, which will be discussed in the next chapter, is the clearest demonstration of the policy of strategic diversity. Uncomfortable with the prospect of China becoming Russia's monopoly customer in Asia, Moscow would like to build the pipeline to the Pacific Ocean from where it would be able to access the wider Asia-Pacific energy market.

Thus far, however, attempts to pursue strategic diversity have been unsuccessful. Russian policy toward Asia is more Sinocentric than ever, a function not only of the expansion of "strategic partnership" with China but also of the deterioration in relations with Japan since the late 1990s. The territorial dispute remains deadlocked; the political atmosphere is poisoned by the lack of movement over the islands; and, notwithstanding the increase in bilateral trade, commercial ties remain modest, particularly compared with Sino-Russian trade. Moscow is leaning toward the Chinese route for the East Siberian oil pipeline, and there are doubts over the security of Japanese investments in offshore projects such as Sakhalin-2.[28] Add to this a nasty escalation of disputes over fishing rights[29] and differences over issues such as Iraq and theatre missile defense, and the picture looks almost uniformly grim.

As long as relations with Japan show no significant improvement, Putin will be unable to realize his vision of strategic diversity. There will be no such improvement, however, without progress on the territorial question, a remote prospect given how far the islands have become identified in both countries with matters of national honor, territorial integrity, and historical record. The continuing stalemate between Moscow and Tokyo benefits China, which as a result remains Russia's sole "strategic partner" in East Asia. Whereas Moscow is becoming increasingly China-dependent, Beijing is able to manage the bilateral relationship from a position of strength: as just one of several foreign policy options in the region—and by no means the most important.

The "Concert of Asia"

The "Concert of Asia" is not a formal or even informal institution so much as a philosophical construct.[30] Its basic principle—that the big players should deal collectively with the big issues[31]—is strongly implicit in the interaction between great powers in different parts of the world. The elitist modus operandi of the "Concert" is evident in the UN P-5, the G-8, and regional forums such as the Middle East "Quartet" of the United States, the EU, Russia, and the UN. It also assumes more ad hoc forms, as in the tripartite "coalition of the unwilling"—Russia, France and Germany—in the lead-up to the Iraq war.

Russia has a vested interest in development of the Concert idea.[32] On its own it has very limited capacity to shape events or the policies of major (or even minor) players in East Asia. It is arguably best served, instead, by an arrangement in which several powers "manage" the region on the basis of consensus or a condominium. For much the same reason that Moscow hopes for parity between China and Japan, so it would like to see a strategic architecture of checks and balances in East Asia. This would have two cardinal virtues. It would restrain the exercise of hegemonic influence, whether emanating from Washington or Beijing. And it would allow secondary actors, such as Russia, a greater say in regional decisionmaking than would be the case in an environment dominated by either the United States or China.

The Kremlin's approach to the Korean question illustrates this thinking. On the one hand, as already mentioned, Russia has the least influence of any of the participants in the Six-Party talks. On the other hand, its very participation—something for which it fought long and hard[33]—gives it a foot in the door of regional decisionmaking, and without having to assume responsibility for concrete outcomes. Paradoxically, Russia's relative insignificance—and unthreatening profile—in East Asia enables it to play a useful if modest role as an intermediary in the negotiations process. In June 2007 Moscow was able to expedite a U.S.-brokered deal to end production at the Yongbyon nuclear plant by arranging the transfer of $U.S.25 million to North Korean leader Kim Jong-il from a previously frozen account.[34]

One of Putin's more successful initiatives has been to "equalize" Russian policy toward the two Koreas. Whereas the Soviet Union allied itself with the Pyongyang regime through the 1961 Treaty of Friendship, Cooperation and

Mutual Assistance,[35] and Yeltsin sided unequivocally with Seoul, Putin has managed the considerable feat of simultaneously improving relations with both the Koreas.[36] This balancing act not only highlights the Kremlin's commitment to strategic diversity but also reflects an understanding that the best chance of playing an active part in East Asian affairs is to portray Russia as a "good regional citizen" committed to positive-sum outcomes. Moscow's offer to host intra-Korean talks[37] and its role in transferring Kim Jong-il's funds are part of this team approach, as is its generally discreet profile—useful in allaying possible Chinese suspicions that it might be seeking to usurp Beijing's special relationship with Pyongyang.

However, despite some partial successes, the notion of a Concert of Asia has not taken root. There are two major impediments. The first is the continuing absence of a collective regional identity[38] and tradition of transnational cooperation, and the consequent resort to competing approaches to regional problems. For all the cant about common threats and challenges, there is little unity of purpose among the major powers when it comes to addressing the specifics of international terrorism and WMD proliferation. In a climate where the instinct for strategic competition far outweighs the spirit of cooperation, the notion of a Concert of Asia—or some variant of it—is a non-starter.

Second, realization of a Concert of Asia presupposes a rough equivalence between the major powers. The original Concert of Europe comprised several more or less equal entities—Great Britain, Prussia, the Russian Empire, the Austro-Hungarian Empire—as well as a re-emergent absolute monarchy in France. No such parallel exists in contemporary East Asia. Not only is the United States the clear regional leader and China the designated challenger, but Russia is a marginal and often disregarded presence. Even if some kind of pan-regional accommodation were to emerge over time, it is hard to envisage that Russia would be accorded a role and respect similar to that of the other powers.[39] Moreover, talk of a strategic architecture of checks and balances begs the question whether, or indeed why, the stronger powers would accept constraints on their freedom of action. As Nicholas Khoo and Michael Smith observe, China "would never agree to be constrained internationally,"[40] and this is even more true of the United States.

Given the improbability of a regional consensus or self-limitation by the leading powers, Moscow's interests may be best served by a semi-permanent state of "controlled tension" between them—in other words, a condition of "neither peace nor war." On the one hand, an escalation of strategic rivalries could lead to conflict spreading to Russian territory and threaten the security of the RFE. It would also disrupt Russia's energy and natural resource markets in China, Japan, and South Korea. On the other hand, Moscow might lose out from the transformation of East Asia into a zone of "peace and prosperity."[41] While Russian energy exports could benefit—although this is far from certain (see chapter 8)—the uncompetitiveness of its manufacturing sector suggests that its strategic and economic weight would decline relative to the more advanced economies in the region: the United States, Japan, South Korea (or a possibly reunified Korea).

Most worryingly, a stable and prosperous East Asia would extend China's "twenty-year period of strategic opportunities," identified by President Jiang Zemin at the 16th Communist Party Congress in November 2002.[42] China's continued rise is predicated on regional and global stability.[43] Russian foreign policy, by contrast, thrives on a degree of uncertainty that enables it to pretend to a greater influence than is actually the case. The Iraq crisis of 2002–03 provides an instructive analogy here. During the build-up to war, Russia played up its international standing—as a member of the UN P-5, as part of the "coalition of the unwilling," and as a self-appointed mediator in negotiations with Saddam Hussein. Although its real impact was minimal, for a time it was able to assume the guise of a major player—a pretence unsustainable during the relatively peaceful 1990s, notwithstanding its friendly relations with the Iraqi president, and again after the American-led military intervention in March 2003. Such sleight of hand is much more difficult in East Asia. Nevertheless, when the other powers are in a state of "controlled" but tense balance, even a modest Russian input can prove surprisingly effective, as in the transfer of Kim Jong-il's missing $25 million.

Multilateral engagement

The Kremlin's awareness of the limitations of Russian influence explains its growing interest in Asia-Pacific multilateral institutions. Although it is far more comfortable using bilateral channels, this force of habit is mitigated by the realization that Russia can do little in Asia purely on the basis of individual relationships with the major powers. In practice bilateralism would entail excessive dependence on Chinese good will, while a transparent Sinocentrism is unhelpful in building ties with other key actors. More generally Moscow faces a stiff task in overturning Asian preconceptions of Russian foreign policy, the most damning of which is that it has little interest in Asia as such, but views it as just another theatre of great-power competition with the United

States.[44] This judgment is a legacy of the Cold War, but owes its durability to the crude instrumentalism of the Yeltsin years, when the administration misused the China card in attempting to extract concessions from the West. Moscow is under pressure to show that it is interested in more than geopolitics and the balance of power, and is willing to subscribe fully to the politics and economics of consensus—the so-called ASEAN way.[45]

Putin has done a good job of bolstering Russia's Asian credentials. It is a mark of Moscow's heightened commitment that while president he attended nearly all the major Asian multilateral summits, either as a full participant or as an observer, and visited a raft of Asia-Pacific nations—not only the big two of China and Japan, but also both Koreas, Mongolia, Vietnam, Malaysia, Thailand, and Indonesia. At the same time he soft-pedaled on Russia's great-power credentials while emphasizing its commonalities with the region.[46]

Nevertheless, Russia's stature in the Asia-Pacific remains very modest. To a large extent this "failure" is unavoidable. Russia is not an Asia-Pacific nation by most criteria. Historically and culturally, it is incontrovertibly a European civilization. And politically, economically, and in terms of strategic culture, it looks far more to the West than the East. It will take more than a few years of clever diplomacy to break down such long-standing realities. And it will require several more decades (at least) to convince the Asians that Russia is not just a European country that happens, through historical and imperialist "accident," to have some of its territory in Asia.

Moscow's ability to forge a larger role in the Asia-Pacific is also hamstrung by the elitist mindset of Russian foreign policymaking. Although it makes use of international institutions, it remains a reluctant multilateralist at heart. Genuine multilateralism, as opposed to multipolarity and pseudo-multilateralism, involves many parties in collective decisionmaking. Russia has little aptitude or liking for such arrangements.[47] It continues to believe that the real business of international relations takes place bilaterally or in select forums, such as the P-5. It prefers to deal directly with the other great powers on an equal ("Concert") basis, rather than treat with multiple parties where the policy lines are often unclear[48] and there is always the risk of being outnumbered and outvoted by smaller nations. Unfortunately for Russia, on most Asia-Pacific issues it is a relatively unimportant player. This confronts it with a real dilemma. On the one hand, it needs to participate more substantively in Asian multilateral institutions if it is to become fully accepted in the region. On the other hand, to engage successfully in regional forums it must accept a much lower status than it has hitherto been used to, a concession that is deeply counter-intuitive.

The final impediment to Russia's multilateral diplomacy in Asia is a disjunction between rhetoric and action. Although Putin has worked hard to change Russia's image in Asia from geopolitical great power to positive-sum contributor, some of its policies in the region have proved counterproductive. The starkest example is the controversy over arms exports to China. Although Moscow insists that such arms are "defensive"[49] and do not destabilize regional security, other countries—the United States, Japan, and several ASEAN states—take a different view.[50] The weapons Russia sells to China— Kilo-class submarines, Sovremenny-class destroyers, Su-30 MKK fighters— are precisely the sort of hardware that improves China's power projection capabilities, not only vis-à-vis Taiwan, but also deep into the South China Sea and close to key shipping lanes. Russia's complacent response to these concerns does not sit well with its efforts to portray itself as a good citizen of the Asia-Pacific.[51]

Chinese reactions to Russia's Asian policy

All three policy approaches described above—strategic diversity, the Concert of Asia, and multilateral engagement—are intended in different ways to reduce Russia's dependence on China. As such, they raise questions about Beijing's responses, both in the current climate and in the longer term.

Beijing is scarcely an ingénu when it comes to evaluating Russian attitudes. It is aware that many in the Russian elite are discomfited by China's rise in East Asia (and beyond) and the changing balance within the bilateral relationship. However, since the Communist leadership is not surprised that Russia should seek to reassert its "rights" as an Asia-Pacific power, it has reacted calmly, almost passively. This relaxed response reveals several important aspects of China's approach. The first arises from the belief that Russia is not so much a long-term strategic ally as a difficult, but important, partner in selected areas. Beijing is prepared to make allowances provided there is no serious damage to core Chinese interests. In this connection, it helps that expectations of Russian behavior are not high, so that the leadership can manage any disappointment and look to the bigger picture. Thus when Moscow reneged on the May 2003 agreement over the East Siberian oil pipeline, Beijing was careful not to condemn it. It continued to chip away at the Kremlin, offering improved financial inducements while waiting for the

Russia-Japan deal to unravel—as indeed happened (see chapter 8). In the meantime, by way of "compensation," it was able to secure a substantial increase in oil imports, as well as several other concessions, including agreement to conduct joint military exercises ("Peace Mission 2005").[52]

This laissez-faire attitude toward Russian involvement in Asian affairs owes much, also, to the correct judgment that it poses little threat to Chinese interests. Russia remains a weak player in the region with few friends, unless of course one counts China itself. Beijing is confident there will be no strategic shift in Russia's relations with Japan, the United States, either of the Koreas, or the ASEANs.[53] Despite Putin's commitment to strategic diversity, Russia's orientation in Asia is becoming more, not less, "China-dependent."[54] China can afford to be "generous" and offer formalistic support to Russian involvement in the Asia- Pacific, because it knows this will be peripheral at best. In any case, it would be counterproductive to obstruct such engagement, breeding resentment to no useful purpose and with no guarantee of success. It matters little how frequently Russian delegations attend meetings of APEC and the ARF, because whatever happens there Russia will remain a bit player, neither disposed nor able to undermine China's leading position in these forums. More generally, Beijing understands that in the current international climate there is no likelihood of a great power consensus arrangement, a "Concert of Asia," let alone one that includes Russia as an "equal" player. For if there is one area where the great Asian powers (the United States, China and Japan) agree, it is that the region does not need the added complication of a state whose sense of entitlement greatly exceeds its real contribution.[55]

China's priority is to derive maximum benefit from its relationship with Russia, not to "compete" with it in East Asia. Indeed, the very notion of strategic rivalry here is absurd, given the disparity in their respective influence. Beijing is willing to indulge Russian vanity if this smoothes the way to achieving important objectives elsewhere, such as consolidating China's "strategic rear" and securing better access to oil and other natural resources. While this tacit bargain falls well short of a strategic partnership, it nevertheless remains a most convenient and useful arrangement.

The expedient relationship

All that said, East Asia continues to be a volatile region where there are few certainties. The accommodation between Moscow and Beijing could unravel in the face of various pressures: the rise of a dominant China; a reassertive Japan; the implosion of the Pyongyang regime and possible Korean reunification; Sino-American conflict over Taiwan; and the downsizing of the American strategic presence in East Asia. The final chapter of this volume explores several scenarios in Sino-Russian relations, but it is worth flagging some issues that may arise specifically in the East Asian context.

The largest potential variable is China's transformation into regional leader and global player. This could have two major consequences for relations. First, Moscow might feel sufficiently threatened that it would swallow its pride and work more closely with the United States and Japan in balancing Chinese power. This scenario has been suggested by liberal Russian commentators,[56] yet remains a minority view. Neither Russia nor the Western powers have shown any interest in "neo-containment."[57] Moreover, as Bates Gill and Yanzhong Huang have noted, "a neo-containment policy to prevent China's rise . . . could become a self-fulfilling prophecy by provoking Beijing to step away from the favourable aspects of its soft power and focus instead on throwing around its growing military and economic weight."[58] Instead there is a broad consensus within the Russian political class that there is more to gain by engaging with China than confronting it, echoing Zheng Bijian's sentiment that China's "peaceful rise" is "not a threat but an opportunity."[59] Although this cooperative mindset is not immutable, it would most likely change only if China's rise were to take a much more virulent form.

Somewhat more plausible is the suggestion that the growing asymmetry in the relationship could lead China to become increasingly offhand toward Russian interests. This might occur, for example, in the context of international efforts to broker a settlement on the Korean peninsula. Russia's already marginal role would be further reduced as the Chinese leadership concludes that Moscow no longer serves any useful purpose in the negotiations and, indeed, is a hindrance. A dominant China could also become more demanding over energy imports and arms transfers and look to other suppliers. The place of Russia in China's "Asia-view" could dwindle to near-anonymity.

Although this scenario cannot be excluded, it is unlikely to unfold soon. For the time being it benefits Beijing—and costs it little—to accommodate Moscow. Russian energy and weapons technology will remain important, at least until China establishes alternative sources for these key components of modernization. The Communist leadership understands, too, that it cannot deal with Russia in East Asia in isolation from the wider bilateral relationship.

An essentially cooperative attitude toward Russian interests in the region is a quid pro quo for Moscow's acquiescence in increased Chinese engagement in Central Asia.

Destabilization of the larger environment in East Asia would present a different set of challenges. In the event of escalating Sino-American tensions over Taiwan or North Korea, or a stand-off between Beijing and Tokyo, Moscow might be tempted to take advantage of the confusion to promote itself as an honest broker. Ideas of strategic diversity, of Russia as the "swing" power, and the Concert of Asia, could gain new impetus. Serious tensions might then arise between Moscow and Beijing, as the latter tires of Russia's game-playing and suspects it of complicity in a larger conspiracy to "keep China down."[60] If Moscow were to identify too closely with Western and Japanese interests, the Chinese leadership—especially under pressure from populist nationalism[61]—could react sharply. Even if Russia's real contribution were slight, the symbolism inherent in a close association with Washington and Tokyo could deal a potentially fatal blow to the edifice of "strategic partnership." Unlike after 9/11, enhanced cooperation between Moscow and Washington in East Asia would be seen by China as impacting on *primary* geopolitical and security interests. The result would not be equalization of the great powers through a Concert of Asia arrangement but the accentuation of regional fault-lines.

This quasi-doomsday scenario is predicated, however, on a sea-change in the quality of Russia's interaction with the West, which is difficult to imagine today. The main obstacle is not so much the deterioration in recent years of Russia's relations with the United States, the EU, and Japan;[62] the record of the post-Soviet period shows that relations can fluctuate dramatically.[63] The more serious impediment is the perception among American and Japanese policymakers that even a well-disposed Russia has little to contribute to security-building in East Asia. The comparison with Central Asia is instructive, for there Moscow's extensive ties in the region give it leverage. No analogous situation exists in East Asia, nor is it likely to do so anytime soon.

While Beijing may become irritated by Russian attempts to take advantage of a more fractured regional environment, it would be unlikely to over-react, short of a major and very concrete provocation. If Moscow were to flirt with Washington and Tokyo, this would undermine levels of trust. But it would scarcely tell the Chinese anything they did not already know or suspect. The suspension of disbelief that helps to sustain the "strategic partnership" across the board applies especially to the two countries' relations in

East Asia. Both sides claim they share common objectives and perspectives because, in different ways, the pretence of likemindedness suits their respective interests: Russia gains profile and the illusion of influence, while China obtains energy, natural resources, and arms. In short, the relationship works precisely because it is based on expediency, pragmatism, and no small degree of cynicism.

CHAPTER EIGHT

THE GEOPOLITICS OF ENERGY

"We anticipate . . . in the next 10–15 years . . . that around 30 percent of Russian oil exports will go to Asian countries."

—VLADIMIR PUTIN, September 2006[1]

"One moment Russia is saying they have made a decision, the next saying that no decision has been made. To date, there has been no correct information. This is regrettable. . . . Currently, the Sino-Russian pipeline question is one step forward, two steps back. Today is cloudy with a chance for sun while tomorrow is sunny with a chance for clouds, just like a weather forecast."

—ZHANG GUOBAO, Vice-Minister,
National Development and Reform Commission, March 2006[2]

Energy, perhaps more than any other single factor, has come to symbolize the new geopolitics of the twenty-first century. At one level its prominence signals a profound change from the traditional reliance on military and political power. Yet at the same time it is no less an instrument of competition than nuclear weapons or large armies were during the Cold War. The means of international influence today are more diverse and sophisticated, but many of the goals remain as "old-fashioned" as ever: national security, the projection of power, control over space, and the pursuit of strategic superiority or parity.

In very different ways energy is fundamental to the rise of Russia and China as re-emerging powers. For Russia, possession of vast oil and gas resources is the power-equivalent of nuclear weapons in the Soviet era. In fact, energy seems a much more flexible and usable form of power. Whereas the world once feared possible nuclear confrontation, now many countries, the mighty and not so mighty, both fear *and need* Russian energy. When Kremlin officials speak of Russia being an "energy superpower,"[3] the message they mean to convey is that it is back as a global, multidimensional, and above all *modern* superpower. Energy is not just an instrument of influence in itself, but impacts on other dimensions of power: military, political, economic, technological, even cultural and normative.

Energy is no less vital to China, but from the opposite standpoint. Without energy China's modernization and rise as the next superpower would grind to a halt, and the ruling Communist Party would be severely undermined.[4] Beijing has responded to these realities by making the worldwide search for energy its number one foreign policy priority. Just as Russia will rely on energy exports for the foreseeable future, so China will remain a net importer of most sources of energy, particularly oil.[5] Energy and geopolitics are as closely intertwined in China's case as they are for Russia—with one notable difference. For Beijing, energy is not an instrument of geopolitical ambition, but the principal rationale for an ever more assertive foreign policy, one that has truly global ramifications.[6] The Asia-Pacific region, Middle East, Africa, Russia, Central Asia, Latin America—there is virtually no part of the world left untouched by China's resource hunger.

Imperfect complementarities

At first sight the Sino-Russian energy relationship appears to be based on an almost ideal complementarity: on one side, the world's biggest exporter of oil and gas;[7] on the other, the world's second largest consumer of energy after the United States.[8] Add to this a flourishing bilateral relationship and public commitment to developing energy ties, and there seems no impediment to the closest possible partnership based on convergent interests. Moscow and Beijing regularly talk up the potential for cooperation. Indeed, energy has become emblematic of the evolution of their relationship from the largely political partnership of the 1990s to today's more "pragmatic and business-like" interaction.

But despite this favorable context, the energy relationship has been dogged by problems. The most fundamental is that Moscow and Beijing have very different understandings of energy security. For the former it means *security of demand*, particularly for pipeline gas.[9] Oil and gas account for over 60 percent of Russia's exports in value terms and over half of federal budget revenues. A loss of overseas markets, improbable though this may seem at a time of global resource hunger, would be catastrophic for economic prosperity and political stability. China's conception of energy security, on the other hand, is centered in the more conventional understanding of *security of supply*.[10] If anything, Beijing is even more anxious than Western consumers on this point. Reliable, long-term access to energy is indispensable to its ability to meet the enormous challenges of sustaining the most rapid and comprehensive modernization in history. It is also crucial to the regime's survival.

These polarized understandings of energy security translate into an imperfect complementarity. An important structural disconnect separates the world's largest energy exporter from its fastest growing energy consumer: Moscow would like to sell natural gas to China, whereas Beijing is much more interested in buying Russian oil. Gazprom views China as the next great gas market, an obvious consumer for potentially huge reserves in Eastern Siberia. Yet natural gas comprises a mere 3 percent of total Chinese primary energy consumption, a figure expected to increase to a still modest 8 percent by 2020.[11] Russian gas exports to China are statistically insignificant, a state of affairs unlikely to change in the near future given major disagreements over pricing (see below) and the long lead-time needed to develop reserves in Eastern Siberia and build pipelines to China.[12]

Beijing is pressing Moscow instead to increase oil exports, principally through the much-touted East Siberian–Pacific Ocean (ESPO) branch pipeline to Daqing, the main Chinese terminal in Heilongjiang province. Yet this project remains problematic and its completion uncertain.[13] In the meantime Moscow is dragging its feet over rail deliveries, which have risen less than anticipated.[14] The volume of oil exports to China remains unimpressive. In 2006 Russia accounted for 11 percent of its total imports, after Saudi Arabia (16.4 percent), Angola (16.2 percent), and Iran (11.6 percent).[15] This share is set to fall as China steps up deliveries from Africa, Latin America, and Central Asia, while continuing to import the bulk of its requirements from the Persian Gulf. Significantly, it is Africa, not Russia, that has emerged as the centerpiece of China's forward overseas energy strategy.[16]

Unsurprisingly, there is a significant discrepancy between declared intent and actual outcomes. Putin's visit to Beijing in March 2006 saw a number of bilateral agreements on energy cooperation,[17] yet there has been little concrete progress. Long-term agreements remain years, even decades away from implementation. In addition to the problems over ESPO, the planned Kovykta gas pipeline, which had been scheduled to send gas to China and Korea by 2011,[18] is in abeyance. Even if the project proceeds, the indications are that the gas will serve the Russian domestic market. Meanwhile Gazprom's hopes of tapping into the Chinese LNG (liquefied natural gas) market have been undermined by ongoing problems with the Sakhalin-2 project,[19] the prior commitment of export volumes to Japanese and Korean buyers, and Beijing's preference for LNG imports from Australia.[20]

The role of energy in Russian foreign policy

In order to understand why Sino-Russian energy cooperation has not developed as expected, we need to consider its role within the overall foreign policies of Moscow and Beijing. For the former, this can be summed up in terms of three broad objectives: maximization of national wealth and private profit; recognition of Russia as a reliable energy supplier and leading member of the international community; and power projection. These objectives are not always compatible, and the contradictions between them have proved to be a major brake on the effective use of energy as a foreign policy tool. Nevertheless, in different ways they have shaped—and continue to shape—Russia's approach.

The importance of profit

Western critics of Putin tend to assume that everything the Kremlin does these days is geopolitically motivated, a conclusion that has led them to underestimate the importance of commercial considerations in Russian decisionmaking. Gazprom's decision to raise gas prices for Ukraine and Georgia during 2005–06, for example, was viewed as part of a larger campaign to undermine the Yushchenko and Saakashvili administrations in Kyiv and Tbilisi respectively, and thereby restore Moscow's writ over the former Soviet space.[21] In fact, while political agendas are important, the Russian government and major energy concerns such as Gazprom, Rosneft, and Lukoil are keenly interested in profit *for its own sake*. The explosion of wealth in post-Soviet Russia has demonstrated that Russians are as capitalistic as anyone.[22] The price hike for Belarus, hitherto the Kremlin's closest ally, in December 2006 highlighted the growing importance of commercial considerations. Political "friends" continue to receive preferential rates, while enemies are "punished" by having to pay European prices. But *all* consumers—allies, friends, and others—are being asked to pay much more than before.[23] Even the most favored, such as Belarus, have been put on notice that they will be required to pay normal commercial rates by 2011.[24] Both the Russian government and big business—in many respects one and the same[25]—are increasingly averse to accepting restrictions on profit-making.

The profit motive is a similarly powerful driver of Russian policy toward China, one often overlooked in the rush to judge the relationship in geopolitical terms. Although neither the Kremlin nor Russian energy companies view China in terms of "one billion customers," they are aware that it is the world's fastest expanding energy market. As such it is a natural growth area for Russian oil, gas, and nuclear exports. Only 3 percent of Russian oil and gas exports go to Asia, a derisory amount given that China, Japan, and the Republic of Korea are three of the world's largest importers of fossil fuels. There is an undeniable economic logic, then, in the government's commitment in its *Energy Strategy 2020* to raising Asia's share of total Russian oil exports to 30 percent and its share of gas exports to 15 percent.[26]

Market expansion in East Asia is consistent with the Kremlin's conception of energy security. In their concern about disruption to gas supplies, the Europeans tend to disregard Russia's own worries about the fragility of demand. Yet the dependence of the Russian economy on the energy sector means that Moscow cannot afford to ignore opportunities for market diversification. It makes sense to reduce Russia's reliance on Europe, which takes up 90 percent of total energy exports.[27]

Nevertheless, much as Moscow would like to "Asianize" its energy markets, it is unwilling to sell itself short. Beijing's attempts to obtain gas at discounted rates, using the cost of domestic coal extraction as a benchmark,[28] have acted as a major disincentive. Commercially Europe remains a far more attractive proposition. The Europeans pay premium rates for gas, linked to escalating oil prices—in practice, upward of U.S.$350 per 1,000 cubic meters—while the dense network of pipelines in western Russia makes it easier and cheaper to transport energy to European consumers. It is a similar story with oil, where there are ongoing tensions between Rosneft and the China National Petroleum Company (CNPC) over price,[29] and where the lack of pipeline infrastructure in Eastern Siberia severely limits the volumes that can be exported to China.[30]

A significant expansion in the Chinese and other Asian energy markets would require massive additional investments in exploration, pipeline infrastructure, and time. The commercial argument for extracting potentially sizable oil and gas reserves in eastern Siberia remains unproven, while there are very few pipelines east of West Siberia. Given that Russian energy companies prefer to buy downstream assets overseas rather than develop new deposits at home, it is hardly surprising that the potential of the Asian market remains unfulfilled. For all the talk about diversifying supply, immediate profit considerations remain uppermost in the minds of Russia's energy companies and the senior Kremlin figures who sit on their boards.

A responsible energy supplier?

Moscow's anxiety to preserve its reputation as a secure energy supplier is another significant obstacle to the reorientation of oil and gas exports. The obvious drawback to playing off East and West (see below) is that both may come to view Russia as untrustworthy. Such a perception could push existing customers to look to other suppliers or even explore alternative forms of energy—"clean coal," nuclear power, renewables—to meet their primary consumption requirements.[31] Moscow is therefore keen, at least officially, to delink exports from political ups and downs. Putin has pointed out that Russia (and the Soviet Union before 1991) has maintained the flow of energy to Europe "without a single day's interruption," even at the height of the Cold War and during the disintegration of the USSR.[32]

This emphasis on reliability is all the more important at a time when Russia's relations with the West are experiencing a severe downturn. Although the Putin regime has become largely impervious to external criticisms of its authoritarian tendencies, it remains acutely sensitive to imputations of *commercial* unreliability. When the Europeans blamed Moscow, rather than Kyiv, for disrupting gas deliveries during the Russia-Ukraine crisis of January 2006, the Putin administration quickly released the pressure it had exerted on President Yushchenko.[33] The need to safeguard Russia's reputation as a supplier trumped short-term profit and geopolitical considerations.

Russia would also like the West's respect. Part of this aspiration is motivated by the materialist rationale of not jeopardizing markets or provoking the creation of a notional energy consumers' cartel.[34] But there is a larger normative consideration as well: positioning Russia as an integral member of the community of "civilized" nations. Putin has a long-term vision of Russia as a modern great power whose influence is more constructive than threatening.[35] In energy policy, this means emphasizing the carrot—Russia's value as a prime source of oil, gas, and nuclear and electrical power—rather than the stick: the threat of cutting or reducing supply. In this spirit, Putin has abjured the expression "energy superpower." Dismissing it as a Cold War anachronism, he has stated merely that Russia has "more possibilities than almost any other country in the world" and that it is committed to working with others in establishing a "just" set of international rules governing energy supply and consumption.[36]

That said, Putin believes Russia should play a decisive role in determining international best practice. EU efforts to pressure it to ratify the European Energy Charter Treaty have run into the sand, as Moscow shows no sign of acceding to demands to liberalize the domestic gas market. Secure in the conviction that Russia will remain the world's leading supplier, it is confident that it is operating from a position of some strength. The objective of showcasing Russia as a responsible player is therefore a qualified aim. Moscow is interested in mutually beneficial arrangements—with a strong preference for maintaining the current system of long-term bilateral contracts[37]—but there are limits to what it will concede by way of conditions, degree of transparency, or constraints on its freedom of action.

Finally, international approbation serves concrete purposes. The consolidation of Russia's image as a reliable energy supplier is important in strengthening Moscow's hand vis-à-vis Beijing. Such a Russia has more options than one whose behavior has alienated its primary customers. In the latter event, Moscow would find itself more vulnerable to Chinese pressure. A good international reputation is therefore not just an abstract aim, but a critical factor that plays into the commercial relationship with Beijing.

Energy as power projection

To many observers, energy has become the most potent source of power in the post-modern world. Whereas the limitations of military might have frequently been exposed—during the Cold War and more recently in the American-led interventions in Iraq and Afghanistan—the "energy weapon" appears to have few constraints in an era of growing resource hunger. Certainly Putin has acted on this assumption. From the outset he has sought to exploit Russia's energy resources and infrastructure to promote its economic, security, and geopolitical interests, principally in the former Soviet space but also globally. In a very real sense his approach has been one of "geopoliticizing" Russia's economic priorities.[38]

The use of energy as a tool of geopolitical influence is at once an act of conscious will and an "accident" forced on Russia by the circumstances of its post-Soviet development. The collapse of Soviet military power (amid a general devaluation of military power worldwide); the concomitant decline in strategic fortunes; the economic crisis during the 1990s; a growing technological lag relative to the industrialized economies of the West (and, increasingly, the emerging Asian powers); and a crumbling moral reputation—all these have left Moscow with little choice. Putin may envisage Russia as a multi-dimensional global power, but for the time being the only really effective means of projecting influence is through the careful management of energy assets.

Inevitably Putin has played the energy card for all it is worth—and then some. He has exploited the dependency of the former Soviet republics. Differential pricing for allies (Belarus), "friends" (Armenia), and critics/opponents (Georgia) reflects a determination to reassert Russia's influence in its neighborhood. Gazprom may be more commercially driven these days, but it is also a servant of the administration's strategic objectives in the region. Under Putin, Gazprom and other big energy concerns—the state oil company Rosneft, United Energy Systems (electricity), and private companies such as Lukoil—have been active foreign policy players, more influential than conventional entities such as the Ministry of Foreign Affairs.

Energy, however, is a double-edged sword. Its incautious exploitation damages Russia's reputation as a reliable supplier and places at risk its chief source of external revenue. Exercising leverage through the manipulation of resources, infrastructure, and prices can become self-negating, since countries targeted or otherwise affected may look to alternatives.[39] Mindful of this, Moscow has tended more recently to prefer the option of sowing "creative doubt," alternating between a conciliatory and a hardline stance. On the one hand, Russia portrays itself as the best-choice source of oil and gas for the world, a safe alternative to the perpetually unstable Persian Gulf.[40] On the other hand, it likes to remind others of the potentially heavy cost of disregarding its interests.

The essence of the policy of creative doubt is to foster in customers a measure of "controllable uncertainty," of neither complacency nor panic. Such a policy sends out a dual message: that Russia's approach to energy exports is responsive, for better or worse, to the policies of others; and that Moscow seeks accommodation wherever possible. The common denominator in all this, however, is the maximization of Russian influence in regional and global affairs.

China occupies a central place in these maneuverings. Putin and other senior administration figures have spoken increasingly about its possibilities as an expansion market, juxtaposing this with criticisms of the reluctance by some EU member-states to allow Russian energy concerns to buy downstream assets. The implication is that China may one day challenge Europe's traditional monopoly of Russian energy exports.[41] More immediately, the China card is useful in neutralizing pressure from Brussels about Russia's problematic interaction with Georgia and Ukraine and refusal to ratify the European Energy Charter Treaty. China offers a form of geopolitical insurance: in the worst case, an alternative to the West should commercial (and political) relations with the latter deteriorate badly, but more plausibly as a means of keeping the Europeans "honest." For Russian policymakers do not wish to "abandon" the West so much as modify its behavior in line with Russian interests.[42]

In this scheme creative doubt plays a pivotal role. For reasons that will become clear, the threat to divert oil and gas exports from Europe is bogus. Moscow is anxious to retain its most lucrative markets and is building new pipelines to the West such as Nord Stream and South Stream.[43] Unsurprisingly, however, it wishes to renegotiate the terms of its energy relationships,[44] and for this the specter of a resource-hungry China serves as useful leverage. The latter's presence as a huge potential market strengthens Russia's hand vis-à-vis the EU, a body whose internal divisions, tendency to panic, and lack of common strategy[45] allow Moscow much more latitude than is warranted. Without China any threat to reorient exports could simply be dismissed.

Of course, the policy of sowing creative doubt involves considerable brinkmanship. It is predicated on a Sino-Russian context that is almost entirely favorable and on a partner willing to be used as geopolitical ballast even though it knows it will inevitably take second place to Europe as a recipient of Russian energy. Although the upswing in bilateral relations and China's resource hunger allow Moscow some leeway, this approach is vulnerable to longer-term uncertainties about the "strategic partnership" and to Beijing's growing energy diversification.

Another risk is that the distinction between substantive threat and elaborate bluff may become lost on the Europeans. Their melodramatic reaction to the temporary cessation of gas deliveries in January 2006 highlighted the risks. Almost overnight several EU member-states questioned Russia's reliability as a supplier and suggested that its mishandling of the crisis with Ukraine demonstrated the need to find alternative sources of gas, as well as develop new forms of energy.[46] Moscow clearly failed to anticipate this turn of events. Although the Europeans will continue to buy significant quantities of Russian gas, in the long run they will look to diversify energy supplies. Political uncertainties could translate into the decline of Russia's primary markets without sufficient compensation from the Asia-Pacific region. In alienating the Europeans, Russia might thus end up as the victim of the China card rather than its master—commercially and politically dependent on Beijing and left with little option except to fuel the modernization of its most powerful neighbor.

Just business—Chinese energy policy

Compared with the complex motivations shaping Russian energy policy, China's aims are straightforward. It seeks to maximize imports—principally crude oil, but also nuclear energy, cheap pipeline gas, and LNG—in order to sustain the process of domestic transformation. Unlike Russia, it has no geopolitical axe to grind here; energy is not a means of external power projection, but a vital national need. The contradictions in Moscow's relations with the West may prove helpful in increasing Chinese oil (and eventually gas) imports and in enhancing the prospects of obtaining these at advantageous prices. But neither the leadership nor China's state energy companies have shown the slightest inclination to become embroiled in disputes between Moscow and the West—and with good reason. Any attempt to stir up further trouble would be not only superfluous but also counterproductive for China's vastly more substantial economic ties with Europe and the United States.

Beijing has preferred instead to accentuate the positives. In the first place, this means playing up the "strategic partnership," flattering Russia's self-esteem, and overlooking the vagaries of its decisionmaking. The expression "strategic patience," coined originally to describe the Clinton administration's Russia policy in the 1990s,[47] applies also to Beijing's watchful approach toward energy cooperation with Moscow. Certainly, it is frustrated by the fecklessness and sometimes bad faith of the Russian government. Continuing uncertainties over the ESPO and Kovykta pipeline projects; the difficulties Chinese companies face in buying equity in Russian enterprises;[48] Moscow's crude attempts to use China as leverage against the Europeans; and the failure to translate worthy intentions regarding long-term cooperation into tangible progress—all these are vexing.

But such irritations are of secondary consequence when weighed against the main objective, which is to extract as much oil as possible from the Russians. Pipeline projects and equity acquisitions facilitate the realization of this overarching aim; they are not objectives in themselves, nor are they intended to serve geopolitical agendas. So long as Beijing can secure Russian oil deliveries, it is philosophical about the lack of movement elsewhere in the energy relationship.

China's equanimity is assisted by the fact that it does not see Russia as its principal strategic energy partner, but as only one of a growing number of suppliers that service its needs.[49] While it would like to increase imports of Russian oil, these are not indispensable. In complementing its continuing dependence on the Persian Gulf, Beijing has significantly increased imports from Africa, Latin America, and Central Asia and pursued a multi-continental approach to acquiring equity in energy ventures.[50] It is also addressing issues of energy conservation, partly out of environmental concerns, but also because it wants to rely less on external sources.[51]

Oil and Gas Pipelines in Eastern Siberia and the Far East

China's eclectic quest for energy is prompted principally by its reluctance to trust any one supplier or region, as well as by concerns about the security of shipping routes.[52] While on the face of things it should trust Russia more than most, given the generally healthy state of relations, such faith is lacking. Beijing's mistrust or "strategic caution" is mainly a reaction to the proven unreliability of Russia as an energy partner, highlighted during the long-running sagas of the ESPO and Kovykta projects.[53] The Chinese leadership has found that commercial contracts, intergovernmental agreements, and public assurances count for little unless they are supported by political will and private self-interest. Experience has shown, however, that these fluctuate wildly in response to changing domestic circumstances (as in the Yukos affair) or external inducements, such as Tokyo's mooted financial package over the ESPO (see next section). Although Chinese interests have not been directly caught up in Sakhalin-2 and other cases where foreign companies have been in dispute with the Russian government, they can hardly have failed to notice Moscow's increasingly arbitrary approach to external partners.

Over the longer term, Beijing has no interest in Russia becoming a monopoly or strategic supplier of its energy needs. It will endeavor to maximize oil imports and, as far as it can, reinforce these arrangements through binding bilateral agreements on deliveries, pipeline construction, and equity ownership. But even in the improbable event that it manages all this, China will continue to view Russia as a "limited-use" partner, of far less importance than its main sources in the Persian Gulf and Africa.[54]

More problems than solutions—the ESPO saga

The case of the East Siberian–Pacific Ocean oil pipeline is a parable of the many flaws in the Sino-Russian energy relationship and the "strategic partnership" more generally. The starting-point for the project was an agreement signed by then Russian prime minister Yevgeny Primakov and his Chinese counterpart, Zhu Rongji, in February 1999. The agreement provided for an initial feasibility study for an oil pipeline with a capacity of 20–30 million tonnes a year (mty) from Angarsk near Lake Baikal to Daqing. Early progress was good and in March 2003 Mikhail Khodorkovsky, the CEO of Yukos, then Russia's largest oil company, concluded an agreement with CNPC to proceed with construction. The agreement, endorsed by Putin and Hu Jintao two months later, envisaged that 700 million tonnes of Russia crude (then worth $150 billion) would be pumped to China over a period of twenty-five years.

It did not take long for the Yukos-CNPC agreement to unravel. Several factors were instrumental. First, the Kremlin arrested Khodorkovsky and other senior Yukos executives in the summer and autumn of 2003. The arrests were motivated by Putin's determination to reassert his political authority against the challenge, real and perceived, of large business interests (the "oligarchs"), of which Khodorkovsky was the most prominent representative.[55] Although Khodorkovsky was criticized for concluding the CNPC agreement, this had little to do with his arrest. The effect of his incarceration, however, was to put the agreement on hold and, eventually, to cancel it altogether.

Another reason for the collapse of the agreement was the intervention of the Japanese government. In January 2003 Tokyo offered Moscow a lucrative financial package to build a much longer pipeline from Angarsk to the Russian Pacific port of Nakhodka, bypassing China altogether, and with a much larger capacity (80 mty). The proposal envisaged a $5 billion investment for construction of the pipeline, plus a further $7.5 billion to explore potential reserves in eastern Siberia.[56] The Japanese package not only seemed commercially attractive, but was also consistent with Putin's commitment to strategic diversity (see previous chapter). If the pipeline were built to the Pacific, then Russia could export oil to the whole of the Asia-Pacific region. The Daqing route, by contrast, would effectively make China the monopoly customer, putting it in prime position to pressure Moscow over the terms and conditions of oil deliveries.[57] The longer route to the Pacific Ocean had the additional advantage of supporting the broader strategic objective of Russia's integration into the Asia-Pacific.

Concerns about the security of the Russian Far East also played an important, if indirect, role. A pipeline reaching out to China alone would increase Russia's "China-dependence" and open its eastern provinces to further Chinese influence.[58] But a transnational project involving several Asian countries—Japan, China, the two Koreas—might establish a collective vested interest in the RFE as a zone of cooperation and stability, rather than a sphere of competition or target of irredentist ambition.

In public Moscow resorted to the largely bogus excuse of "environmental concerns" while it considered its options. Although there were legitimate fears that the pipeline would pass dangerously close to Lake Baikal, the Kremlin's real intention was to play off Beijing and Tokyo against each other in order to obtain the best possible financial and investment package.[59] Delaying a decision might also help to position Russia strategically between China and Japan, a foretaste of the idea of Russia as the swing power in East Asia (see chapter 7).

Of course, procrastination could only continue for so long, and in December 2004 Prime Minister Mikhail Fradkov finally announced that the oil pipeline would be built along the Japanese-backed route, starting at Taishet, 250 km northwest of Angarsk, and traveling to Perevoznaya Bay, not far from the original terminus at Nakhodka. That should have marked an end to the horse-trading and the beginning of pipeline construction and exploration of the east Siberian oil deposits. However, just as the earlier agreement with China had fallen apart, so the Russia-Japan arrangement imploded during 2005–06. Again, there were a number of reasons—political, commercial, and strategic—that turned the tide back in Beijing's favor.

As before, changes within the Russian body politic were crucial. The original Yukos–CNPC deal had prospered and then withered along with Khodorkovsky's political fortunes. Now the Russo-Japanese arrangement unraveled as senior Kremlin figures, principally Igor Sechin, deputy head of the Presidential Administration, became increasingly involved in state energy policy and the ESPO project in particular. The emergence of "Kremlin Inc.," whereby the private interests of key *siloviki* (figures from the Russian state security apparatus such as Sechin[60]) became virtually indistinguishable from the public good, altered the terms of the debate. Direct commercial considerations, both public and private, now assumed much greater importance. The Daqing line would be far cheaper to build than the longer trunk route to the Pacific Ocean and its planned capacity was more appropriate to the estimated volume of oil that would be pumped through it.

The shift in the Russian position was aided by a hardening of Japanese attitudes. Tokyo pulled back on several aspects of its financial package, including the financing of exploration activity in eastern Siberia.[61] It also insisted that Moscow rule out construction of the Daqing route, as this would compete with the main pipeline for limited quantities of oil.[62] At the same time Beijing improved its own financial package. Whereas initially it had promised only to fund the section of the pipeline from Daqing to the Russian border town of Skovorodino,[63] it now offered to subsidize the whole length from Taishet to Daqing.[64]

The contrasting dynamic of Russia's larger relationships with China and Japan proved more influential still. During 2005–06 the atmosphere between Moscow and Tokyo deteriorated owing to the aggravation of the territorial dispute. The Putin and Koizumi administrations adopted strongly nationalist positions and the islands became, more than ever, a focal point for patriotic sentiment on both sides. The issue impinged heavily on all areas of the relationship, including economic cooperation. Over the same period Sino-Russian ties expanded considerably. Whereas Moscow's interaction with Tokyo was trapped in an apparent time-warp, partnership with Beijing went from strength to strength, establishing a context conducive to deal-making. The prospects for Sino-Russian energy cooperation were further boosted by developments elsewhere: demarcation of the common border, Kremlin anxieties over the color revolutions, and the souring of Russia's relations with the United States and the EU.

Against this backdrop strategic diversity as a core principle of Russia's Asian policy foundered on the reality that China was far better disposed toward Russia than a disgruntled Japan. The evolution in Putin's thinking can be charted in two meetings he held with Western Russia-watchers in September 2005 and September 2006. In 2005 he suggested that the Daqing line would be given priority, but insisted that he was committed to developing both routes given the importance of strategic diversity.[65] In the later meeting he did not mention the concept at all, emphasizing instead logistical and commercial considerations: the practical difficulties of extracting oil from unproven fields in eastern Siberia; issues of pipeline capacity; and the importance of profit.[66] Putin was simply bowing to the inevitable. Dreams of strategic "balancing" in East Asia were unrealizable given the respective state of Russia's relations with China and Japan. In the circumstances it seemed that the only feasible option was to make good on the Chinese proposals to finance the Taishet–Daqing branch line.

Learning the lessons

The ongoing saga of the East Siberian oil pipeline offers a number of insights into the current state and future prospects of Sino-Russian energy ties. It highlights, first, the central importance of political and strategic factors. These were behind the original decision to switch from the Yukos-CNPC project to the Japanese-backed pipeline, and they were instrumental two years later in the reversion to the Chinese proposal. In 2003 the Putin administration still harbored hopes of a special relationship with the West and a fresh start with Japan.[67] By 2005 the political context had changed radically, and over the next two to three years the pendulum continued to swing toward China. By early 2008 the gulf in fortunes between Russia's two major Asian relationships appeared as wide as at any time in the past fifty years, and the Taishet-Daqing branch line was consequently the more likely of the two routes to be built.[68]

The second conclusion from the vicissitudes of ESPO follows from the first. The politicization (and "geopoliticization") of the project means that any decision on its future is not irrevocable. It would not take much to resurrect Kremlin fears about the "China threat" in one form or another and for strategic diversity once again to become a determining principle of Russian energy policy in the Asia-Pacific. Koizumi's departure in September 2006 opened up the notional possibility of an improvement in Russo-Japanese relations, although continuing political uncertainties in Tokyo are likely to block any early movement for the better.[69] While it would take more than a successful summit or two to revive the Japanese-backed route, the ESPO experience shows that the situation can change quickly in response to developments elsewhere in the bilateral relationship.

The disproportionate impact of political considerations underlines the unpredictability of Russian decisionmaking. As noted in chapter 1, "the national interest" and "permanent national interests" are loose constructs that mask private and often competing agendas. If there is a guiding principle to Russia's approach to energy relations, then it is perhaps a variant on the notorious aphorism "what's good for General Motors is good for America." Today what is good for state energy companies managed by government insiders frequently passes for the "public interest."[70] This style of decisionmaking is not only morally delinquent, but is also by its very nature volatile—a serious drawback in a sector that relies on long-term, stable understandings.[71] The mixture of political, commercial, and personal interests means, too, that decisions may often be at variance with business logic.[72]

Because Beijing recognizes that Russian policymaking is susceptible to various pressures—venal private agendas over the public good, political motives over national economic interest—it knows better than to assume that everything has been settled, either on ESPO or in the wider energy relationship. It has therefore adopted a two-track approach. Operationally, it looks to maximize Russian oil imports and make the pipeline project work to this purpose, even if it has to foot the bill. Strategically, however, it has kept demand for Russian oil to non-dependent levels. This means continuing to diversify oil suppliers both regionally (Central Asia) and globally (Africa and South America); consolidating ties with the Persian Gulf states; expanding the use of new or relatively new forms of energy, such as LNG and "clean coal"; stepping up efforts at energy efficiency; and establishing a strategic petroleum reserve.

China's flexible approach toward energy cooperation with Russia is a natural response to the non-strategic nature of their interaction. While both understand that cooperation serves their interests, they are not bound by a common sense of purpose; indeed, their priorities and objectives differ fundamentally. Inevitably this has hindered the implementation of major projects, such as ESPO and the Kovykta gas pipeline. The consistent political will and close policy coordination that are the prerequisites of success have been absent, particularly on the Russian side. Far from there being a long-term plan for Russia's development as a strategic energy supplier for China and the Asia-Pacific region—as suggested by the 2020 Energy Strategy—Moscow is motivated more than ever by short-termism.[73]

The tribulations of the East Siberian oil pipeline exemplify the unfulfilled promise of Sino-Russian cooperation. A project that might have taken their partnership to a new level has become symptomatic of its shortcomings. Moreover, the window of opportunity for a strategic energy relationship may be closing. For while China will continue to import Russian oil and the ESPO pipeline could well be built in the next few years, Beijing is already looking elsewhere for the resources needed to sustain China's transformation.

Russia between East and West

More than any other single factor, the post-1999 boom in world oil prices has been responsible for Russia's re-emergence as a great power. The combination of abundant energy resources and the world's resource hunger appears to have given it an unprecedented opportunity to occupy center stage in regional and global decisionmaking. Unsurprisingly the Russian establishment has talked up the possibilities, at times investing the "energy weapon" with almost magical properties.[74] In contrast to the pessimistic commentaries on Russia's prospects in the 1990s, today's tone is triumphalist. Senior government figures routinely declare that the West must get used to a strong Russia reasserting its influence in world affairs,[75] and argue that it is uniquely placed to exercise leverage over the West by threatening to "go East" with its oil and especially gas.[76]

Such talk is overblown and mistakes the image of power for the real thing. The very notion of an "energy superpower" is delusional, as is the belief that energy can be the catalyst for Russia's development as a multidimensional global power. Although oil and gas have increased its international influence, the use of energy for geopolitical ends has considerable limitations.

In the first place, since 90 percent of oil exports are bought and sold freely on world spot markets, the question of leverage only has meaning in relation to natural gas. Genuine leverage, however, presupposes a credible alternative market in the Asia-Pacific region—China—that would absorb Russia's redirected exports. Yet this does not exist, nor will it for many years.

Europe enjoys at least four key advantages as the main market for Russian gas. First, its energy relationship with Russia (and previously the Soviet Union) is long-established, dating back four decades.[77] It has proved remarkably resilient in the face of political shocks, transcending ideological and strategic confrontation as well as the collapse of the USSR. Compared with this network of relationships and understandings, commercial trust between Russia and China is in its infancy. And recent experience with joint energy ventures, such as ESPO, suggests that it will take many years to develop.

Second, Europe is a far larger and more secure market than China. Moscow knows that the Europeans will continue to consume Russian gas in substantial volumes, particularly with the depletion of the North Sea fields.[78] There is no such confidence with the Chinese market. Although gas is predicted to rise from 3 percent of total primary energy consumption to 8 percent by 2020, a number of variables make it unwise to count on this. Beijing is exploring other energy sources, including nuclear power and advanced coal technology; it is importing LNG from Australia and Indonesia; and it has become increasingly wary of relying on Russia. The Russian government too has serious doubts about the size and profitability of the Chinese market. The TNK-BP project for Kovykta, for example, had envisaged piping gas to China and South Korea—600 billion and 300 billion cubic meters respectively over a thirty-year period.[79] But Moscow has since indicated that Kovykta gas, if and when it comes online, will go to the domestic market.[80] As German Gref (minister for economic development and trade, 2000–07) admitted in 2005, the decision on whether to go east or west will be "based on sales prospects"—a gentle but unambiguous signal of Moscow's continuing preference for Europe.[81]

Third, the European market is much more lucrative than China's. Whereas the Europeans pay above U.S.$350 per 1,000 cubic meters (cm),[82] the Chinese are seeking to import Russian gas on the cheap—at around U.S.$100 per 1,000 cm.[83] This is even cheaper than the rate paid by Belarus, the lowest for any of Russia's customers. Gazprom has no intention of making such a drastic concession, while China's interest in Russian gas is not so great as to persuade it to pay more than the cost of extracting domestic coal.

Fourth, logistics overwhelmingly favor continued substantial exports to Europe. Most of Russia's proven gas reserves are located in northern Russia and western Siberia, in fields such as Shtokman and Yamal-Nenets, rather than in eastern Siberia, where Kovykta remains an uncertain proposition.[84]

Crucially, the existing network of Russian and Russia-controlled pipelines is set up to meet European, not Asian, demand. Although there are plans to build more pipelines to service the latter, notably a new route from the Altai to Xinjiang, these are less advanced than projects to develop additional westward pipelines, such as Nord Stream.[85] A geographically "balanced" export strategy is a seductive notion but would require colossal investment to develop difficult-to-access deposits and the accompanying infrastructure. There is little sign of this occurring. On the contrary, the industry still suffers from severe under-investment, with capital continuing to flow toward equity acquisitions overseas rather than into new fields.[86]

Faking it—Russia as an "energy superpower"

There is, in short, no "China option" on the table. If Europe faces competition, then it will come not from Asia but from Russian domestic consumers. The Putin administration had stated its intention to raise internal gas prices to "European" levels by January 1, 2011, although it has since pulled back on this commitment.[87] If significant price liberalization were introduced, it might make the domestic market more enticing to Gazprom (and Russia's independent producers) and, potentially, reduce the gas available to outside consumers. The squeeze on resources is expected to become critical over the medium term with the decline of Gazprom's non-Yamal fields by 2020.[88] In these circumstances, it is improbable that China will become a major market for Russian gas anytime soon. The 15 percent target for gas exports to Asia in the 2020 Energy Strategy looks all the more unachievable given the inadequate investment in new fields and infrastructure in eastern Siberia, the softness of Chinese demand, and the considerable logistical and commercial advantages of the European market.

Such energy leverage as Russia is able to exert is more psychological than material. The Kremlin has skillfully exploited the short-sightedness of EU member-states, whose failure to pursue a common strategy toward Russia has enabled Moscow to pick them off by appealing to individual national interests.[89] In fact, Moscow's position is much weaker than it looks. Even though Russia and Europe are interdependent and would both suffer from a "gas war," it is Russia that is more vulnerable and has fewer options. Vladimir Milov, the former Russian deputy energy minister, has shown that Europe is less dependent on Russian gas than is commonly supposed. For example, while Poland imports nearly all its gas from Russia, this accounts for less than 7 percent of total primary energy consumption (which is overwhelmingly dominated by coal). Germany has long had a "special" relationship with Moscow, yet Russian gas comprises less than 10 percent of its primary energy consumption.[90] Russia, on the other hand, is almost entirely dependent (more than 90 percent) on Europe as a destination for its gas exports.

Moscow can scarcely contemplate reducing supply to its highest paying and most reliable customers. Quite apart from the enormous financial losses involved,[91] any cessation of deliveries would have a long-term impact on consumer confidence. The disputes with Ukraine in January 2006 and Belarus in January 2007 resulted in only the briefest of interruptions to European energy supply, yet cast a large shadow over Russia's reputation for reliability.[92] The crises exposed the self-defeating character of energy leverage: the more Russia uses—or is seen to use—energy as a weapon, the more its customers will look to other sources of supply, even if these take some time to develop.

It is relevant, too, that the EU-27 accounts for well over 50 percent of Russia's total trade turnover, nearly ten times China's share, whereas Russia contributes only 8–9 percent of the EU's external trade.[93] The asymmetry between EU and Russian investment is likewise huge, with EU countries accounting for more than 90 percent of total foreign investment in Russia. By comparison, Chinese investment in Russia remains relatively insignificant, despite recent improvement.[94] Moscow continues to be much more welcoming to European investors, and nowhere more so than in the energy sector.[95]

Growing asymmetry

Russia is potentially the biggest loser from the geopolitics of energy, even as it continues to present a bold front to the international community. Vladimir Putin has sought to promote a vision of Russia as a modern great power, as constructive as it is influential. Energy was to have been the key to this transformation. Instead, rather like nuclear weapons during the Cold War, energy has become identified with aggressive power. It has given Russia the confidence to be assertive, but not the wherewithal to make a positive contribution to the world around it.

China, on the other hand, profits from the political and economic uncertainties in Russia-EU relations. Although it can scarcely hope to cut into Europe's dominant share of Russian gas exports, it can look forward to continued oil deliveries and perhaps in time relatively cheap gas from Sakhalin.[96] It is in the enviable position of benefiting from, yet not depending on, Russia. Its policy of diversifying sources and types of energy has alleviated concerns over access, and it is increasingly in a position to influence the terms of bilateral energy cooperation.

Indeed, in energy as in many other areas of the relationship, a shift in power is taking place. Although Moscow has no pressing economic need to export oil and gas to China, there is an emerging political imperative. Beijing plays a pivotal role in facilitating Russia's pursuit of an "independent" foreign policy by reinforcing Moscow's self-confidence vis-à-vis the West. However, the Russian government is under mounting pressure to offer a quid pro quo by giving substance to energy ties.[97] Without tangible progress here it will be unable to sustain the myth of a "China alternative" and to exercise leverage over the Europeans, let alone realize its larger ambition of becoming the interface between East and West.[98] In effect Chinese geopolitical insurance has become more valuable to Moscow than Russian energy is to Beijing.

This reflects a larger asymmetry in the two countries' relations with the outside world. Today Russia has few friends. While its regional and global influence should not be underestimated, much of this is tied to control over energy resources and the implicit (sometimes explicit) threat of exploiting these to advance its interests. Russia's international image continues to be predominantly that of a "hard" power that relies more on pressure than persuasion—an impression reinforced by the Georgia crisis.[99]

China, by contrast, is a nation with which other countries, great and small, wish to engage. Although many fear its rise and disapprove of its values, this has not stopped them from embracing cooperation with it.[100] A growing number of states are willing to allow access to Chinese economic interests because they are confident that any relationship will be commercially rather than geopolitically driven. Beijing's accumulation of international political capital has widened its options and also influenced its attitude to energy ties with Moscow. A comparison with the period of the Sino-Soviet "unbreakable friendship" is instructive. In the 1950s China had many enemies and few friends and found itself almost totally dependent on the Soviet Union for external assistance. These days it has the luxury of choice as foreign governments and big business rush to pay court.

The differences in Russian and Chinese perspectives can be partly reconciled at the level of basic supply and demand, but they are not conducive to a strategic energy partnership. For here Beijing has more in common with Washington than with Moscow. The United States and China are the two largest consumers and importers of energy; both have a vested interest in a stable and open international environment that would encourage the free flow of imports; and both would like to see a fall in world prices.[101] Russia, on the other hand, benefits from an uncertain global context (including a volatile Middle East), from a constricted market dominated by a few exporting countries, and from high oil and gas prices.

Moscow and Beijing are constantly looking to tilt the bilateral energy relationship to suit their comparative advantages: Russia's control of resources versus China's range of options. This has led them to pursue contradictory and even competing policies. Thus Moscow wants to keep Beijing as dependent as possible by restricting Chinese access to other energy sources in Eurasia, while Beijing is stepping up its engagement with the Central Asian states. The Kremlin hopes to implement strategic diversity in the Asia-Pacific by developing ties with Japan and South Korea; the Communist leadership is keen to maintain China's position as the dominant consumer of Russian energy in the region. Russia sees itself as a genuinely strategic—in other words, indispensable—energy supplier to China. The Chinese, however, are undertaking a whole host of measures to ensure that they never become hostage to Russian fortune. Both sides talk up the "strategic" character of energy cooperation, yet ultimately their relationship is one of strategic opposites.

CHAPTER NINE

THE GRAND CHESSBOARD REVISITED—RUSSIA, CHINA, AND THE UNITED STATES

"We will dictate to the world!"
—BORIS YELTSIN, Beijing, December 1999[1]

"China would be the senior partner in any serious Russian effort to jell . . . an 'anti-hegemonic' coalition [against the United States]. Being more populous, more industrious, more innovative, more dynamic, and harboring some potential territorial designs on Russia, China would inevitably consign Russia to the status of a junior partner."
—ZBIGNIEW BRZEZINSKI, *The Grand Chessboard*, 1997[2]

Today, more than at any other time in the past twenty years, geopolitical competition dominates global politics. Two great waves of internationalism—the first in the wake of the Soviet demise, the second in the aftermath of 9/11—have exhausted themselves and given way to increasingly overt strategic rivalries. The language may still be of positive-sum interdependency, universal values, and common interests. But everyday realities routinely expose the shallowness of such slogans. Multilateral organizations and mechanisms multiply, yet we live in a neo-Westphalian epoch in which the nation-state remains the primary unit of world politics—selfish, assertive, and ever more influential.[3]

In this climate the emphasis is on the advancement of "vital national interests" rather than "universal" or supranational solutions. The United States, "the first, only, and last truly global superpower," according to Zbigniew Brzezinski,[4] has failed to realize its post–Cold War vision of an American-centered "new world order."[5] Its authority as global leader has declined steadily over the past decade. The most recent military intervention in Iraq, in particular, has destroyed the myth of American invincibility and given hope and opportunity to other great powers, both those that are emerging and those seeking to restore former glories.

It is no surprise that Russia and China should figure so prominently among these aspiring great powers, nor that their interaction has assumed special significance for Western policymakers. There is a growing conviction that a major shift has taken place in Moscow's thinking from its traditional Western focus toward a more multi-vectored foreign policy, in which China occupies a position of equal eminence. Some observers view the Sino-Russian rapprochement as a work in progress whose endpoint will be nothing less than a full-blown political-military alliance directed against the United States and its European allies.[6] Such concerns have been fueled by various statements from Moscow and Beijing. Since Boris Yeltsin and Jiang Zemin first announced in April 1997 their intention "to promote the multipolarization of the world and the establishment of a new international order,"[7] the two governments have constantly reiterated their vision of a more "democratic," non-American-centered model of international relations. The July 2005 Sino-Russian joint declaration "On the twenty-first century world order" could hardly have been more pointed: "The international community . . . should abjure confrontational or bloc thinking, should not strive to monopolize or dominate world affairs, and should not divide states into leaders and subordinates."[8]

Such statements suggest a geopolitical world in which the authority of the United States as global leader is under concerted attack from the non-Western powers, China and Russia at the forefront. And yet the real situation is much more complicated than it seems. Moscow and Beijing present a façade of strategic convergence and normative likemindedness. But, as previous chapters have shown, theirs is a partnership characterized by divided loyalties, ulterior motives, and often conflicting agendas. The Russia-China-U.S. triangle, in turn, is a story of shifting allegiances and tactical expediency.

The "Grand Chessboard"

The starting point of our discussion of the dynamic between Moscow, Beijing, and Washington is the "Grand Chessboard," outlined by Brzezinski a little over a decade ago. The Grand Chessboard comprised the greater Eurasian continent, stretching from Lisbon to Vladivostok.[9] Brzezinski's vision was dominated by several large realities. The first, and most important, was the benign hegemony of the United States, the world's "only truly global power."

Second, Eurasia would remain the central arena for "the struggle for global primacy." Third, the continent would face the threat of "global anarchy"—war, ethnic and religious hostilities, WMD proliferation, the population explosion, and so on. This put a premium on a well-conceived and comprehensive American "geostrategy for Eurasia" to ensure global stability. Finally, Brzezinski emphasized the importance of pursuing "geopolitical pluralism," which he defined as ensuring that "no state or combination of states gains the capacity to expel the United States from Eurasia or even to diminish significantly its decisive arbitrating role."[10] In practice geopolitical pluralism would entail constructive interplay between the United States, "geostrategic players" such as Russia and China, and smaller "geopolitical pivots."[11]

Brzezinski's overall prognosis was cautiously optimistic. He acknowledged that there were limits to American power and that this power would inevitably erode over time. Nevertheless, with constructive management Washington could ensure stability on the Eurasian continent and repel any threats to America's global primacy. Specifically, Brzezinski envisaged three stages of development in the short, medium, and long term respectively: (i) consolidation of the existing geopolitical pluralism and prevention of any anti-American coalitions; (ii) the steady development of a network of strategic partnerships with key regional players; and (iii) the fostering of a genuine sense of "shared political responsibility."[12]

A decade later many of Brzezinski's arguments stand up well to critical scrutiny, no mean feat considering the revolutionary developments that have taken place in the intervening period. China's accelerated transformation from modest regional actor to global player; the rise of India; 9/11; the arrival of the United States in Central Asia; Washington's military intervention in Iraq; the spread of Islamic extremism; the erosion of American influence; Russia's resurgence under Putin; the boom in oil and commodity prices; and the emergence of climate change as a truly global priority—all have had far-reaching consequences for today's world and will continue to shape international politics well into the twenty-first century.

At the same time key continuities survive from the mid-1990s. The United States, despite the fiasco of Iraq and signs of "imperial overstretch,"[13] remains the only global superpower in its various dimensions.[14] Despite the emergence of China and India, there is no evidence that they will be able or even willing to mount a serious challenge to Washington's global leadership for many years to come. The world is scarcely more "multipolar" than it was a decade ago, a reality denied by Moscow but readily acknowledged in Beijing.[15] Russia's own revival, impressive as it seems, is only a relative success—modest compared with that of other emerging powers[16]—and one that rests on fragile foundations.

The single greatest continuity from the 1990s is that the Eurasian continent remains the Grand Chessboard—the disparate and anarchic theatre of global geopolitics. The relative position of the different great powers may have changed, but two constants have survived. The first is the primacy of geopolitical contestation, whose instruments have become more diverse, but whose underlying aims—power projection and the expansion of national influence—are as compelling as ever. The second constant is the centrality of the Russia-China-U.S. strategic triangle within this geopolitical contestation. Triangularism has evolved considerably from the primitive models of the Cold War era, but today, more than ever, it exerts a decisive influence on the complex interaction between Moscow, Beijing, and Washington.

Strategic triangularism: genesis and development

Strategic triangularism between Russia, China, and the United States dates back to the beginnings of Communist China in 1949. Mao Zedong's dependence on Soviet economic and military assistance ensured that in the early years of the People's Republic there would be a "leaning to one side," toward Moscow against the United States and its European and Asian allies.[17] This foreign policy bias was reinforced by the circumstances of the Korean War (1950–53), which spawned two decades of strategic confrontation between Washington and Beijing.

The Soviet leadership took comfort in Chinese ideological and political support, although Beijing's real contribution was very limited. As noted in chapter 2, the Sino-Soviet "friendship" was never comfortable. Mao's emphasis on national self-reliance during this time reflected, in part, a suspiciousness toward the Soviet Union as a past and present imperial power that had rarely missed an opportunity to exploit Chinese weakness. Moscow's retention of its Far Eastern provinces and consolidation of Mongolia as a satellite state provided grist to an already active mill. Following Stalin's death the early promise of the Khrushchev era gave way to a further and decisive deterioration by the late 1950s. The protracted Sino-Soviet split after 1960 killed off any slim hopes of a partnership directed against the United States.

In the first two decades following the establishment of the PRC, triangularism was consequently a theoretical rather than practical proposition. The realities of the Cold War—the centrality of U.S.–Soviet strategic bipolarity, ongoing Sino-U.S. tensions over Taiwan—and Beijing's domestic preoccupations (the Great Leap Forward, the Great Proletarian Cultural Revolution) marginalized China in global geopolitics. Although it was a large and populous nation, with a massive standing army, its weaknesses together with Mao's unpredictability made China a most unattractive partner. At best it was a second-line regional power with a strongly isolationist mentality, whose ability to project influence beyond its borders was severely circumscribed.

The situation began to change in 1970–71. A softening of the excesses of the Cultural Revolution; the consequent (if limited) opening-up of China to the world, symbolized by the PRC's replacement of Taiwan at the United Nations; and Washington's desperation to extricate itself from the Vietnam War led to a rethinking of American policy toward China. With the Sino-Soviet border clashes of 1969 fresh in memory, the Nixon administration saw an opportunity to stretch the Soviet Union on two fronts, forcing it into strategic concessions across the globe from Europe to Southeast Asia.[18] Beijing's aims were complementary: to safeguard its "strategic rear" and contain Soviet power, while gaining access to much-needed Western trade, investment, and technology. Nixon's 1972 visit to China, the first by an American president, put triangularism back on the geopolitical agenda. The Soviet leadership reacted to the Sino-American rapprochement by pursuing its own policy of détente with Washington.[19] This initiated a period of reduced tensions between the two superpowers that lasted until the Soviet invasion of Afghanistan in December 1979.

Triangularism during the era of détente was essentially defensive. Moscow sought to minimize the impact of Sino-American rapprochement, while Washington viewed China as a useful check on Soviet ambition. From the outset, however, the Russia-China-U.S. triangle was lopsided, owing to the overwhelming preponderance of military might in the two superpowers. As a strategic minnow in a bipolar world, China had only limited influence. The Sino-Soviet freeze led to the permanent stationing of large numbers of Soviet troops in the Far East—some 46 divisions by 1980[20]—but neither Chinese hostility toward Moscow nor its flirting with Washington did much to curb Soviet behavior. On the contrary, the 1970s saw the aggressive expansion of Soviet power to Africa, Latin America, and, most notoriously, Afghanistan.

The strategic triangle was asymmetrical in another sense as well. Although in theory China was in the position of swing power, able potentially to maneuver between Moscow and Washington,[21] the unevenness of its respective relationships with the United States and the USSR made this unfeasible. There was never any likelihood of Moscow and Beijing making common cause to counterbalance American power, since each was the other's most implacable enemy. Instead both looked to the United States—resolutely anticommunist but also more "rational"—as their external point of reference and sometimes succor.

In such a context ideas of strategic leverage and "balancing" were pipe-dreams. Neither Moscow nor Washington could plausibly threaten the other with the China card since this was of marginal value and, in any event, could not be readily deployed. It was equally futile for the PRC and the Soviet Union to use rapprochement with Washington to pressure each other into more cooperative policies. The most that could be done was to buttress the existing policy of mutual containment—and this too proved of dubious and short-lived value. In sum, the triangularism of the Cold War era was distorted, asymmetrical, and incomplete. At no stage did it threaten to become a more structured arrangement, and its impact, such as it was, was largely symbolic. It would take a radical reordering of the global balance of power for triangularism to acquire a measure of credibility.

Triangularism in the post–Cold War era

The collapse of the USSR in December 1991 appeared to provide just such an opening. A vibrantly self-confident United States emerged as the undisputed global leader; a demoralized Russia became a "black hole,"[22] neither powerful in the traditional political-military sense nor a significant contributor to the post–Cold War order; and China arose cautiously but steadily out of its semi-isolationist shell.[23] The resultant equalization of Russia and China gave new life to strategic triangularism.[24]

Initially Moscow aspired to a condominium arrangement with the United States while sidelining China.[25] However, Washington's refusal to indulge Yeltsin's fantasies of equality led to early disillusionment and the search for other ways to restore Russia to its "rightful" position as a great global power.[26] By autumn 1993 geopolitics had regained its central position in Kremlin thinking.[27] The emphasis on concepts such as "multivectorialism," "geographic balance," and a "multipolar" world highlighted a reversion from positive-sum interdependency to more familiar balance-of-power notions. Triangularism again became fashionable in policymaking circles, along with ideas of Russia as both balancer and bridge between East and West.[28]

That said, Russian foreign policy continued to be overwhelmingly Westerncentric during the first half of the 1990s. Although relations with China improved substantially, the "eastern vector" remained a sideshow and strategic balancing largely non-existent. The situation changed with the appointment of Yevgeny Primakov as foreign minister in January 1996. Unlike his predecessor Andrei Kozyrev, who had interpreted multipolarity as an essentially cooperative enterprise with the United States and other Western powers, Primakov imbued it with a strongly competitive spirit. Multipolarity assumed the form of a "revised bipolarity" (see chapter 2).[29] Russia alone could not contain the hegemonic behavior of the United States, but it might mitigate its effects by working with other major players similarly disturbed by Washington's monopoly of power. Since the Europeans had already been co-opted into the Clinton administration's internationalist agenda,[30] Moscow turned increasingly to the non-Western powers, China and (to a lesser extent) India.[31]

Relations with a rising China served several purposes for Moscow in the triangular context. First, they offered the prospect of greater strategic flexibility by diluting its reliance on the United States. Second, rapprochement might persuade Washington to be more responsive to Russian interests. A "turn to the east" would stoke extant fears of "Russia going bad," of becoming undemocratic and confrontational.[32] Third, closer ties with a strong China could boost Russia's chances of becoming a "bridge between civilizations" or "guarantor" of European security against a possible, if distant, threat from the East. Finally, the spectacle of Moscow and Beijing working toward a common purpose—the "multipolarization of the world and the establishment of a new international order"[33]—enhanced Russia's credentials as an "indispensable" global power, without which no international issue could be resolved.[34]

For the remainder of the Yeltsin presidency, the Russian government consistently employed the China card in its relations with the United States. The "strategic partnership" with China became valuable principally as a counterweight to Washington's hegemonic power. It was an anti-relationship, whose focus was Americacentric rather than Sinocentric. For at the same time as the Yeltsin administration was trumpeting the virtues of multipolarity and geographical balance, it signed the Founding Act with NATO, joined the G-8, and remained fixated on the West.

The bankruptcy of triangularism

Moscow's crude attempts to exploit the Russia-China-U.S. triangle were an utter failure. Far from gaining strategic flexibility and influence, it achieved the opposite, closing off options with the West without strengthening Russia's position in the Asia-Pacific. The China card was ineffective in softening Western policies on the issues that mattered. Against strenuous Russian objections,

NATO enlargement in central and eastern Europe proceeded apace, the alliance intervened militarily over Kosovo in 1999, Washington initiated a national missile defense program, and the United States and Britain launched air-strikes against the Saddam Hussein regime in Baghdad. American interests became increasingly active in Russia's neighborhood, while also stepping up criticisms of the Yeltsin administration's misgovernment, corruption, and brutal campaigns in Chechnya. Yeltsin's claims that the world community needed Russia sounded ever more implausible and his intemperate utterances—Russia and China "will dictate to the world!"[35]—underlined the extent to which a once great power had lost its way at home and abroad. In these circumstances the comparison with China only highlighted the two countries' contrasting fortunes: on one side, an "empty superpower," marginalized by East and West alike; on the other, a rising international presence, increasingly able to engage on a global as well as regional level.

The Primakovian vision failed so comprehensively during the 1990s because it was based on a strategic culture out of step with most of the developed and indeed developing world. Although President Clinton's message of positive-sum cooperation was not always well received, it contained aspects that appealed even to its opponents. Thus while China cared little for the "unipolar moment" in history,[36] it benefited from a buoyant America in terms of trade and investment. Beijing understood, too, that attempting to challenge the United States directly would undermine its own modernization project. The Communist leadership was pragmatic enough to transcend geopolitical tradition and identify a larger national self-interest.

As a result, the gap widened between Primakov's semi-confrontational stance and the more accommodating philosophy of China's "peaceful rise." Crucially, while Beijing did not allow the rhetoric of multipolarity to impinge on its growing engagement with Washington, Moscow tended to take such affirmations at face value. The delusional nature of Primakovian triangularism reached its nadir with his suggestion during a visit to New Delhi in December 1998 that Russia, China, and India should form an axis to constrain American power. Primakov's proposal showed an almost willful ignorance of the foreign policy motivations and interests of China and India.[37]

Triangularism in the 1990s also failed for the same reason as in the 1970s and 1980s, namely the manifestly unequal relationships between the United States, Russia, and China. During the Cold War Chinese weakness ensured that U.S.-Soviet bipolarity would remain the dominant strategic paradigm. The fall of the USSR and subsequent equalization of Russia and China appeared to provide the conditions for the re-emergence of triangularism.

However, two factors militated against this. The first was the dominance and self-assurance of a "victorious" United States, which did not so much crush as co-opt (or ignore) its putative rivals. As Gilbert Rozman has observed, "power had become very unbalanced with no counterweight to the United States."[38] The second was that the equalization of Sino-Russian relations was only momentary, as a rapidly ascendant power intersected with one in sharp decline. By the end of the decade it was apparent that China had no interest in tying itself to a feeble Russia in opposition to a seemingly invincible United States. The strategic triangle was to all intents and purposes defunct.

A new lease of life

It is all the more striking, then, that in recent years ideas of triangularism have resurfaced, driven by the perception that the three powers are now more equal than at any time in their shared history. It is not only a question of "a self-confident America . . . being transformed into a fear-driven nation,"[39] but of others exploiting its travails in Iraq and Afghanistan to reassert themselves. The emerging powers Russia, China, and India, as well as leading European states such as France and Germany, are participating much more actively in international decisionmaking. The Iraq war has demonstrated that the United States can no longer function as the "single pole," supported only by a small coterie of pliant allies—the "coalition of the willing."

The strategic opportunity opened up by America's difficulties has coincided with Russia's resurgence. The consolidation of Putin's political authority, the boom in world oil prices, consistently high economic growth since 1999, and sensible macroeconomic management have given Moscow the confidence to play on the world stage. It has been able to disregard Western criticisms of Russian domestic developments, take advantage of the continuing dependence of the former Soviet republics, and portray Russia as an integral player in the growing international consensus pressing the United States for greater consideration.

The decisive element in the new triangular framework, however, is the rise of China. In his 1997 book Brzezinski downplayed China's potential, pointing to various contradictions within its polity and economy that were likely to hinder its progress. He questioned whether it would necessarily become "a central global power"[40] and thought that by 2020 it would merely be "well on the way to becoming the preponderant *regional* [original italics] power in East Asia."[41] Brzezinski's prognosis underestimated the speed of

China's physical and psychological transformation. Today, although still predominantly a regional power, it is rapidly globalizing its outlook and interests. Beijing's voracious search for energy and natural resources has ensured that China these days is an actor whose domestic and international policies have worldwide implications.[42] While it continues to suffer from major problems—a resources deficit, environmental degradation, the disjunction between economic liberalization and political authoritarianism—it seems destined to become the next global superpower some time in the first half of this century.

Certainly the mere possibility that this may occur has altered the dynamic between the United States, Russia, and China. For the first time in decades the notion of triangularism appears to have some basis in reality. Although China will not overtake the U.S. as the world's leading power anytime soon, there is a very real sense that the gap between them is narrowing and that one day Beijing will challenge American leadership, not just in the Asia-Pacific region, but also beyond.[43] The strategic triangle would in that event assume new significance. Already in 2003, before the full extent of the Iraq imbroglio became apparent, Mikhail Margelov, chair of the International Affairs committee in the Federation Council, emphasized the nexus between the Sino-Russian relationship and the Russia-China-U.S. triangle.[44] Margelov merely hinted at the return of competitive global geopolitics. More recently, however, the Russian government has become much more open about its ambitions in this regard. In August 2006 a senior Foreign Ministry official asserted with undisguised satisfaction that "interaction in the world arena between Russia and China . . . grows into a real geopolitical factor which other global 'players' cannot but reckon with."[45] The oblique reference to the United States revealed the belief that, after a hiatus of nearly two decades, Moscow could once again contest America's global leadership.

Putin's agenda for a resurgent Russia

Russia's current approach to triangularism borrows much from the original Primakov vision.[46] Strategic leverage and balancing have acquired renewed currency, as has the notion of Russia as a bridge—not only between East and West, but also between the developed North and developing South.[47] The salience of such ideas reflects a tacit understanding that Russia, notwithstanding its energy riches, can only become an influential global player with the help of others.

As in the 1990s China represents the most plausible partner in such an enterprise. Moscow sees the two countries forming a strategic axis, but one with its own individual characteristics. Crucially, China's principal utility is instrumental rather than intrinsic: to strengthen Russia's hand in its primary relationships with the United States, the EU, and the major European powers. Much as Moscow desires a productive partnership with Beijing, the West continues to supply the main external points of reference. Putin's claim that Russia belongs to mainstream European civilization reflects the extent to which its national consciousness is bound by long-standing political, economic, and cultural links with Europe. Equally the United States will retain its pre-eminent place in Russian strategic culture, even if China manages to close the gap. Russia seeks to renegotiate the terms of its interaction with the West, not to jettison it.[48]

Although such instrumentalism is more understated than under Yeltsin, geopolitics continues to be the main driving force behind the expansion of ties with Beijing. Consequently the "strategic partnership" has tended to fluctuate in inverse proportion to the state of Moscow's relations with Washington. It was underplayed in the year after 9/11 when Putin bought into the Bush administration's cooperative security agenda, but has benefited greatly from the severe deterioration in Russia-U.S. relations since then.[49]

Ideally Putin would like Russia to become the "third pole" in the emerging global multipolar order—retaining a distinct strategic identity, balancing between the United States and China, and being an "equal partner" to both. He therefore has a strong interest in ensuring that relations with the West do not deteriorate so far as to make Russia over-dependent on the Chinese. At the same time, close ties with Beijing enable Moscow to demonstrate to the West (and to itself) that it is not without options and can sustain an "independent" foreign policy. Russia benefits from the ambiguity in U.S.-Chinese relations, even if its influence here is minimal. In much the same way that "controlled tension" in East Asia allows it to maneuver in the margins and exploit regional uncertainties (see chapter 7), so the mix of suspicion and cooperation between Beijing and Washington feeds Russian aspirations to play the part of the balancer.

Moscow's worst nightmare is to be relegated to the status of junior partner to either (or both) of the other sides in the triangle. Two considerations make this prospect especially unpalatable. The first is a deep conviction in Russia's natural destiny as a great global power. Against this background the last twenty years are seen as an aberration, a modern "Time of Troubles,"[50] following which Russia is resuming its normal course. Such thinking is well described in Dmitri Trenin's "back to 1913" thesis, which argues that Russian policymakers are pursuing today what they would have done a century ago had World War I and the Bolshevik Revolution not intervened to turn everything on its head.[51]

That Russia might become a junior partner to China is of particular concern.[52] Whereas there is ample precedent for Washington's global leadership, the notion of Chinese pre-eminence is profoundly alien to an elite accustomed to regarding China as weak, backward, and often subordinate. Although the latter's dazzling rise and the concomitant decline of Soviet power have undermined such stereotypes, the possibility that China could become the senior partner in the relationship remains difficult to swallow, all the more so given Russia's own revival.

Moscow is therefore wary of doing too much to facilitate China's rise. The perfect scenario is for the United States and China to treat Russia as an essential partner in countering the other's hegemonic ambitions. To this purpose Moscow emphasizes multipolarity and the "democratization" of international relations, but simultaneously talks up Russia's European and Western credentials.[53] This reflects an appreciation that Russia's best chance of recognition as the "indispensable power" is to position itself between East and West. It is revealing, in this connection, that senior Kremlin figures oppose suggestions that the G-8 should be expanded to a G-14 to include emerging non-Western powers such as China, India, and Brazil.[54] Opening up membership of such an elite club would undermine Russia's claims to be the natural bridge between America, Europe, and Asia.

Beijing's globalist agenda

In principle, Beijing shares an interest with Moscow in counterbalancing the hegemonic power of the United States. Yet this apparent likemindedness hides multiple differences in perspective, interests, and priorities. The Communist leadership underplays the competitive elements of triangularism and denies that China has either the capacity or the inclination to overtake the United States. It is modest about Chinese achievements and highlights many unresolved problems. Self-effacing statements such as "China is the world's largest developing country,"[55] "it will take at least decades for China to catch up with the Western world,"[56] and "the United States will remain the world's only global hegemonic power for decades to come"[57] differ markedly in substance and spirit from the self-aggrandizing pronouncements of many Russian politicians and commentators.

This linguistic gulf reflects the contrasting ways in which Russia and China have chosen to interact with the United States. The re-emergence of Moscow's competitive mindset has led it to contest American influence wherever it can, even when this is self-defeating.[58] With the exception of Putin's endorsement of the U.S. troop deployment in Central Asia after 9/11, Moscow has tended to view American actions on the Eurasian continent as motivated chiefly by a desire to undermine Russian interests, for example, over Georgia.

China has adopted a more relaxed stance. Although it retains a strong geopolitical mindset and views the Eurasian chessboard as a fiercely competitive arena, it differs substantially from Russia in its policy *responses* to these strategic surroundings. Slogans such as "multipolarization" and "a new and just world order" serve formalistic purposes, but meanwhile Chinese state and business interests are frantically expanding cooperation with the "global hegemon." The pragmatic bent of Chinese foreign policy is exemplified by the fact that its second and third largest trading partners—the United States and Japan—are also countries with which it has uncomfortable and sometimes hostile political relations.[59] Despite public criticisms and occasional insults, Beijing's ties with Washington and Tokyo are far more substantial than its "close and warm" links with Moscow.[60]

Beijing is not disposed to challenge U.S. interests and actions except where it feels there is a pressing need to do so, such as over Taiwan and theatre missile defense. Even on priority issues the Chinese modus operandi is less confrontational than Russia's. In Central Asia it has taken a softly-softly approach to countering American influence: allowing Russia to take the "anti-hegemonic" lead; working through the multilateral mechanisms of the SCO; and emphasizing pan-regional economic cooperation. The Chinese agree with the Russians on the negative implications of many American policies—in Central Asia, Iran, Iraq, Israel/Palestine. Yet their distaste for Washington's behavior rarely stops them from doing business with it.[61] They are able to quarantine concrete interests from ideological and philosophical objections, something the Russians have not managed to do in recent times.

In terms of the bigger picture this means that Beijing is able to reconcile the development of Sino-Russian partnership with closer ties with the United States. Unlike Moscow it has little interest in competitive balancing involving the other two sides of the triangle, since this would exacerbate frictions and limit its options. Concepts such as "peaceful rise"/"peaceful development" (see chapter 5) are intended to promote China as a constructive international actor committed to cooperation with *all* countries on the basis of common interests (as opposed to shared values). Ganging up with Russia against America would contradict this aim and incur unwarranted political and economic risks.[62] In Russia, by contrast, anti-American sentiment is part of the genetic make-up of much of the elite and a feature of mainstream political discourse.[63]

Beijing's reluctance to become entangled in competitive triangularism also owes much to careful evaluation of the limits of partnership with Moscow. There are serious doubts as to how far Russia would move on Taiwan or in the event of Sino-American confrontation. Yevgeny Bazhanov has admitted that "Moscow may very easily get cold feet,"[64] and it is indicative that it insisted on changing the venue for the "Peace Mission 2005" military exercises to the Shandong peninsula and Vladivostok—in other words, as far away as possible from the tense environment of the Taiwan Straits (see chapter 3). Putin's failure to consult with Beijing before making several critical decisions affecting Chinese interests—endorsement of the American military presence in Central Asia; acceptance of Washington's withdrawal from the ABM Treaty—underscores the dangers of relying on Russia.

Given these uncertainties Beijing has largely eschewed a balancing strategy in favor of an inclusive, non-aligned approach to international relations. Proceeding on the assumption that no single partner can be entirely trusted, it compensates by developing as many options as possible. In the triangular context, this means engaging positively with Russia and the United States, while avoiding any damage—direct or collateral—that might arise from geopolitical game-playing.

If forced to choose, however, Beijing might end up leaning toward Washington rather than Moscow. The United States, as the sole superpower, holds the key to China's most vital interests: economic modernization, the fate of Taiwan, the flow of energy resources through secure sea-lanes, markets for consumer products, the nation's physical security, access to high technology and high-quality tertiary education. Despite its difficulties in Iraq and Afghanistan, the United States remains the clear global leader. As China's modernization continues its frenetic pace, together with the liberalization and globalization of its society (if not polity), the Americacentric tendency in official and popular attitudes will only strengthen.[65]

In many respects, for the Chinese Russia represents the past: a former superpower harking back to earlier glories and living off its natural assets; an erstwhile ally of suspect reliability whose relevance to China's domestic and foreign policy goals is restricted to a few sectors only.[66] Although Beijing observes the diplomatic proprieties of "strategic partnership," it views Russia more as a "limited partner"[67] than as a state with which it seeks comprehensive and deep engagement. It is the reverse with the United States. Despite being a much more difficult, less "friendly" interlocutor, America is truly China's indispensable partner.

Strategic balancing versus strategic inclusion

To date China's more inclusive approach in international relations has proved notably more effective than Russia's strategic balancing. Kremlin efforts to play the China card have "succeeded" to the extent that the Europeans are worried about Russia "turning East," notably in relation to energy supply. But this approach has become increasingly self-defeating. There is no sign of the EU or the United States softening their opposition to Russian policies in key areas—whether in the former Soviet space, in central and eastern Europe, or over Iran—and Moscow risks further deterioration in relations with the West without obtaining adequate "compensation" from its partnership with China.

By contrast, Beijing's emphasis on positive engagement has enabled it to enjoy the benefits of partnership with Russia without detracting from flourishing ties with the United States and Europe. Its restrained handling of issues as diverse as Taiwan and Central Asia has given it the strategic flexibility that Moscow craves but has failed to achieve. Indeed, within the Russia-U.S.-China triangle, it is China that has benefited most in recent years, effectively usurping Russia's place as the second "indispensable" power in Eurasia.

The duality in China's relations with the United States and Russia—the former critical to its interests across the board, the latter a limited partner only—will become more pronounced over time. In many respects—economic, technological, societal—the Chinese leadership and especially the Chinese people have moved on from Russia to embracing the next challenge: catching up with the West, and the United States in particular.[68] As China's horizons and capabilities expand, triangularism will lose much of its relevance as a conceptual tool, to be replaced by a new Sino-American bipolarity.

That said, radical change is not imminent. The triangle will remain in place while the Chinese leadership uses the current "strategic window of opportunity"[69] to complete the process of modernization. Moscow and Beijing will continue to oppose America's "hegemonic" influence in Eurasia. However, the very different priority each attaches to this overarching but vague objective means that such cooperation will remain half-hearted and largely ineffectual. Each side will pursue separate and sometimes competing agendas. Russia will reiterate its "European-ness," attempt to reassert regional leadership in Central Asia, and look to carve out some sort of role in the Asia-Pacific. China will focus on expanding its presence across Eurasia, aspire to regional leadership in East Asia, tone down anti-Americanism to a ritualistic minimum, and quietly undermine Russian efforts to become the hegemon in Central Asia and an influential actor in East Asia.

The re-emergence of strategic anarchy

Despite suffering numerous setbacks in the past decade, the United States remains the only global power. Its authority is frequently questioned, sometimes successfully, but there is no serious threat to its primacy. Evidence of a concerted challenge from the other major powers is notably lacking. Moscow talks a confident game, but in practice recognizes significant limitations on Russian power; its ambition is to be accepted as *one of* the world's leading players, not to compete for top spot with the United States. Meanwhile the thrust of recent Chinese foreign policy has been toward engagement rather than competition, as Beijing focuses mainly on domestic and regional priorities. Speculation about "a struggle for global primacy" between the major powers is overblown. China, Russia, and perhaps India will look to undermine America's dominance and limit the exercise of its "hegemonic" power, but this will be an evolutionary (and uncoordinated) process rather than a seismic shift.

Nevertheless, the diminution of American moral and political influence has facilitated the emergence of a more disparate, "anarchic" strategic environment. The nature of this anarchy is twofold. First, the threats identified by Brzezinski have become more apparent. Islamic extremism, in particular, has emerged as one of the greatest challenges to American *authority* in Eurasia. Sovereign states may still be "the basic units of the world system,"[70] but non-state actors and processes are increasingly vying with established institutions.

The second anarchic feature that distinguishes contemporary Eurasia is more Hobbesian in its import. Since Washington's capacity to coerce or persuade others is much reduced, other players—major powers and minor actors alike—have more scope for independent action. If it is true that no single entity or even loose coalition of interests is able to overturn American primacy, then equally the United States is less able to shape the attitudes and actions of others. American influence in Russia is at its lowest ebb since the late

Gorbachev period; its political leverage on Beijing is limited; the U.S. presence in Central Asia is under pressure from many quarters; the Middle East is more than ever a cauldron of uncertainties; WMD proliferation remains a huge threat; and even close allies such as Japan and South Korea have become more assertive in their dealings with Washington.

Brzezinski's "ordered geopolitical pluralism" has given way to its disorderly cousin, one strongly resistant to American influence. Other major players, including Russia and China, have exploited this to promote their national agendas to an extent inconceivable a decade ago, when there seemed few limits to American power and self-belief. Writing in 2005, Brzezinski captured the change well: "while no major international problem can be resolved without America, America cannot resolve any major international problem on its own."[71] The only way of restoring global stability—and America's political and moral authority—was to find "partners," which required a less hubristic, more historically and culturally aware approach.[72]

Evolution of the Grand Chessboard

The issue of partners raises the question of where Russia and China now stand on Brzezinski's Grand Chessboard. In 1997 he argued that Europe was "Russia's only real geostrategic option—the option that could give Russia a realistic international role and also maximize the opportunity of transforming and socially modernizing itself." This was largely because the alternatives were unrealistic: a strategic condominium with the United States; restoration of the Soviet Union; and "anti-hegemonic" coalition-building.[73]

Brzezinski overestimated the rational-actor element in Russian foreign policy. Many of the ideas he dismissed as illogical and self-defeating have remained influential nonetheless. Although Moscow disavows any intention to revive the USSR, it is committed to projecting Russian power throughout the former Soviet space.[74] More than at any time since the collapse of the USSR, Russia's approach to its neighborhood reveals a patrimonial mentality.[75] Meanwhile it continues to peddle Primakovian ideas of "counterbalancing" coalitions directed against the United States, even in the face of lukewarm interest from China and India.[76] Russia has not only failed to take up its "only real geostrategic option," but has become increasingly alienated from a postmodern, institutionalized Europe.[77] Putin may insist that it is "an integral part of European civilization," but the integrationist vision has been put firmly on the back burner.[78]

In fact, Russia as a Eurasian actor has become much as Dmitri Trenin has described—a twenty-first-century version of the last Tsarist regime. It is geopolitically self-contained, "independent" in the sense that it is not beholden to the West, and assertive. It has few friends or allies but is not particularly concerned by this. It believes that it has considerable license on the Eurasian continent, even if the consequences of its actions turn out to be self-harming. Russia these days acts in the manner of a global power, one that feels able to ignore the constraints of its limited capacities through an unshakable faith in its central importance in world affairs.[79]

China, in many respects, remains a regional rather than a truly international player—a function of still modest capabilities, natural caution, and an introspective tradition in foreign policy. But the trends are unmistakable: China is increasingly thinking and acting global. The pace of this attitudinal change has been extraordinary and its implications are far-reaching. While Beijing's more ambitious outlook has yet to translate into overt rivalry with the United States, its activist and multidirectional foreign policy has reinforced the "pluralization" of the Eurasian geopolitical environment in ways that run directly counter to Brzezinski's vision of a Washington-led consensus.

Brzezinski was right in judging that "geopolitical pluralism in Eurasia as a whole will [be] neither . . . attainable nor stable without a deepening strategic understanding between America and China."[80] The difficulty is getting there. In a world without a defined international system—unipolar, multipolar or multilateral[81]—consensus is unlikely, particularly if it is to be achieved, as Brzezinski hoped, on the basis of China accepting a subordinate role as Washington's lieutenant.

Much more probable is that China will become steadily (if cautiously) more assertive, initially in East Asia and Central Asia, but eventually across much of Eurasia. It will engage constructively with the United States and Russia, but with a larger objective in mind: China as the eventual leader of a new continental consensus. This may take a very long time to materialize but would represent in its view an alternative route out of Eurasia's present anarchic condition and the constraints and shortcomings of American leadership. Such a Beijing-centered order would not be a hegemonic arrangement so much as a Concert of Great Powers, with China being *primus inter pares*.

For the time being, however, the Grand Chessboard will remain a theatre of untidy geopolitical interaction. The emergence of a strategic consensus, whether led by Washington or Beijing, is a distant prospect, and Brzezinski's dream of a Trans-Eurasian Security System[82] will remain just that—a dream.

The "brief window of historical opportunity" to achieve "global peace" on American terms[83] has shut and the "universalization" of Western norms and values appears as hopelessly utopian as ever.[84] But it will be decades, if ever, before China is able to substitute its own vision of order and prosperity.

The most plausible prognosis, then, is for an extended period of transition and uncertainty, dominated not by stable interstate relations—such as strategic partnerships—but by arrangements that are flexible and opportunistic. The players on the Grand Chessboard will remain much the same, but their interaction will change constantly in response to evolving regional and international conditions. Tactical expediency, not common strategic purpose, will be the hallmark of the new Eurasian geopolitics, and the Russia-China axis of convenience will reflect the spirit of the age.

CHAPTER TEN

CONCLUSION—FROM "STRATEGIC PARTNERSHIP" TO STRATEGIC TENSION

"Some Russian politicians like to taunt the West and Japan with the notion that Russia might team up with China in an anti-Western axis . . . the wariness and suspicion between these two neighbors (indeed, for many Russians, fear) and the strength of their separate interests in and with the West . . . make this an improbable scenario. It is more likely that, over time, nervousness about China's growing power could impel Russia to seek closer relations with the West."

—*Trilateral Commission Report on Russia*, 2006[1]

"Thus far, China has pursued a non-expansionist and non-aggressive foreign policy; this will continue over the next decade. Yet, China's size and growth rates pose a standing problem to Russia. The difference between the two countries' potentials has increased, and the problem of the depopulation and economic stagnation of Siberia and Russia's Far East is becoming psychologically difficult for Moscow to bear."

—SERGEI KARAGANOV, 2005[2]

The story of Sino-Russian relations over the past twenty years is a remarkable one. Two once bitter foes have developed a mutually beneficial partnership in the face of an unfortunate shared history, cultural and racial prejudice, political misunderstandings, ideological differences, and geopolitical rivalry. If ever there was a relationship that seemed destined to fail, this was it. It is easy to forget just how bad the atmosphere was even as late as the mid-1980s. In his memoirs, long-time Chinese foreign minister and vice-premier Qian Qichen described the thirty-year period before Gorbachev's famous 1989 visit to Beijing as "ten years of debate from 1959 to 1969, ten years of confrontation from 1969 to 1979, and ten years of negotiation from 1979 to 1989." During this time, "there were both cold and hot wars."[3] If anything, Qian was putting a gloss on things. The "ten years of debate" were a period of ideological and political confrontation, while the "ten years of negotiation" were also a very tense time, during which the Soviet occupation of Afghanistan, Moscow's support for the Vietnamese occupation of Cambodia, and heavy troop concentrations along the Sino-Soviet frontier were major sources of friction.[4]

In July 1986 in Vladivostok, Gorbachev articulated a new cooperative vision that became the basis of Sino-Russian rapprochement. However, the weight of mutual suspicion and the disintegration of the Soviet Union proved to be serious obstacles to progress, and initially Yeltsin's new Russia and a post-Tiananmen China regarded each other with considerable distaste. Although the relationship improved steadily in the course of the 1990s, attitudes remained highly ambivalent. Moscow and Beijing proclaimed their "strategic partnership" and commitment to a new "global multipolar order,"[5] yet senior Russian figures continued to speak openly of the "China threat." During this period, the Kremlin's world-view remained thoroughly Westerncentric and China occupied a secondary position in its foreign policy priorities.

The first years of the twenty-first century have witnessed the strengthening of positive trends, with past problems and difficulties being set aside and, in some cases, removed altogether. When Vladimir Putin and Hu Jintao declare that relations have never been better, they are making no idle boast. The "strategic partnership" is more multidimensional and substantial than at any time in the two countries' history, including the period of "unbreakable friendship." The degree of political, strategic, and normative convergence that has been achieved is impressive. Even economic ties, traditionally the weakest part of the relationship, have undergone considerable expansion in the last few years.

In summing up the Sino-Russian partnership, then, it is important to place any observations about its shortcomings in context. Not only is it a largely effective relationship in its own right, but it also represents the greatest Russian foreign policy achievement of the post-Soviet period, as well as a landmark in Beijing's strategy for China's "peaceful rise"/"peaceful development" and the building of a "harmonious world." It is, for all its faults, one of the more convincing examples of positive-sum international relations today.

Finding a middle way

Many observers of developments in Russia and China tend to evaluate them in terms of boom or bust, rise and fall.[6] This is similarly the case with views of the bilateral relationship, which, depending on one's perspective, is either a "strategic partnership for the twenty-first century,"[7] a de facto political-military alliance, or an increasingly difficult interaction whose contradictions foreshadow a potentially devastating schism.[8] This book has attempted to steer between these overdrawn assessments by recognizing the achievements of the relationship while highlighting its limitations. The progress between Russia and China has been exceptional. At the same time it is important not to swallow the official line that this is truly a strategic partnership, one that sets a new template for international relations.

This concluding chapter pulls together some of the themes explored earlier. It focuses on the key drivers and characteristics of Sino-Russian partnership, as well as the main obstacles inhibiting its development. For these elements, positive and negative, not only define the current relationship but will continue to shape it over coming decades.

A "normal" relationship

The first and perhaps most important point to make is that the partnership is surprisingly "normal." Like most relationships, it is a mix of good and bad, the successful along with the less successful. There is a strong public commitment to expanding cooperation, but this positive mindset is constantly undermined by prejudice, myopia, lack of political will, private agendas, and dysfunctional decisionmaking (especially on the Russian side).

The "strategic partnership" is not a "relationship of a new type,"[9] but one that is fairly conventional in structure, style, and thought. Moscow and Beijing have injected considerable realism into their interaction. They recognize that some problems and tensions remain, but this does not stop them from doing business. Although their summit statements are full of extravagant commitments, on the whole this is an unsentimental affair, driven less by ideational convergence than cold-eyed perceptions of national interests.

As such it represents something of a throwback to the nineteenth-century model of great-power relations. Palmerston's famous maxim, "nations have no permanent friends or allies, they only have permanent interests,"[10] might have been invented with today's Sino-Russian relationship in mind. The convergence between Moscow and Beijing is not the result of a mutual epiphany, intrinsic likemindedness, or empathy with "universal" principles of global interdependency, but reflects the abiding importance of traditional *realpolitik* imperatives: national security, power projection, management of the strategic balance. Ideas serve principally instrumental purposes—to rationalize and legitimize the pursuit of concrete national interests. Thus the neo-Westphalian emphasis on the primacy of state sovereignty supplies a normative veneer to efforts to contain the West's multidimensional influence while maximizing their own.

The primacy of geopolitics

Another indicator of the "normality" of Sino-Russian relations is that geopolitics retains its central importance in the world-view of both leaderships. Although many in the West are wont to dismiss geopolitics as anachronistic, it is an entirely logical modus operandi for two countries that possess vast territories, have suffered repeatedly from invasion, and have been accustomed at different times in their history to being the hegemon in their region (and, in Russia's case, beyond). The ruling elites in Moscow and Beijing have been brought up in a realist strategic culture that emphasizes the element of struggle in an often viciously competitive world, where power relations dominate at the expense of allegedly universal values. Given the volatility of the contemporary international environment, it is no surprise that Russia and China have been so wary of Western liberal conceptions of positive-sum interdependency.

The geopolitics of the twenty-first century is a much more sophisticated and variegated phenomenon than its nineteenth-century predecessor. Indeed, Moscow and Beijing eschew its vocabulary, preferring to couch their objectives in more modern and inclusive language. Soft power, interdependency, globalization, and "universal threats and challenges" have displaced zero-sum calculus, the balance of power, and spheres of influence as the lingua franca of international relations. Russia and China recognize, moreover, that traditional political-military means are blunt and unwieldy, all the more so when their respective military capabilities are either too degraded (in Russia's case) or underdeveloped (China) to be credible instruments of regional and global influence. Instead the two governments have played to their strengths: Russia relying on its control of energy and commodity resources; China on its vast potential as the world's fastest growing economy, at once mass producer and mass consumer.

As we noted at the outset, this "new geopolitics" is only new in the means employed to achieve its objectives, not in the constructs themselves, which remain much the same as in their nineteenth-century heyday. The preservation of geopolitical space and the projection of power remain central priorities in Moscow and Beijing. The significance both leaderships attach to Central Asia illustrates this dichotomy well; the terms of expression and institutional processes differ from the past, but the motivations do not. Geopolitical calculus is never far from the surface of bilateral relations as well. Russia views China as a potential long-term threat in the Russian Far East and Central Asia, while China values a stable relationship with Russia as a means of protecting its strategic rear in East and Central Asia.

Sino-Russian geopolitical convergence is predominantly defensive in spirit. At first sight this seems hard to square with the twin phenomena of China's spectacular rise and Russia's resurgence, or with the two countries' stated intention of establishing a new global order. Yet these two great powers associate with one another more out of a desire to enhance national security (in the widest sense of the term) and safeguard their position in the world than to facilitate the prosecution of an expansionist agenda. Although they retain assertive foreign policy instincts, neither side counts on the other for support when it comes to the hard issues of power projection. Russia has no interest in becoming embroiled in a crisis over Taiwan or taking sides in a possible Sino-American confrontation. China is equally averse to being exploited as a glorified bargaining chip in Russia's relations with the West, while it is increasingly a direct competitor in Central Asia. Crucially, both partners pay far more attention to the West than they do to each other.

A limited partnership

It serves Moscow and Beijing to talk up their relationship, both as a means of self-affirmation and to maximize their clout in a Western-dominated world. Russia, in particular, has used the China card to resurrect its international profile after the collapse of the USSR and the domestic and foreign policy disasters of the 1990s. Although the talking-up of the "strategic partnership" provokes international concern as well as respect, from Moscow's perspective this is not necessarily a bad outcome. As the Georgia crisis has demonstarted, many in the political establishment subscribe to Machiavelli's dictum that it is better to be feared than loved (and ignored).

But we should have no illusions about the warmth of Sino-Russian ties. This is not so much a strategic partnership as a limited partnership—limited in scope, in depth, and above all in mutual trust. Earlier chapters have focused on various fault-lines: uncertainty over the long-term future of the Russian Far East; Moscow's anxieties about China's economic capabilities; incipient rivalry in Central Asia; competing visions of strategic architecture in East Asia; and different perceptions of the world and China's and Russia's roles in it.

One of the relationship's most serious weaknesses is its lack of substance, notwithstanding the progress of recent years. Many achievements are relative and partial. Trade and economic ties are a fraction of China's with the United States, and Russia's with the EU. The much-trumpeted convergence on international issues such as Iran, Central Asia, and U.S. "hegemonism" masks significant differences of emphasis and of specific interests. If the importance of a relationship were measured by the frequency of high-level visits or number of intergovernmental agreements, then we might conclude that the Sino-Russian partnership was each country's most important foreign policy priority. Yet the lack of content in many of these agreements, on the rare occasions they are implemented, suggests that both sides are often just going through the motions.

The importance of asymmetry

Much of the difficulty in translating rhetoric into substance stems from the growing asymmetry in perspectives, interests, and capabilities. More than any other factor, this has hindered the development of a long-term common sense of purpose. The two sides have different, and often competing, agendas. Putin's absolute foreign policy priority is to restore Russia as a great global power. Such a mission implies fulfillment of two other key objectives: first, Russia's re-emergence as the "regional superpower"—the dominant player in the former Soviet space; and, second, international recognition of Russia as an equal partner in its relationships with the other major powers. Beijing's view on these matters is somewhat different. It holds a lower opinion of Russia's influence in world affairs. While it recognizes that Russia's importance has grown substantially under Putin, *in practice* it does not regard it as a genuinely global actor or even as the dominant player in the former Soviet Union.

These opposing perceptions have a critical impact on the policies of both countries. Russia's bullish self-perception translates into an assertive approach in Central Asia, an unhealthy fixation on the geopolitics of energy, "balancing" between Asia and Europe, and attempts to revive Russia-China-U.S. triangularism as a way of positioning Moscow at the center of global decisionmaking. Such an ambitious program is at odds with China's approach, which treats Russia as a secondary bilateral rather than primary global partner, and as a source of energy rather than a close collaborator in an anti-Western or non-Western caucus of great powers. The practical consequence of these divergent views is that Beijing sees diminishing constraints to expanding China's presence in Central Asia, sidelining Russia in the Asia-Pacific, or ignoring its pretensions to be the global pivot between the United States and China.

Although such asymmetry does not threaten an early crisis, it poses questions about the longer-term evolution of their relationship—of which more later. Suffice it to say here that the policy outcomes of this growing imbalance belie official claims that the two sides have "an identity of approaches . . . to the key global problems."[11] Russia and China may be able to agree on some general principles—notably the primacy of national sovereignty and the undesirability of U.S "unipolarity"—but they diverge on many levels: strategic orientation, general approach to international relations, and specific policies.

These differences translate into a mutual wariness. Beijing sees no reason to restrict its options by tying itself too closely to a state whose increasingly confrontational approach toward the West and the former Soviet Union is a major source of international tension. The last thing it needs as it seeks to persuade the world of its good intentions is "guilt by association." For Moscow, concerns about China's rise, not to mention its own Western-oriented world-view, make it cautious about committing itself to a state whose long-term intentions remain a mystery. The number of thorny issues involving one or the other or both parties—Taiwan, Central Asia, the geopolitics of energy, Iran, North Korea, Georgia—represents a further disincentive to a closer relationship. Underlying all this is a pervasive mistrust. Many Russian policymakers still operate on the basis of a potential "China threat" (military, economic, or demographic), while Beijing has learned from experience that Moscow can be a most unreliable partner.

A fragile friendship

One of the principal claims of the "strategic partnership," often cited as proof of its existence, is that Moscow and Beijing have managed to resolve all outstanding bilateral problems. In particular, the border agreement of October 2004 carried immense symbolic importance, signifying that the two countries had put the past behind them and could now turn their attention toward an active agenda of cooperation.

In fact, as a number of Russian commentators have pointed out, nothing has been settled definitively. Although the border agreement is a landmark achievement that opens the way to a more substantive relationship, it has done little to dampen Russian suspicions of Chinese irredentism.[12] There continues to be widespread suspicion that China will move into the near void of the Russian Far East as soon as it feels able, irrespective of what agreements or understandings have been reached. This may not happen for decades, particularly while the Communist leadership remains preoccupied with domestic modernization and reunification with Taiwan. But there may eventually come a time when these tasks are completed and Beijing turns its gaze elsewhere—and where more likely than the RFE, once part of the Qing Empire?

No matter how often the Chinese leadership denies any territorial ambitions, significant elements in the Russian elite will continue to believe the worst. This skepticism, founded in the conviction that "nature abhors a vacuum,"[13] reflects an abiding geopolitical mindset: Russia fears the Chinese strategic and demographic threat in its eastern provinces precisely because it considers such behavior as instinctive to any major power. "Those who can, do," especially when vital natural resources are at stake. On a less existential level, Russia's secondary importance in China's world-view focuses attention on the increasingly exploitative character of their relationship. Putin's complaint about the unbalanced structure of trade—Russian natural resources in exchange for low-grade Chinese manufactured goods[14]—reflects a larger concern that it is being "used" rather than valued as a partner.

Such attitudes have a knock-on effect. Since Russian policymakers never entirely trust the Chinese, they seek to limit their dependency on Beijing and explore strategic options elsewhere. In the Central Asian context, that means reinforcing political, economic, and military ties with key regional players such as Kazakhstan and Uzbekistan. In East Asia, it entails ideas of a Concert of Asia as well as expanding links with Japan as a counterbalance to Chinese influence. And globally it is reflected in the emphasis on Russia's "Europeanness" and pretensions to be the Eurasian bridge. Such ambiguous behavior heightens Chinese perceptions of Russia's limited utility as a partner, on whom it is unwise to depend too much. Beijing therefore takes out of the relationship what it can, without obsessing too much over the sincerity of their "friendship." What really matters in the end is the effective pursuit of specific interests: consolidating China's strategic rear and ensuring the flow of oil, timber, and other commodities.

The axis of convenience

Russia and China bring very different perspectives, assumptions, and expectations to the "strategic partnership." They emphasize the identity of their positions on bilateral and international questions, and yet there is virtually no area of the relationship where the two sides "are in complete agreement."[15] Closer inspection reveals apparent strengths to be weaknesses as well. Thus the positive of rapid trade expansion is diluted by the negative of its "distorted" structure. Agreement on the desirability of squeezing the Americans out of Central Asia is offset by different visions of a post-American order. Moscow and Beijing identify the need to challenge U.S. "hegemonic" power, but not how to do this. There is consensus on the utility of "strategic partnership," but not on what this entails, how it should develop, and on whose terms. In short, the Sino-Russian relationship is characterized by numerous gaps, misunderstandings, and dividing lines.

The wonder, then, is how both sides have managed to make it work. The Russians and Chinese retain ambivalent views of each other—to put things at their kindest—yet they have managed to rise above such misgivings to their mutual profit. How have they defied the odds?

The main answer is that the relationship is an axis of mutual *convenience*. It helps that neither side has excessive expectations of the other; at no stage has the relationship been overtaxed by optimism. Since the initial hopes were relatively modest, there has been limited scope for disappointment. The two sides have found each other useful, albeit in different ways, but have benefited from having no honeymoon period. Contrast this to the highs of Russia-U.S. relations in the aftermath of the Soviet collapse and post-9/11, both of which were followed by equally dramatic lows—the 1999 Kosovo crisis and the current state of semi-confrontation.[16]

The improvement in Sino-Russian relations has been steady and linear. There have been important signposts on the way: progressive demarcation of the border, along with security confidence-building measures; the 2001 Treaty of Good Neighborliness and Friendly Cooperation; the establishment and expansion of the SCO; the growth of economic ties. Much of the progress has been unspectacular, but it has always been *useful*. It has also been politically palatable. Whereas the Kremlin's relations with the United States have often been controversial, even China-critics within the Russian elite support the development of functional ties with Beijing.[17] Similarly, while RFE provincial administrations have opposed some of the detail of the border agreements, they have favored close economic links with China, if only as a means of survival.

The relationship has benefited greatly from having a ready external reference point. The dominant presence of the United States in regional and global affairs has been a critical bonding factor. Moscow and Beijing have been able to establish a common language and understanding at the level of broad, "anti-hegemonic" principle. In Russia this has deflected attention away from the "China threat," which even in the worst-case scenario is a remote one, to the more immediate priority of Western strategic "encroachment" in Russia's neighborhood. The "anti-relationship" dimension of the partnership is less important to China, but is still useful in enabling it to concentrate on what unites the two countries rather than what divides them. Thus incipient strategic competition in Central Asia can be masked by a (more or less) common front against a long-term American presence in the region. And problems in developing energy cooperation or the overall economic relationship do not seem quite so significant when the spotlight lies instead on the Bush administration's attempts to assert global leadership. In this context it matters relatively little that Beijing is more interested in cooperation than confrontation with Washington. By appearing to empathize with Moscow, it enhances the prospects of realizing priority objectives in their relationship.

Of course, to achieve such an accommodation both sides have had to stress the pluses of interaction while underplaying the minuses—a task demanding tolerance, the suspension of disbelief, and strategic patience, especially on the Chinese side. Beijing's muted reaction to the Kremlin's failure to consult over endorsement of the American troop deployment post-9/11 and to the cancellation of the Yukos-CNPC pipeline agreement reflected a willingness to take long views. The Chinese saw that a publicly negative reaction would achieve nothing, whereas a more conciliatory approach might reap dividends over time. This judgment proved correct in both cases.[18]

Moscow and Beijing have generally been able to manage their differences through the simple expedient of not airing them in public. In this respect, as in many others, their approach compares well with the dramatizing of Russia's disagreements with the West. Russia and China are direct competitors for influence in Central Asia. Yet there is barely a whisper of this, with both sides instead stressing the importance of cooperation against the "three evils" of terrorism, separatism, and extremism. Likewise Russian concerns over the latent Chinese demographic threat in the Far East are soft-pedaled through the institutional device of joint arrangements regulating cross-border traffic. The exercise of such discretion is facilitated by the closed nature of decision-making in both countries. Whereas transparency and accountability in Western democracies can constrain policymakers, this is not the case in Russia and China, where foreign policy has always been an elite preserve.[19]

Ultimately, the axis of convenience functions because Moscow and Beijing understand that it benefits them to rise above any differences for the sake of the greater—or at least more urgent—good. Crudely put, Russia "needs" China as a strategic counterweight to the United States, to maximize its foreign policy options, and in support of its aspirations to play an increasingly influential role in the world. China looks to Russia as a key source of oil, timber, and military technology. Although these objectives and the attitudes underpinning them are highly asymmetrical, both countries are bound by a common interest in pursuing cooperation rather than being distracted by a debilitating rivalry.

The future

This perception of a larger common interest is likely to stay in place over the next ten years. Although their partnership is becoming more unbalanced, Moscow and Beijing will continue to find it useful in meeting their primary objectives. Importantly, the tensions that exist between them are not immediately critical; there is no deal-breaker on the horizon. Strategic rivalry in Central Asia is in its preliminary stages, while the issue of Chinese "demographic expansion" has been defused for the time being. Both sides will work together against the threat of Islamic radicalism and reject Western criticisms of anti-democratic trends in their countries. The energy relationship may— or may not—develop according to the ambitious agreements signed by Putin and Hu at the March 2006 summit. But either way Russia will remain a significant source of Chinese oil imports. Military-to-military cooperation will expand following the qualified successes of "Peace Mission 2005" and "Peace Mission 2007." There will be public solidarity on most international issues, and the United States will remain a convenient focus for anti-hegemonic sentiment. Overall the logic of cooperation will continue to outweigh the negatives in the relationship.

Five scenarios for the long term

What is less clear is how the partnership will evolve beyond the next decade. Although many of the problems discussed in preceding chapters are unlikely to lead to an early crisis, neither will they simply recede with "goodwill" and the fading of historical memory.[20] On the contrary, they may become more difficult to manage as wider regional and global developments impact increasingly on the relationship.

Attempting to project longer-term trends is necessarily a speculative enterprise, because forecasts depend on a whole host of variables whose influence is difficult to predict. Nevertheless, scenario-building is useful in highlighting the binding forces and fault-lines in the relationship and in enabling us to contemplate a wide range of possibilities for its future development. With this in mind, we now turn our attention to five long-term scenarios for the evolution of the Sino-Russian "strategic partnership": (i) strategic convergence; (ii) political-military alliance; (iii) "the end of history"; (iv) confrontation; and (v) strategic tension.

Strategic convergence

Strategic convergence is about positive continuity. It is based on the assumption that Moscow and Beijing will build on the rapprochement of the post-Soviet period to enhance cooperation in all spheres and at all levels of the relationship. The deficiencies that inhibit ties and undermine mutual trust would gradually be reduced and eventually eliminated. Strategic convergence would be an essentially linear and relatively smooth process. Solutions to existing problems might require some time to take effect, perhaps many years, but would ultimately be successful. The end-result would be a fully functional strategic partnership, characterized by normative likemindedness and close policy coordination, but without threatening a renewed confrontation with the West along the lines of the Cold War.

Specifically, strategic convergence would involve the following elements. First, the two countries would hold virtually identical views on nearly all regional and global questions: Central Asia, engagement with the West, the Korean situation, energy security, Iran, Iraq. Second, convergence would mean the resolution of outstanding bilateral differences. The notion of a "China threat" would become obsolete; the RFE would become the center of a new regional boom, driven by transnational energy and infrastructural projects; and economic links would flourish. Third, there would be geopolitical accommodation. Russia and China would not only work together, and with other like-minded powers, to restrain American "hegemonic" power, but each would find its niche on the Eurasian continent. China would become the leading power in East Asia, Russia in Central Asia. However, Russia would also play a growing role in Asia-Pacific affairs, while China would become a more significant player in Central Asia. There would be no new "Great Game" between Moscow and Beijing, in large part because both would defuse any tensions through increasingly effective multilateral institutions such as the SCO.

Strategic convergence is one of the more convincing scenarios because it is a logical extrapolation of current positive trends in the relationship. Its core premise, that both sides will continue to find cooperation beneficial, is reasonable. As a non-confrontational course, it is also geopolitically flexible. It would not prevent Russia and China from developing good relations with other partners, such as the United States and EU.

However, plausible though this scenario is in many respects, it under-estimates several important factors. The first is the growing asymmetry in Russian and Chinese capabilities. The extraordinary speed of China's trans-formation and rise as a global power will ensure that an already unequal rela-tionship becomes even more so. This will lead to increased friction between Moscow and Beijing, no matter how hard the respective leaderships strive to contain this. Inevitably the Russian elite (and general population) will become more concerned about the fate of the "empty" eastern provinces. Meanwhile, China could revert to an overt Middle Kingdom mentality, lead-ing it to treat Russia in an offhand and neo-colonial fashion—as a source of raw materials and little else.

The second potentially disruptive element arises out of internal develop-ments in Russia and China. Strategic convergence assumes a stable and pros-perous future in both countries, yet there are many doubts on this score. Part-nership could hardly be insulated from the consequences of domestic political or economic crisis. Such a crisis could exacerbate extant nationalist sentiments—as happened between Russia and Japan in the 1990s—and find a ready outlet in interethnic tensions in the RFE or rivalry in Central Asia.[21] Moscow's continuing failure to address the socioeconomic problems of the RFE, in particular, provides a natural focus for re-emergent tensions.

Finally, the strategic convergence scenario does not give sufficient weight to external factors. Putin himself has admitted that "the disposition of polit-ical forces and development trends in the world" will have a crucial impact on the future of the partnership.[22] Sino-American relations will be especially piv-otal in this regard, where three alternative sub-plots suggest themselves. In the first, the dynamic between Beijing and Washington would remain much as it is: a mixture of cooperation, competition, and containment.[23] In the second, there would be a major escalation of tensions, almost certainly over Taiwan, resulting in confrontation between China and the United States. The third sub-plot envisages Sino-American rapprochement, involving the compre-hensive development of relations and even strategic convergence.

Of the three sub-plots, all but the first would cause Moscow considerable concern. Sino-American confrontation would force it to make undesirable foreign policy choices and expose the underlying fragility of its partnership with Beijing. Russia would almost certainly be asked to demonstrate its good faith by making good on hitherto rhetorical expressions of support. And yet it is difficult to imagine the Kremlin mortgaging Russia's future to an aggres-sive China, especially one which it suspects might next turn its attention to the RFE.

Still worse would be a strategic convergence between China and the United States. Russia's peripheral role in the Asia-Pacific would be further minimized, while its primacy in Central Asia would be challenged simultaneously by the world's two leading powers. Globally a Sino-American condominium would marginalize Russia from international decisionmaking, leaving it as little more than a secondary regional power. In this event, the "strategic partnership" would become a dead letter, replaced by a relationship of "tactical convenience" almost wholly on Beijing's terms.[24]

Chapter 7 referred to Moscow's preference for a state of "controlled tension" in East Asia. This idea is applicable to Russian foreign policy interests across the board. Moscow has a large stake in status quo international politics, whereby it can pretend to an influence that appears more impressive than it is. With China some way from completing its transition from regional to global power, and America's global leadership undermined by recent developments, Russia can exploit the partial vacuum of international authority to position itself as an "indispensable" power. But in the event of either open conflict or stabilization of the global geopolitical environment, the limits of Russian influence would be ruthlessly exposed. Sino-Russian strategic convergence is therefore best served if there are no radical changes, *for better or worse*, to the international system and its constituent interstate relations. Even in that case, however, partnership would be selective, limited, and asymmetrical.

Political-military alliance

One of the loose ends in the strategic convergence scenario is the matter of its endpoint. Assuming steady progress, could the relationship evolve eventually into an alliance arrangement: either an updated version of the 1950 Sino-Soviet treaty, or perhaps a more "modern" set-up, such as the "special" relationships the United States enjoys with the United Kingdom and Japan?

Moscow and Beijing have consistently denied any intention to enter into a formal alliance, which would signal a return to the bloc politics they publicly condemn. Such assurances may or may not be believed. What is more relevant is whether there exists any logic for transforming the "strategic partnership" into a *political-military alliance*. The answer is an emphatic no.

The biggest problem with an alliance is that it is an inflexible course of action that demands considerable commitment. It would, for example, oblige Russia and China to come to each other's aid in the event of conflict with a third party—such as the United States over Taiwan. This would be a Russian military planner's worst nightmare.[25] Despite the deterioration in Russia-U.S.

relations, Moscow has no interest in allowing this to reach the point of confrontation. Not only would it clearly lose from a new Cold War, but its political, economic, and security interests are closely tied to cooperative engagement with the West, and will remain so for decades.

An alliance would be similarly foolhardy for the Chinese. The whole point of Chinese foreign policy in the post-Mao era—"peaceful rise"/"peaceful development"—has been to create the optimum external conditions for domestic modernization. To this end Beijing has exerted great efforts to demonstrate that its intentions are benign. Forming an alliance with an aggressive Russia would send out all the wrong signals. It would also serve no useful purpose. China already receives advanced Russian weaponry and military technology, while any hopes of an end to the EU arms embargo would vanish if Beijing were to conclude an alliance with Moscow. Having Russia as an ally would not enhance China's capabilities, but would on the contrary overextend them. The United States and its allies, such as Japan, would adopt a much more aggressive strategic posture: at the very least, a policy of overt and comprehensive containment, but possibly extending to a more direct approach that could include interdiction of the sea-lanes on which the Chinese economy so depends.

Speculation about a possible alliance is somewhat hypothetical given latent Russian concerns about the "China threat," and PLA suspicions of Moscow's long-term agenda in Eurasia.[26] It is no coincidence that bilateral cooperation is least well developed in the military sphere.[27] The nascent state of military-to-military ties reflects a long history of strategic suspicion between the two countries. For all the public criticism of NATO enlargement and Western "encroachment" into the former Soviet Union, Russian planners still see China as the more likely (if still distant) *military* threat. They recall the disastrous failure of the original 1950 Sino-Soviet Treaty as well as the border clashes of 1969, a confrontation that almost went nuclear. It would require a massive change in strategic culture and circumstances for the option of an alliance to gain renewed consideration on either side.

"The end of history"

In his 1989 essay "The End of History?" the political philosopher Francis Fukuyama speculated that the world might be witnessing "the universalization of Western liberal democracy as the final form of human government."[28] Within a decade, however, it became apparent that the U.S.-led message of political democracy, a transparent market economy, and civil society had fallen on barren soil in many parts of the world, including Russia and China.[29]

Today, more than ever, Western norms are being challenged by other value-systems: Islamic fundamentalism, authoritarian and semi-authoritarian models of modernization, and even a revived radical socialism in Latin America.

It may seem odd, then, to suggest that the end of history thesis, and its central idea of a global democratic consensus, might one day serve as the basis for a new convergence between Moscow and Beijing. Under Putin there has been a return of state control in many areas of Russian public life and a significant rollback of political pluralism, while Hu Jintao has sought to reinforce the authority of the Chinese Communist Party and rein in the liberal "excesses" of the 1990s.[30] Nevertheless, a substantial if uneven process of modernization has occurred in both countries. The *personal* freedoms of the respective populations are greater than at any time in their history, and most Russians and Chinese enjoy a vastly improved quality of life.[31] Economic management remains dirigiste in many respects, but there has also been considerable liberalization. Deng Xiaoping's concern that the open window "would let in the flies"[32]—meaning that liberalization would admit subversive foreign influences—has been amply justified by the experience of both countries over the past two decades.

For the time being the ruling regimes in Moscow and Beijing have managed to enforce a distinction between economic modernization on the one hand and democratic political rights and a civil society on the other. But this may not always prove feasible. Many China-watchers, in particular, argue that the Communist Party will be unable to sustain the economic growth necessary for its continued legitimacy unless there is genuine democratization. The opening-up of the Chinese economy is already generating societal pressures so intense that Beijing will have no choice but to loosen state controls or else risk a political and social explosion.[33]

A similar argument can be applied to Russia. Putin's statism has been popular because it has coincided with prolonged economic growth—and also because of the Russian people's hankering for stability after the chaos of the late Gorbachev and Yeltsin years. However, this comfortable state of affairs may not last. Even if growth is maintained at present levels—a far from certain prospect—an ever more cosmopolitan Russian society could become increasingly exigent and demand a real political voice and choice.[34]

Extrapolating further, democratization in Russia and China could act as a force binding the two countries. A new democratic consensus might not only defuse tensions in the bilateral relationship, but also strengthen Moscow's and Beijing's engagement with the West. There would be a considerable diminution of geopolitical rivalries, and positive-sum interdependency would become the driving force of world politics. Sino-Russian strategic convergence would reinforce, and be reinforced by, a larger international convergence centered on "universal" (actually Western) democratic norms and values.

This optimistic scenario is not completely out of the question, yet it remains a distant prospect. The sheer difficulty of democratic transition in Russia and China makes it almost unimaginable that they would be able or willing to converge on such an alien basis. Even if political change were to proceed relatively smoothly in China—a huge assumption in itself—it is likely to be some decades before it becomes a democratic polity in the Western liberal sense. Similarly it would take at least a generation, most probably longer, for transparent, accountable government and a Western-style civil society to develop in Russia.

Somewhat more plausible is the emergence of some hybrid form of democratization.[35] There would be no democratic "end of history" as such and domestic reforms would be imperfect at best. Nevertheless, *the process itself* might stimulate a shift in strategic culture away from the traditional geopolitical emphasis on the balance of power and spheres of influence, toward a more inclusive international agenda. Against this backdrop Moscow and Beijing would find more to unite than divide them. But even this modified scenario depends on many variables unfolding in an almost entirely favorable way.

Confrontation

Unlike the "end of history," the *confrontation* scenario has historical precedent to support it. The Sino-Soviet rupture and the border clashes of 1969 showed how quickly and drastically the relationship can deteriorate. It was only ten years after the signing of the 1950 treaty that Khrushchev withdrew all Soviet advisers from China. And it was only a decade later that conflict erupted at several points along the border. A repeat of such worrying developments appears out of the question until one recalls that confrontation must also have seemed an extremely remote possibility when the original Sino-Soviet treaty was signed.

There are, of course, major differences between the current relationship and its context, and the situation in the 1960s: no Cold War; a far more globalized and interdependent world; more predictable and responsible leadership on both sides; and a much stronger bilateral relationship, politically and institutionally. All the same, it would be unwise to dismiss the potential for confrontation altogether. There are several variables, in particular, that merit consideration. The first is the unresolved situation in Central Asia and the RFE. In the former case there is an obvious conflict of interest between Moscow's determination to reassert regional leadership and Beijing's desire to maximize Chinese influence. Similarly, in the RFE, the combination of long-standing Russian security anxieties, Moscow's neglect of the region, local misgovernment, and the steady expansion of Chinese economic influence makes for an unstable mix.

The second potential source of trouble stems from heightened nationalist pressures. In China, the Communist Party has used nationalism as a legitimizing quasi-ideology to replace, in practice, an obsolete communist doctrine.[36] Given the uncertainties of political and economic transition, it is reasonable to allow for the possibility of a more assertive and even aggressive foreign policy. As the Sino-Russian relationship becomes increasingly unequal, Beijing may feel emboldened to take on new strategic challenges in Central Asia and the RFE.

Russia's nationalist conundrum in relation to China is somewhat different. A recession, such as might result from the depletion of energy resources[37] or a slump in world commodity prices, could revive a siege mentality whereby Russia turns in on itself and sees threats everywhere. In this event, a self-confident China would represent a natural object for Russian fears. The end-result could be a self-fulfilling prophecy: Moscow preempts the notional threat of Chinese "expansionism" by adopting a hostile strategic posture, which provokes Beijing to respond in kind.

Advocates of the confrontation theory identify a third source of potential trouble: acute political and economic crisis in China arising out of a failed modernization process. Some Russian scholars, in particular, envisage the implosion of the Communist regime and the country's consequent descent into chaos.[38] There would no longer be the capacity or will to deal with China's huge floating population. The subsequent upsurge in the numbers of Chinese in the RFE would create an incendiary situation. Low-level local disturbances could quickly escalate into something far more serious.

Although the confrontation scenario contains grains of truth, it is highly speculative and rests on a number of suspect assumptions. The most dubious is that the respective ruling elites would be willing to incur extraordinary risks, up to and including military confrontation with another nuclear weapons state. This is improbable. The mere threat of nuclearization, not to mention the mass of destructive conventional weaponry at hand, is a huge deterrent to military adventurism.

Second, both countries have far more effective means of projecting power and influence than military action. For example, while China is committed to playing a prominent role in Central Asia, it believes it can best do this by stressing security interdependency and pan-regional economic cooperation. Similarly, ratcheting up tensions in the RFE would run counter to Beijing's priority interests: to maximize imports of Russian oil and timber and to protect China's strategic rear.

Third, the confrontation scenario is based on the perception of China as a naturally expansionist power. The evidence to support this thesis is flimsy. Although there have been occasional periods of territorial expansion in its history—such as during the late Ming and early Qing dynasties—for the most part China has been an "imperialist" power only in the sense of seeing itself as the Middle Kingdom around which the rest of the universe revolved.[39] It would require a considerable psychological shift for Beijing to abandon its own imperial tradition for one that is not only alien, but likely to have uncertain and potentially catastrophic consequences.

Fourth, the "chaos theory" underestimates the regime's resilience and resourcefulness. Throughout the post-Mao era the CCP has consistently demonstrated a capacity to reinvent itself. Many of the problems China faces will defy solutions for decades, and its rulers will face a constant challenge of popular legitimacy. But it does not necessarily follow that everything will fall apart and revert to the anarchy of the warlord era of the 1920s and 1930s.[40]

Finally, even in the unlikely event of a meltdown in China, there is no historical basis to anticipate a mass influx of Chinese into Russia. Such fears reflect the paranoia and xenophobia of some Russians, rather than reality. In the Chinese mind, the RFE and Central Asia have always been "barbarian" outlands—places of exile and desolation, not sought-after prizes of conquest or even outflow areas.[41] This remains the case. The critical mass that might transform a source of tension into a *casus belli* is unlikely to emerge.

In sum, the interest of Moscow and Beijing in cooperation is so compelling and the consequences of conflict so grave that it is difficult to envisage confrontation between them, even in the longer term. Both sides understand that if this were somehow to occur, it would be a case of the ultimate negative-sum game, in which everyone stood to lose—and lose big.

Strategic tension

The improbability of conflict does not mean that the relationship will be without its problems in coming decades. In fact, the *strategic tension* scenario—the most persuasive in our view—rests on two central, if seemingly contradictory, propositions. First, the weaknesses and limitations of the relationship will become increasingly apparent. Second, bilateral tensions will remain broadly manageable and not escalate to the point of conflict.

Strategic tension is the direct opposite of *strategic convergence*. Whereas the latter imagines a steady improvement in relations, strategic tension foresees the strengthening of negative elements and a gradual alienation between Moscow and Beijing. Instead of the eventual emergence of a strategic partnership, it envisages an interaction shaped increasingly by tactical expediency. A limited partnership would become even more so, as Beijing restricts its cooperation with Russia to areas of particular need, such as ensuring the supply of energy and natural resources. There would be some coordination of international policies on a case-by-case basis, but no overall identity of view. The "fragile friendship" referred to earlier would become more brittle and superficial.

Under this scenario a number of fault-lines would open up over time. Rivalry in Central Asia would move from its present tacit phase to a more overt competition for influence.[42] Utterances about a "global multipolar order" and "anti-hegemonism" would become more formalistic, and Russia and China (in particular) would frame their foreign policies with little consultation or reference to each other. There would be a geopolitical accommodation of sorts, but based more on forbearance and necessity than common purpose. More likely, as China completes its transformation into a global actor, Russia would find itself steadily marginalized—a situation it would not accept with good grace. Russia's frustrations, for example over its inability to play an influential role in Asia-Pacific affairs, would be reflected in a growing, if impotent, resentment.

Strategic tension predicts a lack of positive movement in key areas, such as cooperation on energy and infrastructural projects. The structure of bilateral trade would become more unbalanced, and Russia would be reduced to a raw materials appendage of China. Arms transfers, once the mainstay of the economic relationship, would dwindle to near-insignificance, as Beijing looks elsewhere for more advanced technology and builds its own state-of-the-art weapons. Russian energy exports might even decline, as China further diversifies its sources of fossil fuels, explores new forms of energy, and engages seriously in energy efficiency. In general, the economic relationship would become more narrow and less substantial.

The demographic question would become more acute. Russian suspicions of Beijing's irredentist ambitions would increase and the normative gap would widen as both countries—particularly China—turn increasingly to the West as the main source of popular culture, high technology, and money.[43] Cultural and human contacts, along the lines of the much-publicized "Year of Russia in China" (2006) and "Year of China in Russia" (2007), would be limited to the official or quasi-official sphere and fail to resonate with the public in either country.[44]

Strategic tension offers a somewhat pessimistic vision of the future. Yet this scenario is more stable and functional than most. It posits that despite many unresolved problems, there will be no major crisis or sudden downturns. Like *strategic convergence*, it is based on the premise that Russia and China will find it beneficial to maintain some level of cooperation. There may be little in the way of creative approaches to problems and the quality of engagement will be somewhat disappointing, but Moscow and Beijing will find ways to muddle through. To this end they will lean heavily on the "suspension of disbelief" and continue pretending that their relationship is closer, warmer, and more substantial than is the case. Where necessary they will engage in crisis prevention, taking care to ensure that controversial issues such as the demographic imbalance and Chinese "illegal migration" do not become over-politicized. Moscow and Beijing will also manage their strategic rivalry, camouflaging competing agendas in the inclusive vocabulary of "common interests," "shared views," and "strategic partnership."

In this scenario the chief threat to the relationship would not be conflict or confrontation, but *indifference*.[45] As China becomes a global actor, engaging fully in all dimensions of international relations, the importance of partnership with Russia will diminish. The latter would no longer be viewed as a putative strategic partner (or rival), but as a power of tangential relevance to Chinese interests. Moscow could react to this state of affairs in one of two ways. It might persist in trying to position itself as a distinct strategic pole and "global balancer" between East and West. Or more pragmatically, given the limitations of Russian power, it could gravitate slowly back to Europe and become part of a larger Western consensus.[46]

In either case, the Sino-Russian relationship would become a reduced version of its current self. There would be no crisis, but also no strategic partnership. There would be a loss of momentum, and even occasional minor spats. But Moscow and Beijing would continue to do business with each other in selected areas—energy, natural resources, security confidence-building, strategic disarmament. The bilateral dynamic would be mistrustful and unsatisfactory in many respects, but also relatively predictable and useful.

Final thoughts

There is an understandable temptation to invest the Sino-Russian relationship with earth-shattering importance, to view it as nothing less than an axis that threatens the West's strategic supremacy and the global leadership of the United States.[47] From this belief emerges the conclusion that good relations between Moscow and Beijing are fundamentally inimical to the West's interests and to international stability.[48]

The reality is far more complex. The "strategic partnership" is the embodiment of ambivalence and ambiguity, in which little is as it seems. At heart it is an opportunistic arrangement—an *axis of convenience*. What drives it is not a shared vision, but expediency, the constantly shifting forces of national interests as defined by the respective ruling elites, and external circumstances. Moscow and Beijing believe that it benefits them to play up the importance and strength of their relationship. But at the same time its numerous limitations undermine this façade. The negating impulse that supplies much of the rationale for partnership will come under increasing pressure from within and without. In the longer term Moscow and Beijing will need to find a more constructive basis for engagement if the current *ersatz* strategic partnership is to become the genuine article. This will require not only vision, but also the political will and perseverance to see the task through.

It cannot be stressed too much that good relations between Russia and China do not pose a threat to the West. On the contrary, their partnership—such as it is—provides for a measure of stability and predictability that assists the building of a safer world. If James Baker's original vision of a security belt from Vancouver to Vladivostok[49] is ever to be realized, then some form of Sino-Russian entente or understanding will be integral to it. Conversely, a major deterioration in relations between Moscow and Beijing, marked by growing strategic rivalry, would add to the long list of destabilizing elements on the Eurasian continent and in the wider international environment. For all the anti-hegemonic and multipolar bombast, Russia and China's chief preoccupations and interests are with the West, not each other. Their partnership is intended to supplement, not supplant, cooperation with the United States and Europe.

The interaction between Moscow and Beijing, then, is neither as impressive as both sides claim, nor as threatening as Western critics allege. It is a great-power relationship of a somewhat traditional type, defined as much by its flaws and limitations as by its strengths and possibilities. As such it is quite "normal," although scarcely in the post-modern fashion of the early twenty-first century. The big question in coming decades is not whether such a partnership will undermine the established international order, but whether it can adapt and prosper in an ever more globalized, interdependent world.

NOTES

Chapter One

1. Joint Declaration of the Russian Federation and the People's Republic of China, Moscow, March 26, 2007—http://kremlin.ru/text/docs/2007/03/120807.shtml [accessed April 3, 2007]; www.fmprc.gov.cn/eng/wjdt/2649/t309361.htm.

2. Meeting with the International Valdai Discussion Club, Novo-Ogarevo, September 9, 2006—www.kremlin.ru/text/appears/2006/09/111114.shtml.

3. According to Dmitry Polikanov, director of Opinion and Market Research of PBN, 52.69 percent of Russians believed that China benefited the most from bilateral economic cooperation, compared with 8 percent who thought that Russia was the prime beneficiary, and 24.81 percent who believed that both sides benefited equally—"A measure of confidence," *Russia Profile*, vol. 3, no. 8 (October 2006): 18.

4. Ross Terrill notes that "[a]n empire is not merely a large and far-flung realm. As a political construction, it is by nature repressive, because it requires mechanisms and/or myths to hold together diverse cultures. . . . By this definition of empire, the PRC, an autocratic Chinese state ruling a land nearly half of which was historically inhabited by non-Chinese people, is indeed an empire of our time. . . . It consistently uses the techniques of the autocratic side of Chinese imperial tradition and its goals partake of imperial goals. The final dynasty, the Qing (Manchu), took form by military conquest, and it is this China that the Chinese Communists control today."—Ross Terrill, *The New Chinese Empire—and What It Means for the United States* (New York: Basic Books, 2004), pp. 2–3.

5. "China is big, it is growing, and it will influence the world in the years ahead. For the United States and the world, the essential question is—how will China use its influence? To answer that question, it is time to take our policy beyond opening doors to China's membership into the international system: We need to urge China to

become a *responsible stakeholder* in that system. China has a responsibility to strengthen the international system that has enabled its success." Deputy Secretary of State Robert B. Zoellick, "Whither China: From Membership to Responsibility?" Remarks to the National Committee on US-China Relations, New York City, September 21, 2005—www.state.gov/s/d/former/zoellick/rem/53682.htm.

6. See, for example, the Declaration of the SCO Summit in Astana, July 5, 2005: "Every people must be properly guaranteed to have the right to choose its own way of development"; "in the area of human rights it is necessary to respect strictly and consecutively historical traditions and national features of every people"—www.sectsco. org/html/00500.html.

7. Charles Krauthammer, "The Unipolar Moment," *Foreign Affairs*, vol. 70, no. 1 (1991): 22–33.

8. The idea of spheres or zones of "vital interests" was encapsulated by Andranik Migranyan in August 1992, when he claimed that Russia, rather than the United States or NATO, had the right to determine "the fate of the geopolitical space of the former USSR"—"Podlinnye i mnimye orientiry vo vneshnei politike," *Rossiiskaya gazeta*, August 4, 1992, p. 7.

9. The original Chinese expression is "to sleep in the same bed while dreaming different dreams." In an interesting inversion, however, the Chinese-American scholar Yu Bin has described Russia-China relations as a case of "dreaming the same dream from different beds"—presentation at a conference on "China's Growing International Security and Diplomatic Role," Wilton Park, U.K., March 17, 2007.

10. As the international relations theorist Hedley Bull put it, "the only rules or principles which, for those in the Hobbesian tradition, may be said to limit or circumscribe the behaviour of states in their relations with one another are rules of prudence or expediency. Thus agreements may be kept if it is expedient to keep them, but may be broken if it is not"—*The Anarchical Society: A Study of Order in World Politics*, 3d ed. (Basingstoke, U.K.: Palgrave, 2002), p. 24.

11. "A *society of states* (or international society) exists when a group of states, conscious of certain common interests and common values, form a society in the sense that they conceive themselves to be bound by a common set of rules in their relations with one another, and share in the working of common institutions"—Bull, *The Anarchical Society*, p. 13.

12. As enshrined in Article VII of the 1975 Helsinki Final Act (Conference on Security and Cooperation in Europe) and the United Nations Universal Declaration of Human Rights.

13. One of Russia's leading security thinkers in the post-Soviet era, Andrei Kokoshin, argued in 1998 that "Russia's international objectives should be targeted toward identifying and effectively utilizing its options for participating in assorted alliances and coalitions, learning to operate in a multidimensional environment while being governed by its own long-term national interests, and firmly sticking to its chosen course of policy"—*Soviet Strategic Thought, 1917-91* (MIT Press, 1998), p. 200.

Kokoshin did not elaborate on the practical difficulties of implementing such an all-encompassing approach.

14. Robert Kagan counterposes this "association of autocracies" with the Western-led "axis of democracy"—*The Return of History and the End of Dreams* (London: Atlantic Books, 2008), pp. 53, 71–74. See also Mark Leonard, *Divided World: The Struggle for Primacy in 2020* (London: Centre for European Reform, January 2007), p. 17; Peter Ferdinand, "Russia and China: Converging Responses to Globalization," *International Affairs*, vol. 83, no. 4 (July 2007): 655–80.

15. Most famously in the 2003 Goldman Sachs report by Dominic Wilson and Roopa Purushothaman, *Dreaming with BRICs: The Path to 2050* (Goldman Sachs Global Economics Paper 99, October).

16. For some instructive and, from a Russian perspective, depressing insights, see Julian Cooper, "Of BRICs and Brains: Comparing Russia with China, India, and Other Populous Emerging Economies," *Eurasian Geography and Economics*, vol. 47, no. 3 (May–June 2006): 255–84.

17. Dmitri Trenin and Bobo Lo, *The Landscape of Russian Foreign Policy Decision-Making* (Carnegie Moscow Center, 2005), p. 13.

18. The most well-known—and notorious—of these is Li Zhisui's *The Private Life of Chairman Mao* (London: Chatto & Windus, 1994).

19. See, for example, Olga Kryshtanovskaya on the attitudes of the *siloviki* (figures from the security apparatus, such as Putin)—*Anatomiya Rossiiskoi elity* (Moscow: Zakharov, 2004), pp. 262–86.

20. Trenin and Lo, *The Landscape of Russian Foreign Policy Decision-Making*, p. 9.

21. Mark Leonard, *What Does China Think?* (London: Fourth Estate, 2008), pp. 89–92.

22. John O'Loughlin and Paul F. Talbot, "Where in the World is Russia? Geopolitical Perceptions and Preferences of Ordinary Russians," *Eurasian Geography and Economics*, vol. 46, no.1 (January 2005), p. 47.

23. Speech at a conference on "Prospects for the Development of the Far East and Zaibaikal Region," Blagoveshchensk, July 21, 2000—www.kremlin.ru/text/appears/2000/07/28796.shtml.

24. Joshua Cooper Ramo defines the Beijing consensus as "a path for . . . nations around the world who are trying to figure out not simply how to develop their countries, but also how to fit into the international order in a way that allows them to be truly independent, to protect their way of life and political choices in a world with a single massively powerful centre of gravity"—*The Beijing Consensus* (London: Foreign Policy Centre, 2004), p. 3. In reality the essence of the Beijing consensus lies not in this somewhat tendentious summation, but in the conviction that economic and social modernization can take place in a non-democratic political system, such as in China (and, increasingly, Russia). Indeed, according to this understanding, the absence of Western-style political pluralism and civil society may actually facilitate modernization.

25. Wilson and Purushothaman, *Dreaming with BRICs*, p. 3.

26. Imperial Russia did not finally subjugate the whole of Central Asia until 1895. By the end of the 1860s, however, Tashkent and Samarkand had fallen to the Tsar, whose forces were repeatedly victorious against the emirate of Bokhara (annexed in 1873) and the khanate of Kokand (annexed in 1876).

27. Samuel P. Huntington, *The Clash of Civilizations and the Remaking of World Order* (London: Touchstone Books, 1998).

28. The ten-member ASEAN also has ten dialogue partners, with which it meets to discuss issues of mutual interest. They are Australia, Canada, China, the European Union, India, Japan, the Republic of Korea, New Zealand, the United States, and Russia. The EAS has a very similar membership—the ten ASEAN member-states, plus Australia, China, Japan, India, New Zealand, and the Republic of Korea. Russia, which is currently only an observer, has pushed hard for full membership of the EAS with Chinese support, but so far without success.

29. Zbigniew Brzezinski, *The Grand Chessboard: American Primacy and Its Geostrategic Imperatives* (New York: Basic Books, 1997).

Chapter Two

1. http://intermongol.net/poetry/foreign.html.

2. Joint Declaration of the Russian Federation and the People's Republic of China, Moscow, March 26, 2007—http://kremlin.ru/text/docs/2007/03/120807.shtml [accessed April 3, 2007]; www.fmprc.gov.cn/eng/wjdt/2649/t309361.htm.

3. A VTsIOM survey of August 2007 asked respondents to identify the countries with which Russia would have "the most friendly relations in the next 10–15 years." China ranked first with 21 percent, ahead of Belarus and Germany (both 12 percent) and the United States (10 percent). Its negative rating was also very low. Only 3 percent of those surveyed thought that Russia's "most tense and hostile" relations would be with China, compared with the United States (24 percent) and Georgia (19 percent). See VTsIOM Press Release no. 756, August 30, 2007—http://wciom.ru/novosti/press-vypuski/press-vypusk/single/8690.html.

4. See Alexander Lukin, *The Bear Watches the Dragon: Russia's Perceptions of China and the Evolution of Russia–Chinese Relations since the Eighteenth Century* (Armonk, New York: M.E. Sharpe, 2003), pp. 20–25.

5. Marshall T. Poe, *The Russian Moment in World History* (Princeton University Press, 2003), pp. 26–27.

6. That said, there were times when Russia was able to "break out." For example, Isaiah Berlin argued that its "triumph over Napoleon and the march to Paris . . . made Russia aware of her national unity, and generated in her a sense of herself as a great European nation, recognized as such; as being no longer a despised collection of barbarians teeming behind a Chinese wall, sunk in medieval darkness, half-heartedly and

clumsily imitating foreign models"—"Birth of the Russian Intelligentsia," in Isaiah Berlin, *Russian Thinkers* (Harmondsworth, U.K.: Penguin, 1978), p. 118.

7. Lukin, *The Bear Watches the Dragon*, pp. 16–17.

8. Iver Neumann, *Russia and the Idea of Europe* (London and New York: Routledge, 1996), p. 25.

9. For an example of this overwrought distinction, see Fedor Shelov-Kovedyaev, "Russia, an Engine for Global Development," *Russia in Global Affairs*, vol. 4, no. 3 (July–September 2006). Shelov-Kovedyaev was briefly deputy foreign minister at the beginning of the Yeltsin era.

10. Russian perceptions of Chinese backwardness are fueled by incidents such as the leakage of 100 tonnes of benzene into the Songhua river in December 2005. The accident, which resulted from an explosion in a petrochemical factory in Jilin city, contaminated water supplies along a 190 km stretch of the river. It also caused a major scare in Khabarovsk, which lies on the Amur into which the Songhua flows. See "Toxic Leak Reaches Russian City," BBC News item—http://news.bbc.co.uk/1/hi/world/europe/4551842.stm.

11. Soloviev acknowledges this tacitly in his poem "Pan-Mongolism" by referring to "China's defeated walls." Genghis Khan launched his campaign against the Jin Dynasty in northern China in 1211, 25 years before the Mongols under Batu Khan attacked the Rus principalities in force.

12. Su Fenglin, "Questions Regarding Past and Present Sino-Russian Cultural Exchange," in Akihiro Iwashita, *Eager Eyes Fixed on Eurasia*, vol. 2 (Sapporo: Hokkaido University, 2007), p. 94.

13. Under the Treaty of Nerchinsk, Russia gave up its claims to the Amur valley in return for substantial caravan trading rights—see John J. Stephan, *The Russian Far East: A History* (Stanford University Press, 1994), pp. 31–32.

14. Victor Larin, "Russia's Eastern Border: Last Outpost of Europe or Base for Asian Expansion?" *Russian Expert Review*, vol. 18, no. 4 (October 2006)—www.rusrev.org/eng/content/review/print.asp?ids=136&ida=1464.

15. See Jonathan D. Spence, *The Search for Modern China*, 2d ed. (New York and London: W.W. Norton, 1999), pp. 117–19. Most of the imperial court's external dealings were handled by the Ministry of Rituals, which looked after relations with China's Asian neighbors, or by the imperial household, which supervised European missionary activity.

16. See Stephan, *The Russian Far East*, pp. 41–45.

17. The remarkable Nikolai Nikolaevich Muraviev-Amursky (1830–81) was primarily responsible for extending the borders of the Russian Empire to the Pacific Ocean. As governor-general of Eastern Siberia between 1847 and 1861, he secured the unwilling agreement of the Chinese to the 1858 Treaty of Aigun, which effectively reversed the outcomes of the Treaty of Nerchinsk and paved the way for the full annexation of the Russian Far East—see Stephan, *The Russian Far East*, pp. 44–49.

18. Westernizing thinkers such as Petr Chaadaev, Vissarion Belinsky, and Aleksandr Herzen were especially scathing about China, seeing it as the embodiment of stagnation and tyranny. However, even Sinophiles such as Prince Ukhtomsky believed that Russia had a god-given duty to rule over China in order to "protect" its civilization—see Lukin, *The Bear Watches the Dragon*, pp. 16–32.

19. Under the Treaty of Aigun, Russia regained the left bank of the Amur that had been conceded at Nerchinsk in 1689. Two years later at the Treaty of Peking, the Manchus surrendered the right bank of the Amur river, and large parts of Manchuria and Ussuri, now Primorsky, *krai* (territory). The Treaty of Tarbagatai in 1864 saw the further transfer of 440,000 square kilometers in the region northwest of Xinjiang province, up to and including Lake Balkhash.

20. Lukin, *The Bear Watches the Dragon*, pp. 69–70.

21. Gilbert Rozman, "Russia in Northeast Asia: In Search of a Strategy," in *Russian Foreign Policy in the 21st Century and the Shadow of the Past*, edited by Robert Legvold (Columbia University Press, 2007), p. 362.

22. The term "unbreakable friendship" appears to have first been used in a letter from Stalin to Mao, dated September 2, 1951. Stalin wrote that "the Soviet Union's unbreakable friendship with the People's Republic of China serves and will continue to serve as a guarantee of peace in the Far East against all and any aggressors"—http://hrono.rspu.ryazan.ru/libris/stalin/16-45.html.

23. For a superb account of the May 4, 1919, movement and its impact on modern China, read Rana Mitter, *A Bitter Revolution: China's Struggle with the Modern World* (Oxford University Press, 2005).

24. Ibid., pp. 136–38.

25. Gao Wenqian, *Zhou Enlai: The Last Perfect Revolutionary* (New York: Public Affairs, 2007), p. 32.

26. In 1921 the People's Government of Mongolia was formed; this was followed three years later by the establishment of the Mongolian People's Republic.

27. See Robert Service, *Stalin: A Biography* (Basingstoke and Oxford: Macmillan, 2004), pp. 391–92; also William Taubman, *Khrushchev: The Man and His Era* (New York and London: W.W. Norton, 2003), pp. 335–36.

28. Mao especially resented Stalin's insistence that he take the fight against Chiang Kai-shek to the cities (in accordance with Leninist rather than Chinese tradition). The result was the near-extinction of the Communists as an effective fighting force, a fate avoided only by the decision to undertake the Long March. See Li Zhisui, *The Private Life of Chairman Mao* (London: Chatto & Windus, 1994), p. 116.

29. In the "Xian incident" in December 1936, the northern warlord Zhang Xueliang imprisoned a visiting Chiang Kai-shek, demanding that he give priority to fighting the Japanese instead of pursuing the civil war against the Communists. The latter were keen to eliminate Chiang Kai-shek or, at the very least, form a united anti-Japanese front with Zhang Xueliang. Stalin, however, insisted that they secure

Chiang's release and put themselves under his leadership—see Spence, *The Search for Modern China*, pp. 408–09.

30. Bates Gill and Taeho Kim, *China's Arms Acquisitions from Abroad: A Quest for "Superb and Secret Weapons,"* SIPRI Research Report 11 (Oxford University Press, 1995), pp. 28–29.

31. Taubman, *Khrushchev*, pp. 336–37.

32. Li Zhisui, who was Mao's personal doctor for twenty-two years, recalls that the Chinese leader "turned bitterly hostile, convinced that the new Soviet leader had violated a fundamental tenet of revolutionary morality—that of unswerving loyalty"—*The Private Life of Chairman Mao*, p. 115. The expression "China's Khrushchev" was later used to condemn senior leaders who might threaten Mao's hold on power. These included head of state Liu Shaoqi, who was purged during the Cultural Revolution—Gao, *Zhou Enlai*, p. 92.

33. The Chinese claimed that the abrupt Soviet withdrawal caused the cancellation of 343 major contracts and 257 other technical projects—Spence, *The Search for Modern China*, p. 558.

34. Taubman, *Khrushchev*, p. 605.

35. Gill and Kim, *China's Arms Acquisitions from Abroad*, pp. 29–30.

36. "During the 1960s . . . China found herself without a significant ally and confronted with the possibility of hostile action by either or both super powers . . . the spectre of a super-power 'condominium' against China seemed a very real possibility"—Barry Naughton, "The Third Front: Defense Industrialization in the Chinese Interior," *The China Quarterly*, no. 115 (September 1988): 368.

37. Mao claimed that the Soviet system was no longer socialist, but "social imperialist." References to Soviet revisionism ended when Deng Xiaoping came to power in 1979—see Carol Lee Hamrin, "China Reassesses the Superpowers," *Pacific Affairs*, vol. 56, no. 2 (Summer 1983): 222.

38. *The Military Balance 1969-1970* (London: Institute for Strategic Studies), pp. 7, 39.

39. The most serious clashes took place on Damansky/Zhenbao island in the Ussuri river, on the border between Heilongjiang and Primorye, in March 1969.

40. Igor Sutyagin, "The Soviet–Chinese conflict of 1969," in *The Role of Nuclear Weapons and Its Possible Future Missions*, www.otan.nato.int/acad/fellow/94-96/sutyagin/02-03.htm.

41. Lukin, *The Bear Watches the Dragon*, pp. 140–43.

42. See chapter 9.

43. Qian Qichen, long-time Chinese foreign minister (1988–98) and later vice premier (1993–2003), referred in this connection to the saying "It takes more than one cold day to freeze the ice three feet thick"—*Ten Episodes in China's Diplomacy* (New York: Harper Collins, 2005), p. 1.

44. The discrepancy between Soviet-Japanese and Soviet-Chinese trade was particularly pronounced during the late 1970s and early 1980s. Whereas the former was in

the range of U.S.$4–5 billion, the latter was some ten to fifteen times lower. Sino-Soviet trade did not pass the one billion dollar mark until 1984—see *Direction of Trade Statistics Yearbook* (Washington, DC: International Monetary Fund, 1985), p. 392.

45. Before Gorbachev, Khrushchev was the last Soviet leader to visit China—in September 1959 for the 10th anniversary of the founding of the PRC.

46. See Yevgeny Primakov, *Russian Crossroads: Toward the New Millennium* (Yale University Press, 2004), p. 36.

47. Mikhail Gorbachev, *Izbrannye rechi i stati*, vol. 4 (Moscow: Politizdat, 1987), p. 27.

48. Vladivostok was opened to visits by foreigners on January 1, 1992.

49. Gorbachev, *Izbrannye rechi i stati*, vol. 7 (Moscow: Politizdat, 1987), p. 558.

50. New thinking reflected a profound shift from an emphasis on superpower rivalry to ideas of interdependency and international cooperation. Gorbachev asserted that security could only be achieved through "political decisions and disarmament." Security, he insisted, was "indivisible. It is either equal security for all or none at all. The only solid foundation for security is the recognition of the interests of all peoples and countries and of their equality in international affairs." Crucially, Gorbachev called for the de-ideologization of international relations: "ideological differences should not be transferred to the sphere of interstate relations, nor should foreign policy be subordinate to them, for ideologies may be poles apart, whereas the interest of survival and prevention of war stand universal and supreme"—Mikhail Gorbachev, *Perestroika: New Thinking for Our Country and the World* (London: Collins, 1987), pp. 141–43.

51. In his memoirs, Qian Qichen emphasized that the Chinese side insisted on the removal of "three major barriers" as a precondition to improving relations: (i) the downsizing of Soviet troops present in Mongolia and along the Sino-Soviet frontier; (ii) Soviet withdrawal from Afghanistan; and (iii) the success of Soviet efforts to persuade the Vietnamese to withdraw their troops from Cambodia—*Ten Episodes in China's Diplomacy*, pp. 5–17.

52. Primakov recounts that "the Chinese leadership feared this visit might excite the imagination of the intelligentsia and particularly the students, who obviously were stirred by the introduction of glasnost in the Soviet Union. As it turned out, their fears were well founded. Passions flared in Beijing during Gorbachev's visit"—*Russian Crossroads*, p. 36.

53. The disputed areas included numerous islands in the Amur, Ussuri, and Argun rivers, as well as the Tumen river basin. The most intractable question concerned two islands in the Amur river, Bolshoi Ussuriisky (Heixiazi in Chinese) and Tarabarov (Yinlong), whose sovereignty was not resolved until 2004.

54. John Gittings, *The Changing Face of China: From Mao to Market* (Oxford University Press, 2005), pp. 246–49.

55. One prominent Chinese scholar puts it succinctly, if simplistically: "The Chinese reform program focused on economics, a strategy that led to twenty-five years of

sustained growth. In contrast, the Soviet reform program was aimed at politics as well as economics, a strategy that led to the disintegration of the Union of Soviet Socialist Republics in 1991"—Shiping Hua, "The Deng Reforms (1978–1992) and the Gorbachev Reforms (1985–1991) Revisited: A Political Discourse Analysis," *Problems of Post-Communism*, vol. 53, no. 3 (May/June 2006): 1.

56. The "Washington consensus" is a common but much misunderstood term. Originally applied to economic reforms aimed at Latin American countries in the late 1980s, it became synonymous with IMF market prescriptions for Eastern Europe and the former Soviet Union during the 1990s. In Russia it was the (foreign) scapegoat for the ineptitude and corruption of the Yeltsin administration.

57. In an address at the Russian foreign ministry in October 1992, Yeltsin called for a "full-scale foreign policy with multiple vectors. While developing our relations with Western countries . . . we must work with equal diligence in the eastern direction"—"Chto skazal Eltsin rossiiskim diplomatam," *Rossiiskie vesti*, October 29, 1992, p. 1.

58. "Rossiya khochet otkryt novuyu eru v otnosheniyakh s Kitaem," *Kommersant*, December 18, 1992—www.kommersant.ru/doc.aspx?DocsID=33872.

59. Jeanne L. Wilson, *Strategic Partners: Russian-Chinese Relations in the Post-Soviet Era* (Armonk, New York: M.E. Sharpe, 2004), pp. 27–30.

60. The Russian Foreign Policy Concept of June 2000 observed that the main task in Sino-Russian relations was to bring "the scale of economic interaction in conformity with the level of political relations"—*Kontseptsiya vneshnei politiki Rossiiskoi Federatsii*, June 28, 2000 (www.mid.ru/ns-osndoc.nsf/0e9272befa34209743256c630042d1aa/fd86620b371b0cf7432569fb004872a7?OpenDocument).

61. See table 5-1. The figures for Russia-Japan trade over the same period were marginally lower, falling from a high of nearly U.S.$6 billion in 1995 to around U.S.$4 billion in 1998–99—www.economy.gov.ru/merit/japan.html [August 21, 2003].

62. During 1991–92, several Russian political figures visited Taipei, including Gavriil Popov, head of the Moscow City Soviet (later mayor); Deputy Finance Minister Andrei Zverev; and Valentin Fedorov, the governor of Sakhalin *oblast* (province). The most serious initiative came from former deputy premier Oleg Lobov, who received Taiwan's deputy foreign minister, Chang Hsiao-yen, in April 1992. Lobov and Chang signed a protocol on establishing joint Economic and Cultural Coordination Commissions, which was subsequently confirmed by Yeltsin. Following vigorous protests from Beijing, Yeltsin issued a decree in September 1992 affirming Moscow's commitment to the "one China policy," effectively killing off the Lobov initiative. See Lukin, *The Bear Watches the Dragon*, pp. 267–71.

63. Predictably, the stiffest criticisms of the West came at the December 1999 summit, which took place in the aftermath of the NATO military intervention in Kosovo, Washington's decision to proceed with a strategic missile defense program, and President Clinton's strident criticisms of the second post-Soviet Chechen war. The summit statement asserted that a "negative momentum in international relations continues to grow" and criticized attempts to force the international community "to accept

a unipolar world pattern and a single model of culture, value concepts and ideology." In this connection, it highlighted the "jeopardizing of the sovereignty of independent states using the concepts of 'human rights are superior to sovereignty' and 'humanitarian intervention'"—www.mfa.gov.cn/eng/wjb/zzjg/dozys/gjlb/3220/3221/t16727.htm.

64. In his *Midnight Diaries*, Yeltsin referred nostalgically to his trips to China: "It was in China, during all of our visits abroad, where we felt ourselves to be light and free. We came away from Beijing with only the happiest of emotions." On an even more personal note, Yeltsin described one occasion when he and Jiang "sat in the armchairs and contemplated our long lives already gone by. We remembered the past, the 1950s, when [Jiang] did his student apprenticeship in Moscow at ZIL automakers. We recalled those hungry, merry student days"—Boris Yeltsin, *Midnight Diaries* (London: Phoenix, 2000), pp. 162–63.

65. Li Peng studied at the Moscow Power Institute for six years (1948–54). Qian Qichen completed his studies at the Central Communist Youth League School in 1954–55, before serving two diplomatic postings in Moscow (1955–62 and 1972–74).

66. Rajan Menon defined "strategic convergence" as "multifaceted cooperation and a convergence of views and interests on important questions of international security"—"The Strategic Convergence between Russia and China," *Survival*, vol. 39, no. 2 (Summer 1997): 101–25.

67. See note 53 above.

68. Wilson, *Strategic Partners*, pp. 104–05, 107–08.

69. Ilya Bulavinov, "Rossiya i Kitai mezhdu proshlym i budushchim," *Kommersant-Daily*, April 22, 1997, p. 2.

70. Igor Korotchenko, "Igor Rodionov vystupil za sozdanie oboronnogo soyuza stran SNG," *Nezavisimaya gazeta*, December 26, 1996.

71. Ironically, one of Russia's leading Sinologists argued this in conversation with the author in December 1995, focusing in particular on the "danger" of Chinatowns sprouting in Russia as in the West.

72. Former prime minister Gaidar regularly emphasized the dichotomy between the "democratic West" and the "poor, non-democratic countries" of the East, of which China was the most threatening—see Lukin, *The Bear Watches the Dragon*, pp. 242–44.

73. Bobo Lo, *Russian Foreign Policy in the Post-Soviet Era: Reality, Illusion and Mythmaking* (Basingstoke and New York: Palgrave Macmillan, 2002), pp. 18–19.

74. Yeltsin's vision of "integration," however, might be described as "selective" or *à la carte*—Russia would be part of the Western community, but on an equal footing with the United States and Europe.

75. Yeltsin's divide-and-rule approach to power led him to favor different elite factions at different times. The resultant uncertainty was most evident in domestic policymaking, but it also crippled—or "anaesthetized"—Russian foreign policy, which came to be defined principally by a resentful but impotent conservatism—see Lo, *Russian Foreign Policy in the Post-Soviet Era*, p. 154.

76. As distinct from Kozyrev's vision of cooperative multipolarity. In 1994, well before Primakov made multipolarity fashionable, Kozyrev insisted that the United States "does not have the capability to rule alone." The only adequate response to the challenges of the post-Cold War world was "a joint strategy of partnership between the democratic nations of East and West"—Andrei Kozyrev, "The Lagging Partnership," *Foreign Affairs*, vol. 73, no. 3 (May/June 1994): 64

77. Primakov spoke of Russia's role as a "counterbalance to the negative trends . . . in international relations"—"Rossiya ishchet novoe mesto v mire," interview in *Izvestiya*, March 6, 1996, p. 3.

78. Foreign Minister Igor Ivanov noted soon after his appointment in September 1998 that Russia should aim to establish "favorable external conditions for solving our internal problems" ("Ya ne predstavlyayu sebe nashu stranu v sostave NATO," interview in *Izvestiya*, October 28, 1998, p. 6). Similarly, in his report to the 15th Party Congress in September 1997, Jiang Zemin emphasized that "in carrying out the socialist modernization program, we need a long-term peaceful international environment and, above all . . . to maintain good relations with . . . surrounding countries"—www.fas.org/news/china/1997/970912-prc.htm.

79. Wang Jisi, "China's Changing Role in Asia," The Atlantic Council of the United States, January 2004, p. 15.

80. Yu Bin argues that the Sino-Russian relationship is currently more equal than at any time in its history. However, he also notes that China "is rising to be more powerful for the first time in [its] 400-year history of interactions"—"In the Search for a Normal Relationship: China and Russia into the 21st Century," *China and Eurasia Forum Quarterly*, vol. 5, no. 4 (November 2007): 79.

81. This is particularly the case in relation to the Russian Far East—see Viktor Larin, "Tikhookeanskaya politika Rossii v nachale XXI veka," *Svobodnaya Mysl*, vol. 10, no. 2 (February 2007): 142.

82. In October 1860 British and French troops occupied the imperial capital and burned down the Summer Palace. The emperor was forced to express "his deep regret" for the arrest and killing of British emissaries; the northern city of Tianjin was made a treaty port, and the Kowloon peninsula was given to Hong Kong. See Spence, *The Search for Modern China*, pp.182–83.

83. Qian, *Ten Episodes of Chinese Diplomacy*, p. 189.

84. This was a recurrent theme in the author's conversations with Chinese diplomats in Moscow during the second half of the 1990s.

Chapter Three

1. Hu Jintao and Vladimir Putin joint press conference, Kremlin, July 1, 2005—www.kremlin.ru/appears/2005/07/01/1908_type63377type63380_90631.shtml.

2. Meeting with the International Valdai Discussion Club, Novo-Ogarevo, September 9, 2006—www.kremlin.ru/text/appears/2006/09/111114.shtml.

3. Putin's remarks to the Valdai Discussion Club, Novo-Ogarevo, September 9, 2006—www.kremlin.ru/text/appears/2006/09/111114.shtml.

4. http://english.mofcom.gov.cn/aarticle/statistic/ie/200802/20080205371690. html. There is a substantial discrepancy between the Russian and Chinese figures for bilateral trade. In 2007 Russian customs statistics (www.customs.ru/ru/stats/stats/popup. php?id286=364) estimated total trade at nearly U.S.$41 billion, compared to the Chinese figure of U.S.$48 billion. (In 2006 the respective numbers were U.S.$29 billion and U.S.$33 billion.) One of China's leading Russianists suggested to the author in May 2007 that this discrepancy was due to the "failure" of Russian customs to count all cross-border trade. In May 2003 Putin estimated "unofficial" trade to be in the order of U.S.$10 billion—www.strana.ru/print/182092.html.

5. In 2006 China accounted for 6.8 percent of Russia's total trade, a long way behind the European Union's 54.8 percent, but ahead of Ukraine (5.7 percent), Turkey (4.0 percent), and the United States (3.6 percent)—http://trade.ec.europe.eu/doclib/docs/2006/september/tradoc_113440.pdf.

6. A senior official from China's National Development and Reform Commission (NDRC) estimated that oil imports from Russia grew from just over 2 million tonnes in 2003—less than two percent of total oil imports—to 12 million tonnes in 2006, around 10 percent of total imports—Zhang Jianping, "Chinese Perceptions of Energy Security and Strategy for the Future of Northeast Asia," *ERINA Report*, vol. 77 (September 2007), p. 6. Other sources, including China's Ministry of Commerce, give a higher figure for Russian oil exports to China in 2006—15 million tonnes—but the percentage remains about the same (11 percent)—http://english. mofcom.gov.cn/aarticle/newsrelease/significantnews/200703/20070304.

7. In an interesting twist on an old theme, Russian foreign minister Sergei Lavrov advocates a "global 'orchestra' of the leading powers . . . [that] would be able to consolidate the collective principles in global politics and put an end to the practice of creating various kinds of balances of forces in the world"—"The Rise of Asia, and the Eastern Vector of Russia's Foreign Policy," *Russia in Global Affairs* (July/September 2006): 76.

8. Author's conversation with Ji Zhiye, deputy director of the China Institute of Contemporary International Relations, Beijing, May 2007.

9. Andrei Piontkovsky, *East or West? Russia's Identity Crisis in Foreign Policy* (London: Foreign Policy Centre, January 2006), p. 18.

10. Peter Ferdinand, "Russia and China: Converging Responses to Globalization," *International Affairs*, vol. 3, no. 4 (July 2007): 674; Willy Wo-Lap Lam, *Chinese Politics in the Hu Jintao Era: New Leaders, New Challenges* (Armonk and London: M.E. Sharpe, 2006), p. 272.

11. Viktor Larin, "Tikhookeanskaya politika Rossii v nachale XXI veka," *Svobodnaya mysl*, vol. 10, no. 2 (February 2007): 144.

12. Putin's assertion of Russia's "European-ness" was a consistent theme throughout his presidency. While still acting president, he declared that "we are part of Western European culture. In this lie our values. Wherever our people live, in the Far East

or in the south, we are Europeans"—*Ot pervogo litsa: razgovory s Vladimirom Putinym* (Moscow: Vagrius, 2000), p. 156.

13. These included agreements between Transneft and China National Petroleum Company; Rosneft and CNPC; Gazprom and CNPC; United Energy Systems (Russia) and the State Grid Corporation of China; Russian Railways and the Railways Ministry of the PRC—www.kremlin. ru/eng/text/docs/103472.html [accessed March 31, 2006].

14. For example, at different times during the 1990s Moscow claimed "strategic partnerships" with China, India, Iran, CIS member-states, and, most implausibly, Cuba. See Bobo Lo, *Russian Foreign Policy in the Post-Soviet Era: Reality, Illusion and Mythmaking* (Basingstoke and New York: Palgrave Macmillan, 2002), p. 94.

15. Andrei Kokoshin, *Soviet Strategic Thought, 1917-91* (MIT Press, 1998), pp. 199–200.

16. Although the Bolshevik regime managed to survive the Russian Civil War (1918–21) and the intervention of the foreign powers, it was left very weak and isolated. The situation gradually improved in the course of the 1920s. Stalin's mass industrialization of the country after 1929 was critical in raising the Soviet Union's international profile and influence (even if this was viewed almost entirely negatively).

17. Strictly speaking, the Sino-Japanese relationship is not a "strategic partnership" so much as a "strategic relationship of mutual benefit"—a somewhat cooler appellation. See remarks by PRC State Councillor Tang Jiaxuan in Tokyo, February 21, 2008—www.fmprc.gov.cn/eng/wjdt/zyjh/t413428.htm.

18. The Russian foreign ministry refers to partnership rather than strategic partnership, despite noting that the relationship with the United States is "one of the priorities of Russian foreign policy and an important factor in international stability," December 21, 2007—www.mid.ru/ns-rsam.nsf/1f773bcd33ec925d432569e7004196 dd/16dd0c29bd3ef47343256a2c0040bfb4?OpenDocument.

19. www.russia.org.cn/eng.

20. Ibid.

21. Joint Declaration of the Russian Federation and People's Republic of China, March 21, 2006—www.mid.ru/ns-rasia.nsf/1083b7937ae580ae432569e7004199c2/432569d80021985fc3257139002ea173?OpenDocument.

22. See Mikhail Margelov, "Russian-Chinese Relations: At Their Peak?" *International Affairs* (Moscow), vol. 49, no. 6 (2003): 80.

23. Foreign Minister Lavrov claims that Russia's role as a "cultural and civilizational bridge . . . is needed as never before." Perhaps mindful of the occasionally negative connotations of the term "bridge," he adds that "it would be more correct to speak of interfacing the interests of the West and the East for the purpose of solving acute problems of the present"—"The Rise of Asia," p. 71.

24. Jeanne L. Wilson, *Strategic Partners: Russian–Chinese Relations in the Post-Soviet Era* (Armonk, New York: M.E. Sharpe, 2004), pp. 11–12.

25. Alexander Lukin observes that "Russians cannot get used to the idea that Chinese, who were poorer than Russians only 2 or 3 decades ago, are now becoming

richer and are looking on Russians not as 'older brothers,' but as strange people, European in appearance, but somehow unable to better their life"—"Facing China," *Kommersant.ru*, November 9, 2006.

26. Pavel Felgengauer, *The Moscow Times*, July 19, 2001, cited in Frank Umbach, "The Wounded Bear and the Rising Dragon. The Sino-Russian Relationship at the Beginning of the 21st Century: A View from Europe," *Asia Europe Journal*, vol. 2, no. 1 (2004): 58.

27. See Joshua Kurlantzick, "China's Charm: Implications of Chinese Soft Power," Carnegie Endowment for International Peace, Washington, DC, *Policy Brief* 47 (June 2006), p. 4.

28. For example, China's trade with Africa has leapt from nearly U.S.$10 billion in 2000 to U.S.$74 billion in 2007, making it the continent's third largest trading partner after the United States and France—http://english.mofcom.gov.cn/aarticle/statistic/ie/200802/20080205371690.html; Chris Alden, *Terms of Endearment: From Marxism to Materials*, CLSA Special Report on China and Africa, Shanghai, September 2006, p. 5.

29. James McGregor, *One Billion Customers: Lessons from the Front Lines of Doing Business in China* (London: Nicholas Brealey Publishing, 2005).

30. Vladimir Skosyrev, "Neudobny sosed," *Nezavisimaya gazeta*, March 26, 2007—www.ng.ru.

31. In 2006 Sino-Iranian trade exceeded U.S.$14 billion, a 43 percent increase on the previous year (www.iran.ru/rus/news_iran.php?act=news_by_id&news_id=48227). By contrast, Russia's trade with Iran in the same year was a very modest U.S.$2 billion (Putin press conference, Tehran, October 16, 2007—www.kremlin.ru/appears/2007/10/16/1747_type63377type63380_148431.shtml).

32. This remains the case, despite some evidence of a tougher line in Moscow toward the Iranians and EU disenchantment with Chinese obstructiveness in the UN Security Council. Crucially, the Russian presence is highly visible in the two most controversial areas of Tehran's security policy: its active nuclear program and its acquisition of advanced weaponry.

33. Zheng Bijian, "China's New Road of Peaceful Rise and Chinese–U.S. Relations," address at the Brookings Institution, June 16, 2005, in *China's Peaceful Rise: Speeches of Zheng Bijian, 1997-2005* (Brookings, 2005), pp. 8–9.

34. As Zhao Huasheng has observed, "China's greatest strategic pressure comes from possible U.S. support of Taiwan independence and U.S. containment of China's rise. . . . Therefore, China concentrates its main resources on the major strategic front and keeps other fronts stable and tranquil"—"China, Russia, and the United States: Prospects for Cooperation in Central Asia," *China-Eurasia Forum Quarterly* (February 2005), p. 23.

35. In 2006 China imported more oil from Saudi Arabia (16.4 percent of total imports), Angola (16.2 percent) and Iran (11.6 percent) than from Russia (11 percent)—http ://bg2.mofcom.gov.cn/aarticle/aboutchina/economy/200703/20070304453287.html.

36. Nevertheless, one does not have to look very far to find alarmist references to "hundreds of thousands" and even "millions" of Chinese flooding into the Russian Far East and directions west. See Vladimir Ovchinsky, "The 21st Century Mafia: Made in China," *Russia in Global Affairs* (January–March 2007): 91; also Alexander Khramchikhin, "'Tretim raduyushchimsya' byt ne udastsya," *Nezavisimoe voennoe obozrenie* (December 22, 2006) (http://nvo.ng.ru).

37. "Rossiyane khotyat druzhit s Kitaem, no na rasstoyanii" ("Russians want to make friends with China, but from a distance"), VTsIOM press release no. 674, April 16, 2007. It is important to distinguish between Russian attitudes toward China in the abstract and responses toward the Chinese at a directly personal level.

38. A number of scholars have pointed out that the local RFE economies cannot absorb hundreds of thousands of new workers—see Fiona Hill and Clifford Gaddy, *Siberian Curse: How Communist Planners Left Russia Out in the Cold* (Brookings, 2003), pp. 186–87; also Larin, "Tikhookeanskaya politika Rossii v nachale XXI veka," p. 152.

39. Remarks by General Yury Baluyevsky, then chief of the Russian General Staff—Aleksei Georgiev, "Uchenie. 'Mirnaya missiya' vypolnima," *Voenno-promyshlenny kurer,* August 24, 2005, p. 2.

40. Although Zhejiang province is not especially close to Taiwan, it is part of the Nanjing Military District, which covers Taiwan. By contrast, the Shandong peninsula falls within the purview of the Jinan Military District.

41. *East Asian Strategic Review 2006* (Tokyo: National Institute for Defense Studies, June 2006), p. 183.

42. I am indebted for this information to a senior military attaché based in Beijing.

43. See Shinji Hyodo, "Russia, China and the SCO: 'Peace Mission 2007,'" *RUSI Newsbrief,* July 6, 2007 (www.rusi.org/publication/newbrief/ref:A468E5C6Cb8B26/); also Erica Marat, "Fissures in the Force—Multilateral Cooperation Can Only Go So Far," *Jane's Intelligence Review,* June 2007, jir.janes.com.

44. In practice, "strategic resources" can cover almost anything, but they certainly include energy and other natural resources.

45. Nicklas Norling, "Russia's Energy Leverage Over China and the Sinopec-Rosneft Deal," *China and Eurasia Forum Quarterly* (November 2006), p. 35.

46. The biggest success story of cooperation between Russia and foreign multinationals is the creation of TNK-BP in September 2003, establishing Russia's third largest oil company (measured by level of production and reserves)—www.tnk-bp.com/company/history/. More recently, however, TNK-BP has been riven by a bitter dispute between BP and its Russian partners.

47. The barring of CNPC from the Slavneft auction in December 2002 foreshadowed CNOOC's (China National Offshore Oil Company) failed take-over of UNOCAL in 2005.

48. *Moscow Defense Brief,* no. 1, 2006, Centre for Analysis of Strategies and Technologies (CAST)—www.isn.ethz.ch/pubs/ph/details.cfm?v21=109021&lng=en&v33=106753&id=15841. In May 2006 a senior European diplomat insisted to the author

that Russian arms sales to China had been considerably under-reported and amounted, in fact, to around U.S.$4 billion.

49. Umbach, "The Wounded Bear and the Rising Dragon," pp. 59–60.

50. Dmitri Trenin has pointed out the contradictions in Moscow's position: on the one hand, portraying the deployment as a direct threat to Russian security; on the other, dismissing it as having no effect on the Russian deterrent—see "Russia's Strategic Choices," Carnegie Endowment for International Peace, Washington, DC, *Policy Brief* 50 (May 2007), p. 2.

51. The opportunity for Moscow to exploit potential divisions is all the greater given a coalition government in Germany. Chancellor Merkel supports missile defense—albeit within the NATO framework rather than as a U.S.-driven bilateral arrangement. Her coalition partners, however, do not. Kurt Beck, leader of the Social Democratic Party, has asserted that "we do not need new missiles in Europe. . . . There are enough problems around the world for us to deal with . . . poverty, climate change, and terrorism. New missiles and weapons systems will not help there"—"Debatte über US-Abwehrschild: Beck stellt sich gegen Merkel," *Süddeutsche Zeitung*, March 18, 2007—www.sueddeutsche.de/deutschland/artikel/162/106056/.

52. A PRC foreign ministry press release of May 21, 2007, emphasized China's particular concern about "emerging missile defense cooperation in [the] Asia-Pacific region" and reaffirmed its opposition to external attempts "to provide assistance or protection related to missile defense to the Taiwan region of China by whatever means"—www.fmprc.gov.cn/eng/wjb/zzjg/jks/kjlc/wkdd/ddfy/t321027.htm.

53. According to the International Institute for Strategic Studies, China has 46 intercontinental ballistic missiles (ICBMs), 35 intermediate-range ballistic missiles (IRBMs), and 725 short-range ballistic missiles (SRBMs)—see *The Military Balance 2007* (London: IISS), p. 346.

54. Following the Clinton administration's decision in 1999 to proceed with development of national missile defense (NMD), Moscow pushed hard for a pan-European theatre missile defense system in which Russia would play a central role. See "Zamysel i etapy sozdaniya obshcheevropeiskoi sistemy protivoraketnoi oborony"—www.armscontrol.ru/start/rus/docs/evropro.htm; also "NATO–Russia TMD Cooperation in New Phase" (www.armscontrol.org/act/2003_06/briefs_june 03.asp).

55. "Russia proposes space arms treaty," BBC News, February 12, 2008—http://news.bbc.co.uk/1/hi/world/europe/7240796.stm. For details of the proposal, see Foreign Minister Lavrov's speech to the UN Disarmament Conference in Geneva, February 12, 2008—www.mid.ru/brp_4.nsf/2fee282eb6df40e643256999005e6e8c/ef2b bef46ae2344ec32573ed006c584c?OpenDocument.

56. Putin described the decision as "mistaken," and stated that it would have no impact on Russia's nuclear weapons capabilities—see "Vladimir Putin Believes in Positive Development of Russian–US Relations," December 24, 2001—http://english.pravda.ru/world/2001/12/24/24294.html.

57. Article 8 of the July 2001 Sino-Russian statement described the ABM Treaty as a "cornerstone of strategic stability and the basis of the reduction of strategic offensive weapons"—Russian foreign ministry press release of July 18, 2001.

58. Putin press conference at the conclusion of the Russia-U.S. summit in Sochi, April 6, 2008— www.kremlin.ru/text/appears/2008/04/163185.shtml. See also "Russia stresses new demand on missile defense . . . ," *RFE/RL Newsline*, April 9, 2008— www.rferl.org/newsline/2008/04/090408.asp.

59. Yevgeny Primakov thus recalls: "During meetings with Jiang Zemin in Beijing early in 2002, I understood that China's leaders were seriously concerned about [the US bases in Central Asia]. They feel that the long-term U.S. military presence in Central Asia completes the process of surrounding China with U.S. bases"—*Russian Crossroads: Toward the New Millennium* (Yale University Press, 2004), p. 71. See also Vasily Mikheev, ed., *Kitai: ugrozy, riski, vyzovy razvitiyu* (Carnegie Moscow Center, 2005), p. 365.

60. Andrei Kozyrev, "The Lagging Partnership," *Foreign Affairs*, May/June 1994; Andrei Kozyrev, "Rossiya i SShA: Partnerstvo ne prezhdevremenno, a zapazdyvaet," *Izvestiya*, vol. 73, no. 3 (March 11, 1994): 66.

61. See Robert Kagan, *The Return of History and the End of Dreams* (London: Atlantic Books, 2008), pp. 59–80; Mark Leonard, *Divided World: The Struggle for Primacy in 2020* (London: Centre for European Reform, January 2007), pp. 18–19.

62. In 1859 Marx identified "the Asiatic, ancient, feudal and modern bourgeois modes of production . . . as epochs marking progress in the economic development of society"—*A Contribution to the Critique of Political Economy* (London: Lawrence and Wishart, 1971), p. 21. Yegor Gaidar saw a more modern Asiatic mode of production as defined by "the absence of fully-fledged private property; the indivisibility of property and administrative power with the latter undoubtedly dominating; power relations as a ubiquitous substitute for all social relations; the economic and political dominance of the bureaucracy (often taking despotic forms)"—*Gosudarstvo i evolyutsiya: kak otdelit sobstvennost ot vlasti i povysit blagosostoyanie Rossiyan* (St. Petersburg: Nauka, 1997), p. 11.

63. In a press conference in London on July 12, 2004, then defense minister Sergei Ivanov claimed that Western democracy was not the only model of democracy: "if Western democracy exists, then so does Eastern democracy and Southern democracy"—http://rian.ru/politics/20040712/631635.html.

64. Ferdinand, "Russia and China: Converging Responses to Globalization," pp. 673–74.

65. In this connection, Yu Bin notes that "the 20th century presented at least three distinctive 'Wests' for China: Europe, Russia, and America. Each plays a vital role for China's internal and external dynamics. All exert powerful influence in the minds of Chinese political and intellectual elites. None, however, has completely overwhelmed China's own self-identity as a non-Western cultural-political paradigm"—in "China Perceives Two Wests: Europe-America-China Trio into the 21st Century—and Some

Modest Proposals for 'Empire Moderation,'" paper for a conference on "History as a Guide to the New International Order—The United States, Europe and China in the 21st Century," St. Anne's College, Oxford, August 12–18, 2006, pp. 40–41.

66. See Yong Deng, "Remolding Great Power Politics: China's Strategic Partnerships with Russia, the European Union, and India," *Journal of Strategic Studies*, vol. 30, no. 4–5 (August 2007): 882. On January 12, 2007, Russia and China joined forces in vetoing a draft resolution calling on the Myanmar government to cease attacks on ethnic minorities and begin a political dialogue with the opposition—www.un.org/News/Press/docs/2007/sc8939.doc.htm.

67. Zbigniew Brzezinski, *The Grand Chessboard: American Primacy and Its Geostrategic Imperatives* (New York: Basic Books, 1997), pp. 116–17, 170; see also Umbach, "The Wounded Bear and the Rising Dragon," p. 47.

68. Dmitri Trenin, "'Osennii marafon' Vladimira Putina i rozhdenie Rossiiskoi vneshepoliticheskoi strategii," *Carnegie Moscow Center Briefing Paper*, November 15, 2001, p. 6.

69. In September 2006 a senior Kremlin official told a group of foreign academics and journalists, including the author, that he opposed expansion of the G-8 into a G-14 that would bring in some of the key non-Western powers, such as China, India, Brazil, and South Africa. By way of justification, he argued that although the G-8 countries might have their policy differences, they nevertheless "spoke a common language" and retained special bonds of trust. This "special atmosphere" had apparently dissipated when they were joined by the non-G8 leaders (including Hu Jintao and Indian prime minister Manmohan Singh).

70. Several scholars have remarked on the converging pattern of voting between the two countries in the UN—see Peter Ferdinand, "Sunset, Sunrise: Russia and China Construct a New Relationship," *International Affairs*, vol. 83, no. 5 (September 2007): 858–60.

71. The fact that this modernization model is called Beijing consensus (rather than, say, Moscow consensus) is unlikely to gladden Russian policymakers. Unsurprisingly, Putin and senior Russian figures do not use this term whenever they speak of Sino-Russian likemindedness.

Chapter Four

1. Speech at a conference on "Prospects for the Development of the Far East and Zaibaikal Region," Blagoveshchensk, July 21, 2000—www.kremlin.ru/text/appears/2000/07/28796.shtml.

2. As Dmitri Trenin has observed, "it is precisely this eastern dimension that makes it Russia rather than Muscovy"—*The End of Eurasia: Russia on the Border Between Geopolitics and Globalization* (Carnegie Moscow Center, 2001), p. 227.

3. F. Kazemzadeh, review of W.S. Vucinich, ed., *Russia and Asia: Essays on the Influence of Russia on the Asian People* (Stanford, Calif.: Hoover Institution, 1972), in *The Journal of Modern History*, vol. 47, no. 1 (March 1975): 173.

4. Viktor Larin divides the Russian Far East into three zones of economic activity: (i) a "technical-industrial production" zone, covering Khabarovsk, Komsomolsk-na-Amure, and the Pacific port of Vanino; (ii) a "resources-raw materials" zone in southern Sakhalin; and (iii) a "scientific-educational, finance, and transport-leisure" zone in southern Primorye—"Tikhookeanskaya politika Rossii v nachale XXI veka," *Svobodnaya mysl*, vol. 10, no. 2 (February 2007): 153.

5. "For the [Russian] state, the Far East has always been a military outpost and strategic border in the east that ought to be adapted and defended, but not necessarily economically developed"—Victor Larin, "Russia's Eastern Border: Last Outpost of Europe or Base for Asian Expansion?" *Russian Expert Review*, vol. 18, no. 4 (October 2006).

6. Dmitri Trenin, *Integratsiya i identichnost: Rossiya kak "novy zapad"* (Moscow: Evropa, 2006), pp. 169–70.

7. As Rajan Menon has memorably put it, "buffoons, crooks and xenophobes have attained positions of power with enough regularity to give bad governance deep roots"—"The Sick Man of Asia: Russia's Endangered Far East," *The National Interest* (Fall 2003): 99.

8. This was a frequent refrain in the author's conversations with Russian policymakers and commentators in the 1990s.

9. www.kremlin.ru/text/appears/2000/07/28796.shtml.

10. During his initial address to the Federal Assembly (both houses of parliament) on July 8, 2000, Putin emphasized strengthening the "executive vertical" and ensuring "a single united strategy of domestic and foreign policy"—www.kremlin.ru/appears/2000/07/08/0000_type63372type63374type82634_28782.shtml.

11. Nazdratenko was appointed minister of fisheries in February 2001, before being transferred to the position of deputy secretary of the Security Council in April 2003—this in the wake of a scandal over the alleged misallocation of fishing quotas—www.nupi.no/cgi-win/Russland/krono.exe?6215.

12. In his Blagoveshchensk speech, Putin complained that local production was often uncompetitive and warned that failure to take advantage of the region's natural resources would leave them mere observers of the housing boom on "the opposite bank of the river," that is, in China—www.kremlin.ru/text/appears/2000/07/28796.shtml.

13. Elizabeth Wishnick, "The Securitization of Chinese Migration to the Russian Far East: Rhetoric and Reality," paper presented at the annual meeting of the International Studies Association, Honolulu, March 5, 2005, www.idss-nts.org/PDF/Elizabeth_Wishnick.pdf, p. 2. The Vladivostok journalist Oleg Ssylka estimates that the population has now fallen to just over 6 million—"Authorities Hope Chinese Investment Will Bring Russians Back to Far East," *Russian Analytical Digest*, no. 7 (October 3, 2006): 13.

14. Fiona Hill and Clifford Gaddy, *The Siberian Curse: How Communist Planners Left Russia Out in the Cold* (Brookings, 2003), p. 177.

15. Wishnick, "The Securitization of Chinese Migration to the Russian Far East."

16. Alex Rodriguez, "Chinese reap opportunity, rancor in Russia's Far East," *Chicago Tribune*, September 27, 2006—www.amren.com/mtnews/archives/2006/09/chinese_reap_op.php.

17. The figure of 2 million was already being suggested to the author in the mid-1990s. Although there is a huge disparity in the various estimates of the Chinese population in the RFE, all agree that it has increased substantially during the post-Soviet period. One anonymous—and absurd—estimate speaks of "three million illegal Chinese immigrants"—"The Round-Up of Chinese Immigrants," *Sakhalin Times*, March 25, 2005.

18. "Russian official alarmed by illegal immigration from China," *RIA Novosti*, March 15, 2006—http://en.rian.ru/russia/20060315/44341799-print.html.

19. Vladimir Portyakov, "Russian Vector in the Global Chinese Migration," *Far Eastern Affairs*, vol. 34, no.1 (2006): 51.

20. Sergei Prikhodko, "My ne dolzhny boyatsya Kitaya," *Izvestiya*, March 21, 2004—www.izvestia.ru/russia/article45535/index.html.

21. Mikhail Alexseev, "Chinese Migration into Primorskii Krai: Economic Effects and Interethnic Hostility," in *Slavic Eurasia's Integration into the World Economy and Community*, edited by Shinichiro Tabata and Akihiro Iwashita (Sapporo: Slavic Research Center, Hokkaido University, 2004), p. 336.

22. Vilya Gelbras, "Chinese Migration in Russia," *Russia in Global Affairs*, vol. 3, no. 2 (April–June 2005): 179.

23. Alexseev, "Chinese Migration into Primorskii Krai," pp. 333–34; see also interview with Vladimir Suprun, "Kitai rvetsya v Ameriku, no zaselyaet Sibir," *Nezavisimaya gazeta*, February 6, 2006—www.ng.ru/printed/65122.

24. Gelbras, "Chinese Migration in Russia," p. 179.

25. Ibid., p. 182.

26. "O roznichnykh rynkakh i o vnesenii izmenenii v trudovoi kodeks Rossiiskoi Federatsii," Federal Law no. 271-F3, December 30, 2006—www.rg.ru/2007/01/10/ryhki-dok.html.

27. Several sources confirmed this development to the author during his visit to Vladivostok and Khabarovsk in June 2007.

28. Article 5 of the Passport Law of April 29, 2006—www.bjreview.com.cn/document/txt/2006-12/14/content_50706.htm.

29. The U.S.$1.35 billion Baltic Pearl project in St. Petersburg is symptomatic of the westward trend—and greater ambition—of Chinese investment in Russia.

30. Gelbras, "Chinese Migration in Russia," p. 182.

31. Ibid., pp. 183–86.

32. See Putin's remarks to the Russia-China Economic Forum in March 2006—www.kremlin.ru/appears/2006/03/22/1123_type63376type63377type82634_103471.shtml.

33. See note 3 to chapter 1.

34. We should note, however, that *as consumers* local inhabitants appreciate the price-lowering impact of Chinese consumer imports. They were quick to complain about rising prices following the introduction of the law on market trading—author's conversations in Vladivostok, June 2007.

35. "The Round-Up of Chinese Immigrants."

36. Alexseev estimates that nearly 90 percent of migrant laborers in Primorye work in these sectors—"Chinese Migration into Primorskii Krai," p. 336.

37. According to Oleg Ssylka, local employers "can pay the Chinese workers half as much as the Russian average and still the salaries are attractive by Chinese standards. In the forestry sector, Chinese workers earn 5,000-6,000 rubles a month and can accumulate 50,000 rubles a year. With these funds they can build a house in China and pay for their children's education"—"Authorities Hope Chinese Investment Will Bring Russians Back to Far East," p. 14.

38. In an interesting survey from 2003, RFE inhabitants attributed the following major characteristics to the Chinese: "hardworking"—65 percent of respondents (compared with 48 percent for the Japanese, 49 percent for the Koreans, 5 percent for people from the Caucasus, 20 percent for Russians); "enterprising"—48 percent (29 percent/Japanese, 31 percent/Koreans, 34 percent/Caucasus, 16 percent/Russians); "cunning"—41 percent (11:17:40:15 percent); and "aggression"—21 percent (4:6:63:12 percent). In other words, Chinese were seen as the most hardworking, enterprising, cunning, and also the most aggressive of the Asian peoples. Strikingly, the "cunning" rating for the Chinese exceeds even that of people from the Caucasus, the most common target for Russian xenophobia. See Viktor Larin, *V teni prosnu-vshegosya drakona* (Vladivostok: Dalnauka, 2006), pp. 274–75.

39. In fact, the extent of mixed Sino-Russian marriages in the RFE may have been exaggerated. According to some estimates, over the past decade only 200 Chinese have formally married Russian women and remained in the country—Ssylka, "Authorities Hope Chinese Investment Will Bring Russians Back to Far East," p. 14. On the other hand, the Russian market trading law of December 2006 (see note 26 above) has allegedly led to an increase in marriages between "Chinese entrepreneurs" and Russian women—Libor Kroska and Yevgenia Korniyenko, "Chinese Investments in Russia: Where Do They Go and How Important Are They?" *China and Eurasia Forum Quarterly*, vol. 6, no. 1 (February 2008): 46.

40. Anastasia Nazarova, "Can China be trusted?" *Sakhalin Times*, September 2, 2005.

41. Ibid.

42. Although Russia has a long history as a multinational country, with more than a hundred ethnic groupings, this is hardly the same thing as a genuinely multicultural society. The Slavic and later Soviet (*homo sovieticus*) paradigms have exerted an overwhelming dominance over Russian political, economic, and cultural life for the last 400 years.

43. Anatoly Vishnevsky predicts that "migrants and their descendants will comprise more than a third of the country's population by 2050, while by the end of the 21st century, the posterity of contemporary Russians will obviously be in the minority"—"The Specter of Immigration," *Russia in Global Affairs*, vol. 3, no. 2 (April–June 2005): 161.

44. Larin, *V teni prosnuvshegosya drakona*, p. 278.

45. James Kynge, *China Shakes the World* (London: Weidenfeld & Nicolson, 2006), p. 52.

46. According to a joint report by the Center for Strategic and International Studies (CSIS) and the Institute for International Economics (IIE), the number of migrant laborers exceeded 140 million in 2004, a figure that was only likely to increase in the short term—C. Fred Bergsten, Bates Gill, Nicholas R. Lardy, and Derek Mitchell, *China: The Balance Sheet—What the World Needs to Know Now about the Emerging Superpower* (New York: Public Affairs, 2006), p. 163.

47. According to Larin, "tourism" remains the main source of growth in the permanent, as well as temporary, Chinese presence in Russia—*V teni prosnuvshegosya drakona*, p. 390.

48. Gelbras, "Chinese Migration in Russia," p. 184.

49. Kavel A. Afrasiabi and Natalia Gold, "Russia's WTO hopes on borderline," *Asia Times Online*, April 8, 2008—www.atimes.com/atimes/Central_Asia/JD08Ag02.html.

50. Aleksandr Khramchikhin, "'Tretim raduyushchimsya' byt ne udastsya," *Nezavisimoe voennoe obozrenie*, December 22, 2006—http://nvo.ng.ru/printed/7042.

51. Portyakov, "Russian Vector in the Global Chinese Migration," p. 48.

52. V. Smolensky, "Kakaya Podnebesnaya im nuzhna," *Profil*, March 20, 2006, p. 32.

53. Gelbras, "Chinese Migration in Russia," p. 178. Larin estimates that half a million Chinese work abroad on contract—*V teni prosnuvshegosya drakona*, p. 381.

54. See Tamara Stark and Sze Pang Cheung, *Sharing the Blame: Global Consumption and China's Role in Ancient Forest Destruction*, Greenpeace International, March 28, 2006—www.illegal-logging.info/item_single.php?item=document&item_id=369&approach_id=19; also Justin Gills and others, "Corruption Stains Timber Trade: Forests Destroyed in China's Race to Feed Global Wood-Processing Industry," Washington Post Foreign Service, April 1, 2007—www.illegal-logging.info/item_single.php?item=news&item_id=1991&approach_id=19.

55. Alexander Lukin, "Kitai: opasny sosed ili vygodny partner?" *Pro et Contra* (November–December 2007): 85.

56. "O vozmozhnostyakh po organizatsii bezvizovykh gruppovykh turistskikh poezdok v Rossiiskuyu Federatsiyu," press release of the Russian Embassy in Beijing, May 7, 2007—www.russia.org.cn/rus/?ID=1333.

57. See note 38 above.

58. Lukin, "Kitai," p. 86. The usefulness of the Chinese as scapegoats is reflected in the political longevity of some RFE provincial leaders. The notoriously corrupt Naz-

dratenko remained governor of Primorye for well over a decade, before being moved to the lucrative position of minister of fisheries. Governor Ishaev in Khabarovsk has been even more successful as one of the longest-serving of all Russia's regional leaders (1991 to the present).

59. This shift is due mainly to Putin's decision to move from electing to appointing governors. Nevertheless, as the author discovered during a trip to Vladivostok and Khabarovsk in June 2007, anti-Chinese sentiment is rarely far from the surface.

60. Vladimir Putin, address to the Federal Assembly, May 10, 2006—www.kremlin.ru/text/appears/2006/05/105546.shtml. It is symptomatic of the Kremlin's concern that Putin devoted the largest part of his address to this theme. On the other hand, some Western experts believe that Russia's demographic situation in Siberia and the Far East is a natural response to regional climatic and economic conditions—see Hill and Gaddy, *The Siberian Curse.*

61. *Towards a Knowledge-based Society*, UNDP Development Report for the Russian Federation 2004 (Moscow, 2004), p. 55. *The 2006 World Population Data Sheet* gives a slightly higher projection—110.3 million (Washington: Population Reference Bureau, 2006—www.prb.org/pdf06/06WorldDataSheet.pdf, p. 11). Since 2006, anecdotal evidence has emerged suggesting that new financial incentives introduced by the Kremlin to encourage more births are beginning to pay off; maternity wards are said to be packed.

62. *The 2006 World Population Data Sheet*, for example, projects that China's population will rise from its current 1.311 billion to 1.476 billion in 2025 (as compared with Russia's 130 million), before tailing off slightly to 1.437 billion (Russia's 110 million), pp. 9–10. Other estimates suggest that it may already have reached 1.5–1.6 billion.

63. One small comfort is that the rate of out-migration has slowed in recent years—author's conversation with Viktor Larin in Vladivostok, June 2007.

64. On June 26, 2006, Putin signed a decree "On measures to assist the voluntary repatriation back to the Russian Federation of compatriots residing abroad"—Vladimir Kuzmin, "Zhuravlevy vozvrashchayutsya," *Rossiiskaya gazeta*, June 27, 2006, p. 1.

65. Of course, the picture is far from uniform. During his trip to Vladivostok and Khabarovsk in June 2007, the author was struck by the disparity in the two cities' fortunes. Whereas the former appeared as run-down as it had been in the 1990s, Khabarovsk exuded provincial prosperity and civic pride.

66. Vladimir Portyakov, "New Chinese Migrants in Russia as a Phenomenon of Reality and Research," 2003—http://192.38.121.218/issco5/documents/Portyakovpaper.doc; see also Larin, "Tikhookeanskaya politika Rossii v nachale XXI veka," p. 153.

67. Larin, "Russia's Eastern Border."

68. Larin, *V teni prosnuvshegosya drakona*, p. 121.

69. The border free trade zones have existed for some years, yet remain almost entirely undeveloped on the Russian side. The most established is Suifenhe-Pogranichny, but even this development is languishing. Although the Chinese have

built a five-star hotel, a trade exhibition center, and a shopping arcade, the Russian side has only a chapel—unclassified report from a Western diplomatic source, June 2007.

70. The Vladivostok APEC 2012 project is an extraordinarily ambitious undertaking by any standard. It involves, *inter alia*, the construction of two bridges from the Primorye peninsula to Russkii Ostrov (Russian Island), as well as the more routine requirements of providing five-star accommodation for the visiting APEC delegations. According to Japanese sources, there is very little likelihood that the bridges can be constructed in time. There are also suggestions that the foreign delegations will be housed in several cruise liners in the bay, thereby avoiding the risk of building five-star hotels that would end up as white elephants (author's conversations in Vladivostok, June 2007).

71. Menon, "The Sick Man of Asia," p. 100.

72. The *okrug* (district) of Khanty-Mansiisk is perhaps the most signal illustration of the benefits of being an oil-producing region; conversely, Chechnya (as opposed to individual Chechen warlords) has derived few benefits from being an oil transit region, even in times of peace.

73. *Itogi sotsialnogo razvitiya Primorskogo kraya 2007*, Department of Economic Development, Primorsky *krai* (www.primorsky.ru/files/6420.pdf); *Primorskii krai 2005: statisticheskii ezhegodnik* (Vladivostok: Rosstat, 2005), p. 262.

74. *Khabarovskii krai—vneshnyaya torgovlya*—www.adm.khv.ru/invest2.nsf/pages/ru/ftradechar.htm.

75. Larin, *V teni prosnuvshegosya drakona*, p. 233.

76. *Khabarovskii krai—vneshnyaya torgovlya*—www.adm.khv.ru/invest2.nsf/pages/ru/ftradechar.htm.

77. Larin claims that the RFE border regions rely on China for 60–80 percent of foodstuffs (meat, vegetables, fruit) and consumer items (clothes, footwear, household appliances)—"Tikhookeanskaya politika Rossii v nachale XXI veka," pp. 146–47.

78. A senior advisor in the Khabarovsk provincial administration told the author in June 2007 that the regional authorities were looking to Japanese rather than Chinese investment in the *krai*. Chinese business interests were considered rather low-level.

79. Vladimir Ovchinsky, "The 21st Century Mafia: Made in China," *Russia in Global Affairs*, vol. 5, no. 1 (January–March 2007): 93–94; also Alexander Lukin, "Facing China," *Kommersant.ru*, November 9, 2006.

80. Andrei Zabiyako, quoted in Paul Abelsky, "An Exaggerated Invasion," *Russia Profile*, vol. 3, no. 8 (October 2006): 34.

81. See Alexseev, "Chinese Migration into Primorskii Krai," p. 341; also Viktor Larin, *Rossiisko-kitaiskie otnosheniya v regionalnykh izmereniyakh* (Moscow: Vostok zapad, 2005), pp. 382–83; and "Tikhookeanskaya politika Rossii v nachale XXI veka," p. 146. The sense of vulnerability remains acute at the highest provincial levels. Khabarovsk governor Ishaev has repeatedly called on Moscow to foster the growth of

secondary industry in order to prevent the region—and the RFE more generally—from becoming a mere supplier of raw materials to China. See "Khabarovsk region Governor insists on changes in economic policy," *DV Times*, September 20, 2007—http://dvtimes.org/?news_print,88870.

The trade dependence of the RFE regions bordering China varies considerably. At one end of the scale, Amur is especially reliant; in 2007 China accounted for nearly all of its imports—U.S.$261 million out of U.S.$278 million—while receiving more than half its exports (www.amurobl.ru/index.php?m=24597&r=2&c=2711&p=2731). On the other hand, while 48 percent of Primorye's exports went to China, Chinese goods and services comprised a comparatively modest 37 percent of imports in value terms, behind Japan with 39 percent—www.primorsky.ru/files/6420.pdf. The apparent discrepancy between these figures and those cited by Larin in note 77 above is most likely due to the huge increase in Japanese high-value car imports.

82. Elizabeth Wishnick notes the propensity of regional administrations to play up the China threat around election time—see "The Securitization of Chinese Migration to the Russian Far East."

83. The distinguished Khabarovsk scholar Pavel Minakir explained Governor Ishaev's restraint as an outcome of the recentralization of power that had occurred under Putin. Once powerful governors had become *chinovniki*—compliant "officials" of the Putin administration (conversation with the author, Khabarovsk, June 2007).

84. There are indications that Moscow is finally beginning to understand the scale of the effort needed to revive the RFE. In August 2007 the Council of Ministers approved a 430-billion-ruble package (then equivalent to U.S.$16.8 billion) to support regional economic development in the period up to 2013 ("$17Bln for Far East Approved," *Moscow Times*, August 3, 2007—www.themoscowtimes.com/stories/2007/08/03/ 047-print.html). It remains to be seen whether these promised resources are fully disbursed and, if so, whether they are allocated to the areas of greatest need. Past experience encourages considerable skepticism on both scores (author's conversation with Viktor Larin, Vladivostok, June 2007).

85. Author's meetings in Vladivostok, June 2007. The situation remains especially bad in Primorye, where Nazdratenko's protégé, Sergei Darkin, is governor. Following the introduction of gubernatorial appointments (in lieu of elections), Darkin was the first governor to be formally endorsed by Putin, in January 2005.

86. Larin, "Tikhookeanskaya politika Rossii v nachale XXI veka," p. 151.

87. Ibid., p. 154.

88. Recent estimates of Chinese *urban* unemployment alone are in the range of 20–25 million—see Bergsten and others, *China: The Balance Sheet*, p. 32. On the other hand, the development of new industries (IT, tourism, financial and insurance services) and sectors (privately owned and individual enterprises) is likely to result in an easing of unemployment pressures over coming decades—Angang Hu, *Economic and Social Transformation in China: Challenges and Opportunities* (London and New York: Routledge, 2007), p. 207. Some commentators even argue that China is likely to suffer

from labor shortage if current growth rates are maintained—Boris Kuzyk and Mikhail Titarenko, *Kitai-Rossiya 2050: Strategiya sorazvitiya* (Moscow: Institute of the Far East/Institute of Economic Strategies, 2006), pp. 255–57.

89. Alexei Arbatov, "Natsionalnaya bezopasnost Rossii v mnogopolyarnom mire," report to the Presidium of the Russian Academy of Sciences, *Vestnik Rossiiskoi Akademii Nauk*, vol. 70, no. 11 (2000)—http://vivovoco.rsl.ru/vv/journal/vran/ arbatoff.htm. Yury Fedorov has also raised the same possibility in conversation with the author.

90. Alexei Voskressenski, "The Rise of China and Russo-Chinese Relations," in *Eager Eyes Fixed on Eurasia*, vol. 2, edited by Akihiro Awashita (Hokkaido University, Sapporo, 2007), p. 28. See also Menon, "The Sick Man of Asia," pp. 102–03.

Chapter Five

1. *China's Peaceful Rise: Speeches of Zheng Bijian, 1997–2005* (Brookings, 2005), p. 30. Zheng Bijian is one of the Communist Party's leading ideologists and the author of the concept of "peaceful rise." In 1992 he was appointed executive vice president of the Central Party School, in which capacity he worked very closely with Hu Jintao (then president of the school).

2. *Annual Report to Congress on the Military Power of the People's Republic of China 2006* (Office of the Secretary of Defense, 2006), p. 7.

3. Ross Terrill, *The New Chinese Empire—and What it Means for the United States* (New York: Basic Books, 2003), pp. 67–72.

4. "Peaceful rise" and "peaceful development" are essentially synonymous, but resonate very differently. The latter term is seen as less threatening and as such has become officially endorsed. "Peaceful rise," however, is a more accurate reflection of China's foreign policy vision and is still widely used by academics and other commentators. See Susan L. Shirk, *China: Fragile Superpower* (New York: Oxford University Press, 2007), pp. 108–09; also Bates Gill, *Rising Star: China's New Security Diplomacy* (Brookings, 2007), p. 8.

5. In 1999 Dmitri Trenin suggested that "somewhere between 2010 and 2015, parity in the number of nuclear warheads may emerge between the PRC and the Russian Federation at the level of 700 to 1,000 warheads"—*Russia's China Problem* (Carnegie Moscow Center, 1999), p. 31. Other experts have highlighted China's superiority along the Sino-Russian border: "For the foreseeable future, Russian military capabilities in the Far East will not match those of the Chinese"—Yury Galenovich, Vasily Mikheev, Mikhail Nosov, and Yury Fedorov, *Perspektivy Kitaya* (Moscow: Institute for Applied International Research, 2003), p. 88.

6. Comments by President Putin at a meeting with the International Valdai Discussion Club, Novo-Ogarevo, September 6, 2004. The author was present at the meeting.

7. In August 2000 the nuclear submarine *Kursk* suffered an explosion in its forward torpedo room. Well-publicized rescue efforts by British and Norwegian teams failed, and in the end the full complement of 118 crew died, some agonizingly slowly. The

incident was a public relations disaster for Putin, not least because of his decision to continue holidaying at his summer residence in Sochi.

8. Alexei Arbatov, "Russian Military Policy Adrift," *Carnegie Moscow Center Briefing Papers*, vol. 8, no. 6 (November 2006): 1–10.

9. David Shambaugh, *Modernizing China's Military: Progress, Problems, and Prospects* (University of California Press, 2004), pp. 1–3.

10. There has been a considerable reduction in the size of the PLA—from 2.3 million in 1991 to 1.6 million in 2007. See *The Military Balance 1990–91* (Oxford University Press for International Institute for Strategic Studies), p. 149 and *The Military Balance 2007* (London: IISS), p. 347.

11. David Shambaugh, "China's Military Modernization: Making Steady and Surprising Progress," in *Strategic Asia 2005-06—Military Modernization in an Era of Uncertainty*, edited by Ashley J. Tellis and Michael Wills (Seattle and Washington, DC: National Bureau of Asian Research 2005), p. 81.

12. Ibid., p. 91.

13. The Pentagon's 2006 report on the military power of the People's Republic of China revealed growing concern that the PLA was developing sufficient capability not only to undertake offensive operations against Taiwan, but also to deter U.S. involvement in the event of conflict—p. 6. However, a number of commentators believe that this threat is overstated, given Taiwan's air superiority and the PRC's lack of sea lift capacity. Interestingly, the most recent (2008) Pentagon report is fairly relaxed in its assessment, observing that "[a]n invasion of Taiwan would strain the capabilities of China's untested forces and would almost certainly invite international intervention"—*Annual Report to Congress on the Military Power of the People's Republic of China 2008* (Office of the Secretary of Defense, 2008), p. 44. Earlier, it notes that recent improvements in Taiwanese defense capabilities have "reinforced Taiwan's natural defensive advantages in the face of Beijing's continuing military build-up" (ibid., p. 40).

14. *Annual Report to Congress on the Military Power of the PRC 2008*, p. 1.

15. *The Military Balance 2008* (London: Routledge for International Institute for Strategic Studies, February 2008), p. 212.

16. Arbatov notes that despite the parlous state of Russia's armed forces, "China does not represent a military threat to Russia, at least in the mid-term perspective. The nuclear deterrent, and the planned growth in Chinese dependence on Russian oil, serve as guarantees of security for the uncertain long-term future"—"Russian Military Policy Adrift," p. 3.

17. *Annual Report to Congress on the Military Power of the PRC 2008*, p. 22.

18. See *East Asian Strategic Review 2006* (Tokyo: National Institute of Defense Studies), p. 184.

19. The most frequently cited example here is the outbreak of the First World War, which has been attributed, among other causes, to the vagaries of European railway timetables—see A. J. P. Taylor, *War by Timetable: How the First World War Began* (Lon-

don: Macdonald, 1969). However, even in this case "rational causes"—namely, great power rivalry between Britain, France, Germany, and Russia—were far more important factors.

20. *Annual Report to Congress on the Military Power of the PRC 2008*, p. 22.

21. Vasily Kashin, "Will China Repeat Stalin's Success?" *Moscow Defense Brief* 2 (2004)—http://mdb.cast.ru/mdb/2-2004/di/wcrs/.

22. Mikhail Margelov, "Russian-Chinese Relations: At Their Peak?" *International Affairs* (Moscow), vol. 49, no. 6 (2003): 80, 85.

23. *China's Peaceful Rise*, p. 30.

24. Some experts argue that even in the event of a unilateral declaration of independence, Beijing would still be most reluctant to undertake military action. Such a declaration would have little practical effect, and Taiwanese independence would not be recognized even by its closest ally the United States.

25. Typical of this view is the fear, expressed by Arbatov in 1999, that "new [Chinese] leaders might come to power and a re-evaluation of national interests could hypothetically push Beijing toward an expansionist policy in relation to the [Russian] Far East and Siberia, or against Kazakhstan and other Central Asian allies of Moscow" —*Rossiiskaya natsionalnaya ideya i vneshnyaya politika*, Scientific Report 53 (Moscow Social-Scientific Fund, 1998), p. 39. Boris Nemtsov and Vladimir Milov are even more explicit regarding China's allegedly hostile intent and warn of the potentially disastrous consequences of Putin's "capitulationist" policy toward Beijing—"Putin. Itogi" (Moscow: Novaya gazeta, 2008), pp. 54–57.

26. Gill, *Rising Star*, pp. 142–43.

27. Article 8 of the Anti-Secession Law, passed by the National People's Congress in March 2005, notes that "in the event that the 'Taiwan independence' secessionist forces should act . . . to cause the fact of Taiwan's secession from China, or that major incidents entailing Taiwan's secession from China should occur, or that possibilities for a peaceful reunification should be completely exhausted, the state shall employ non-peaceful means and other necessary measures to protect China's sovereignty and territorial integrity"—*People's Daily Online*, http://english.people.com.cn/200503/14/eng20050314_176746.html.

28. Susan Shirk notes, for example, that various internal Chinese sources argue that military action against Taiwan would set back the cause of modernization from at least three to ten years—*China: Fragile Superpower*, p. 183. In fact, given the degree of economic interdependency between the Chinese and American economies (not to speak of other major Asian economies such as Japan, South Korea, and the ASEANs), the impact on China's modernization could be far more drastic.

29. Cross-strait trade exceeded U.S.$124 billion in 2007, including more than U.S.$100 billion in Taiwanese exports to the mainland—Chinese Ministry of Commerce statistics (http://english.mofcom.gov.cn/aarticle/statistic/ie/200802/2008 0205371690.html). There are an estimated one million Taiwanese business people

and their families on the mainland—Gill, *Rising Star*, p. 143. In May 2007 the author was told by several sources that there were 500,000 Taiwanese living in the Shanghai region (*shi*) alone.

30. Except perhaps in a defensive sense. Shambaugh claims that Chinese military planners retain anxieties about Russian capabilities and intentions—*Modernizing China's Military*, p. 303.

31. Victor Larin, "Russia's Eastern Border: Last Outpost of Europe or Base for Asian Expansion?" *Russian Expert Review*, vol. 18, no. 4 (October 2006)—www. rusrev.org/eng/content/review/print.asp?ids=136&ida=1464.

32. According to its alleged originator, Senior Colonel Huang Shuofeng, comprehensive national power represents the aggregate of "a variety of factors, such as territory, natural resources, military force, economic power, social conditions, domestic government, foreign policy, and international influence"—*Zonghe guoli lun* (Beijing: Zhongguo shehui kexue chubanshe, 1992), p. 7.

33. *China's National Defense in 2006* (Beijing: Information Office of the State Council of the PRC, December 2006)—http://english.people.com.cn/whitepaper/ defense2006/defense2006.html.

34. *Annual Report to Congress on the Military Power of the PRC 2006*, p. 17.

35. Paradorn Rangsimaporn, "Russia's Debate on Military-Technological Cooperation with China," *Asian Survey* (May/June 2006), p. 488. Baluyevsky's assessment reflects the extent to which thinking about China has evolved at the highest levels of the Russian military. In 1996 then defense minister Igor Rodionov claimed that China was attempting to expand its strategic influence at Russia's expense—see Igor Korotchenko, "Igor Rodionov vystupil za sozdanie oboronnogo soyuza stran SNG," *Nezavisimaya gazeta*, December 26, 1996, p. 1.

36. "Transfers of major conventional weapons," SIPRI (Stockholm International Peace Research Institute) Arms Transfers Database, information generated on June 11, 2007.

37. *Annual Report to Congress on the Military Power of the PRC 2008*, p. 21.

38. In the period 2002–06 China accounted for 45 percent of Russian arms sales, almost double that of India (25 percent)—*SIPRI Yearbook 2007: Armaments, Disarmament and International Security* (Oxford University Press, 2007), p. 392.

39. Viktor Litovkin, "Voenno-eksportny tupik," *Nezavisimaya gazeta*, January 29, 2008, pp. 1, 6.

40. In the decade 1997–2006 the PRC sold weapons to twenty-five different countries, from Algeria to Zimbabwe—see SIPRI Arms Transfers Database, information generated on June 11, 2007.

41. "Beijing confident Moscow will allow use of engines on jets sold to Pakistan," *Financial Times*, November 9, 2006, p. 10.

42. A senior PLA officer put it to the author in March 2007 that "one cannot buy modernization."

43. The arms embargo has affected other major arms exporters. For instance, although Israel has sold China equipment in the past, it is constantly being constrained by Washington—see Shambaugh, "China's Military Modernization," p. 74.

44. In the end, the combination of Washington's vigorous opposition and Beijing's ill-advised decision to push through the Anti-Secession Law ensured that the decision to lift the embargo was deferred—Robert G. Sutter, *Chinese Foreign Relations: Power and Policy Since the Cold War* (Lanham, Md.: Rowman & Littlefield, 2008), p. 347.

45. Richard Weitz, "The Sino-Russian Arms Dilemma," *China Brief*, vol. 6, no. 22 (November 8, 2006)—http://jamestown.org/china_brief/article.php?articleid= 2373238. The past year has seen a massive drop in Russian arms exports to China. Yu Bin notes that there have been no new contracts since 2006, a state of affairs he attributes to three factors: (i) the postponement of the delivery of 40 Ilyushin cargo planes to China; (ii) "the near saturation of China's market by a large quantity of airplanes and naval vessels"; and (iii) "the lack of breakthrough in military technology cooperation and technology transfers"—"In the Search for a Normal Relationship: China and Russia into the 21st Century," *China and Eurasia Forum Quarterly*, vol. 5, no. 4 (November 2007): 79.

46. The 2003 Goldman Sachs report on the BRICs underestimates the enormous differences between the "emerging powers," not only in development structure but also political values, economic potential, and strategic orientation.

47. Bobo Lo, *Russian Foreign Policy in the Post-Soviet Era: Reality, Illusion and Mythmaking* (Basingstoke and New York: Palgrave Macmillan, 2002).

48. "Advance Comprehensive Cooperation in Pursuit of Sustainable Development," speech by Hu Jintao at the APEC Summit in Sydney, September 6, 2007—www.mfa.gov.cn/eng/wjdt/zyjh/t359776.htm.

49. As encapsulated in Deng Xiaoping's "12-character" strategy: "observe calmly; secure our position; cope with affairs calmly; hide our capacities and bide our time; be good at maintaining a low profile; and never claim leadership"—"Deng Puts Forward New 12-Character Guiding Principle for Internal and Foreign Policies," Ching Pao (Hong Kong), no. 172, pp. 84–86, November 5, 1991, FBIS HK0611100091.

50. As of July 1, 2007, the World Bank estimated China's GDP at U.S.$2.668 trillion, placing it behind the United States ($13.201 trillion), Japan ($4.340 trillion), and Germany ($2.907 trillion)—World Development Indicators database, http://site resources.worldbank.org/DATASTATISTICS/Resources/GDP.pdf.

51. In fact, the World Bank argues that China reached this position in 1995, measured in terms of purchasing power parity (PPP)—C. Fred Bergsten, Bates Gill, Nicholas R. Lardy, and Derek Mitchell, *China: The Balance Sheet—What the World Needs to Know Now about the Emerging Superpower* (New York: Public Affairs, 2006), p. 163.

52. The Goldman Sachs report is even more optimistic, projecting that China's GDP will surpass that of the United States by 2041—Dominic Wilson and Roopa Purushothaman, *Dreaming with BRICs: The Path to 2050* (Goldman Sachs Global Economics Paper 99, October), p. 3.

53. The World Bank estimates China's per capita income at U.S.$2,010—ranking it 129th out of 209 countries. By comparison, the United States has a per capita income of $44,970 (ranking 10th) and Russia $5,780 (79th). When judged by PPP, China's figures are somewhat better—$7,740, ranking 102nd—but still very low by the standards of the developed Western economies and even Russia. See World Development Indicators database, World Bank, September 14, 2007—http://siteresources.worldbank.org/DATASTATISTICS/Resources/GNIPC.pdf.

54. *China's Peaceful Rise*, p. 20.

55. James Kynge, *China Shakes the World: The Rise of a Hungry Nation* (London: Weidenfeld & Nicolson, 2006), p. 7.

56. Bergsten and others, *China: The Balance Sheet*, p. 50. According to the latest (2006) World Bank figures, China's literacy rate has reached 95 percent for men and 87 percent for women—http://devdata.worldbank.org/wdi2006/contents/Table2_13.htm.

57. Bergsten and others, *China: The Balance* Sheet, p. 50. According to UNESCO, China had 2.4 million graduates in 2006, more than the top three OECD countries combined—the United States (1.4 million), Japan (0.6 million) and France (0.3 million). Interestingly, the Russian figure is also quite impressive—1.1 million. See UNESCO Institute for Statistics, "Highlights from the UIS Report: Education Counts—Benchmarking Progress in 19 WEI [World Education Indicators] Countries," no. 2 (September 2007), pp. 1–2.

58. *China Statistical Yearbook 2007* (Beijing: China Statistics Press, October 2007), pp. 787, 789.

59. Bergsten and others, *China: The Balance Sheet*, p. 100.

60. Ibid., pp. 99–108.

61. *China's Peaceful Rise*, p. 26.

62. Kynge, *China Shakes the* World, pp. 108–15.

63. Kerry Brown, *The Rise of the Dragon: Inward and Outward Investment in China in the Reform Period 1978–2007* (Oxford: Chandos, 2008), pp. 63–67.

64. According to the OECD, oil and gas accounted for 62 percent of total Russian exports in 2005, compared with 52 percent in 2000—*OECD Economic Surveys 2006: Russian Federation*, Organisation for Economic Cooperation and Development, vol. 2006/17 (November 2006), p. 50. According to Matthew Sagers of Cambridge Energy Research Associates (CERA), the share of oil and gas had increased to 65.1 percent in 2006—panel presentation at a conference on "The Economics and Geopolitics of Russian Energy," Georgetown University, October 29, 2007.

65. Putin's address to the Federal Assembly, April 26, 2007—www.kremlin.ru/text/appears/2007/04/125339.shtml.

66. Sechin was deputy head of the Presidential Administration under Putin and regarded by many as his *éminence grise*. He became deputy prime minister in May 2008 after Medvedev succeeded Putin as president. At the time of Medvedev's appointment to the board of Rosneft, he (Medvedev) was one of two first deputy

prime ministers (along with Sergei Ivanov). Since becoming president, he has resigned from Rosneft, although this move appears to be motivated almost entirely by the need to pay lip-service to constitutional propriety.

67. Vasily Mikheev has rightly observed that "in contrast to Europe, Russian business does not view China as a strategically significant partner"—"Vizit V. Putina v Kitai," March 2006, www.eurasianhome.org/xml/t/expert.xml?lang=ru&nic=expert& pid=591.

68. China's oil consumption has doubled since 1993, the year it first became a net oil importer—Kamila Proninska, "Energy and security: regional and global dimensions," *SIPRI Yearbook 2007*, p. 226. Oil, oil products, and timber generally account for at least two-thirds of Russian exports to China. The 80 percent increase in Chinese exports to Russia in 2007 is due almost entirely to manufacturing and consumer goods—see Ministry of Commerce statistics, http://english.mofcom.gov.cn/aarticle/statistic/ie/200802/20080205371690.html.

69. China Ministry of Commerce statistics—http://english.mofcom.gov.cn/a article/statistic/ie/200802/20080205371690.html.

70. Mao and his senior comrades on the Long March comprised the first generation of Chinese leaders. Deng Xiaoping embodied the second generation and Jiang Zemin the third. Hu Jintao leads the present, "fourth generation" of Chinese leaders.

71. The children of Hu Jintao, Wen Jiabao, and former prime minister Zhu Rongji are either living in or have been educated in the United States. On the provenance of the fifth-generation leaders, see Vasily Mikheev, "East Asia and Russia's Development Strategy," *Russia in Global Affairs*, vol. 5, no. 1 (January–March 2007): 75.

72. Address to the Russia-China Economic Forum, Beijing, March 2006—www.kremlin.ru/appears/2006/03/22/1123_type63376type63377type82634_103471.shtml.

73. Yu Bin, "Russia Says 'No' to the West, and 'Sort Of' to China," *Comparative Connections*, vol. 9, no. 1 (April 2007): 149.

74. See note 45 above; also Yu Bin, "China–Russia Relations: Partying and Posturing for Power, Petro, and Prestige . . . ," *Comparative Connections*, vol. 9, no. 2 (July 2007): 162— www.csis.org/media/csis/pubs/0702qchina_russia.pdf.

75. Alexander Lukin, "Kitai: opasny sosed ili vygodny partner?", *Pro et Contra* (November–December 2007): 80–81.

76. Yu Bin, "China-Russia Relations," p. 161.

77. China is looking for cheap electricity, while Russia's United Energy Systems is insisting that the Chinese pay at least as much as local inhabitants in the Russian Far East—15 percent above the Russian average. See Elena Medvedeva and Kira Latukhina, "RAO EES ne puskayut v Kitai," *Vedomosti*, February 8, 2008.

78. See http://english.mofcom.gov.cn/aarticle/statistic/ie/200802/2008020537 1690.html. The picture is even more grim if one uses Russian statistics. Russian exports to China stagnated ($15.76 billion in 2006, $15.89 billion in 2007), while Chinese exports nearly doubled (from $12.91 billion in 2006 to $24.91 billion in 2007)— www.customs.ru/ru/stats/stats/popup.php?id286=364.

79. *China's Peaceful Rise*, p. 35.

80. Ibid., p. 1.

81. As Wang Jisi observes, "The Chinese leadership is conscious of the ambivalent feelings in neighboring countries as well as in the United States and Europe about the growth of Chinese power"—"China's Changing Role in Asia," Atlantic Council of the United States, January 2004, p. 3.

82. Demonstrated most recently by its hard-line stance on Kosovo independence.

83. As Lukin observes, "Russia plays a far lesser role in Chinese policy than China plays in Russian policy", "Kitai," p. 74. See also Frank Umbach, "The Wounded Bear and the Rising Dragon. The Sino-Russian Relationship at the Beginning of the 21st Century: A View from Europe," *Asia Europe Journal*, vol. 2, no. 1 (2004): 60; and Dmitri Trenin, "Rossiya mezhdu Kitaem i Amerikoi," p. 52.

84. Yury Fedorov in conversation with the author.

85. This has been a consistent theme in the author's conversations with Chinese diplomats, academics and journalists over more than a decade. As one Chinese diplomat complained during the darkest days of Russia's economic crisis in the late 1990s, "What gives them the right to look down on us?"

86. See Strobe Talbott, *The Russia Hand: A Memoir of Presidential Diplomacy* (New York: Random House, 2003).

87. Alexander Lukin, "Facing China," *Kommersant*, November 9, 2006—www.kommersant.ru.

Chapter Six

1. Zhao Huasheng, "China, Russia, and the United States: Prospects for Cooperation in Central Asia," *China and Eurasia Forum Quarterly* (Winter 2005): 20.

2. www.sectsco.org/502.html.

3. The expression "the Great Game" is thought to have originated in 1831 in a letter from Lieutenant Arthur Connolly to a friend—see Peter Hopkirk, *The Great Game: On Secret Service in High Asia* (London: John Murray, 2006), p. 123.

4. Moscow's influence in Xinjiang was very strong during the 1930s and 1940s, first with the warlord Sheng Shicai and then, after he went over to the Nationalists, in backing a Uighur-led revolt that led to the Second Republic of East Turkestan—Graham Hutchings, *Modern China: A Guide to a Century of Change* (Harvard University Press, 2000), pp. 470–71.

5. Shanghai Convention on Combating Terrorism, Separatism, and Extremism, June 15, 2001—http://english.scosummit2006.org/en_bjzl/2006-04/20/content_87.htm.

6. Zhao, "China, Russia, and the United States," 23.

7. The East Turkestan Islamic Movement (ETIM) emerged in the 1990s, partly as a manifestation of a resurgent Uighur desire for self-determination and self-expression, and partly in response to the victory of the Taliban in neighboring

Afghanistan. China, Russia, and the United States view it as a terrorist organization and claim that it has close links with al-Qaeda. It has been blamed for a number of terrorist incidents in Xinjiang. See John Z. Wang, "East Turkistan Islamic Movement: A Case Study of a New Terrorist Organization in China," *International Journal of Offender Therapy and Comparative Criminology*, vol. 47, no. 5 (2003): 574–75; Seva Gunitskiy, "In the Spotlight: East Turkestan Islamic Movement (ETIM)," Center for Defense Information Terrorism Project, December 9, 2002—www.cdi.org/terrorism/etim.cfm.

8. Dmitri Trenin, "'Osennii marafon' Vladimira Putina i rozhdenie Rossiiskoi vneshnepoliticheskoi strategii," *Carnegie Moscow Center Briefing Paper*, November 15, 2001, p. 6.

9. Putin's decision was made against the advice of the majority of Russia's senior political figures. See presentation by Grigory Yavlinsky at the Carnegie Endowment for International Peace, Washington DC, January 31, 2002—www.cdi.org/russia/johnson/6061.txt.

10. See James M. Goldgeier and Michael McFaul, *Power and Purpose: U.S. Policy Toward Russia after the Cold War* (Brookings, 2003), pp. 305–25.

11. Uzbekistan, Kyrgyzstan, and Tajikistan indicated strong interest, while Kazakhstan allowed limited landing rights at three airfields. Only Turkmenistan abstained, adhering instead to a "positive neutrality"—see Martha Brill Olcott, *Central Asia's Second Chance* (Washington, DC: Carnegie Endowment for International Peace, 2005), p. 5.

12. The Jackson-Vanik amendment linked the granting of the Soviet Union's Most Favored Nation (MFN) trading status to its progress in allowing Jews to emigrate freely from the USSR. This obviously anachronistic amendment has little practical impact—Russia's MFN status is routinely renewed every year—but retains considerable symbolic resonance. It remains a major irritant in Russia-U.S. relations.

13. See Putin meeting with news agency heads from the G-8 member-states, Novo-Ogarevo, June 2, 2006—www.kremlin.ru/text/appears/2006/06/106430.shtml.

14. Yevgeny Primakov, *Russian Crossroads: Toward the New Millennium* (Yale University Press, 2004), p. 71.

15. For many Chinese, of course, the most crucial development in the region was the collapse of the USSR in 1991. It is certainly true that since then China "has been continually rethinking its interests and policy in the region"—Huasheng Zhao, "China and Central Asia," in *Central Asia: Views from Washington, Moscow, and Beijing*, edited by Eugene Rumer, Dmitri Trenin, and Huasheng Zhao (Armonk, N.Y.: M.E. Sharpe, 2007), p. 138. Nevertheless, Russia remained the dominant power in Central Asia in the 1990s. As one Chinese observer noted, Beijing had "no wish to jeopardize the Sino-Russia strategic partnership by making too many bold moves in Central Asia (Shiping Tang, "Economic Integration in Central Asia: The Russian and Chinese Relationship," *Asian Survey*, vol. 9, no. 2 [March/April 2000]: 368). After 9/11 and the entry of the United States into the region, however, the strategic situation changed completely.

16. See, for example, Alec Rasizade, "The Specter of a New 'Great Game' in Central Asia," *Foreign Service Journal* (November 2002): 48–52; Subodh Atal, "The New Great Game," *The National Interest* (Fall 2005): 101–05; J. Peter Pham, "Beijing's Great Game: Understanding Chinese Strategy in Central Eurasia," *American Foreign Policy Interests*, no. 28 (2006): 53–67; Dmitri Trenin, "Russia and Central Asia," in *Central Asia*, edited by Rumer, Trenin, and Zhao, p. 84.

17. The balance of power informs Moscow's approach to the region even at the trivial level. Thus it reacted to the establishment of the U.S. base in Manas by persuading the Kyrgyz government to allow it to build a tiny base in Kant, a mere 30 km away. The new base had little operational significance in the "war on terror," but was symbolically important in "balancing" the much larger U.S. military presence.

18. See Trenin, "Russia and Central Asia," pp. 81–82. It is revealing, in this connection, that the well-known political scientist Andranik Migranian has found renewed favor with the Kremlin in recent times. Back in 1992 Migranian called for Russia to implement its own Monroe doctrine (*doktrina Monro*) in relation to the former Soviet Union—"Podlinnye i mnimye orientiry vo vneshnei politike," *Rossiiskaya gazeta*, August 4, 1992, p. 7.

19. The establishment in February 2006 of a new Bureau of South and Central Asian Affairs at the State Department reflected Washington's view that Central Asia should no longer be viewed within the conceptual framework of the former Soviet Union—www.state.gov/r/pa/prs/ps/2006/60885.htm. This step was consistent with the sentiments expressed by former assistant secretary of state Strobe Talbott, in a famous speech in July 1997: "For the last several years, it has been fashionable to proclaim, or at least to predict, a replay of the 'Great Game' in the Caucasus and Central Asia. . . . Our goal is to avoid and actively to discourage that atavistic outcome. In pondering and practicing the geopolitics of oil, let's make sure that we are thinking in terms appropriate to the 21st century and not the 19th. Let's leave Rudyard Kipling and George MacDonald Fraser where they belong—on the shelves of historical fiction"—"A Farewell to Flashman: American Policy in the Caucasus and Central Asia," address at the Johns Hopkins School of Advanced International Studies, Baltimore, Md., July 21, 1997—www.state.gov/www/regions/nis/970721talbott.html.

20. Richard Weitz, "Averting a New Great Game in Central Asia," *The Washington Quarterly* (Summer 2006): 155–56.

21. Niklas Swanström, "China and Central Asia: A New Great Game or Traditional Vassal Relations?" *Journal of Contemporary China*, vol. 45, no. 14 (November 2005): 576.

22. See Pham, "Beijing's Great Game," pp. 61–62, 65.

23. See table 6-1.

24. Lukoil, in particular, is very heavily involved in various oil projects in Kazakhstan—Karachaganak, Kumkol, Dostyk—while Gazprom monopolizes Turkmenistan's gas exports (45 billion cubic meters per annum) and aspires to part-ownership of Uzbekistan's natural gas resources. See Trenin, "Russia and Central Asia," pp. 106–09.

25. The flagship of this new Russian cultural diplomacy is Russkii mir, the Kremlin's attempt to offer an analog to institutions such as the British Council, Alliance Française, Goethe Institute, and Confucius Institutes.

26. Trenin, "Russia and Central Asia," pp. 81–82.

27. The Single Economic Space (SES) was established on September 19, 2003, at the Yalta CIS summit. Its stated intention was to ensure the free movement of goods, services, capital, and labor between the four member countries. However, there were significant differences in deciding what this entailed specifically. The SES was particularly contentious in Ukraine, where many feared that it would deflect Kyiv from the much more important objective of WTO accession. The Orange Revolution in December 2004 ended Ukrainian participation, effectively killing off the SES.

28. Although the term "peaceful offensive" is generally used in connection with mainland policy toward Taiwan, it also seems appropriate to describe the increasingly active Chinese involvement in Central Asia.

29. According to a November 2007 agreement, Russia will supply 5 million tonnes of oil through the Atasu-Alashankou pipeline, which currently has a capacity of 10 million tonnes (expected to double by 2011). See Sergei Kulikov and Mikhail Sergeev, "Rossiiskaya neft potechet v Kitai mimo zheleznoi dorogy," *Nezavisimaya gazeta*, November 27, 2007, p. 4.

30. See Vitaly Naumkin, "Uzbekistan's State-Building Fatigue," *The Washington Quarterly*, vol. 29, no. 3 (Summer 2006): 134–35.

31. Joshua Kurlantzick, "China's Charm: Implications of Chinese Soft Power," Carnegie Endowment for International Peace, Washington, DC, *Policy Brief* 47 (June 2006), pp. 2–3.

32. Zhao Huasheng rightly observes that China "wants to avoid giving the impression that it is challenging any great power; it makes every effort to dispel the idea that it seeks to eject and replace any foreign power in the region"—"China and Central Asia," p. 157.

33. Ibid., p. 153.

34. Beijing's fears are reflected in the claim that U.S. and European attempts "to forcibly transplant the Western mode . . . in an attempt to change the current governments in the region . . . [have] resulted in a more or less turbulent situation in some Central Asian countries"—Shi Ze, "Relations Between China and Central Asian Countries Face Opportunity of All-Round Development," *China International Studies* (Winter 2005): 83.

35. Alexander Lukin, "Kitai: opasny sosed ili vygodny partner?" *Pro et Contra* (November–December 2007): 81; Stephen Blank, "China, Kazakh Energy, and Russia: An Unlikely Ménage à Trois," *China and Eurasia Forum Quarterly* (November 2005): 207. The eminent Kazakh scholar Kamal Burkhanov has likewise emphasized the importance of Central Asian energy as an alternative to Russian oil and gas—conversation with the author, Almaty, March 6, 2007.

36. According to the then Turkmen president, Saparmurad Niyazov, Turkmenistan was "ready to supply China with 30–40 billion cubic meters of gas" (Sergei Blagov, "Turkmenistan seeks to strengthen energy ties with China," *Eurasia Daily Monitor*, vol. 49, no. 3, April 10, 2006—www.jamestown.org/edm/article.php?article_id= 2370963). Niyazov's sudden death in December 2006 and his successor's decision to sign a new agreement with Gazprom cast doubt on the implementation of the Sino-Turkmen deal. However, during a first visit to Beijing, in July 2007, the new president, Gurbanguly Berdymukhammedov, reiterated previous assurances that Turkmenistan would supply China with gas. Since then, work has begun on the pipeline.

37. Russia has consistently attempted to undermine Chinese energy interests in Central Asia, including through recourse to the courts in Canada and Sweden—see Sebastien Peyrouse, "The Economic Aspects of the Chinese-Central Asia Rapprochement," *Silk Road Paper* (Washington, DC, and Stockholm: Central Asia-Caucasus Institute and Silk Road Studies Program, 2007), p. 54.

38. Farkhad Tolipov, "East vs. West? Some Geopolitical Questions and Observations for the SCO," *China and Eurasia Forum Quarterly* (July 2005): 22.

39. Zhao, "China and Central Asia," pp. 157–58.

40. Ibid., pp. 158–59.

41. More generally, Beijing has in recent years made far greater use of multilateral mechanisms and processes, most notably with the EU and ASEAN, and in the China-Africa summit—Bates Gill, "China's Evolving Regional Security Strategy," in *Power Shift: China and Asia's New Dynamics*, edited by David Shambaugh (University of California Press, 2005), pp. 252–57.

42. Russian Foreign Ministry website—www.ln.mid.ru/ns-vnpop. nsf/osn_copy/ 10B2E48726C25A62C32570430031545F.

43. Declaration on the Fifth Anniversary of the Shanghai Cooperation Organization, Shanghai, June 15, 2006—www. sectsco.org/502.html. Unsurprisingly, the principles embodying the "Shanghai spirit" closely resemble China's Five Principles of Peaceful Coexistence, originally presented by then premier Zhou Enlai at the 1955 Asia-Africa Summit in Bandung, Indonesia. The principles were: "mutual respect for territorial integrity and sovereignty; non-aggression; non-interference; mutual equality and benefit; and peaceful coexistence"—see Hutchings, *Modern China*, p. 42.

44. Declaration on the Fifth Anniversary of the SCO, Shanghai, June 15, 2006—www.sectsco.org/502.html.

45. Chien-peng Chung, "China and the Institutionalization of the Shanghai Cooperation Organization," *Problems of Post-Communism*, vol. 53, no. 5 (September/October 2006): 5–7.

46. Declaration of the Heads of Member States of the SCO, Astana, July 5, 2005—www.sectsco.org/html/00500.html. It is telling that the RATS has taken nearly four years to come up with a list of "terrorist organizations" in Central Asia, let alone coordinate counterterrorist measures within the SCO framework. See Yu Bin, "Partying

and Posturing for Power, Petro, and Prestige . . . ," *Comparative Connections*, vol. 9, no. 2 (July 2007): 164.

47. Declaration on the Fifth Anniversary of the SCO.

48. "Energy Dominates Shanghai Summit," BBC News—http://news.bbc.co.uk/go/pr/fr/-/1/hi/world/asia-pacific/6949021.stm.

49. Joint Communiqué of the Heads of SCO Member-States, Bishkek, August 16, 2007—www.sectsco.org/html/01721.html.

50. At the CIS Sochi summit in August 2001, Putin told Russian journalists that informal bilateral contacts between leaders of member-states were much more useful than the formal multilateral sessions. "Putin, CIS Leaders Meet Without Ties to Form New Ties," *RFE/RL Newsline*, August 2, 2001—www.rferl.org/newsline/2001/08/1-rus/rus-020801.asp. Subsequently, he was even more explicit in his criticism. "We find ourselves at a crossroads: either we achieve a qualitative strengthening of the CIS and create a functional, globally influential regional structure; or inevitably we will see the dilution of this geopolitical space and, consequently, a decisive falling-off in interest among member-states in the work of the CIS"—opening address at the Security Council session on foreign policy questions in the CIS space, July 19, 2004—www.kremlin.ru/text/appears/2004/07/74648.shtml.

51. Murat Laumulin, "The Shanghai Cooperation Organization as 'Geopolitical Bluff'? A View from Astana," *Russie.Nei.Visions,* July 12, 2006, p. 6.

52. Significantly, even semi-official Chinese sources dismiss such comparisons out of hand—see Wang Haiyun, "Sino-Russia Relationship Signifies Reciprocal Strategic and Coordination Partners," *International Strategic Studies* 3 (2006): 17.

53. Laumulin, "The Shanghai Cooperation Organization as 'Geopolitical Bluff'?" p. 6.

54. Declaration of the Heads of Member States of the SCO, Astana, July 5, 2005—www.sectsco.org/html/00500.html.

55. Article 1 of the SCO Charter—www.sectsco. org/html/00096.html.

56. Weitz, "Averting a New Great Game in Central Asia," p. 164; Oksana Antonenko, "The EU Should Not Ignore the Shanghai Co-operation Organisation," *Centre for European Reform Policy Brief*, May 2007.

57. Weitz, "Averting a New Great Game in Central Asia," p. 164; Antonenko, "The EU Should Not Ignore the SCO."

58. Weitz, "Averting a New Great Game in Central Asia," p. 162.

59. Christopher Brown, "China's Central Asian Reach—The Shanghai Cooperation Organization and the China-Russia Bi-Lateral Relationship," statement to the Subcommittee on Oversight and Investigations, House International Relations Committee, Washington, DC, December 14, 2005.

60. See Eugene B. Rumer, "China, Russia and the Balance of Power in Central Asia," *Strategic Forum* 223 (November 2006), p. 1 (Washington, DC: Institute for National Strategic Studies).

61. Declaration of the Heads of Member States of the SCO.

62. Declaration on the Fifth Anniversary of the SCO. Similarly, the "Bishkek Declaration" of August 2007 rehashed the same themes of "double standards" and the right of a sovereign state "to choose independently its way of development based on its unique historical experience and national features." The Bishkek declaration also endorsed the idea of a Central Asia Nuclear-Weapon-Free Zone, in an interesting echo of Soviet disarmament initiatives of the 1980s. See www.sectsco.org/html/01753.html.

63. Weitz, "Averting a New Great Game in Central Asia," p. 165.

64. The rent paid by the United States for the Manas base increased in 2006 from under U.S.$30 million to more than U.S.$200 million—see Martha Brill Olcott, "Eyes on Central Asia: How to Understand the Winners and Losers," in *Eager Eyes Fixed on Eurasia*, vol. 2, edited by Akihiro Iwashita (Sapporo: Slavic Research Center, Hokkaido University, 2007), pp. 7–8.

65. See Roger McDermott, "The Rising Dragon: SCO Peace Mission 2007," *Jamestown Foundation Occasional Paper* (October 2007), p. 13.

66. Stephen Blank, "China in Central Asia: The Hegemon in Waiting?" in *Eurasia in Balance: The US and the Regional Power Shift*, edited by Ariel Cohen (Burlington, Vt.: Ashgate, 2005), p. 170.

67. Yu Bin writes of "the survival of the slowest," arguing that "the SCO's resilience is . . . derived from rather than compromised by its weakness and slowness"—"Central Asia Between Competition and Cooperation," *Foreign Policy in Focus Commentary*, December 4, 2006—www.fpif.org/fpiftxt/3754.

68. Zhao, "China, Russia, and the United States," p. 31.

69. For a detailed exposition of the concept of "regional superpower," see Leon Aron, "The Foreign Policy Doctrine of Postcommunist Russia and Its Domestic Context," in *The New Russian Foreign Policy*, edited by Michael Mandelbaum (New York: Council on Foreign Relations Press, 1998), p. 33.

70. The consolidation and development of inter-elite ties have acquired fresh impetus in the circumstances of Russia's new-found economic power. As Celeste Wallander puts it, the Putin regime is pursuing "transimperialism" as an extension of Russian "patrimonial authoritarianism into a globalized world." This relies on "selectively integrating transnational elite networks . . . and replicating the patron-client relations of power, dependency, and rent seeking and distribution at the transnational level"—"Russian Transimperialism and Its Implications," *The Washington Quarterly*, vol. 30, no. 2 (Spring 2007): 117–18.

71. Although Russia's trade with the five Central Asian states has grown substantially in recent years, the increase in China–Central Asia trade has been even more spectacular. During the 1990s, this remained under U.S.$1 billion, but by 2007 it had risen to U.S.$19.66 billion (see table 6-2).

72. According to the Chinese scholar and diplomat Shi Ze, China and the Central Asian countries "should promote the flow of commodities, technology, finance and labor between the two sides in order to finally form a free trade area within the framework

of the SCO so as to further speed up the development of economy in Central Asia" ("Relations Between China and Central Asian Countries Face Opportunity of All-Round Development," p. 85). Significantly, he does not mention Russia in this context. In the circumstances, it is hardly surprising that Moscow, as well as the Central Asians, has proved unreceptive to the idea.

73. The extraordinary growth in China's trade with other SCO member-states shows little sign of slowing. The 2007 figures show huge increases in Chinese exports to Central Asia: 56.7 percent with Kazakhstan, 73.5 percent Kyrgyzstan, 68 percent Tajikistan, 86.1 percent Turkmenistan, and 88.6 percent Uzbekistan. Chinese imports from Central Asia are more uneven, not surprising given that its economic interest is essentially limited to energy. Nevertheless, the increases for Kazakhstan (78.2 percent) and especially Turkmenistan (213.3 percent) are eye-catching—http://english.mofcom. gov.cn/column/print.shtml?/statistic/ie/200802/200802053 71690.

74. In fact, this is already happening. Between 2003 and 2006, the share of raw materials in Central Asian exports to China increased from 84.4 percent to 90.2 percent. Over the same period the share of manufactured goods in Central Asian imports from China increased from 77.5 percent to 92 percent—Vladimir Paramonov and Aleksey Strokov, "Economic Involvement of Russia and China in Central Asia," *Central Asian Series* 07/12(e) (May 2007) (Swindon: Conflict Research Centre, Defence Academy of the United Kingdom), p. 5.

75. Author's conversation in March 2007 with Kamal Burkhanov, director of the Institute of History and Ethnology, Almaty, Kazakhstan. See also Xuanli Liao, "Central Asia and China's Energy Security," *China and Eurasia Forum Quarterly* (November 2006): 68.

76. Weitz, "Averting a New Great Game in Central Asia," p. 163.

77. Declaration of the Heads of Member States of the SCO.

78. The CSTO arose out of the decision in May 2002 to transform the 1992 Agreement on Collective Security (signed by Armenia, Belarus, Kazakhstan, Kyrgyzstan, Russia, and Tajikistan) into an "international regional organization." The main task of the new organization was "to coordinate and deepen military-political interaction," but the overall thrust of its activities soon turned to the ubiquitous "struggle against international terrorism" and other "non-traditional security threats"—www.dkb.gov. ru/start/index.htm.

79. Interview with CSTO general secretary Nikolai Bordyuzha, *Moskovskie novosti*, May 15, 2007—www.dkb.gov.ru/start/index.htm. See also CSTO Summit Declaration "On Further Perfecting and Improving the Organization's Effectiveness," May 2005— www.dkb.gov.ru/start/index.htm.

80. Bordyuzha notes somewhat tritely that "economy is unthinkable without security, or security without economy"—in "CSTO, Regional Security Guarantor," *RIA Novosti*, September 22, 2006—http://en.rian.ru/analysis/20060922/54178637-print.html.

81. Ibid.

82. Trenin, "Russia and Central Asia," p. 100.

83. Three battalions each from Russia and Tajikistan, two each from Kazakhstan and Kyrgyzstan—www.odkb.gov.ru/g/l.htm.

84. Shinji Hyodo, "Russia, China and the SCO: 'Peace Mission 2007,'" *RUSI Newsbrief*, July 6, 2007, p. 3.

85. Stephen Blank, "China and the Shanghai Cooperation Organization at Five," *China Brief*, June 21, 2006—http://jamestown.org/terrorism/news/article.php?article id=2373196.

Chapter Seven

1. Samuel P. Huntington, *The Clash of Civilizations and the Remaking of the World Order* (London and New York: Touchstone Books, 1998), p. 218.

2. Bates Gill and Yanzhong Huang, "Sources and Limits of Chinese 'Soft Power,'" *Survival*, vol. 48, no. 2 (Summer 2006): 30–31.

3. www.kremlin.ru/appears/2005/11/17/1213_type63382_97334.shtml.

4. It is estimated that there are only 76,000 troops (73,500 ground and airborne; 2,500 naval infantry) in the entire Far Eastern Military District—*The Military Balance 2007* (London: IISS, 2007), p. 203.

5. Report of the 2001 Trilateral Commission, cited in Wang Jisi, "China's Changing Role in Asia," *The Atlantic Council*, January 2004, p. 5.

6. Huntington, *The Clash of Civilizations*, p. 218.

7. Bobo Lo, "Rossiiskaya politika v vostochnoi Azii: Evolyutsiya i preemstvennost," *Yaderny Kontrol*, vol. 8, no. 6 (November–December 2002): 38.

8. Robert Kagan, "The world divides . . . and democracy is at bay," *The Sunday Times*, September 2, 2007—www.timesonline.co.uk/tol/comment/columnists/guest_contributors/article2367065.ece.

9. As Vasily Mikheev notes, "China plays the role of a regional 'disturber of the peace' as it seeks to strengthen its political influence on the basis of its growing economic might, its important and sometimes even leading role on world markets, and the active expansion of its capital abroad"—"East Asia and Russia's Development Strategy," *Russia in Global Affairs*, vol. 5, no. 1 (January–March 2007): 72. See also Alexei Voskressenski, "The Rise of China and Russo-Chinese Relations," in *Eager Eyes Fixed on Eurasia*, vol. 2, edited by Akihiro Iwashita (Sapporo: Slavic Research Center, Hokkaido University, 2007), pp. 37–38.

10. Gill and Huang, "Sources and Limits of Chinese 'Soft Power,'" pp. 30–31.

11. Evan S. Medeiros, "Strategic Hedging and the Future of Asia-Pacific Stability," *The Washington Quarterly* (Winter 2005–06): 148–53.

12. In 2007 Japan spent U.S.$43.65 billion on defense, the most outside the big five nuclear weapons states (the United States, Russia, China, the United Kingdom, France)—*The Military Balance 2008* (London: Routledge for International Institute of Strategic Studies, February 2008), p. 384. In May 2007 the Japanese Upper House approved a bill setting out steps for a referendum on revising the constitution to allow

Japan's Self-Defense Force to undertake military operations overseas—"Japan Approves Constitution Steps," http://news.bbc.co.uk/1/hi/world/asia-pacific/6652 809.stm.

13. Under the terms of the Yalta agreement of February 1945, Stalin agreed that the Soviet Union would enter the war in the Pacific three months after the end of the war in Europe. In return, the USSR would be allowed to regain territories lost to Japan in the 1904–05 Russo-Japanese war. Stalin fulfilled his part of the bargain, but took the opportunity to add to the Soviet Union's territorial winnings by annexing several islands—Iturup, Kunashiri, Shikotan, and the Habomais—that had belonged to Japan even before the Russo-Japanese war.

14. Comment to the author by a senior Russian Foreign Ministry official, Moscow, November 1998.

15. It is symptomatic of the difference in America's approach to Europe and Asia that in the latter case Washington has soft-pedaled on democracy-building and resigned itself to moral relativism, embodied in the concept of "Asian values."

16. Wang, "China's Changing Role in Asia," p. 12.

17. Russia became a full member of APEC in 1998, largely as the result of strong political support from the United States and China.

18. The term "multivectorialism" entered into public discourse following an address by Yeltsin to senior Foreign Ministry officials in October 1992—"Chto skazal Eltsin rossiiskim diplomatam," *Rossiiskie vesti*, October 29, 1992, p. 1.

19. Andrei A. Kokoshin, *Soviet Strategic Thought, 1917–1991* (MIT Press, 1998), pp. 199–200.

20. Bobo Lo, *China and Russia: Common Interests, Contrasting Perceptions*, CLSA Special Report (Shanghai: May 2006), p. 15.

21. In the past century, Russian, Soviet, and Japanese troops have clashed in the 1904–05 Russo-Japanese war, during the Japanese military intervention in the Russian Far East (1918–21), at the battles of Lake Khasan (1938) and Khalkin Gol (1939), and, most notoriously, at the end of the Second World War when the Red Army intervened to mop up the remnants of the Kwantung Army and annex Manchuria, Sakhalin, and the South Kuriles/Northern Territories.

22. See chapter 4, note 38.

23. See chapter 8, note 48.

24. Bobo Lo, *Against the Tide: Difficult Times for Moscow and Tokyo*, CLSA Special Report (Shanghai: February 2006), p. 7.

25. For example, then foreign minister Primakov was excluded from the Krasnoyarsk summit. This was a source of considerable annoyance to MFA officials, who feared that Yeltsin would concede too much to the Japanese in his desire to conclude a peace treaty (source: author's conversations with senior MFA officials in November 1997). The Russian side comprised, in addition to Yeltsin, Deputy Prime Minister Boris Nemtsov and Press Secretary Sergei Yastrzhembsky—both of whom strongly favored Tokyo over Beijing.

26. Paragraph 9 of the 1956 Joint Declaration of Japan and the USSR stated that the latter "agrees to hand over to Japan the Habomai Islands and the island of Shikotan. However, the actual handing over of these islands to Japan shall take place after the conclusion of a peace treaty between Japan and the Union of Soviet Socialist Republics"—www.mofa.go.jp/region/europe/russia/territory/overview.html. Of course, the continuing failure to agree a peace treaty means that Moscow feels under no obligation to hand over Shikotan and the Habomais.

27. See "Japan leader forges ties with old, new Russian leaders," *Channel News Asia*, April 27, 2008—www.channelnewsasia.com/stories/afp_asiapacific/print/343907/1/.html.

28. The Japanese companies Mitsui and Mitsubishi had previously held 25 percent and 20 percent, respectively, of shares in the Sakhalin Energy Investment Company (SEIC), the consortium responsible for developing the Sakhalin-2 project. The remaining 55 percent of shares were held by Royal Dutch Shell. Following two years of intense pressure from the Kremlin, the three foreign companies were forced to admit Gazprom to a 50 percent plus one share participation in the project and, as a consequence, to halve their equity.

29. In August 2006 the Russian coastguard fired on the Japanese fishing vessel *Kisshin Maru* in the waters around the disputed territories. One of the Japanese crew members was killed (the first such death in half a century), the captain put on trial in Vladivostok, and the boat impounded. The captain was released after paying a large fine.

30. Amitav Acharya noted in 1999 that "a concert system, even one that is geared primarily to the management of the great-power balance itself, need not be multilateral in any formal sense. It could consist of a series of overlapping and cross-cutting bilateral relationships which are non-exclusionary and not directed against any member of the great-power system. Nor does concert require very harmonious relationships between the major powers. . . . While the [19th-century European] concert did not lead [the great powers] to renounce their individual interests, it did produce a more moderate form of great-power rivalry than would normally be the case with a balance-of-power system"— Amitav Acharya, "A Concert of Asia?" *Survival*, vol. 41, no. 3 (Autumn 1999): 89.

31. Bobo Lo, *Russian Foreign Policy in the Post-Soviet Era: Reality, Illusion and Mythmaking* (Basingstoke and New York: Palgrave Macmillan, 2002), p. 67.

32. Acharya, "A Concert of Asia?" p. 96.

33. These efforts date from 1969, when Leonid Brezhnev first proposed the notion of an "Asian Collective Security Pact" that would cover Northeast Asia—see Arnold L. Horelick, "The Soviet Union's Asian Collective Security Proposal: A Club in Search of Members," *Pacific Affairs*, vol. 47, no. 3 (Autumn 1974): 269–85.

34. In February 2007 Pyongyang agreed to "shut down and seal" its Yongbyon heavy water nuclear reactor in exchange for 1 million tonnes of heavy fuel oil. The agreement hit a major snag, however, when Kim Jong-il demanded that the United States enable the transfer of U.S.$25 million of personal funds held in an account

with Banco Delta Asia, a bank based in Macao and blacklisted by the U.S. government for money-laundering on behalf of the DPRK. No foreign banks were willing to transfer the money for fear of incurring American sanctions. The impasse was finally resolved when Moscow arranged for an obscure Khabarovsk-based bank, Dalkombank (Far Eastern Commercial Bank), to act as the financial conduit in return for U.S. assurances that no sanctions would be imposed.

35. This was a mutual defense pact valid for thirty-five years. When the treaty expired in 1996, Moscow was reluctant to renew it and emphasized that a new treaty should not contain any mutual defense commitments. After several years of stalemate, there was some belated movement toward the end of the Yeltsin administration, and in February 2000 Putin signed the Treaty of Friendship, Good-Neighborly Relations and Cooperation with Kim Jong-il. Importantly, however, the document contained no military provisions and was largely formalistic.

36. One should emphasize, of course, that this improvement is asymmetrical: political in the case of Russia-DPRK relations, economic in Russia-ROK relations. Unsurprisingly, there is an enormous disparity in Russian trade with the two Koreas: in 2006 Russia-DPRK turnover was a miserable U.S.$210 million, compared with U.S.$9.3 billion with the ROK—www.gks.ru/free_doc/2007/b07_11/25-05.htm. Keun-Wook Paik points out that moves by Gazprom to send pipeline gas to the DPRK have yet to bear fruit, and even promised exports of crude oil have not been confirmed—private communication with the author, December 22, 2007.

37. "Russia announces Koreas talks," BBC News item—http://news.bbc.co.uk/1/hi/world/asia-pacific/3139441.stm.

38. Nicholas Khoo and Michael Smith rightly note that "advocates of a concert system for Asia overlook an important ingredient that accounts for what is said to be its success in nineteenth century Europe, namely, the homogeneous nature of the continent's political regimes"—"A 'Concert of Asia'?" *Policy Review* 108, August 2001—www.hoover.org/publications/policyreview/3476536.html.

39. In this vein, one senior Japanese diplomat put it to the author in February 2007 that Russia's involvement in the Korean Six-Party talks was "more nuisance than value."

40. Khoo and Smith, "A 'Concert of Asia'?"

41. "Peace and prosperity" was the name of former South Korean president Roh Myung Moon's policy of engagement, which aimed to bring peace to the Korean peninsula and prosperity to both the Koreas. See Ko Jae-nam, "The Policy of Peace and Prosperity and South Korea-Russia Cooperation," *East Asian Review*, vol. 16, no. 3 (Autumn 2004): 3–16.

42. See Wang, "China's Changing Role in Asia," p. 4.

43. *China's Peaceful Rise: Speeches of Zheng Bijian, 1997–2005* (Brookings, 2005), pp. 17–18.

44. It is telling that Chinese academics view Russia not as a bridge between East and West or even as a Eurasian nation, but as the "Third West" after Europe and the United States—conversation with Yu Bin in Shanghai, May 2006.

45. See Rodolfo Severino, secretary-general of ASEAN, "The ASEAN Way and the Rule of Law," address in Kuala Lumpur, September 3, 2001—www.aseansec.org/2849.htm.

46. Vladimir Putin, "Rossiya i ATES: k ustoichivomu i stabilnomu razvitiyu Aziatsko-Tikhookeanskogo regiona," address at the APEC summit, Sydney, September 7, 2007—www.kremlin.ru/text/appears/2007/09/143334.shtml.

47. Crucially, the Russian experience of multilateralism has been limited largely to (i) pseudo-multilateral bodies such as the Warsaw Pact, COMECON, the CIS; or (ii) organizations where it preserves the right of veto, e.g., the UN Security Council and the OSCE.

48. It is notable, for example, that Moscow has always preferred to deal with individual EU member-states rather than with the EU as such.

49. See, for example, interview by the Chief of the General Staff, General Yury Baluyevsky, in *Nihon Keizai Shimbun*, February 10, 2006—www.old.mil.ru/print/articles/article12187.shtml.

50. Sherman Garnett, "Limited Partnership," in *Rapprochement or Rivalry? Russia–China Relations in a Changing Asia*, edited by Sherman Garnett (Washington, DC: Carnegie Endowment for International Peace, 2000), p. 13. Mikheev observes that the growth of China's defense spending will ensure that other Asia-Pacific countries follow suit: "Although the 'status' nature of the new stage in the arms race will not lead directly to military conflicts, it will increase rivalries and threaten cooperation in international relations in East Asia"—"East Asia and Russia's Development Strategy," p. 77.

51. Indeed, one can reasonably argue that Moscow sees enhanced opportunities to capitalize on the security concerns of a number of ASEAN member-states. Most recently, in September 2007, Rosoboronexport (the Russian arms exports agency) provided the Indonesian government with a credit line of U.S.$1 billion to purchase a range of Russian military equipment, including two Kilo-class submarines, 20 BMP-3 armored personnel carriers, 5 Mi-35 combat-transport helicopters, and 10 Mi-17 transport helicopters. According to press reports, Jakarta intends to buy Su-35 multipurpose fighters in the near future—"Rossiya beret Indoneziyu na vooruzhenie," *Kommersant-Daily*, September 7, 2007, p. 2.

52. See Lionel Martin, "Do Oil and Weapons Make a Marriage?" *Eurasia Daily Monitor*, vol. 2, no. 3, January 5, 2005—www.jamestown.org/edm/article_id.php?article_id=2369045.

53. If there is any shift, then it is likely to be one of growing indifference: "As China consolidates its economic and political positions in the region, East Asia's political and economic interest in Russia will tend to decline"—Mikheev, "East Asia and Russia's Development Strategy," p. 80.

54. Bobo Lo, "Putin's Oriental Puzzle," *The World Today*, vol. 61, no. 12 (December 2005): 15–16.

55. Gilbert Rozman, "Russia in Northeast Asia," in *Russian Foreign Policy in the 21st Century and the Shadow of the Past*, edited by Robert Legvold (Columbia University Press, 2007), p. 385.

56. Dmitri Trenin and Vasily Mikheev, *Russia and Japan as a Resource for Mutual Development: A 21st-Century Perspective on a 20th-Century Problem* (Carnegie Moscow Center, 2005), p. 4. According to Alexei Arbatov, "the key to the security of Siberia and the [Russian] Far East, along with a reasonable defense capability, is the development of balanced relations with other regional powers, Japan in the first instance"—*Rossiiskaya natsionalnaya ideya i vneshnyaya politika* (Moscow Social-Scientific Fund, 1998), p. 39.

57. The term "neo-containment" emerged in the mid-1990s to denote a more modern and nuanced version of strategic (Cold War) containment. *The Economist* defined it as "not . . . an overarching strategy for dealing with an overriding threat...[but as] a series of mini-containments" in response to an increasingly difficult Russia. During the 2000 U.S. presidential campaign, some of George W. Bush's advisers advocated neo-containment as an alternative to the Clintonian mission of democratic transformation. See "Introducing neo-containment," *The Economist*, May 6, 1995; Angela Stent, "Russia and America: How Close an Embrace?" *World Policy Journal*, vol. 20, no. 4 (Winter 2003/04)—www.worldpolicy.org/journal/articles/wpj 03-4/stent.html.

58. Gill and Huang, "Sources and Limits of Chinese 'Soft Power,'" p. 31.

59. *China's Peaceful Rise*, p. 1.

60. Peter Hays Gries observes that "the ways Chinese imagine their 'Century of Humiliation' at the hands of Western imperialists in the past have a powerful influence on the nature and direction of Chinese nationalism today"—*China's New Nationalism: Pride, Politics, and Diplomacy* (University of California Press, 2005), p. 19.

61. Gries notes the emergence in the 1990s of a "genuinely popular nationalism . . . that should not be conflated with state or official nationalism." This radical, sometimes uncontrolled nationalism was especially evident in the public reaction to the U.S. bombing of the Chinese Embassy in Belgrade on May 8, 1999—ibid., p. 20.

62. For an excellent account for the reasons behind the worsening of Russia's relations with the West, see Dmitri Trenin, "Russia Leaves the West," *Foreign Affairs* (July/August 2006): 87–96.

63. Bobo Lo, "Evolution or Regression? Russian Foreign Policy in Putin's Second Term," in *Towards a Post-Putin Russia*, edited by Helge Blakkisrud (Oslo: Norwegian Institute of International Affairs, 2006), pp. 71–72.

Chapter Eight

1. Putin remarks to the International Valdai Discussion Club, Novo-Ogarevo, September 9, 2006—www.kremlin.ru/text/appears/2006/09/111114.shtml.

2. Tom Miles and Emma Graham-Harrison, "Frustrated China seen getting no promises of Putin," *Toronto Star*, March 20, 2006.

3. "Sovereignty Is a Political Synonym for Competitiveness," speech by Deputy Head of the Presidential Administration Vladislav Surkov, at the Party Personnel Training and Education Centre of the United Russia Party, February 7, 2006—www.edinros.ru/news.html?id=111148.

4. Daniel Yergin notes that "the primary concern for both China and India is to ensure that they have sufficient energy to support economic growth and prevent debilitating energy shortfalls that could trigger social and political unrest"—"Ensuring Energy Security," *Foreign Affairs*, vol. 85, no. 2 (March/April 2006): 77.

5. Zha Daojiong, "China's Energy Security and Its International Relations," *China and Eurasia Forum Quarterly*, vol. 3, no. 3 (November 2005): 42.

6. Ibid., p. 48.

7. In 2007 Russia produced 490.83 million tonnes of oil, of which it exported 258.96 million tonnes. Gas production in the same year was 650.76 billion cubic meters (bcm), while exports totaled 191 bcm—"O tekushchei situatsii razvitiya promyshlennogo proizvodstva (janvar-dekabr 2007)," Russian Ministry of Industry and Energy, February 6, 2008—www.minprom.gov.ru/activity/light/stat/8/print.

8. In 2006 China's oil consumption was 349.8 million tonnes, while coal consumption reached 1191.3 million tones—www.bp.com/liveassets/bp_internet/globalbp/globalbp_uk_english/reports_and_publications/statistical_energy_review_2007/STAGING/local_assets/downloads/pdf/statistical_review_of_world_energy_full_ report _2007.pdf.

9. Putin remarks to the International Valdai Discussion Club.

10. Yergin, "Ensuring Energy Security," p. 77.

11. See David Fridley, "Natural Gas in China," in *Natural Gas in Asia: The Challenges of Growth in China, India, Japan and Korea*, 2nd ed., edited by Jonathan Stern and Ian Wybrew-Bond (Oxford Institute of Energy Studies, 2008), p. 59.

12. The Russian Ministry of Industry and Energy's "Eastern Gas Strategy" contains ambitious projections for exports to China and the Republic of Korea: 25–50 bcm of pipeline gas from 2020; 21 bcm of LNG by 2020, rising to 28 bcm by 2030—"Vostochnaya gazovaya programma— utverzhdena!," Ministry press release, September 7, 2007—www.minprom.gov.ru/activity/news/329/print. The vast range in the estimates for pipeline gas exports suggests they are dictated more by wishful thinking than by scientific calculation.

13. In July 2007 Deputy Industry and Energy Minister Andrei Dementyev stated that completion of the East Siberian oil pipeline would remain "on hold" until at least 2015 or even 2017, pending development of the East Siberian oil fields—"Siberia-Pacific Pipeline Put on Hold," *Radio Free Europe/Radio Liberty Newsline*, July 20, 2007—www.rferl.org/newsline/1-rus.asp?po=y.

14. There was an initial rapid rise from 3 million tonnes in 2002 to nearly 11 million tonnes in 2004. Since that time, growth has been uneven. Russian oil exports to China stayed at approximately the same level during the following year, before jumping to 15 million tonnes in 2006. In 2007, however, there was a decline, with exports

down 10 percent during January–October compared with the same period in 2006—
"Postavki rossiiskoi nefti v Kitai za 10 mesyatsev 2007g sokratilis na 10%—torgpred
Rossii"—Interfax news item, November 13, 2007.

15. "Oil Imports from All Sources on the Increase," press release from the PRC
Ministry of Commerce, March 6, 2007—http://vienna2.mof com.gov.cn/aarticle/
chinanews/200703/20070304442570.htm.

16. The PRC Ministry of Commerce press release emphasizes that China's imports
of crude oil from Venezuela and Kazakhstan "soared up tremendously." Imports from
Africa climbed to 31 percent of the total during 2006, a 14.2 percent increase over the
previous year—http://vienna2.mofcom.gov.cn/aarticle/chinanews/200703/20070304
442570.htm.

17. These included a Rosneft-CNPC agreement on "Basic Principles for the Creation of Joint Ventures"; a Protocol between Transneft and CNPC; an agreement
between United Energy Systems and the State Grid Corporation of China to carry out
a feasibility study for a project to supply electricity to the PRC; and a Memorandum
of Understanding between Gazprom and CNPC on deliveries of natural gas—
www.kremlin.ru/eng/text/docs/103472.shtml.

18. Viktor Vekselberg, executive director for gas business at TNK-BP, noted that
even according to "the most optimistic predictions," export supplies to China and
South Korea would begin "no sooner than 2012 or 2013"—"Viktor Vekselberg: Nothing Will Be for Free," *Kommersant*, May 5, 2006—www.kommersant.ru. A subsequent
report was even more pessimistic, claiming that the Russian government "does not
intend in the near future to construct the gas pipeline from Kovykta to China." It
quoted a government source as saying that the North European and Trans-Caspian
gas pipelines were the priorities and that the pipeline to China would not be built
"anytime soon"—see Andrei Lavrov, "Gazovaya OPEK sozdana," *Gazeta* 130, July 19,
2007— http://gzt.ru/business/2007/07/18/220012.html. With the impending sale of
TNK-BP's assets to Gazprom, the prospects for the pipeline look even dimmer.

19. In December 2006 the Kremlin used the twin excuse of project cost overruns
and "environmental concerns" to force Shell, the operating company of Sakhalin-2, to
sell half its shares to Gazprom for U.S.$6.75 billion (see chapter 7, note 28). For an
account of this sorry—and disruptive—affair, see Michael Bradshaw, "The Sakhalin
End Game: Two Wrongs Don't Make a Right," *Pacific Oil and Gas Report*, vol. 10, no. 1
(Spring 2007): 11–16.

20. In 2007 China imported 2.91 million tonnes of LNG through its Guangdong
terminal, a threefold increase from the previous year. 85 percent of the LNG came
from Australia's Northwest Shelf, with the rest bought on world spot markets—*Platts
Energy* news item, January 24, 2008—www.gasandoil.com/goc/news/nts80769.htm.

21. At a breakfast meeting with State Department correspondents on January 5,
2006, U.S. secretary of state Condoleezza Rice remarked that "it was not a good week
from the point of view of Russia's demonstrating that it is now prepared to act . . . as
an energy supplier in a responsible way. . . . Perhaps even they were a little surprised

at how clearly the point was made by European states in particular, that would have suffered from what appeared to us to be politically motivated efforts to constrain energy supply to Ukraine. The game just can't be played that way"—www.state.gov/secretary/rm/2006/58725.htm.

22. The "profit motive" in this context refers both to the desire of state-controlled companies to be commercially profitable and to the personal interest of Putin's inner circle in making money. Philip Hanson notes the Kremlin's predilection for offshore and opaque intermediary firms in energy deals, the most notorious example being the establishment of RosUkrEnergo in the wake of the January 2006 Russia-Ukraine gas crisis (communication with the author, November 27, 2007).

23. Dmitri Trenin, "Russia Redefines Itself and Its Relations with the West," *The Washington Quarterly*, vol. 30, no. 2 (Spring 2007): 99.

24. According to the terms of the Russia-Belarus gas deal of January 1, 2007, Minsk agreed to pay Gazprom U.S.$100 per 1,000 bcm (up from U.S.$46.68 in 2006) and to sell it half of Beltranshas. After further wrangling over import duties for Russian oil, which led to the temporary cut-off of the Druzhba pipeline, it was agreed on January 12 that Belarus would pay duties of U.S.$53 per tonne of imported oil. See David Marples, "Is Russia-Belarus Friendship Over?" *Eurasia Daily Monitor*, vol. 4, no. 10, January 15, 2007—www.jamestown.org/edm/article.php?article_id= 2371806.

25. It is not for nothing that Putin's Kremlin was known by many as "Kremlin Inc." Celeste Wallander describes a system of "patrimonial authoritarianism"—"a political system based on holding power in order to create, access, and distribute rents." Its inherent corruption "is not merely a feature of the system; it is essential to the very functioning of political power"—Celeste Wallander, "Russian Transimperialism and Its Implications," *The Washington Quarterly*, vol. 30, no. 2 (Spring 2007): 116.

26. *Energeticheskaya strategiya Rossii na period do 2020 goda*, part 5 ("Perspektivy sprosa na Rossiiskie energoresursy"), Russian Ministry of Industry and Energy, August 28, 2003—www.minprom.gov.ru/docs/strateg/1/print.

27. Europe accounts for over 90 percent of oil and gas exports from Russia—see http://en.g8russia.ru/agenda/nrgsafety/russianrole/index-print.html; also Roland Götz, "European Energy Foreign Policy and Russian Natural Gas," paper presented at the Transatlantic Workshop on the Role of Russia in European Energy Security, Oslo, December 12–13, 2007, p. 15.

28. Jeaseoung Choi and Gi C. Jung, "New LNG Projects in Asia and Their Effects on Pricing," paper presented at the World Gas Conference, June 2, 2003—http://igu.dgc.dk/html/wgc2003/WGC_pdffiles/10423_1046410594_19013_1.pdf.

29. In 2004 Rosneft and CNPC concluded a deal whereby the Russian side would supply China with 8.9 million tonnes of oil annually during the period 2006–10, all at a stable price. Following the sharp rise in global oil prices, however, Rosneft demanded that CNPC pay a rate more in line with the spot market. Although the two sides eventually agreed a compromise, Rosneft has since advised CNPC that it will not deliver oil to China after 2010 under the present arrangement. See John C. Webb and

Matthew J. Sagers, *From East Siberia to the Pacific: Putin's Oil Pipeline "Project of the Century"* (Cambridge, Mass.: Cambridge Energy Research Associates, March 2008), pp. 3, 32–33. The Chinese are aggrieved because Rosneft reneged on a freely negotiated contract and because the original agreement was quid pro quo for a U.S.$6 billion loan by the Bank of China in 2004. Without this loan, Rosneft would not have been able to buy Yuganskneftegaz, the production arm of Yukos, and transform itself into Russia's largest and richest oil company with a market capitalization value estimated at U.S.$60–80 billion by 2006 (up from U.S.$500 million in the late 1990s). See Yu Bin, "From Election Politics to Economic Posturing," *Comparative Connections,* vol. 10, no. 2 (April 2008), pp. 3–4; Nicklas Norling, "Russia's Energy Leverage Over China and the Sinopec–Rosneft Deal," *China and Eurasia Form Quarterly,* vol. 4, no. 4 (November 2006): 33–34.

30. Cambridge Energy Research Associates estimate that Russian Railways (RZD) can currently manage an annual maximum of 15 million tonnes—Webb and Sagers, *From East Siberia to the Pacific,* p. 32.

31. According to one estimate, China is set to become the world's largest producer of nuclear energy by 2050—David Zweig and Bi Jianhai, "China's Global Hunt for Energy," *Foreign Affairs,* vol. 84, no. 5 (September/October 2005): 36.

32. Meeting with news agency heads from the G-8 member-states, Novo-Ogarevo, June 2, 2006—www.kremlin.ru/text/appears/2006/06/106430.shtml.

33. For a detailed discussion of the dispute see Jonathan Stern, "The Russia–Ukrainian Gas Crisis of January 2006," Oxford Institute for Energy Studies, January 16, 2006.

34. See interview with Valery Chizhov, permanent representative of the Russian Federation at the EU, *Nezavisimaya gazeta,* February 5, 2007—www.russiaeu.mid.ru/in_0502.htm.

35. Bobo Lo, "Evolution or Regression? Russian Foreign Policy in Putin's Second Term," in *Towards a Post-Putin Russia,* edited by Helge Blakkisrud (Oslo: Norwegian Institute of International Affairs, 2006), p. 59.

36. Meeting with the International Valdai Discussion Club, Novo-Ogarevo, September 9, 2006—www.kremlin.ru/text/appears/2006/09/111114.shtml.

37. These are typically twenty-five-year agreements on a "take or pay" basis (whereby the customer pays for a certain amount of gas even if it uses less). Gazprom has agreements with two-thirds of the EU-27, plus Turkey, Serbia, Montenegro, and Bosnia Herzegovina—www.gazprom.ru/eng/articles/article20160.shtml.

38. Defined as the conversion of economic trumps into political-strategic capital—Bobo Lo, *Vladimir Putin and the Evolution of Russian Foreign Policy* (Oxford: Blackwell for the Royal Institute of International Affairs, 2003), p. 67.

39. In January 2006 Georgia reacted to the cut-off in Russian gas supplies by turning to Iran (via Azerbaijan)—Diana Petriashvili, "Gas Crisis Over, Georgia Vows to Diversify Energy Supplies," *Eurasia Insight,* January 31, 2006—www.eurasianet.org/departments/insight/articles/eav013106_pr.shtml.

40. Viktor Khristenko, "Energeticheskaya strategiya Rossii: proryv na vostok," *Vedomosti*, February 6, 2006—www.vedomosti.ru/newspaper/article.shtml?2006/02/06/102474.

41. In the wake of Gazprom's unsuccessful bid to buy into the British gas service provider Centrica, CEO Alexei Miller met with EU ambassadors in Moscow to raise Russian concerns. Gazprom subsequently issued a statement warning that it might redirect supplies to other markets: "It should not be forgotten that we are actively familiarising ourselves with new markets, such as North America and China . . . competition for energy resources is growing." Gazprom spokesman Sergei Kupriyanov told the *Financial Times* that "we just want European countries to understand that we have other alternatives in terms of gas sales. We have a fast-growing Chinese market, and a market for liquefied natural gas in [the United States]. If the European Union wants our gas, then it will have to consider our interests as well"—Neil Buckley and Arkady Ostrovsky, "Gazprom issues threat to EU gas supply," *Financial Times*, April 19, 2006, http://search.ft.com/ftArticle?queryText=gazprom+issues+threat+to+EU+gas+supply&y=3&aje=true&x=18&id=060419011001&ct=0.

42. Lo, "Evolution or Regression?" p. 75.

43. The Nord Stream gas pipeline will extend 1,220 kilometers from Vyborg in Russia to Greifswald on Germany's Baltic coast. It is scheduled to be completed in 2011, with the first deliveries of gas starting the following year—www.nord-stream.com/project.html. The project is highly controversial. Some countries, notably Poland and Ukraine, view it as part of Russian strategy to maximize energy leverage over them. The South Stream project envisages piping gas from Russia's Black Sea coast to Italy via Bulgaria. Two routes are planned: a southern line passing through Greece to southern Italy, and a northern line through Serbia and Hungary and on to northern Italy. The project is still in its very early stages, and there are real doubts as to its commercial feasibility. It too is seen as a highly political exercise—a means of undermining the EU's Nabucco pipeline and, by extension, EU influence in central and southern Europe.

44. The Kremlin's determination to control the terms of engagement with foreign energy interests was especially apparent in its handling of the Shtokman gas project. In September 2006 it declared that it would develop the field without any international participation, dashing the hopes of Chevron and Conoco-Phillips, which had been proposing to take LNG to the United States. In July 2007 Gazprom admitted Statoil (Norway) and Total (France) to the project, but on very unequal terms. Gazprom held a controlling 51 percent share, and the foreign companies were denied any claim of ownership over the reserves. See Jorn Madslein, "Shock as Russia Goes Solo over Gas Field," October 9, 2006—http://news.bbc.co.uk/1/hi/business/6035811.stm; Andrew E. Kramer, "French Oil Giant Agrees to Work on a Russian Natural Gas Project," *The New York Times*, July 13, 2007—www.nytimes.com/2007/07/13/business/worldbusiness/13gazprom.html?scp=1&sq=french+oil+giant+kramer&st=nyt.

45. The formal existence of a Common Strategy of the European Union on Russia has done nothing to minimize the considerable divisions between member-states over how best to engage Moscow.

46. Comments by Chancellor Angela Merkel in *Der Spiegel* on January 9, 2006, cited in "German Chancellor Has 'Concerns' about Russia," *Radio Free Europe/Radio Liberty Newsline*, January 9, 2006—www.rferl.org/newsline/2006/01/090106.asp. See also Katinka Barysch, "Russia, Realism and EU Unity," *Centre for European Reform Policy Brief*, July 2007, p. 5.

47. Strobe Talbott, "Gogol's Troika: The Case for Strategic Patience in a Time of Troubles," address at Stanford University, November 6, 1998—www.fas.org/news/russia/1998/98110607_wlt.html.

48. The most notorious example of this was the blocking of CNPC's participation in the auction for Slavneft in 2002. A more recent example is the limiting of CNPC's purchase of Rosneft shares in the IPO (Initial Public Offering) of July 2006. CNPC had wanted to buy up to U.S.$3 billion worth of shares, but was restricted to U.S.$500 million. Other foreign companies, such as BP and Petronias (Malaysia), were allowed to purchase twice that amount—see Norling, "Russia's Energy Leverage Over China and the Sinopec–Rosneft Deal," p. 34.

49. The number of foreign countries supplying oil to China rose from five in 1989 to thirty-two in 2005—Linda Jakobson and Zha Daojiong, "China and the Worldwide Search for Oil Security," *Asia-Pacific Review*, vol. 13, no. 2 (November 2006): 63.

50. Mikkal E. Herberg, "Asia's Energy Insecurity: Cooperation or Conflict?" in *Strategic Asia 2004-05: Confronting Terrorism in the Pursuit of Power*, edited by Ashley J. Tellis and Michael Wills (Seattle and Washington, DC: National Bureau of Asian Research, 2004), pp. 351–52.

51. To this end the Chinese government has set itself the ambitious target of a 20 percent reduction in energy consumption per unit of GDP and intends to spend U.S.$150 billion on renewable and alternative energy in the period up to 2020—Wen-ran Jiang, "Beijing's 'New Thinking' on Energy Security," *China Brief*, vol. 6, no. 8 (April 12, 2006)—http://jamestown.org/china_brief/article.php?articleid=2373181. Crucially, there is growing evidence that energy efficiency and environmental targets are assuming real importance as performance indicators for local authorities (author's conversations in Shanghai and Beijing, May 2008).

52. See Xuegang Zhang, "China's Energy Corridors in Southeast Asia," *China Brief*, vol. 8, no. 3 (January 31, 2008): 4–7—www.jamestown.org/terrorism/news/uploads/cb_008_003d.pdf.

53. A very senior official in China's National Development and Reform Commission (NDRC) complained to the author in May 2008 that Russia seemed more interested in "games-playing" than in energy cooperation.

54. To put matters into perspective, Russia's share of total Chinese oil imports—11 percent in 2006—is seven times less than the combined figure of the Middle East

(45 percent) and Africa (31 percent)—http://vienna2.mofcom.gov.cn/aarticle/china news/200703/20070304442570.html.

55. As William Tompson has put it, "Khodorkovskii's destruction was a means to a larger end—the re-definition of the Kremlin's relationship with big business"—"Putin and the 'Oligarchs': A Two-Sided Commitment Problem," in *Leading Russia: Putin in Perspective*, edited by Alex Pravda (Oxford University Press, 2005), p. 192.

56. Yu Bin, "The Russian–Chinese Oil Politik," *Comparative Connections*, vol. 5, no. 3 (October 2003): 139. The nature and extent of the Japanese financial package are shrouded in mystery. Some estimates put the total figure as high as U.S.$14 billion—see Sergei Blagov, "Russia's Pacific Pipeline Seen as Double-Edged Sword," *Eurasia Daily Monitor*, vol. 2, no. 8, January 12, 2005—www.jamestown.org/edm/article.php?article_id=2369078. Other sources are more conservative, claiming merely that then Japanese foreign minister Yukio Kawaguchi offered low-interest loans of up to ¥900 billion (equivalent to U.S.$7.5 billion) in the course of a meeting in Vladivostok in March 2003 with Russian deputy prime minister Viktor Khristenko—"Japan Sweetens Offer for Siberian Pipeline," *Alexander's Gas and Oil Connections*, August 8, 2003—www.gasandoil.com/goc/news/ntr33235.htm. Some Japanese sources even assert that Tokyo has never offered the Russians a financial package (Shoichi Itoh, in a meeting at Chatham House on December 14, 2007). This last possibility seems unlikely, however, given both the weight of countervailing evidence and the improbability that the Russian government would undertake the longer and more expensive route without external financial inducements.

57. Russia had already experienced a similar problem with the Blue Stream gas pipeline to Turkey in 2003, when Ankara held up deliveries for six months. See Lyle Goldstein and Vitaly Kozyrev, "China, Japan and the Scramble for Siberia," *Survival*, vol. 48, no. 1 (Spring 2006): 171.

58. Ibid., p. 172.

59. For a detailed account of the environmental issues, see Shoichi Itoh, "The Pacific Pipeline at a Crossroads: Dream Project or Pipe Dream?" *ERINA Report*, vol. 73 (January 2007): 51–53—www.erina.or.jp/en/Publications/er/pdf/Er73.pdf. The view of most foreign and Russian energy experts in Moscow was that the environmental case was essentially a pretext to give the Russian government greater leverage, as well as more time to negotiate a better deal.

60. As chairman of Rosneft, Sechin benefited enormously from the U.S. $6 billion Chinese loan that enabled the company to buy Yuganskneftegaz (see note 29 above).

61. Private communication from Japanese Foreign Ministry official.

62. Itoh, "The Pacific Pipeline at a Crossroads," p. 50.

63. Blagov, "Russia's Pacific Oil Pipeline Seen as Double-Edged Sword."

64. Valeria Korchagina, "China Offers $400m for Oil Pipeline," *Moscow Times*, March 23, 2006, p. 1.

65. Putin's response to a question from the author at a meeting with the International Valdai Discussion Club, Kremlin, September 5, 2005.

66. Putin's meeting with the International Valdai Discussion Club, Novo-Ogarevo, September 9, 2006—www.kremlin.ru/text/appears/2006/09/111114.shtml.

67. In 2003 Moscow was quite optimistic about the possibilities of real movement in several areas of the relationship, including on the territorial question. Fast forward a couple of years, however, and this promise had evaporated in the face of a new militancy on both sides.

68. A third possibility is that neither pipeline will be built. The oil will be piped to Skovorodino (end of ESPO stage 1), and then transported by rail south to China and east to the Russian Pacific coast—Webb and Sagers, *From East Siberia to the Pacific*, p. 31.

69. Koizumi's successor Shinzo Abe lasted less than a year, while the current Japanese prime minister, Yasuo Fukuda, is under considerable pressure from his own Liberal Democratic Party, the political opposition, and plummeting popularity ratings (down to 25 percent). See Purnendra Jain, "Fukuda's political troubles deepen," *Asia Times Online*, May 3, 2008—www.atimes.com/atimes/Japan/JE03Dh01.html.

70. Trenin, "Russia Redefines Itself and Its Relations with the West," p. 95. Putin has justified this conflict of interest by arguing that senior Kremlin figures occupy the most senior (and lucrative) positions in Russia's "national champions" in order to defend the interests of the state—www.kremlin.ru/text/appears/2006/09/111114.shtml.

71. Such as Russia's long-term gas agreements with a number of European countries.

72. I am indebted to John Lough for this insight.

73. Trenin puts it very well: "Aside from a general preference for economic expansion over integration, Moscow is pursuing few long-term strategies. Tactics prevail, medium-term thinking is just emerging, and no national interest worth the name has surfaced"—"Russia Redefines Itself and Its Relations with the West," p. 104.

74. Konstantin Vnukov, "Moscow-Beijing: New Vistas of Cooperation," *International Affairs* (Moscow), vol. 52, no. 3 (August 2006): 43.

75. One of the more extreme expressions of this view came during a presentation by Foreign Minister Lavrov at a closed session of the Federation Council on November 8, 2007. Lavrov allegedly stated that "Russia is on the rise, Western Europe lacks ideological unity, and the United States finds itself in a blind alley." He added that Russia could bring down the international system if it felt so disposed, which would lead to the emergence of a "new system"—see "Foreign Minister Says International Relations Face 'Moment of Truth,'" *Radio Free Europe/Radio Liberty Newsline*, November 9, 2007—www.rferl.org/newsline/1-rus.asp.

76. Notably, Gazprom CEO Alexei Miller—see note 41 above.

77. In 1968 Austria was the first West European country to import Soviet gas. It was followed by Italy in 1969 and West Germany in 1970—see www.gazexport.ru/history/?pkey1=00002.

78. UBS, for example, expects total European gas demand to rise from 510 bcm in 2004 to 577 bcm in 2010 and 645 bcm in 2015. Over the same period, it forecasts that demand for Russian gas will rise from 161 bcm in 2005 to 184 bcm in 2010 and 215 bcm in 2015—*Russian Gas*, UBS Investment Research Report, July 12, 2006, p. 34.

79. "RUSIA Petroleum, CNPC and KOGAS Complete Kovykta International Feasibility Study," *Insight TNK-BP*, December 2003, pp. 6–7.

80. Roman Kupchinsky, "Moscow Mulls Its China Energy Strategy," *Radio Free Europe/Radio Liberty Report*, September 8, 2006—www.rferl.org/features article/2006/9/93A2DB5A-9043-4482-BB4B-681A2BE6F40A.html; also Rifat Kandiyoti, "China's Pipeline Politics," March 27, 2007—www.chinadialogue.net/article/show/single/en/880-China-s-pipeline-politics. In theory Chinese requirements would be met with pipeline gas and LNG from Sakhalin, but this remains a notional proposition. In 2007 Gazprom, supported by the Kremlin, blocked an agreement that would have enabled ExxonMobil to export 8 bcm per annum of Sakhalin-1 gas to China. See Kim Feng Wong and Martin Daniel, "Asia's Gas Conundrum," *Platts Insight*, February 1, 2007—www.platts.com/Magazines/Insight/2007/sep/2HD0070 D90RP716C0y549B_1.xml.

81. "Minister Says Siberian Gas Supplies to Go Where Sales Dictate," *RIA-Novosti*, September 21, 2005—http://en.rian.ru/business/20050921/41461936-print.html.

82. These are expected to rise considerably over the next couple of years, perhaps even to U.S.$500 per 1,000 cm in some cases.

83. According to Vladimir Milov, the former Russian deputy energy minister, Beijing previously hoped to pay only U.S.$40 per 1,000 cubic meters—"How Sustainable is Russia's Future as an Energy Superpower?" summary of presentation at the Carnegie Endowment for International Peace, Washington, DC, March 16, 2006—www.carnegieendowment.org/events/index.cfm?fa=eventDetail&id=860. Recent sources suggest, however, that the Chinese now understand that they must pay something more in line with international prices (or at least the prices paid by countries such as Belarus)—Lin Fanjing, "Russian Duopolies, Poles Apart," *China Oil, Gas & Petrochemicals*, July 15, 2007, p. 16.

84. Götz, "European Energy Foreign Policy and Russian Natural Gas," p. 9. UBS estimates Shtokman's gas reserves at 3.6 trillion cubic meters (tcm) and Yamal's potential reserves at more than 50 tcm. By contrast, Kovykta's reserves are estimated at 2 tcm—*Russian Gas*, pp. 52, 55, 89.

85. The future of the Altai-Xinjiang pipeline is uncertain, to say the least. Aleksandr Ananenkov, deputy head of the Gazprom board, announced in July 2007 that unless gas negotiations with the Chinese were completed that year, implementation of the project would not even start until 2012—"Russia-China gas pipeline project could be delayed," *Alexander's Gas and Oil Connections*, vol. 12, no. 14, July 27, 2007—www.gasandoil.com/goc/news/ntr73056.htm.

86. Vladimir Milov, presentation at the conference on "The Economics and Geopolitics of Russian Energy," Georgetown University, October 29, 2007.

87. As Gazprom puts it, the intention is to raise domestic prices to "the level of the European market, factoring in [i.e., minus] the costs of transportation and customs duties"—www.gazprom.ru/articles/article25604.shtml. Domestic gas prices had been scheduled to increase from U.S.$50.6 per 1,000 cm on July 1, 2007, to U.S.$102 per 1,000 cm by July 1, 2010—Pekka Sutela, "Curbing Domestic Russian Gas Consumption—How and How Likely?" presentation at the Oslo Energy Workshop, December 13, 2007, p. 14. However, the Russian government decided subsequently to postpone the full price liberalization because the sharp rise in international gas prices would have meant higher than anticipated increases at home, with potential political consequences around the time of the 2011–12 election cycle—"Russia Gas: Netback Pushback," *MGA Energy Special Report*, May 6, 2008.

88. Philip Hanson emphasizes that "the real worry [for Europe] is not so much Russian use of energy leverage but Russia's doubtful capacity to increase, or even maintain, its oil and gas supplies to Europe"—"The Sustainability of Russia's Energy Power: Implications for the Russian Economy," *Economics Working Paper* 84, UCL/SSEES Centre for the Study of Economic and Social Change in Europe, London, December 2007, p. 17.

89. Recent notable examples of Russian success in splitting the Europeans include the partnership with Germany's E.ON-Ruhrgas over Nord Stream; the participation of Italy's ENI in South Stream (undercutting the EU's own Nabucco project); and the involvement of France's Total and Norway's Statoil in Shtokman.

90. Vladimir Milov, "Putin's Russia and Its Energy Policy," presentation at Chatham House, London, September 20, 2006.

91. For example, Putin claimed that Russia would lose U.S.$3.3 billion in natural gas revenue as a result of the January 2007 dispute with Belarus—"Putin Warns of Oil-Supply Cuts," *Radio Free Europe/Radio Liberty Newsline*, January 10, 2007—www.rferl.org/newsline/2007/01/100107.asp.

92. German chancellor Angela Merkel and European Commission president José Manuel Barroso were particularly critical when oil supplies were disrupted as a result of the Russia-Belarus stand-off. Merkel warned that the interruption "destroys trust," while Barroso called for the EU to "develop effective solidarity mechanisms to deal with any energy supply crisis and actively develop a common external energy policy"—Ahto Lobjakas, "EU: Proposed Energy Policy Overhaul Accompanies Supply Woes," *Radio Free Europe/Radio Liberty*, January 10, 2007—www.rferl.org/features article/2007/01/f7a61d68-4fc7-453c-b6e8-38f173f01b98.html.

93. In 2006 the EU accounted for 58.9 percent of Russia's total exports and 45.9 percent of its imports. (China took 5.4 percent of Russian exports and contributed 9.8 percent of its imports.) Russia's share of total EU exports was 6.2 percent, while its share of imports was 10.1 percent—http://trade.ec.europa.eu/doclib/docs/2006/september/tradoc_113440.pdf.

94. Total Chinese investment in Russia during 2006 was a modest U.S.$935 million—*RBCC* [Russo-British Chamber of Commerce] *Weekly Observer*, no. 60 (July 23–30, 2007), p. 7. The most significant Chinese investment in Russia is the Baltic Pearl residential complex in St. Petersburg. Scheduled to be completed in 2012, this U.S.$1.35 billion project will eventually provide housing and services for 35,000 people—Yu Bin, "Partying and Posturing for Power, Petro, and Prestige . . . ," *Comparative Connections*, vol. 9, no. 2 (July 2007): 160.

95. Yu Bin, "China–Russia Relations: G-8, Geoeconomics, and Growing 'Talk' Fatigue," *Comparative Connections*, vol. 8, no. 3 (October 13, 2006)—www.csis.org/media/csis/pubs/0603qchina_russia.pdf.

96. Jonathan Stern sees Sakhalin as the future gas hub of East Asia, although he argues that it will be China rather than Russia that will be forced to come to terms—communication with the author, December 2007.

97. Norling, "Russia's Energy Leverage Over China and the Sinopec–Rosneft Deal," p. 36.

98. Foreign Minister Lavrov writes of Russia "interfacing the interests of the West and the East for the purpose of solving acute problems of the present"—Lavrov, "The Rise of Asia, and the Eastern Vector of Russia's Foreign Policy," *Russia in Global Affairs*, vol. 4, no. 3 (July–September 2006): 69.

99. In recent times the Kremlin has become partial to the term "soft power" in relation to Russian foreign policy. Its understanding of soft power, however, differs substantially from that of Joseph Nye, the originator of the concept. Whereas Nye views it as power through persuasion rather than coercion, Moscow interprets it as essentially non-military power. Under this generous definition, the use of economic leverage qualifies as "soft power."

100. Recent Western responses on Tibet illustrate an ability to ring-fence commercial interests from moral outrage. In March 2008 the Chinese authorities suppressed violent demonstrations in Tibet and Gansu province, leading to strong public condemnation from the United States, France, Germany, and many others. The criticism gathered further momentum during the ill-fated Olympic torch relay. However, many of the same countries were quick to assure Beijing of their continuing commitment to economic and political engagement.

101. Zweig and Bi, "China's Global Hunt for Energy," p. 37.

Chapter Nine

1. "Yesterday Clinton permitted himself to pressure Russia. Evidently, he, for a second, a minute, half a minute, forgot what Russia is and that Russia possesses a full nuclear arsenal. So I want to say to Clinton through you that he should not forget what world he lives in! It has never been the case, and never will be, that he alone will dictate to the whole world how it should live, labor, work, rest, and so on. No and once again no! A multipolar world is the basis of everything. That is what I have agreed

with Jiang Zemin, Chairman of the People's Republic of China. We will dictate to the world how to live, and not him [Clinton] alone!"—*Kommersant*, December 10, 1999—www.kommersant.ru/doc.aspx?DocsID=232501&print=true.

2. Zbigniew Brzezinski, *The Grand Chessboard: American Primacy and Its Geostrategic Imperatives* (New York: Basic Books, 1997), p. 117.

3. As defined by Richard Falk, "a neo-Westphalian world order would continue to be understood primarily through the prism of statist geopolitics, although accompanied by a conceptual acknowledgement that normative concerns are integral (relevance of international law and morality) and that transnationalism (localism, regionalism, and cosmopolitanism) is significantly more relevant than in the Westphalian era"—*The Declining World Order: America's Imperial Geopolitics* (New York and London: Routledge, 2004), p. 20.

4. Brzezinski, *The Grand Chessboard*, p. 215.

5. President George H.W. Bush first enunciated the concept of a "new world order" in a speech to the U.S. Congress on January 16, 1991, two hours after the beginning of the first American-led military intervention against Saddam Hussein: "This is an historic moment. We have in this past year made great progress in ending the long era of conflict and cold war. We have before us the opportunity to forge for ourselves and for future generations a new world order, a world where the rule of law, not the law of the jungle, governs the conduct of nations"—www.famousquotes.me.uk/speeches/ George_Bush/.

6. Christopher Marsh, "Russia Plays the China Card," *The National Interest*, no. 92 (November–December 2007)—www.nationalinterest.org/Article.aspx?id=16028; also Constantine C. Menges, *China: The Gathering Threat* (Nashville, Tenn.: Nelson Current, 2005), pp. 364–66.

7. "Russian-Chinese Joint Declaration on a Multipolar World and the Establishment of a New International Order," Moscow, April 23, 1997—www.un.org/ documents/ga/docs/52/plenary/a52-153.htm.

8. "Sovmestnaya deklaratsiya Rossiiskoi Federatsii i Kitaiskoi Narodnoi Respubliki o mezhdunarodnom poryadke v XXI veke," Moscow, July 1, 2005—www.kremlin. ru/text/docs/2005/07/90623.shtml.

9. Brzezinski, *The Grand Chessboard*, p. 35.

10. Ibid., pp. 196–99.

11. Brzezinski defined "geostrategic players"—France, Germany, Russia, China, and India—as "states that have the capacity and the national will to exercise power or influence beyond their borders in order to alter—to a degree that affects America's interests—the existing geopolitical state of affairs." "Geopolitical pivots," on the other hand, were "states whose importance is derived not from their power and motivation but rather from their sensitive location and from the consequences of their potentially vulnerable condition for the behavior of geostrategic players." Geopolitical pivots included Ukraine, Azerbaijan, Turkey, Iran, and South Korea—ibid., pp. 40–41.

12. Ibid., p. 198.

13. Paul Kennedy first coined the term "imperial overstretch" or "the problem of strategical overextension" in relation to the United States. See *The Rise and Fall of the Great Powers* (London: Fontana Press 1989), pp. 666–74.

14. Brzezinski wrote that "the United States stands supreme in the four decisive domains of global power: militarily it has an unmatched global reach; economically, it remains the main locomotive of global growth . . . technologically, it retains the overall lead in the cutting-edge areas of innovation; and culturally, despite some crassness, it enjoys an appeal that is unrivaled"—*The Grand Chessboard*, p. 24.

15. Thus Wang Jisi notes that "the Chinese projection of the 'inevitability of multipolarity' does not prevent them from noting, at least privately, the 'tide of the day' is otherwise—the United States will remain the only global hegemonic power for decades to come. Chinese policy analysts, being realists, have few illusions about the feasibility of formulating a lasting international coalition that could serve as the counterforce to U.S. power." See *China's Changing Role in Asia* (Washington, DC: Atlantic Council of the United States, January 2004), p. 15.

16. Julian Cooper points out that Russia is less competitive than other populous emerging economies. In the World Economic Forum Global Index for 2005–06, it ranked 75th, compared with China (49th), India (50th), and Brazil (65th). In business competitiveness, the respective rankings were 74th, 57th, 31st, and 49th. Moreover, the trend is negative, with Russia having slipped down the rankings since 2003. Cooper observes that Russia "gives the impression of being much less disposed to learn from others," and that its "development as a more knowledge-based economy is also hampered by its security orientation and practices inherited from Soviet times, and given new impetus by the political elite's perception that the country is insecure and that its sovereignty is under threat."—Julian Cooper, "Of BRICs and Brains: Comparing Russia with China, India, and Other Populous Emerging Economies," *Eurasian Geography and Economics*, vol. 47, no. 3 (May/June 2006): 276–79.

17. "The forty years' experience of Sun Yat-sen and the twenty-eight years' experience of the Communist Party have taught us to lean to one side . . . all Chinese without exception must lean either to the side of imperialism or to the side of socialism. Sitting on the fence will not do, nor is there a third road"—Mao Zedong, "On the People's Democratic Dictatorship," speech commemorating the 28th anniversary of the Chinese Communist Party, June 30, 1949—www.marxists.org/reference/archive/mao/selected-works/volume-4/mswv4_65.htm.

18. As Nixon told Kissinger, "we're doing the China thing to screw the Russians and help us in Vietnam . . ."—David Reynolds, *Summits: Six Meetings that Shaped the Twentieth Century* (New York: Basic Books, 2007), p. 240. Kissinger himself opined that "for the next 15 years we have to lean toward the Chinese against the Russians. We have to play this balance of power game totally unemotionally. Right now we need the Chinese to correct the Russians and to discipline the Russians"—*Washington Journal of Modern China*, vol. 8, no. 2 (Spring 2007): 3.

19. Reynolds, *Summits*, p. 242.

20. *The Military Balance 1980-1981* (Oxford University Press for the International Institute of Strategic Studies), pp. 11, 63.

21. See Gilbert Rozman, "A New Sino-Russian-American Triangle?" *Orbis* (Fall 2000): 552.

22. Brzezinski, *The Grand Chessboard*, p. 87.

23. It should be recognized that China's impressive economic growth throughout the 1980s was already giving it the base to become more than just a regional power.

24. Although strategic triangularism may have "virtually vanished from Western discussions of current affairs" (Rozman, "A New Sino-Russian-American Triangle?" p. 552), this was certainly not the case in Russia, judging from the author's many conversations with local academics and journalists during the 1990s.

25. Although Yeltsin's first foreign minister, Andrei Kozyrev, denied any interest in a condominium arrangement, this notion was implicit in his assertion that "the stage is set . . . for Russia and the United States to influence positively the course of world affairs . . . through a constructive partnership"—Andrei Kozyrev, "The Lagging Partnership," *Foreign Affairs*, vol. 73, no. 3 (May/June 1994): 59.

26. As Kozyrev put it: "Russia is doomed to be a great power"—"Rossiya i SShA: Partnerstvo ne prezhdevremenno, a zapazdyvaet," *Izvestiya*, March 11, 1994, p. 3.

27. One critical factor that encouraged the return of geopolitics was NATO's push eastward to include Hungary, Czechoslovakia, and Poland—see Yevgeny Primakov, "Opravdano li rasshirenie NATO?" *Nezavisimaya gazeta*, November 26, 1993, pp. 1, 3.

28. As Andrei Tsygankov points out, "geopolitics was quickly becoming the name of the national discourse, and Westernizers could no longer be taken seriously without framing what they had to say in geopolitical terms"—*Russia's Foreign Policy: Change and Continuity in National Identity* (Lanham, Md.: Rowman & Littlefield, 2006), p. 66.

29. Bobo Lo, *Russian Foreign Policy in the Post-Soviet Era: Reality, Illusion and Mythmaking* (Basingstoke and New York: Palgrave Macmillan, 2002), p. 108.

30. In some cases the Europeans led the way; for example, Germany was the most enthusiastic proponent of NATO enlargement.

31. Lo, *Russian Foreign Policy in the Post-Soviet Era*, p. 108.

32. Strobe Talbott, U.S. assistant secretary of state under Bill Clinton, recounts a meeting with Prime Minister Chernomyrdin in February 1997 at which the latter "reprised threats and warnings we'd been hearing for several years: there would be dire consequences for Russian reform . . . ; there would be military and political countermeasures (no ratification of outstanding arms control treaties, greater Russian reliance on nuclear weapons, stronger ties with Iran and China). He left us in no doubt that Russia would continue relentlessly to exploit any differences between us and our allies"—Strobe Talbott, *The Russia Hand: A Memoir of Presidential Diplomacy* (New York: Random House, 2003), p. 233.

33. www.un.org/documents/ga/docs/52/plenary/a52-153.htm.

34. The notion of Russia's "indispensability" was a common refrain throughout the 1990s, all the more vocally expressed as its domestic and foreign policy weaknesses became ever more apparent.

35. See quotation at the head of this chapter.

36. Charles Krauthammer, "The Unipolar Moment," *Foreign Affairs*, vol. 70, no. 1 (Winter 1990/91), pp. 23–33.

37. Ramesh Thakur and Zhang Yunling, "China, India, Russia: Eyeing New Alignments," *International Herald Tribune*, November 30, 1999—www.iht.com/articles/1999/11/30/edram.t.php. Primakov, of course, was careful to couch his proposal in terms of the three countries working to ensure regional peace and stability—see Amit Baruah, "A chance to take centre stage," *The Hindu*, May 13, 2005—www.hindu.com/2005/05/13/stories/2005051300341000.htm.

38. Rozman, "A New Sino-Russian-American Triangle?" p. 552.

39. Zbigniew Brzezinski, "The Dilemma of the Last Sovereign," *The American Interest* (Autumn 2005), p. 39.

40. Brzezinski, *The Grand Chessboard*, p. 159.

41. Ibid., p. 164.

42. For a most persuasive and entertaining account of China's global impact, see James Kynge, *China Shakes the World* (London: Weidenfeld & Nicolson, 2006).

43. Mikhail Margelov, "Russian-Chinese Relations: At Their Peak?" *International Affairs* (Moscow), vol. 49, no. 6 (2003): 85.

44. Ibid., p. 83.

45. Konstantin Vnukov, "Moscow-Beijing: New Vistas of Cooperation," *International Affairs* (Moscow), vol. 52, no. 3 (2006): 44.

46. Interestingly, Primakov retains an influential if behind-the-scenes role as a key foreign policy adviser to Putin. In July 2007 he led the Russian side in talks with a small U.S. delegation headed by Henry Kissinger on the theme of "Russia-USA: A Look into the Future." In his welcoming address, Putin pointedly remarked that the meeting's findings "should not be brought to our foreign ministries to gather dust there"—an indication perhaps of the relative influence of Primakov and the Ministry for Foreign Affairs. See "Kissinger-led U.S. group attends closed debate at Putin home," *RIA-Novosti*, July 13, 2007—http://en.rian.ru/russia/20070713/68933469.html.

47. Putin's interview with NBC, July 12, 2006—www.kremlin.ru/appears/2006/07/12/1130_type63379_108507.shtml.

48. Bobo Lo, "Evolution or Regression? Russian Foreign Policy in Putin's Second Term," in *Towards a Post-Putin Russia*, edited by Helge Blakkisrud (Oslo: Norwegian Institute of International Affairs, 2006), p. 75.

49. Many commentators believe that relations between Russia and the United States are worse than at any time since the end of the Cold War. Indeed, the Georgian crisis has spawned talk of a "new Cold War."

50. Andrew Kuchins, "Russian Democracy and Civil Society: Back to the Future," testimony before the U.S. Commission on Security and Cooperation in Europe,

February 8, 2006—www.carnegieendowment.org/publications/index.cfm?fa=view &id=18007. The original "Time of Troubles" was the period between the death of Tsar Fedor, the last of the Rurik dynasty, in 1598 and the accession of Mikhail Romanov in 1613. During this period Muscovy was beset by internecine quarrels, political and social anarchy, and foreign invasion.

51. Dmitri Trenin, "What You See Is What You Get," *The World Today*, vol. 60, no. 4 (April 2004): 13–14.

52. Writing in 2000, Rozman remarked that "Russians, from the man on the street to regional political leaders to the Duma, are so fearful of becoming the *junior* partner of China that they really do not want these relations to advance appreciably"—"A New Sino-Russian-American Triangle?" p. 553. China's astonishing rise since then has only reinforced Russian apprehension.

53. Dmitri Trenin posits the idea of Russia's becoming part of the "New West," as distinct from the "Euro-Atlantic West." This New West—comprising Asian, Latin American, East European, and African nations—is focused principally on developing capitalism (including institution-building and secure property rights) rather than Western-style democracy and civil society—*Getting Russia Right* (Washington, DC: Carnegie Endowment for International Peace, 2007), pp. 47, 104–05.

54. See chapter 3, note 69. On the other hand, Brzezinski refers to the "increasingly anomalous G-8" and argues strongly for a G-14 "that would have the added advantage of engaging both China and India" ("The Dilemma of the Last Sovereign," p. 45).

55. Hu Jintao's speech at the Sydney APEC Summit, September 6, 2007—www. mfa.gov.cn/eng/wjdt/zyjh/t359776.htm.

56. Wang, *China's Changing Role in Asia*, p. 3.

57. Ibid., p. 15.

58. An example of this is its unceasing allergic reaction to NATO enlargement. This has only stoked anti-Russian sentiment in central and eastern Europe and vindicated NATO membership for the Visegrad and Baltic states.

59. Although China's relations with the EU are easier than with the United States and Japan, they are by no means problem-free. The proliferation of trade disputes (for example, relating to market access and intellectual property rights), European discontent over under-valuation of the renminbi, the continuing EU arms embargo, and most recently the furor over Tibet indicate otherwise. See Charles Grant with Katinka Barysch, *Can Europe and China Shape a New World Order?* (London: Centre for European Reform, June 2008).

60. In 2007 China's two-way trade with the United States and Japan was U.S.$302 billion and U.S.$236 billion respectively—Ministry of Commerce statistics, http://english. mofcom.gov.cn/column/print.shtml?/statistic/ie/200802/20080205371690.

61. See chapter 3, p. 46.

62. Anti-Americanism is also difficult to manage. For example, the extent and ferocity of popular protests following the 1999 U.S. bombing of the Chinese Embassy in Belgrade and the Hainan "incident" in April 2001 caught the Communist leader-

ship by surprise. The protests became associated with social anarchy and an implicit challenge to its authority—see Peter Hays Gries, *China's New Nationalism: Pride, Politics, and Diplomacy* (University of California Press, 2005), pp. 128–34. The pattern of nationalist outpouring followed by calls for public restraint was repeated in the recent controversy over Tibet and the Olympic torch relay.

63. Public opinion surveys have shown the Russian population to be consistently more pro-American and pro-Western than the elite. A poll conducted in January 2008 found that 51 percent of respondents had a "positive" or "basically positive" attitude toward the United States, as against 39 percent "basically negative" or "very negative" (with 11 percent uncommitted)—www.levada.ru/russia.html. The responses were still more favorable toward the EU—70 percent versus 17 percent, with 13 percent uncommitted. In a November 2007 survey, 75 percent of respondents felt that Russia should strengthen its ties with the West, compared with 14 percent who believed it should keep its distance. This rating has remained remarkably constant throughout the Putin presidency, never straying outside the range of 70–77 percent (and far higher than in 1998–99, when it lay between 35 and 42 percent)—www.levada.ru/inter relations3.html.

64. Yevgeny Bazhanov, "Between Washington and Beijing," *Russia Profile*, vol. 3, no. 8 (October 2006): 36.

65. The general indifference toward Russia among most young Chinese has been apparent to the author during various trips to China. Other commentators have remarked on this apathy and its potential consequences. One of the strongest advocates of the Sino-Russian relationship, Alexei Voskressenski (head of the Department of Asian and African Studies, Moscow State Institute of International Relations—MGIMO), laments "the low level of cross-cultural understanding and the fragility of benign attitudes that may change very quickly to distrust or even hatred"—"The Rise of China and Russo-Chinese Relations in the New Global Politics of Eastern Asia," in *Eager Eyes Fixed on Eurasia*, vol. 2, edited by Akihiro Iwashita (Sapporo: Slavic Research Center, Hokkaido University, 2007), p. 39.

66. It is symptomatic that many Chinese who retain an affection for Russia refer nostalgically to the Russian songs they learned in the 1950s.

67. The term "limited partnership" was first used by Sherman Garnett to describe a partnership that "can only develop so far"—"Limited Partnership," in *Rapprochement or Rivalry? Russia–China Relations in a Changing Asia*, edited by Sherman Garnett (Washington, DC: Carnegie Endowment for International Peace, 2000), p. 30.

68. It is telling that many in the coming generation of Chinese leaders—the so-called "fifth generation"—have either been educated in the West or have considerable experience in engaging with Western policymakers and business.

69. In his report to the 16th Party Congress in November 2002, Jiang Zemin noted that "the first two decades of the 21st century are a period of important strategic opportunities . . . we need to concentrate on building a well-off society of a higher standard in an all-round way. . . . We will further develop the economy, improve

democracy, advance science and education, enrich culture, foster social harmony, and upgrade the texture of life for the people. The two decades of development will serve as an inevitable connecting link for attaining the third-step strategic objectives for our modernization drive as well as a key stage in improving the socialist market economy and opening wider to the outside world"—http://english.people.com.cn/200211/18/eng20021118_106983.shtml.

70. Brzezinski, *The Grand Chessboard*, p. 36.

71. Brzezinski, "The Dilemma of the Last Sovereign," p. 42.

72. Ibid., p. 43.

73. Brzezinski, *The Grand Chessboard*, pp. 118–20.

74. Anatoly Chubais's much-criticized concept of "liberal imperialism" remains pertinent. "Liberal" in this context is mainly synonymous with "economic," although Chubais associated it also with the dissemination of Russian language and culture, as well as "freedom and democracy"—"Missiya Rossii v XXI veke," *Nezavisimaya gazeta*, October 1, 2003—www.ng.ru/printed/42475.

75. Celeste Wallander describes Russia's approach as neither post-imperial nor neo-imperial, but trans-imperial: "Transimperialism is the extension of Russian patrimonial authoritarianism into a globalized world"—"Russian Transimperialism and Its Implications," *The Washington Quarterly*, vol. 30, no. 2 (Spring 2007): 117. See also chapter 8, note 25.

76. Vladimir Skosyrev, "Treugolnaya khimera," *Nezavisimaya gazeta*, November 29, 2006—www.ng.ru.

77. In a famous article in 2000, Vladimir Baranovsky posed the question: "Russia: A Part of Europe or Apart from Europe?"—*International Affairs*, vol. 76, no. 3 (July 2000): 443–58.

78. Dmitri Trenin, "Russia Redefines Itself and Its Relations with the West," *The Washington Quarterly*, vol. 30, no. 2 (Spring 2007): 98.

79. "Russia does not aspire to the role of a superpower . . . but Russia knows its own value. . . . Russia has enough potential to influence the creation of a new world order so that the future architecture of international relations will be balanced and take account of the interests of all members of international society"—Putin interview with *Al Jazeera*, February 10, 2007—www.kremlin.ru/text/appears/2007/02/118108.shtml. See also Sergei Lavrov, address to the 15th Assembly of the Council on Foreign and Defense Policy, March 17, 2007—www.mid.ru/brp_4.nsf/2fee282eb6df40e643256999005e6e8c/f3c5edc2dadb268dc32572a10041ed8f?OpenDocument.

80. Brzezinski, *The Grand Chessboard*, p. 205.

81. Although "multipolar" and "multilateral" have become almost interchangeable in Russian diplomatic-speak, they mean very different things. A multipolar system is elitist and centered in relations between a few great powers. A multilateral system implies a much more open and democratic arrangement, with meaningful participation by minor powers (and others) in international decisionmaking. When Moscow and Beijing speak of the "democratization of international relations," they challenge

U.S. hegemony but remain committed to keeping the magic circle of decisionmakers as exclusive as possible.

82. Brzezinski, *The Grand Chessboard*, pp. 208–09.

83. Ibid., p. 210.

84. Even in 1997 it was difficult to agree with Brzezinski's contention that "the very multinational and exceptional character of American society has made it easier for America to universalize its hegemony without letting it appear to be a strictly national one"—ibid., p. 210. In today's much more difficult international environment, such claims appear more fantastic than ever.

Chapter Ten

1. Roderic Lyne, Strobe Talbott, and Koji Watanabe, *Engaging with Russia: The Next Phase*, Report to the Trilateral Commission (Washington, DC, London, Tokyo, 2006), pp. 177–78.

2. Sergei Karaganov, "Russia and the International Order," in *What Russia Sees*, edited by Dov Lynch, Chaillot Paper 74 (Paris: Institute for Security Studies, European Union, January 2005), p. 28.

3. Qian Qichen, *Ten Episodes in China's Diplomacy* (New York: Harper Collins, 2005), p. 1.

4. Ibid., pp. 4–31.

5. "Russian-Chinese Joint Declaration on a Multipolar World and the Establishment of a New International Order," Moscow, April 23, 1997—www.un.org/documents/ga/docs/52/plenary/a52-153.htm.

6. As reflected in titles such as Gordon Chang's *The Coming Collapse of China* (London: Arrow Books, 2001) and Richard Bernstein and Ross Munro's *The Coming Conflict with China* (New York: Vintage Books, 1998).

7. Joint Declaration by the People's Republic of China and the Russian Federation, Beijing, April 25, 1996—www.nti.org/db/china/engdocs/chru0496.htm.

8. Samuel P. Huntington, *The Clash of Civilizations and the Remaking of World Order* (London: Touchstone Books, 1997), p. 243. Also Alexei Arbatov, "Natsionalnaya bezopasnost' Rossii v mnogopolyarnom mire," Report to the Presidium of the Russian Academy of Sciences, April 25, 2000, *Vestnik Rossiiskoi Akademii Nauk*, vol. 70, no. 11 (2000)—http://vivovoco.rsl.ru//vv/journal/vran/arbatoff.htm.

9. Article 11 of the Sino-Russian Joint Declaration on "The International Order in the 21st Century," Moscow, July 1, 2005—www.kremlin.ru/text/docs/2005/07/ 90623.shtml.

10. Yevgeny Primakov, architect of competitive multipolarity under Yeltsin, frequently cited Palmerston's maxim—see, for example, his interview with Aleksei Benediktov on Radio Ekho Moskvy, December 16, 1999 (www.echo.msk.ru/programs/beseda/10944/). It is no coincidence that Primakov has re-emerged in recent times as Putin's foreign policy counselor.

11. Andrei Denisov, Russian permanent representative to the UN—www.un. int/russia/ppintart/2005/050913edenc.pdf.

12. Vitaly Tsygichko alleges that the border settlement is vulnerable to three factors in particular: (i) "Chinese political practice indicates that it will easily violate any agreement that does not suit it for one reason or another"; (ii) the secrecy of the agreement's provisions; and (iii) the twenty-year validity of the agreement, "after which time the parties must return to negotiations on [the border] question"— Dmitri Trenin and Vitaly Tsygichko, "What Is China to Russia: Comrade or Master?" *Security Index*, vol. 82, no. 2 (Summer/Fall 2007): 114.

13. See Putin's address at the Blagoveshchensk conference on "Development Prospects in the Far East and Zabaikal Regions," July 21, 2000— www.kremlin.ru/ appears/2000/07/21/0000_type63374type63378_28796.shtml.

14. Statement to the Russia-China Economic Forum, Beijing, March 22, 2006— www.kremlin.ru/appears/2006/03/22/1123_type63376type63377type82634_103471. shtml (see chapter 5, note 72).

15. "We are in complete agreement in our discussions of international problems in international forums"—Igor Rogachev, Russian ambassador in Beijing (1992–2005), March 26, 2007—www.kreml.org/interview/145423520.

16. Bobo Lo, "Evolution or Regression? Russian Foreign Policy in Putin's Second Term," in *Towards a Post-Putin Russia*, edited by Helge Blakkisrud (Oslo: Norwegian Institute of International Affairs, 2006), p. 72.

17. See Yegor Gaidar, "Rossiya zainteresovana v stabilnom razvitii Kitaya"—www. gaidar.org/otvet/may02_01.htm.

18. An instructive comparison can be drawn between the Chinese response to the collapse of the Yukos-CNPC agreement and the disproportionate European reaction to the very brief—and unintended—cessation of energy deliveries resulting from Moscow's spats with Ukraine and Belarus in 2006–07.

19. Dmitri Trenin and Bobo Lo, *The Landscape of Russian Foreign Policy Decision-Making* (Carnegie Moscow Center, 2005), p. 6.

20. More optimistic commentators suggest that the relationship will improve with the effect of time. Igor Rogachev, long-time Russian ambassador in Beijing, believes that the current distortions in bilateral trade will resolve themselves as the Russian economy becomes more diversified and its manufacturing industry becomes internationally competitive. Ji Zhiye, deputy head of the China Institute of Contemporary International Relations (CICIR), suggests that time will also have a positive impact on Russian and Chinese popular attitudes toward each other (source: author's conversations in Beijing, May 2007).

21. Nationalism is very much on the rise in Russia and China, even with both economies experiencing impressive growth and rising living standards.

22. Meeting with the International Valdai Discussion Club, Novo-Ogarevo, September 9, 2006—www.kremlin.ru/appears/2006/09/09/1930_type63376type63381_ 111114.shtml.

23. Evan Medeiros notes the predilection to hedging strategies in both Beijing and Washington: "pursuing policies that, on the one hand, stress engagement and integration mechanisms and, on the other, emphasize realist-style balancing"—"Strategic Hedging and the Future of Asia-Pacific Stability," *The Washington Quarterly* (Winter 2005–06): 145.

24. Zbigniew Brzezinski uses the term "partners of tactical convenience" in the context of the George W. Bush administration's promotion of "expedient security arrangements" between Russia and the United States—"The Dilemma of the Last Sovereign," *The American Interest* (Autumn 2005), p. 38.

25. It is telling in this connection that the Russian Defense Ministry rejected as too provocative the PLA's original proposal to hold the "Peace Mission 2005" joint exercises off the coast of Zhejiang province—see chapter 3, p. 48.

26. David Shambaugh, *Modernizing China's Military: Progress, Problems, and Prospects* (University of California Press, 2004), p. 303.

27. The "Peace Mission 2005" exercises were the first ever conducted between the two countries—see chapter 3, pp. 48–49.

28. Francis Fukuyama, "The End of History?" *The National Interest*, no. 16 (Summer 1989): 4.

29. Contrary to the belief of many Putin critics in the West, the process of de-democratization in Russia was already in full swing by the mid-1990s, evident in the securing of Yeltsin's re-election in the summer of 1996. In the space of six months, Yeltsin transformed a popularity rating of around 2–3 percent in January to 53 percent in the July run-off with Communist leader Gennady Zyuganov.

30. Thus Hu has emphasized the concept of "scientific development," based on the "five syntheses" of development—between urban and rural areas; between different regions; between economic growth and social welfare; between the population and nature; and between domestic growth and the open-door policy. The key premise is that economic progress should not benefit some sectors of the population and regions at the expense—or neglect—of others. See Willy Wo-Lap Lam, *Chinese Politics in the Hu Jintao Era: New Leaders, New Challenges* (Armonk, New York: M.E. Sharpe, 2006), pp. 42–44.

31. Dmitri Trenin makes a distinction between the personal and political freedoms of Russians—*Integratsiya i identichnost: Rossiya kak 'novy Zapad'* (Carnegie Moscow Center and Evropa, 2006), p. 200. The same distinction can be applied to the Chinese today, who are better off and more mobile than at any time in their history, but who continue to lack real rights of political participation.

32. "There are those who say we should not open our windows, because open windows let in flies and other insects. They want the windows to stay closed, so we all expire from lack of air. But we say, 'Open the windows, breathe the fresh air and at the same time fight the flies and insects'"—www.time.com/time/subscriber/personofthe year/archive/stories/1985.html.

33. Minxin Pei, *China's Trapped Transition: The Limits of Developmental Autocracy* (Harvard University Press, 2006), pp. 7–16; Ross Terrill, *The New Chinese Empire—And What It Means for the United States* (New York: Basic Books, 2003), pp. 313–18.

34. According to a March 2007 poll by the Levada Center, 75 percent of respondents believed that the political opposition in Russia should have the right to stage rallies and demonstrations. And 65 percent opposed the breaking up of meetings by the OMON riot police, even when permission to hold these had been denied—see "Oppozitsionnye protesty," Levada-Center press release, March 29, 2007—www.levada.ru/press/2007032902.html.

35. One should admit that this "hybrid form" eludes ready definition. A representative of the Xinhua news agency told the International Valdai Discussion Club in September 2007 that China "welcomed all forms of democracy—Western, sovereign, and Chinese." This statement closely resembles Sergei Ivanov's remarks in London in July 2004, which challenged the West's monopoly on democracy—http://rian.ru/politics/20040712/631635.html (see chapter 3, note 63).

36. Terrill, *The New Chinese Empire*, pp. 147–49.

37. The main danger for Russia is not so much the lack of resources *per se* as the lack of political and economic will to invest in developing untapped resources.

38. This view is shared even by academics who view the relationship positively. Alexei Voskressenski argues that "if reforms in China fail, there will be even more problems for Russia and China's neighboring countries." He notes in particular that it will be "practically impossible to contain the migration of huge masses of unemployed people from across the border"—"The Rise of China and Russo-Chinese Relations," in *Eager Eyes Fixed on Eurasia*, vol. 2, edited by Akihiro Iwashita (Sapporo: Slavic Research Center, Hokkaido University, 2007), p. 28.

39. See Jonathan Spence, *The Search for Modern China*, 2d ed. (New York and London: W.W. Norton, 1999), p. 119.

40. Broadly speaking, the warlord era in China encompasses the period from the collapse of the Qing Dynasty in 1911–12 to the final Communist victory in 1949. During this time, central authority was very weak, and powerful military leaders ruled over individual fiefdoms. Although Chiang Kai-shek was able to assert a measure of central control following the Northern Expedition of 1926 and, subsequently, the purge of the Communists in Shanghai and Canton (Guangzhou), various warlords continued to rule vast swathes of China until the late 1940s.

41. Viktor Larin, "Russia's Eastern Border: Last Outpost of Europe or Base for Asian Expansion?" *Russian Expert Review*, vol. 18, no. 4 (October 2006)—www. rusrev.org/eng/content/review/print.asp?ids=136&ida=1464.

42. This could take the form of direct bilateral competition or be reflected at the multilateral level in a more explicit institutional rivalry between the SCO and the CSTO.

43. Yu Bin, "Russia Says 'No' to the West, and 'Sort Of' to China," *Comparative Connections*, vol. 9, no. 1 (April 11, 2007): 149–50—www.csis.org/media/csis/pubs/0701qchina_russia.pdf.

44. A number of commentators testify to the limited impact of such official events—for example, Voskressenski, "The Rise of China and Russo-Chinese Relations," p. 39. More generally, the impact of generational change on attitudes toward

Russia has been largely negative: "Many Chinese, especially the older generation, still have some fond feelings toward Russian culture and literature. . . . However, among the young population of China, the situation is different. The younger generation in general is interested in Russia, but few of them know much about it"—Su Fenglin, "Questions Regarding Past and Present Sino-Russian Cultural Exchange," in *Eager Eyes Fixed on Eurasia*, ed. by Iwashita, p. 104. The author's own experience of lecturing in Shanghai in 2006–07 confirms these impressions.

45. "The worst sin towards our fellow creatures is not to hate them, but to be indifferent to them; that is the essence of inhumanity"—George Bernard Shaw, *The Devil's Disciple*, Act II.

46. Lyne, Talbott, and Watanabe, *Engaging with Russia*, pp. 177–78. Interestingly, senior Russian political figures are re-emphasizing ideas such as a "common European civilization" and Gorbachev's vision of a "common European home"—see Medvedev's remarks at the joint press conference, Russia-EU summit in Khanty-Mansiisk, June 27, 2008—www.kremlin.ru/eng/speeches/2008/06/27/2114_type82914type 82915_203194.shtml.

47. Huntington, for example, claims that "Russia and China united would decisively tilt the Eurasian balance against the West"—*The Clash of Civilizations*, p. 243.

48. This primitive Manichean view of the world was evident in the panicky reaction to the modest "Peace Mission 2005" military exercises in August 2005.

49. "Our objective is both a Europe whole and free and a Euro-Atlantic community that extends east from Vancouver to Vladivostok"—address by Secretary of State James Baker III, Aspen Institute, Berlin, June 24, 1991—http://findarticles.com/p/articles/mi_m1584/is_n25_v2/ai_11218409.

INDEX